PE

Or ... ...

'A prophet who thought the unthinkable and spoke the unspeakable, even when it offended conventional thought' Peter Grosvenor, *Daily Express*

'He saw through everything because he could also see through himself. Many writers and journalists have tried to imitate his particular kind of clarity without possessing anything like his moral authority' Peter Ackroyd, *The Times*

'Orwell's innocent eye was often devastatingly perceptive . . . a man who looked at his world with wonder and wrote down exactly what he saw, in admirable prose' John Mortimer, *Evening Standard*

'Matchlessly sharp and fresh . . . The clearest and most compelling English prose style this century' John Carey, *Sunday Times*

'It is impossible not to be elated by his literary and political writing – and enraged by what he was up against . . . the most lovable of writers, someone whose books can make the reader long for his company' Geoffrey Wheatcroft, *Spectator*

'His intellectual honesty was a virtue . . . it wasn't just the amount of truth he told but the way he told it, in prose transmuted to poetry by the pressure of his dedication' Clive James, *New Yorker*

'The finest English essayist of his century . . . He made it his business to tell the truth at a time when many contemporaries believed that history had ordained the lie . . . His work endures, as lucid and vigorous as the day it was written' Paul Gray, *Time*

ERIC ARTHUR BLAIR (George Orwell) was born in 1903 in India, where his father worked for the Civil Service. The family moved to England in 1907 and in 1917 Orwell entered Eton, where he contributed regularly to the various college magazines. From 1922 to 1927 he served with the Indian Imperial Police Force in Burma, an experience that inspired his first novel, *Burmese Days* (1934). Several years of poverty followed. He lived in Paris for two years before returning to England, where he worked successively as a private tutor, schoolteacher and bookshop assistant, and contributed reviews and articles to a number of periodicals. *Down and Out in Paris and London* was published in 1933. In 1936 he was commissioned by Victor Gollancz to visit areas of mass unemployment in Lancashire and Yorkshire, and *The Road to Wigan Pier* (1937) is a powerful description of the poverty he saw there. At the end of 1936 Orwell went to Spain to fight for the Republicans and was wounded. *Homage to Catalonia* is his account of the civil war. He was admitted to a sanatorium in 1938 and from then on was never fully fit. He spent six months in Morocco and there wrote *Coming Up for Air*. During the Second World War he served in the Home Guard and worked for the BBC Eastern Service from 1941 to 1943. As literary editor of *Tribune* he contributed a regular page of political and literary commentary, and he also wrote for the *Observer* and later for the *Manchester Evening News*. His unique political allegory, *Animal Farm*, was published in 1945, and it was this novel, together with *Nineteen Eighty-Four* (1949), which brought him world-wide fame.

George Orwell died in London in January 1950. A few days before, Desmond MacCarthy had sent him a message of greeting in which he wrote: 'You have made an indelible mark on English literature . . . you are among the few memorable writers of your generation.'

PETER DAVISON is Research Professor of English at De Montfort University, Leicester. He was born in Newcastle upon Tyne in 1926 and studied for a London External BA (1954) by correspondence course. He edited an Elizabethan text for a London MA (1957) and then taught at Sydney University, where he gained a Ph.D. He was awarded a D.Litt. and an Hon. D. Arts by De Montfort University in 1999. He has written and edited fifteen books as well as the Facsimile Edition of the manuscript of *Nineteen Eighty-Four* and the twenty volumes of Orwell's *Complete Works* (with Ian Angus and Sheila Davison). He is a Past-President of the Bibliographical Society, whose journal he edited for twelve years. He was made an OBE in 1999 for services to literature.

CHRISTOPHER HITCHENS is a regular columnist for *Vanity Fair* and the *Nation*. His books include *Blood, Class and Nostalgia: Anglo-American Ironies* (1990) and *No One Left to Lie To: The Triangulations of William Jefferson Clinton* (1998). He is currently Professor of Liberal Studies at the New School for Social Research in New York, and lives in Washington, DC.

Orwell in Spain

1934

The Full Text of Homage to Catalonia *with Associated Articles,*
Reviews and Letters from The Complete Works of George Orwell

Edited by Peter Davison
Introduction by Christopher Hitchens

PENGUIN BOOKS

PENGUIN BOOKS

Published by the Penguin Group
Penguin Books Ltd, 80 Strand, London WC2R ORL, England
Penguin Putnam Inc., 375 Hudson Street, New York, New York 10014, USA
Penguin Books Australia Ltd, 250 Camberwell Road, Camberwell, Victoria 3124, Australia
Penguin Books Canada Ltd, 10 Alcorn Avenue, Toronto, Ontario, Canada M4V 3B2
Penguin Books India (P) Ltd, 11 Community Centre, Panchsheel Park, New Delhi – 110 017, India
Penguin Books (NZ) Ltd, Cnr Rosedale and Airborne Roads, Albany, Auckland, New Zealand
Penguin Books (South Africa) (Pty) Ltd, 24 Sturdee Avenue, Rosebank 2196, South Africa

Penguin Books Ltd, Registered Offices: 80 Strand, London WC2R ORL, England

www.penguin.com

This collection first published 2001
8

The texts in this collection are taken from *The Complete Works of George Orwell*, published by
Martin Secker & Warburg Ltd (vols. 1–9 1986, vols. 10–20 1998). *Homage to Catalonia* previously
published in Penguin Books 1962 and 1989. Some material previously published in different form,
in *The Collected Essays, Journalism and Letters of George Orwell*, Vols. 1–4, in Penguin Books 1970

Homage to Catalonia copyright 1938 by Eric Blair
Other material copyright © the Estate of the late Sonia Brownell Orwell, 1998
Introduction copyright © Christopher Hitchens, 2001
This selection, headnotes, footnotes and the Note on the Text of *Homage to Catalonia*
copyright © Peter Davison, 2001
All rights reserved

The moral rights of the editor and of the author of the introduction have been asserted

Set in 10/12.5 pt Monotype Columbus
Typeset by Rowland Phototypesetting Ltd, Bury St Edmunds, Suffolk
Printed in England by Clays Ltd, St Ives plc

ISBN-13: 978–0–141–18516–3
ISBN-10: 0–141–18516–3

www.greenpenguin.co.uk

Contents

Introduction

The grandeur of George Orwell, in our store of moral and intellectual memory, is to be found partly in his very lack of grandeur. He is remembered, with different and varying degrees of distinctness, as the man who confronted three of the great crises of the twentieth century and got all three of them, so to speak, 'right'. He was right, earlier than most, about imperialism, viewing it as an unjust and unjustifiable form of rule, and also as a cause of war. He was right, early and often, about the menace presented by Fascism and National Socialism, not just to the peace of the world but to the very idea of civilization. And he was right about Stalinism, about the great and the small temptations that it offered to certain kinds of intellectual, and about the monstrous consequences that would ensue from that nightmarish sleep of reason.

He brought off this triple achievement, furthermore, in his lowly capacity as an impoverished freelance journalist and amateur novelist. He had no resources beyond his own, he enjoyed the backing of no party or organization or big newspaper, let alone any department of state. Much of his energy was dissipated in the simple struggle to get published, or in the banal effort to meet a quotidian schedule of bills and deadlines. He had no university education, no credential nor area of expertise. He had no capital. Yet his unexciting pen-name, drawn from a rather placid English river, is known to millions as a synonym for prescience and integrity, and the adjective 'Orwellian' is understood widely and – this has its significance – ambivalently. To describe a situation as 'Orwellian' is to announce dystopia: the triumph of force and sadism and demagogy over humanism. To call a person 'Orwellian' is to summon the latent ability of an individual to resist such triumphs, or at least to see through them and call them by their right names.

Though he is best remembered for his satires upon, and polemics against, the big lie and grand illusion – he properly understood that it was both – of the 'Great Soviet Experiment', Orwell acquired the necessary knowledge and insight for that task as a front-line fighter against the European Right and its 'crusade' (the term actually employed by Franco and his Vatican supporters) to immolate the Spanish Republic. It was while serving in Catalonia that he survived a fascist bullet through his throat while in the trenches, but very nearly did not survive a Communist stab in the back while recuperating in Barcelona. From this near-accidental opportunity to bear witness came the body of work we now understand as 'Orwellian'. This work had been slowly begun in the sullen villages of colonial Burma, and refined in slums and coal-mines and doss-houses and on the picket-lines of the Depression, but the crucible – or the point where the hammer met the anvil – was in Spain.

Introducing the American edition of *Homage to Catalonia* in 1952 (the first such edition, incidentally, since the book did not find a publisher in the United States until fourteen years after it was written and two years after its author had died a virtual pauper), Lionel Trilling made the uncondescending observation that Orwell was not a genius. By this he meant, and stated very finely:

If we ask what it is that he stands for, what he is the figure of, the answer is: the virtue of not being a genius, of fronting the world with nothing more than one's simple, direct, undeceived intelligence, and a respect for the powers one does have, and the work one undertakes to do ... He is not a genius – what a relief! What an encouragement. For he communicates to us the sense that what he has done, any one of us could do.

This judgement strikes me as being simultaneously true and beautiful. Orwell was physically brave in Spain, but not heroically so. He did no more than countless other volunteer soldiers, and suffered very much less than many of them. But when he was put to the test, and stumbled across an important chunk of evidence, he had to confront the strong pressure either to lie or to keep silent. Here again, he was exceptional rather than exemplary. He simply resolved that he would tell the truth as he saw it, and would stipulate that he had only the vantage point of a bewildered and occasionally frightened but none the less determined individual. He repeatedly enjoins the reader, in effect, not to take him upon trust:

It will never be possible to get a completely accurate and unbiased account of the Barcelona fighting, because the necessary records do not exist. Future historians will have nothing to go upon except a mass of accusations and party propaganda. I myself have little data beyond what I saw with my own eyes and what I have learned from other eye-witnesses whom I believe to be reliable.

In this properly provisional verdict, however, he unknowingly erred on the side of pessimism. The history of the May events in Barcelona in 1937 was certainly buried for years under a slag-heap of slander and falsification. Orwell, indeed, derived his terrifying notion of the memory-hole and the rewritten past, in *Nineteen Eighty-Four*, from exactly this single instance of the abolished memory. 'This kind of thing is frightening to me,' he wrote about Catalonia, 'because it often gives me the feeling that the very concept of objective truth is fading out of the world':

After all, the chances are that those lies, or at any rate similar lies, will pass into history . . . The implied objective of this line of thought is a nightmare world in which the Leader, or some ruling clique, controls not only the future *but the past*. If the Leader says of such and such an event, 'It never happened' – well, it never happened. If he says that two and two are five – well, two and two are five.

But in our very immediate past, documents have surfaced to show that his vulgar, empirical, personal, commonsensical deposition was verifiable after all. The recent opening of Communist records in Moscow, and also of closely held Franco-era documentation in Madrid and Salamanca, has provided a posthumous vindication.

The narrative core of *Homage to Catalonia*, it might be argued, is a series of events that occurred in and around the Barcelona telephone exchange in early May 1937. Orwell was a witness to these events, by the relative accident of his having signed up with the militia of the anti-Stalinist POUM (Partido Obrero de Unificación Marxista) upon arriving in Spain. Allowing as he did for the bias that this lent to his first-hand observations, he none the less became convinced that he had been the spectator of a full-blown Stalinist *putsch*, complete with rigged evidence, false allegations and an ulterior hand directed by Moscow. The outright and evidently concerted fabrications that immediately followed in the press, which convinced or neutralized so many 'progressive intellectuals', only persuaded him the more that he had watched a lie being gestated and then born.

Well, now we have the papers of the Soviet Military Archive in Moscow, formally known as the State Military Archive. 'Document Forty-Two', in the series dealing with Spain, provides us with the text of a lengthy unsigned report, delivered on 15 April 1937, and forwarded by Georgi Dimitrov to Marshal Voroshilov. The importance of the traffic is emphasized by this very routing: unimportant messages did not go from the head of the Comintern to the chief of the Red Army and thus almost certainly to Stalin himself. (The actual author may well have been André Marty, the French-born Comintern agent for Spain, memorably etched in at least some of his cold hatefulness by Ernest Hemingway in *For Whom the Bell Tolls*.)

In robotic prose, the author characterizes the non-Communist left in the Spanish Republic and specifically Catalonia as 'fascists or semi-fascists'. He goes on to describe the position of Moscow as 'absolutely correct on every question'. This slavish stuff might be called routine, but just after a paean to the 'natural and indisputable' inevitability of a Communist Party victory, the writer of the report comes to the point. A crisis may be objectively brewing, given the staunchly anti-Russian positions taken by Largo Caballero and his Republican cabinet, but it may still need some subjective assistance. In fact, the duty of the Party involves 'not waiting passively for a "natural" unleashing of the hidden government crisis, but to hasten it and, if necessary, to provoke it'. The date of this proposal, which also announces that 'the Party is waiting for your advice on this question', anticipates the Communist police attack on the Barcelona telephone exchange by a matter of just over two weeks.

The succeeding paper, 'Document Forty-Three', was written on 11 May and is the first report back to the Comintern on the mixed results of the action. Regretting the extent to which the POUM and other forces had been able to resist the Stalinist onslaught, the author (whose identity in this instance is uncertain) relays the demand for 'energetic and merciless repression' by means of a 'military tribunal for the

Trotskyists'.* There is no need for guesswork about the meaning of this; Professor Peter Davison's work on Orwell has already established that a Catalan version of the Moscow show-trials was in preparation, and that George Orwell and his wife Eileen would have been in the dock – an NKVD file unearthed in Moscow and dated 13 July 1937 describes them as 'pronounced Trotskyists' – had they not managed to slip across the border into France. As it was, many of their English comrades were imprisoned and vilely ill-used, and Andrés Nin, the leader of the POUM, was kidnapped by Stalin's agents and tortured to death. With each succeeding disclosure from the records of the period, it becomes clearer that Orwell's free-hand sketch of events was a journalistic understatement.

'Part of his malaise', wrote Jennie Lee, who saw Orwell in those terrible days, 'was that he was not only a socialist but profoundly liberal. He hated regimentation wherever he found it, even in the socialist ranks.' Ms Lee went on to become the wife of Aneurin Bevan, who was also Orwell's editor and patron at *Tribune*. Her choice of the word 'malaise', and her stress upon regimentation, are both oddly paradoxical. To many supporters of the Spanish Republic, especially to foreigners who did not wish to impose themselves (as well as to those who did), it seemed axiomatic that one should first win the war against a fascist mutiny supported by Hitler and Mussolini, and only then discuss the shape of the future. Orwell, the old Etonian and former colonial policeman, and lifetime foe of affectations and posturings, might have been expected to be highly susceptible to this no-nonsense approach. In fact, in his 'Notes on the Spanish Militia', discussing a POUM attack on Huesca, he writes: 'I was not in this show, but heard from others who were that the POUM troops behaved well.' It sounds amazingly like a stiff-upper-lip staff officer ('this show') of the generation before.

Yet when it came to it, this rather insular and reserved Englishman –

---

* These documents, and many others of extraordinary interest, were disclosed as a consequence of an exclusive agreement between the State Military Archive and Yale University Press. They will appear in full in *Spain Betrayed: The Soviet Union and the Spanish Civil War* by Ronald Radosh and Mary R. Habeck (New Haven, Yale University Press, 2001). In view of the fact that I have disagreed strongly in print and in public with Professor Radosh, for his published views on the Spanish conflict, I should like to emphasize the unusual courtesy he showed in sharing his findings with me.

renowned in his own detachment as a bit of a stickler for discipline, whose wife when at the Aragon front wrote yearningly of Crosse & Blackwell pickles and Lea & Perrins sauce and good old English marmalade – brought himself to see that a conventional military victory was an illusion, and that what the place really needed was a thoroughgoing social and political revolution. Moreover, he came to understand that much of the talk about 'discipline' and 'unity' was a rhetorical shield for the covert Stalinization of the Spanish Republic. Undoubtedly, he was assisted to this conclusion by the calibre of the revolutionaries he met, both Catalan and international (he often finds occasion in these pages to speak well of the German comrades). And of course, he could tell in his bones and from experience that the Stalinists were lying. As a consequence, the honour of many decent and brave people was upheld, through his fragmentary but consistent writings, against a positive downpour of calumny and malice. This can sometimes make one feel better about the supposedly hopeless pragmatism, the sheer want of theoretical capacity, of the island race.

Integrity, though, is not just a matter of dogged adherence. It is most striking to see, in these pages, how Orwell continues to fight with the weapons of patience and politeness. Whether it is in combating an anonymous reviewer in *The Listener* (a stolid adherent of the commonsense school, this one, see page 295) or debating with other leftists like Raymond Postgate, he maintains the rules of rational argument and never – except in taking the odd pot-shot at an occasional fascist – descends into mere invective. He monitors reports of the trial of the POUM (page 311), keeps up the search for news of his missing or imprisoned friends and steadily answers all his correspondence. Every now and then, we glimpse another 'flash-forward' to the raw material of *Animal Farm* or *Nineteen Eighty-Four*, as when we read, on page 325, of his old comrade Georges Kopp being tortured by confinement with rats, or when Orwell drily notes that Antonov-Ovseenko, the Soviet commissar in Barcelona charged with the extirpation of Trotskyism, has himself been indicted in Moscow for Trotskyist deviations, or when in Orwell's papers we find Bertram Wolfe's eulogy to Andrés Nin, with its evident influence on the world of Goldstein and Big Brother. The only lacuna – and it is an odd one, given Orwell's sensitivity to colonial questions – concerns the subject of Morocco. It was from this base, and with a heavily Moorish army, that Franco's aggression had been launched. The demand of the Trotskyist Left was that Spanish Morocco should be immediately given its independence, first as a matter of principle and second because it might undermine Franco's imperial rearguard. The Communist line was to oppose this, because such a policy would alienate Britain and France, the other two colonial powers in North Africa. Meanwhile, they used chauvinist propaganda against the employment of dark-skinned infidels by a Catholic crusade. The argument was a very intense one at the time; it is disappointing to find Orwell having so little to say about it.

The intellectuals and writers of enlightened Europe generated shelf upon shelf of prose and poetry during the Spanish Civil War, but it is absolutely safe to say that most of this stuff would not bear reprinting except as a textbook in credulity and/or bad faith. There is barely a sentence, however, in this collection which causes a wince or a shudder. Orwell, who did not share the febrile enthusiasm of the clenched-fist cheerleaders and propagandists (see page 248), none the less had a deeper belief than they did in the capacities of the Spanish people. His work also acts as a prophylactic against the efforts of a certain revisionist school, which now likes to argue that the victory of Franco was preferable after all, because the alternative would have been a prototype 'Peoples' Democracy' of the order of Czecho-slovakia in 1948. Orwell, who had grasped the nature of 'Peoples' Democracy' more acutely than most, argued to the contrary. An awful tyranny was possible in either case, he granted, but:

Given a Government victory, it seems much likelier that Spain will develop into a capitalist Republic of the type of France than into a socialist state. What seems certain, however, is that no regression to a semi-feudal, priest-ridden régime of the kind that existed up to 1931 or, indeed, up to 1936 is now possible. Such régimes, by their nature, depend upon a general apathy and ignorance which no longer exist in Spain. The people have seen and learned too much. At the lowest estimate, there are several million people who have become impregnated with ideas which make them bad material for an authoritarian state.

In the event of a Franco victory, as Orwell also noted, 'the desire for liberty, for knowledge and for a decent standard of living has spread far too widely to be killed by obscurantism or persecution'. Those who assert that Spain would have become Stalinized in the event of a Franco defeat are also fond of arguing that Franco's regime was relatively benign, as against Hitler's, say, and that it gave way in the end to democratic evolution from below. Why could not this be true in the opposing case, and for much the same reasons? The missing element in the calculation is the ability of people to make their own history, an ability which Orwell did not doubt since he had seen it demonstrated. Dystopia might win, but it did not have to, and it might not last. In this sense, the courage and bearing of the Catalans taught Orwell to argue against his own direst premonitions.

He was prescient even in the smaller things, writing in 1943 that it was mistaken to believe, as many did, 'that Franco will fight for the Axis if the Allies invade Europe. Fidelity is not the strong point of the minor dictators.' To combat Franco in 1937 was to hope for a reverse of European fascism *tout court*: once that struggle had been betrayed by Stalin and Chamberlain and Daladier, matters resumed the banal shape of *realpolitik* and local compromise. Excess of zeal is a poor guide, especially for the ideologically inclined.

Just such an excess of wartime enthusiasm, and of the Puritanism that may accompany it, led Orwell to commit his only lapse into demagogy. In May 1937 – that cruellest of months for the cause, as it was to turn out – W. H. Auden published his extraordinary poem 'Spain', which first appeared as a shilling pamphlet with proceeds donated to Medical Aid for the Spanish Republic. In a long and extremely moving evolution of verses, the poet attempted to express his emotion for the martyred country itself ('that arid square, nipped off from hot Africa and soldered so crudely to inventive Europe'), to hymn its centrality in the hearts of thinking and feeling people ('Our thoughts have bodies/ The menacing shapes of our fever/ Are precise and alive') and to register the moral agony that was experienced by intellectuals who abandoned neutrality and decided to support the use of force by their chosen side:

> To-day the deliberate increase in the chances of death;
> The conscious acceptance of guilt in the necessary murder;
> > To-day the expending of powers
> On the flat ephemeral pamphlet and the boring meeting.

In successive articles, one of them written for *The Adelphi* in 1938 and another more celebrated under the title *Inside the Whale*, Orwell emptied the vials of contempt over this stanza in particular. He denounced it as

a sort of thumb-nail sketch of a day in the life of a 'good party man'. In the morning a couple of political murders, a ten-minutes' interlude to stifle 'bourgeois' remorse, and then a hurried luncheon and a busy afternoon and evening chalking walls and distributing leaflets. All very edifying. But notice the phrase 'necessary murder'. It could only be written by a person to whom murder is at most a *word*. Personally I would not speak so lightly of murder . . . The Hitlers and the Stalins find murder necessary, but they don't advertise their callousness, and they don't speak of it as murder; it is 'liquidation', 'elimination', or some other soothing phrase. Mr Auden's brand of amoralism is only possible if you are the kind of person who is always somewhere else when the trigger is pulled.

The laden sarcasm here is more than slightly thuggish; it also reflects one of Orwell's less agreeable habits of mind, which was an instinctive prejudice against homosexuals. (Allusions to 'pansy' or 'nancy' poets elsewhere in his writing are common enough – there's one on page 249. They are usually directed at Auden or his supposed clique, and are the only expletives uttered by Orwell that could also have been authored by Zhdanov or some other Stalinist cultural enforcer.)

Auden of course exemplified nothing of the kind; in order to believe that he was, you would have to find the words (not the phrases) 'liquidation' or 'elimination' to be 'soothing'. His 'brand of amoralism' consisted in trying to be direct and honest about the consequences of going to Spain and overcoming what were essentially pacifist scruples. For example, though he broadcast propaganda for the Republican government from Valencia, he was revolted by the burning of churches – revolutionary actions which Orwell always reports and refers to with the utmost breeziness, as to be expected in time of class warfare and civil strife.

It isn't clear how much immediate effect Orwell's polemic had on Auden, but in 1939 he revised 'Spain' to delete all allusion to such choices, and after the 1950s he would not permit the poem to be anthologized at all. This is in more than one way a pity, because it robs us of a magnificent minor epic in verse, and leaves stranded and isolated a haunting phrase which many people have heard but which fewer and fewer people can 'place'. That phrase – 'History to the Defeated' – forms part of the climax of the poem, and suggests in an elegiac way that the losers will never be granted their meed of honour. To them, history 'May say Alas but cannot help or pardon.' In later life, Auden came, wrongly in my humble opinion, to think of this as an expression of the repulsive idea that impersonal or Hegelian capital-H 'History' was necessarily on the side of the triumphant big battalions.

Yet 'History to the Defeated' is the underlying subject and text of this collection of pages and fragments. Like several others in the 'midnight of the century', the glacial period that reached its nadir in the Hitler–Stalin Pact, Orwell wrote gloomily but defiantly for the bottom drawer. He belongs in the lonely 1930s tradition of Victor Serge and Boris Souvarine and David Rousset – speaking truth to power but without a real audience or a living jury. It is almost tragic that, picking through the rubble of that epoch, one cannot admire him and Auden simultaneously. 'All I have is a voice', wrote Auden in 'September 1, 1939', 'To undo the folded lie, / The romantic lie in the brain . . . And the lie of Authority.' All Orwell had was a voice, and to him, too, the blatant lies of authority were one thing, while the 'folded' lies that clever people tell themselves were another. The tacit or overt collusion between the two was the ultimate foe.

In Catalonia three years ago, the history of the defeated was finally celebrated as a victory. A square near the Barcelona waterfront was named Plaça George Orwell, while a street in the town of Can Rull was named Calle Andrés Nin. Present at the dedications were many veterans of the Barcelona 'May Days' of 1937, who had survived to bear witness because Nin never betrayed any names to his interrogators and murderers. The translations of Dostoyevsky and Tolstoi that are read by Catalan schoolchildren are Nin's translations; he was a figure in Catalonia's literary and linguistic revival, and a lover of Russia for the same reason that he was a hater of Stalin. The history of the Civil War that is taught to Catalan schoolchildren now includes Orwell, and has been wiped clean of any totalitarian or revisionist taint. Truth, it turns out, is great after all, and can prevail. The book you hold in your hands is a modest, individual illustration of that mighty proposition, which will always stand in need of volunteers to vindicate it.

Christopher Hitchens
Palo Alto, California
May Day, 2000

Editorial Note

In the main, the items reproduced here are given in the chronological order in which they were written or published. However, the order of events is sometimes better represented by not following this practice. It will be obvious, from dates and item numbers, where the chronological order has not been followed. Letters are typewritten unless stated otherwise. The titles used for Orwell's essays and articles are not always his own but this distinction is not noted unless there is a special reason to do so.

Almost all the items are drawn from *The Complete Works of George Orwell*, edited by Peter Davison, assisted by Ian Angus and Sheila Davison (Secker & Warburg, 1998). Some explanatory headnotes and many footnotes have been added, amplified and modified. The *Complete Works* did not provide biographical notes of authors of books reviewed but, for this selection, these have been added if the author had a link with Orwell or if they might illuminate the context of Orwell's review. Item numbers from the original edition are given in italics within square parentheses, and a list of volumes in which these items can be found is given in the Further Reading.

Where the text was in some way obscure, the original edition does not modify but marks the word or passage with a superior degree sign (°); in most instances such passages have been silently corrected in this edition but in a few instances the degree sign has been retained, for example, where one of Orwell's idiosyncratic spellings occurs: e.g., 'agressive' or 'adress'.

References to items in the *Complete Works* are generally given by volume, forward slash and item number in italic: e.g.: XV/*953*; page references to *CW* are given similarly except that the page number is in roman: XII/387; page references to this present volume are given as 'p. 57'; references are also made to the companion three volumes: *Orwell and Politics*, *Orwell and the Dispossessed* and *Orwell's England*. References to *Homage to Catalonia* are given to this edition by page and, within square brackets, by the *CW* volume number (VI) and page (the page numbers in *CW* and Penguin Twentieth-Century Classics are identical for the text): e.g.: p. 36 [VI/57].)

The following works are designated by abbreviated forms:

Complete Works and *CW*: *The Complete Works of George Orwell*, edited by Peter Davison assisted by Ian Angus and Sheila Davison, 20 vols. (1998); volume numbers are given in roman numerals, I to XX. Vols. X–XX of a second, enlarged and amended, edition are being published in paperback from September 2000.

CEJL: *The Collected Essays, Journalism and Letters of George Orwell*, edited by Sonia Orwell and Ian Angus, 4 vols. (1968; paperback, 1970)

Crick: Bernard Crick, *George Orwell: A Life* (1980; 3rd edn, 1992)

A Literary Life: P. Davison, *George Orwell: A Literary Life* (1996)

Orwell Remembered: Audrey Coppard and Bernard Crick, eds., *Orwell Remembered* (1984)

Remembering Orwell: Stephen Wadhams, ed., *Remembering Orwell* (1984)

S&A, *Unknown Orwell*: Peter Stansky and William Abrahams, *The Unknown Orwell* (1972)

S&A, *Transformation*: Peter Stansky and William Abrahams, *Orwell: The Transformation* (1979)

Shelden: Michael Shelden, *Orwell: The Authorised Biography* (1991)

The Thirties: Malcolm Muggeridge, *The Thirties* (1940; 1971); reviewed by Orwell, XII/615

Thomas: Hugh Thomas, *The Spanish Civil War* (rev. edn, 1977; Penguin, 1979)

A fuller reading list is given in Further Reading.

Peter Davison,
De Montfort University, Leicester

Acknowledgements

George Orwell's (Eric Blair's) work is the copyright of the Estate of the late Sonia Brownell Orwell. Most of the documents in this edition are held by the Orwell Archive (founded by Sonia Orwell in 1960) at University College London. Gratitude is expressed to the Archive, and particularly its Archivist, Gill Furlong, for the help given the editor. A number of documents are in the possession of others and thanks to the following are gratefully extended: Archivo Histórico Nacional de España, Madrid, for the Spanish originals of the documents referring to Orwell (Blair) and Doran (*374A*); the BBC for the paragraph from the Weekly News Broadcast to India, 22 (*1173*); the British Library for Mss Add. 49384 (Kopp's report on Orwell's wound, *369*); Mrs Bertha Doran and Waverley Secondary School, Drumchapel, Glasgow, for *386*; the Lilly Library, Indiana University, Bloomington, Indiana, for *358* and *365*; Harry Ransom Research Center, University of Texas at Austin, Texas, for *381* and *434*; and Judith Williams for *386A*.

Headnotes, footnotes and the Note on the Text of *Homage to Catalonia* are copyright of Peter Davison.

I wish to add a last acknowledgement to this, my favourite of Orwell's books. Sheila, my wife for over fifty years, has been of inestimable help in the production of this and the other three volumes in this series, *Orwell and the Dispossessed, Orwell and Politics* and *Orwell's England.* Her eyes, much sharper than mine, have spotted many errors in the course of proof-reading, and she has endeavoured to ensure I have written simply and straightforwardly. For this and so much else I am abidingly grateful.

Orwell's Journey to Spain, December 1936

The Spanish Civil War was fought from 1936 to 1939 between the Spanish Republican Government and Nationalist rebels. The Republicans included socialists, communists, anarchists and Catalan and Basque nationalists, but also many moderates; the Nationalists comprised the conservative elements of Spain, including monarchists, Carlists, Falangists (fascists) and the Roman Catholic Church. The Soviet Union gave the Republicans (especially the communists) active support; the Nationalists were given heavier support by Nazi Germany and Fascist Italy. Many foreigners fought on both sides, especially on behalf of the Republicans, notably in the International Brigade. Britain and France were among countries that pursued a non-interventionist policy. General Francisco Franco (1892–1975) played a vital role in ensuring the Nationalist victory. From September 1936 he served as Generalissimo of the Nationalist forces and after the war became dictator of Spain. The ferocity of the war led to heavy loss of life, directly in the fighting, 'behind the lines', and, after the war, in retributive killings and deaths in prison (perhaps some 100,000), a total of some half-million people in all.[1]

On 10 December 1936, George Orwell wrote the first of a series of short letters to his literary agent, Leonard Moore, making arrangements for his journey to Spain, where he intended to fight on behalf of the Republicans. He confirmed that his bank had allowed him to overdraw to the tune of £50 (which Moore had guaranteed). He asked Moore to try to persuade the Daily Herald *(a newspaper that supported the Left) to commission him to write 'a few articles or something like that' (327). No agreement was reached with the* Herald. *The next day he wrote an authorization for his agent giving his wife, Eileen, complete rights over his literary affairs and directed that all payments due to him should be paid to her (328). On 15 December he sent Moore the manuscript of* The Road to Wigan Pier. *This was*

processed very rapidly and on Saturday, 19 December, his publisher, Victor
Gollancz, sent him a telegram asking him to call at Gollancz's offices on the
following Monday, 21 December, to discuss the book's publication. Orwell
telegraphed back to say he would be there at noon and they then discussed
terms for the publication of the book and the inclusion of illustrations (341).
Orwell endeavoured to win the support of Harry Pollitt, Secretary-General
of the Communist Party, for his journey to Spain, but Pollitt, suspicious of
Orwell's political reliability (as he saw it), declined to help him. He did,
however, advise him to obtain a safe-conduct from the Spanish Embassy in
Paris. Orwell also obtained a letter of introduction from the Independent
Labour Party (the ILP) to John McNair, its representative in Barcelona.[2]
Orwell arrived in Barcelona about 26 December. He described the journey
(and an incident in Paris on the way) in his Tribune *column, 'As I Please',*
in 1944. Jennie Lee (1904–88, Baroness Lee of Asheridge, 1970), first
Minister of Arts and wife of Aneurin Bevan (1897–1960), under whose
forceful leadership the National Health Service had been set up in 1948,
described Orwell's arrival in Barcelona in a letter to Margaret M. Goalby,
written shortly after Orwell's death.

1. Hugh Thomas, *The Spanish Civil War* (3rd edn, 1977; Penguin, 1979), 926–7. Thomas provides a large-scale, and very conveniently available, account of the war. The war has naturally attracted a vast literature, not all of it in agreement. For the POUM (with which Orwell fought), see Victor Alba and Stephen Schwartz, *Spanish Marxism vs. Soviet Communism: A History of the POUM* (Rutgers University Press, 1988). Victor Alba edited *El Proceso del P.O.U.M.: Documentos Judiciales y Policiales* (Barcelona, 1989); this gives (in Spanish) many documents associated with the Tribunal Especial, June 1937 to October 1938, including that concerning Orwell (p. 75; see p. 26 below), but not, for example, that concerning Charles Doran, given in an English translation on p. 26. Ken Loach's film, *Land and Freedom*, gives a good impression of the war, chiefly from the point of view of the POUM. Alba and Orwell's friend, Stafford Cottman, were among its advisers.

2. See 'Notes on the Spanish Militias' (*439*), below. For accounts of Orwell in Spain in full-length biographical studies, see S&A, *Transformation*, Part Four: 'An Education in Spain'; Crick, ch. 10, 'Spain and "necessary murder"'; Shelden, ch. 14, 'Soldier in Catalonia'; Peter Davison, *George Orwell: A Literary Life* (1996), ch. 4, 'The Turning Point: Wigan and Spain'; and Jeffrey Meyers, *Orwell: Wintry Conscience of a Generation* (2000), ch 8. Stephen Wadhams, *Remembering Orwell*, ch 3 (based on interviews recorded for the Canadian Broadcasting Corporation's 'George Orwell: A Radio Biography', 1984) has valuable reminiscences.

[2549]

Extract from 'As I Please', 42 [The Journey to Spain]

Tribune, *15 September 1944*

About the end of 1936, as I was passing through Paris on the way to Spain, I had to visit somebody at an address I did not know, and I thought that the quickest way of getting there would probably be to take a taxi. The taxi-driver did not know the address either. However, we drove up the street and asked the nearest policeman, whereupon it turned out that the address I was looking for was only about a hundred yards away. So I had taken the taxi-driver off the rank for a fare which in English money was about threepence.

The taxi-driver was furiously angry. He began accusing me, in a roaring voice and with the maximum of offensiveness, of having 'done it on purpose'. I protested that I had not known where the place was, and that I obviously would not have taken a taxi if I had known. 'You knew very well!' he yelled back at me. He was an old, grey, thick-set man, with ragged grey moustaches and a face of quite unusual malignity. In the end I lost my temper, and, my command of French coming back to me in my rage, I shouted at him, 'You think you're too old for me to smash your face in. Don't be too sure!' He backed up against the taxi, snarling and full of fight, in spite of his sixty years.

Then the moment came to pay. I had taken out a ten-franc note. 'I've no change!' he yelled as soon as he saw the money. 'Go and change it for yourself!'

'Where can I get change?'

'How should I know? That's your business.'

So I had to cross the street, find a tobacconist's shop and get change. When I came back I gave the taxi-driver the exact fare, telling him that after his behaviour I saw no reason for giving him anything extra; and after exchanging a few more insults we parted.

This sordid squabble left me at the moment violently angry, and a little later saddened and disgusted. 'Why do people have to behave like that?' I thought.

But that night I left for Spain. The train, a slow one, was packed with Czechs, Germans, Frenchmen, all bound on the same mission. Up and down the train you could hear one phrase repeated over and over again, in the accents of all the languages of Europe – *là-bas* (down there). My third-class carriage was full of very young, fair-haired, underfed Germans in suits of incredible shoddiness – the first *ersatz* cloth I had seen – who rushed out at every stopping-place to buy bottles of cheap wine and later fell asleep in a sort of pyramid on the floor of the carriage. About halfway down France the ordinary passengers dropped off. There might still be a few nondescript journalists like myself, but the train was practically a troop train, and the countryside knew it. In the morning, as we crawled across southern France, every peasant working in the fields turned round, stood solemnly upright and gave the anti-Fascist salute. They were like a guard of honour, greeting the train mile after mile.

As I watched this, the behaviour of the old taxi-driver gradually fell into perspective. I saw now what had made him so unnecessarily offensive. This was 1936, the year of the great strikes, and the Blum[1] government was still in office. The wave of revolutionary feeling which had swept across France had affected people like taxi-drivers as well as factory workers. With my English accent I had appeared to him as a symbol of the idle, patronising foreign tourists who had done their best to turn France into something midway between a museum and a brothel. In his eyes an English tourist meant a bourgeois. He was getting a bit of his own back on the parasites who were normally his employers. And it struck me that the motives of the polyglot army that filled the train, and of the peasants with raised fists out there in the fields, and my own motive in going to Spain, and the motive of the old taxi-driver in insulting me, were at bottom all the same.

1. Léon Blum (1872–1950) was the first Socialist Prime Minister of France, 1936–7 and 1938; he presided over a Popular Front government which enacted a series of reforms benefiting working men and women. He was imprisoned during the occupation of France by the Germans. He was again Prime Minister, 1946–7.

[355A]

Jennie Lee to Margaret M. Goalby, 23 June 1950: Orwell's Arrival in Barcelona

In the first year of the Spanish Civil War I was sitting with friends in a hotel in Barcelona when a tall thin man with a ravished [*sic*] complexion came over to the table. He asked me if I was Jennie Lee, and if so, could I tell him where to join up. He said he was an author: had got an advance on a book from Gollancz,[1] and had arrived ready to drive a car or do anything else, preferably to fight in the front line. I was suspicious and asked what credentials he had brought from England. Apparently he had none. He had seen no-one, simply paid his own way out. He won me over by pointing to the boots over his shoulder. He knew he could not get boots big enough for he was over six feet. This was George Orwell and his boots arriving to fight in Spain.

I came to know him as a deeply kind man and a creative writer . . . He was a satirist who did not conform to any orthodox political or social pattern . . . The only thing I can be quite certain of is, that up to his last day George was a man of utter integrity; deeply kind, and ready to sacrifice his last worldly possessions – he never had much – in the cause of democratic socialism. Part of his malaise was that he was not only a socialist but profoundly liberal. He hated regimentation wherever he found it, even in the socialist ranks.

1. This advance was of £100 against royalties for *The Road to Wigan Pier* (see *341*).

Orwell in Spain, December 1936

In George Orwell: A Life *(317–18), Bernard Crick quotes from John McNair's typescript, 'George Orwell: The Man I Knew', dated March 1965, in Newcastle upon Tyne University Library. McNair records that Orwell brought him one letter from Fenner Brockway (1888–1988, Lord Brockway, 1964), General Secretary of the ILP, and one from H. N. Brailsford (1873–1958), a socialist intellectual and journalist and leader-*

writer for several newspapers, including the Manchester Guardian*; Orwell later corresponded with him (see below). McNair, a Tynesider, was at first put off by Orwell's 'distinctly bourgeois accent', but, when he realized that this was George Orwell, two of whose books he 'had read and greatly admired', he asked what he could do to help him. 'I have come to Spain to join the militia to fight against Fascism,' Orwell told him. He also told McNair that 'he would like to write about the situation and endeavour to stir working-class opinion in Britain and France'. McNair proposed that Orwell base himself in McNair's offices and suggested he visit Madrid, Valencia and the Aragón front, where the POUM¹ was stationed, 'and then get down to writing his book'. Orwell told McNair that writing a book 'was quite secondary and his main reason for coming was to fight against Fascism'. McNair took him to the POUM barracks, where Orwell immediately enlisted, and introduced him to Victor Alba, then a journalist who would later write a history of the POUM (see, p. 2, n. 1, above); Alba showed Orwell round Barcelona. Orwell did not know, and never knew, that two months before he arrived in Spain, the NKVD's resident in Spain, Aleksandr Orlov, had confidently assured NKVD Headquarters, 'The Trotskyist organization POUM can easily be liquidated'² – by those, the Communists, whom Orwell took to be their allies in the fight against Franco.*

1. POUM, Partido Obrero de Unificación Marxista (Workers' Party of Marxist Unification), was described by Orwell in *Homage to Catalonia* as 'one of those dissident Communist parties which have appeared in many countries in the last few years as a result of the opposition to "Stalinism"; i.e. to the change, real or apparent, in Communist policy. It was made up partly of ex-Communists and partly of an earlier party, the Workers' and Peasants' Bloc. Numerically it was a small party, with not much influence outside Catalonia, and chiefly important because it contained an unusually high proportion of politically conscious members. . . .It did not represent any block of trade unions.' He gives the membership as 10,000 in July 1936; 70,000 in December 1936; and 40,000 in June 1937, but warns that the figures are from POUM sources, and 'a hostile estimate would probably divide them by four'; see pp. 180–81 [VI/202–3].

2. Christopher Andrew and Vasili Mitrokhin, *The Mitrokhin Archive: The KGB in Europe and the West* (1999), 95, quoting John Costello and Oleg Tsarev, *Deadly Illusions* (1993), 281.

[*358*]

Eileen Blair to Leonard Moore
31 January 1937   *Handwritten*

The Stores, Wallington, Near Baldock, Herts

Dear Mr Moore,

I enclose the signed agreement.[1] I am afraid there was a little delay before your letter was forwarded to me – I got it yesterday – but when I read the agreement I was delighted, as I know my husband will be when he hears the details. I had not fully realised before how satisfactory it was; in your office the other day I was being rather single-minded.

There is quite good news in Spain, though it comes very erratically. Eric has been created a 'cabo', which is I think a kind of corporal[2] & which distresses him because he has to get up early to turn out the guard, but he also has a dug-out in which he can make tea. There is apparently no 'proper' fighting as neither side has efficient artillery or even rifles.[3] He says he thinks the government forces ought to attack but are not going to. I hope no crisis will arise needing his decision as letters take from 7 to 10[4] days to get here.

With many thanks,

Yours sincerely,

Eileen Blair

1. The agreement was for the next three novels Orwell was to write after *Keep the Aspidistra Flying* (see *357*).

2. Orwell refers to his promotion in *Homage to Catalonia*, see p. 48 [VI/25].

3. Orwell records that rifles were issued on their third morning in Alcubierre, *Homage to Catalonia*, see p. 42 [VI/16].

4. '10' is possibly '16.' Eileen seems to be more concerned that a battle could affect the publication of her husband's work than that it might endanger his life. Her objectivity, surely deceptive, might be considered in the light of that attributed to Orwell at the end of her life.

'British Author with the Militia'

The Spanish Revolution: Bulletin of the Workers' Party of
Marxist Unification[1] *(POUM), 3 February 1937*

At the beginning of January, we received a visit in Barcelona from Eric
Blair, the well-known British author, whose work is so much appreciated
in all English-speaking left circles of thought. Comrade Blair came to
Barcelona, and said he wanted to be of some use to the workers' cause.
In view of his literary abilities and intellectual attainments, it appeared
that the most useful work he could do in Barcelona would be that of a
propaganda journalist in constant communication with socialist organs of
opinion in Britain. He said: 'I have decided that I can be of most use to
the workers as a fighter at the front.' He spent exactly seven days in
Barcelona, and he is now fighting with the Spanish comrades of the
P.O.U.M. on the Aragón front.

In a postcard which he sent us, he says: 'When I have persuaded them
to teach me something about the machine-gun, I hope to be drafted to
the front line trenches.'

1. *The Spanish Revolution* was published fortnightly from 10 Rambla de los Estudios, Barcelona,
and presented the POUM's case in the propaganda war being waged within the government
forces. It was available in London (from the ILP and the Marxist League) and in New York,
Chicago and Toronto. This issue also had a longer article, 'Fighting Men from Britain', and
one summarizing 'The Stalinist Position', 'The P.O.U.M.'s Position' and 'The Anarchist
Position', under the heading 'If they are not Socialist, nor Communist, nor Marxist, What
Are They?'. In addition to explaining why ILP men were fighting under the POUM banner,
this and later articles reveal a tone strikingly similar to the propaganda fed people at home
during World War I. Training, it was explained, lasted fifteen days, 'and by that time they
should be ready for service at the front'. The food was said to be good but it would 'take
the lads a week to get used to the drinking of wine at practically every meal'. Each man was
given a packet of cigarettes a day 'and the pay received is remarkably good, namely 10
pesetas'. Pay came as a surprise, 'as all of our lads had volunteered to fight and had never
considered the possibility of such a regular sum'. Its frequency is not mentioned. A peseta
was worth about fourpence, pre-metrication (see *363, n. 5*). Orwell kept copies of *The Spanish
Revolution* among his papers until his death.

On 8 March 1937, The Road to Wigan Pier *was published by Victor Gollancz (see 362).*

---

[363]

Eileen Blair to her mother
22 March 1937   Handwritten

Seccion Inglesa, 10 Rambla de los Estudios, Barcelona[1]

Dearest Mummy,

I enclose a 'letter' I began to write to you in the trenches! It ends abruptly – I think I've lost a sheet – & is practically illegible but you may as well have a letter written from a real fighting line, & you'll read enough to get the essential news. I *thoroughly* enjoyed being at the front. If the doctor had been a good doctor I should have moved heaven & earth to stay (indeed before seeing the doctor I had already pushed heaven & earth a little) as a nurse – the line is still so quiet that he could well have trained me in preparation for the activity that must come. But the doctor is quite ignorant & incredibly dirty. They have a tiny hospital at Monflorite in which he dresses the villagers' cut fingers etc. & does emergency work on any war wounds that do occur. Used dressings are thrown out of the window unless the window happens to be shut when they rebound onto the floor – & the doctor's hands have never been known to be washed. So I decided he must have a previously trained assistant (I have one in view – a man). Eric did go to him but he says there is nothing the matter except 'cold, over-fatigue, etc.' This of course is quite true. However, the weather is better now & of course the leave is overdue, but another section on the Huesca front made an attack the other day which had rather serious results & leave is stopped there for the moment. Bob Edwards[2] who commands the I.L.P. contingent has to be away for a couple of weeks & Eric is commanding in his absence, which will be quite fun in a way. My visit to the front ended in a suitable way because Kopp[3] decided I must have 'a few more hours' & arranged a car to leave Monflorite at 3:15 a.m. We went to bed at 10 or so & at 3 Kopp came & shouted & I got up & George[4] (I can't remember which half of the family I write to) went to sleep again I hope. In this way he got 2 nights proper rest & seems much better. The whole visit's unreality was accentuated by the fact that there were *no* lights, not a candle or a torch; one got up & went to bed in black dark, & on the last night I emerged in black dark & waded knee deep in mud in & out of strange buildings until I saw the faint glow from the Comité Militar where Kopp was waiting with his car.

On Tuesday we had the only bombardment of Barcelona since I came. It was quite interesting. Spanish people are normally incredibly noisy & pushing but in an emergency they appear to go *quiet*. Not that there was any real emergency but the bombs fell closer to the middle of the town than usual & did make enough noise to excite people fairly reasonably. There were very few casualties.

I'm enjoying Barcelona again – I wanted a change. You might send this letter on to Eric & Gwen, whom I thank for *tea*. Three lbs of it has just come & will be much appreciated. The contingent is just running out, Bob Edwards tells me. The other message for Eric is that as usual I am writing this in the last moments before someone leaves for France & also as usual my cheque book is not here, but he will have the cheque for £10 within 2 weeks anyway & meanwhile I should be very grateful if he gave Fenner Brockway[5] the pesetas. (In case anything funny happened to the last letter, I asked him to buy £10 worth of pesetas & give them to Fenner Brockway to be brought out by hand. Living is very cheap here, but I spend a lot on the I.L.P. contingent as none of them have had any pay & they all need things. Also I've lent John[6] 500 ps. because he ran out. I guard my five English pounds, which I could exchange at a fairly decent rate, because I must have something to use when we – whoever we may be – cross the frontier again.)

I hope everyone is well – & I hope for a letter soon to say so. Gwen wrote a long letter which was exciting – even I fall into the universal habit of yearning over England. Perhaps the same thing happens in the colonies. When a waiter lit my cigarette the other day I said he had a nice lighter & he said 'Si, si, es bien, es *Inglés*!' Then he handed it to me, obviously thinking I should like to caress it a little. It was a Dunhill – bought in Barcelona I expect as a matter of fact because there are plenty of Dunhill & other lighters but a shortage of spirit for them. Kopp, Eric's commander, longed for Lea & Perrins Worcester Sauce. I discovered this by accident & found some in Barcelona – they have Crosse & Blackwell's pickles too but the good English marmalade is finished although the prices of these things are fantastic.

After seeing George[7] I am pretty confident that we shall be home before the winter – & possibly much sooner of course. You might write another letter to the aunt[8] some time. I have *never* heard from her & neither has Eric,[9] which worries me rather. I think she may be very sad about living in Wallington. By the way, George[10] is positively urgent about the gas-stove – he wanted me to write & order it at once, but I still think it would be better to wait until just before our return, particularly as I have not yet heard from Moore about the advance on the book.[11] Which reminds me that the reviews are better than I anticipated, as the interesting ones haven't come through yet.

I had a bath last night – a great excitement. And I've had 3 superb dinners in succession. I don't know whether I shall miss this café life. I have coffee about three times a day & drinks oftener, & although theoretically I eat in a rather grim pension at least six times a week I get headed off into one of about four places where the food is really quite good by any standards though limited of course. Every night I mean to go home early & write letters or something & every night I get home the next morning. The cafés are open till 1.30 & one starts one's after-dinner coffee about 10. But the sherry is *undrinkable* – & I meant to bring home some little casks of it!

Give Maud[12] my love & tell her I'll write some time. And give anyone else my love but I shan't be writing to them. (This letter is to the 3 O'Shaughnesseys,[13] who are thus 'you' not 'they'.) It is a dull letter again I think. I shall do this life better justice in conversation – or I hope so.

Much love
Eileen

1. Offices of the POUM journal, *The Spanish Revolution*. See 360.

2. Robert Edwards (1906–), unsuccessful ILP parliamentary candidate in 1935, was a Labour and Co-operative MP from 1955 to 1987. In January 1937 he was Captain of the ILP contingent in Spain, linked to the POUM. He left Spain at the end of March to attend the ILP conference at Glasgow, but was unable to return because of the government ban on British nationals' participation in the Spanish Civil War. In 1926 and 1934 he led delegations to the Soviet Union; was General Secretary of the Chemical Workers' Union, 1947–71; National Officer, Transport and General Workers' Union, 1971–6; and Member of the European Parliament, 1977–9. See *Orwell Remembered*, 146–8, and especially Shelden,

264–5, which convincingly demolishes Edwards's accusation that Orwell went to Spain solely to find material for a book.

3. George(s) Kopp (1902–51), Russian by birth, Belgian by nationality, was Orwell's commander in Spain. He was a civil engineer but also something of an impostor. After World War II he farmed in Scotland and in 1944 married Doreen Hunton, Eileen's sister-in-law, Gwen O'Shaughnessy's half-sister. He died in Marseilles. Although Orwell and Kopp remained friends, their relationship cooled in the late 1940s. Doreen Kopp wrote to Ian Angus, 29 April 1967, that when Orwell joined her husband's company, 'he was very intrigued to find one Englishman who described himself as a "grocer". He was anxious to meet an English grocer wishing to fight in Spain! It was of course very typical of George as he always wanted to be taken for a working man.'

4. Eileen started to write 'Eric' but overwrote 'George'. Her brother, Dr Laurence Frederick O'Shaughnessy, a distinguished thoracic surgeon, was called Eric (a shortening of his second name). His wife, Gwen, was also a doctor.

5. Fenner Brockway (1888–1988; Lord Brockway, 1964) was General Secretary of the ILP, 1928, 1933–9, and its representative in Spain for a time. A devoted worker for many causes, particularly peace, he resigned from the ILP in 1946 and rejoined the Labour Party, which he represented in Parliament, 1950–64.

6. John McNair (1887–1968), a Tynesider, was an indefatigable worker for the cause of socialism all his life. He left school at twelve, and ran into trouble with employers because of his left-wing sympathies. In order to find work, he went to France and stayed for twenty-five years, becoming a leather merchant, founding a French football club with eight teams, and lecturing on English poets at the Sorbonne. He returned to England in 1936, rejoined the ILP and was its General Secretary, 1939–55. The first British worker to go to Spain, where he remained from August 1936 to June 1937, he was the representative in Barcelona of the ILP. A constant contributor to the *New Leader*, the weekly organ of the ILP (later *Socialist Leader*). In a footnote to *Homage to Catalonia*, see p. 141 [VI/151], Orwell gives the purchasing value of the peseta as 'about fourpence'; 500 pesetas would be about £8 6s 8d or $41.00. See also p. 16, n. 3.

7. Eileen again began writing 'Eric', over which she wrote 'George'.

8. Almost certainly Orwell's aunt Nellie Limouzin, then living at The Stores, Wallington, the Orwells' cottage.

9. Eileen must here mean her husband.

10. Before writing 'George', Eileen wrote 'Eric', but crossed it out.

11. *The Road to Wigan Pier.*

12. Possibly an aunt of Eileen's whose second name was Maud.

13. Eileen's mother, her brother, 'Eric', and his wife, Gwen.

[364]

To Eileen Blair

[5? April 1937]   *Handwritten; undated*

[Hospital, Monflorite]

Dearest,

You really are a wonderful wife. When I saw the cigars my heart melted away. They will solve all tobacco problems for a long time to come. McNair tells me you are all right for money, as you can borrow & then repay when B.E.[1] brings some pesetas, but don't go beggaring yourself, & above all don't go short of food, tobacco etc. I hate to hear of your having a cold & feeling run down. Don't let them overwork you either, & don't worry about me, as I am much better & expect to go back to the lines tomorrow or the day after. Mercifully the poisoning in my hand didn't spread, & it is now almost well, tho' of course the wound is still open.[2] I can use it fairly well & intend to have a shave today, for the first time in about 5 days. The weather is much better, real spring most of the time, & the look of the earth makes me think of our garden at home & wonder whether the wallflowers are coming out & whether old Hatchett is sowing the potatoes. Yes, Pollitt's review[3] was pretty bad, tho' of course good as publicity. I suppose he must have heard I was serving in the Poum militia. I don't pay much attention to the *Sunday Times* reviews[4] as G[5] advertises so much there that they daren't down his books, but the *Observer* was an improvement on last time. I told McNair that when I came on leave I would do the *New Leader* an article, as they wanted one, but it will be such a come-down after B.E's that I don't expect they'll print it. I'm afraid it is not much use expecting leave before about the 20th April. This is rather annoying in my own case as it comes about through my having exchanged from one unit to another – a lot of the men I came to the front with are now going on leave. If they suggested that I should go on leave earlier I don't think I would say no, but they are not likely to & I am not going to press them. There are also some indications – I don't know how much one can rely on these – that they expect an action hereabouts, & I am not going on leave just before that comes off if I can help it. Everyone has been very good to me while I have been in hospital, visiting me every day etc. I think now that the weather is getting better I can stick out another month without getting ill, & then what a rest we will have, & go fishing too if it is in any way possible.

As I write this Michael, Parker & Buttonshaw[6] have just come in, & you should have seen their faces when they saw the margarine. As to the photos, of course there are lots of people who want copies, & I have written the numbers wanted on the backs, & perhaps you can get reproductions. I suppose it doesn't cost too much – I shouldn't like to disappoint the Spanish machine-gunners etc. Of course some of the photos were a mess. The one which has Buttonshaw looking very blurred in the foreground is a photo of a shell-burst, which you can see rather faintly on the left, just beyond the house.

I shall have to stop in a moment, as I am not certain when McNair is going back & I want to have this letter ready for him. Thanks ever so much for sending the things, dear, & do keep well & happy. I told McNair I would have a talk with him about the situation when I came on leave, & you might at some opportune moment say something to him about my wanting to go to Madrid etc. Goodbye, love. I'll write again soon.

With all my love
Eric

1. Bob (Robert) Edwards.
2. See *Homage to Catalonia*, p. 68 [VI/52–3].
3. Harry Pollitt (1890–1960), a Lancashire boiler-maker and founder-member of the Communist Party of Great Britain in 1920, became its general secretary in 1929. With Rajani Palme Dutt, he led the party until his death. He was, however, removed from leadership in the autumn of 1939 until Germany's invasion of Russia in July 1941, for his temporary advocacy of a war of democracy against Fascism. His review of *The Road to Wigan Pier* appeared in the *Daily Worker*, 17 March 1937.
4. *The Road to Wigan Pier* was reviewed by Edward Shanks in the *Sunday Times* and by Hugh Massingham in the *Observer*, 14 March 1937.
5. Victor Gollancz.
6. Michael Wilton (English), also given as Milton, Buck Parker (South African) and Buttonshaw (American) were members of Orwell's unit. Douglas Moyle, another member, told Ian Angus, 18 February 1970, that Buttonshaw was very sympathetic to the European left and regarded Orwell as 'the typical Englishman – tall, carried himself well, well educated and well spoken'.

[365]

Extract from letter from Eileen Blair to Leonard Moore
12 April 1937

I saw my husband a month ago at the front, where, as this is a revolutionary war, I was allowed to stay in the front line dug-outs all day. The Fascists threw in a small bombardment and quite a lot of machine-gun fire, which was then comparatively rare on the Huesca front, so it was quite an interesting visit – indeed I never enjoyed anything more. Eric was then fairly well, though very tired; since then he has had a rest two miles behind the line as he got a poisoned arm, but I think he is now back in the line and the front has been active for the last week. He is keeping quite a good diary[1] and I have great hopes for the book. Unfortunately the activity on his part of the front has interfered with his leave, which is now long overdue, but I hope he will be down here in a week or two.

1. Orwell's diary was taken from Eileen's hotel room in Barcelona by the police (see p. 151 [VI/164]). It is possibly now in the NKVD Archive in Moscow with the dossier on Orwell compiled by the NKVD. Miklos Kun, grandson of the Hungarian Communist leader, Bela Kun (purged on Stalin's orders about 1939), told the editor that he had seen the dossier but he could not confirm that the diary was with it.

---

[367]

Eileen Blair to Dr Laurence ('Eric') O'Shaughnessy
1 May 1937   Handwritten

10 Rambla de los Estudios, Barcelona

Dear Eric,

You have a hard life. I mean to write to Mother with the news, but there are some business matters. Now I think of these, they're inextricably connected with the news so Mother must share this letter.

George is here on leave. He arrived completely ragged, almost barefoot, a little lousy, dark brown, & looking really very well. For the previous 12 hours he had been in trains consuming anis, muscatel out of anis bottles, sardines & chocolate. In Barcelona food is plentiful at the moment but there is nothing plain. So it is not surprising that he ceased to be well.

Now after two days in bed he is really cured but still persuadable so having a 'quiet day'. This is the day to have on May 1st. They were asked to report at the barracks, but he isn't well enough & has already applied for his discharge papers so he hasn't gone. The rest of the contingent never thought of going. When the discharge is through he will probably join the International Brigade. Of course we – perhaps particularly I – are politically suspect[1] but we told all the truth to the I.B. man here & he was so shattered that he was practically offering me executive jobs by the end of half an hour, & I gather that they will take George. Of course I must leave Barcelona but I should do that in any case as to stay would be pointless. Madrid is probably closed to me, so it means Valencia for the moment with Madrid & Albacete in view but at long distance. To join the I.B. with George's history is strange but it is what he thought he was doing in the first place & it's the only way of getting to Madrid. So there it is. Out of this arises a further money crisis because when I leave Barcelona I shall leave all my affiliations – & my address & even my credit at the bank; & it will take a little time to get connected again perhaps. Meanwhile we spend immense sums of money for Spain on new equipment etc. I did write to you about getting money through banks – i.e. your bank buys pesetas[2] with your pounds & instructs a bank in Barcelona to pay me the number of pesetas you bought. If this can be done will you do it (about another 2000 pesetas[3] I should think), & will you ask the bank to cable. Probably I shall be here for a couple of weeks but I'm not *sure* where I shall go next & I want if possible to have some money in hand before leaving. If the bank business can't be done I frankly don't know what can – i.e. I must use the credit at 60 to the £. before leaving here & find some method of getting money through my new friends, whoever they may be (I have met the Times correspondent at Valencia).

1. Association with the ILP, which was associated with the POUM, made both Eileen and her husband politically suspect. Eileen was working in the ILP office in Barcelona as McNair's secretary (Crick, 327). Both would later be called 'confirmed Trotskyists' in the document prepared for the Tribunal for Espionage and High Treason, Valencia, reproduced under 'Escape from Spain', below.
2. A line has been drawn in the margin by 'bank; & it will take a little time . . . your bank buys pesetas', presumably by Eileen's brother. In January 1937 the US dollar stood at 4.91 to the pound.
3. Exchange rates were suspended during the civil war. In January 1936 there were 36 pesetas

to the pound, and in January 1940, 39 pesetas. Eileen writes of using 'credit at 60 to the £'. At 60, 2,000 pesetas would cost just over £33; at 36, £55 11s. Presumably Eileen hoped for more than 60.

---

[368]

Extract from letter to Victor Gollancz

On 1 May 1937, Orwell wrote to Gollancz from Barcelona to thank him for his introduction to The Road to Wigan Pier, *which he had first seen about ten days earlier. Since then he had been slightly ill and 'then there was 3 or 4 days of street-fighting in which we were all more or less involved, in fact it was practically impossible to keep out of it'. He concludes:*

I shall be going back to the front probably in a few days & barring accidents I expect to be there till about August. After that I think I shall come home, as it will be about time I started on another book. I greatly hope I come out of this alive if only to write a book about it. It is not easy here to get hold of any facts outside the circle of one's own experience, but with that limitation I have seen a great deal that is of immense interest to me. Owing partly to an accident I joined the P.O.U.M. militia instead of the International Brigade,[1] which was a pity in one way because it meant that I have never seen the Madrid front; on the other hand it has brought me into contact with Spaniards rather than Englishmen & especially with genuine revolutionaries. I hope I shall get a chance to write the truth about what I have seen. The stuff appearing in the English papers is largely the most appalling lies – more I can't say, owing to the censorship. If I can get back in August I hope to have a book ready for you about the beginning of next year.

1. The International Brigade was composed of foreign volunteers, mostly Communist, and played an important part in the defence of Madrid. Its headquarters was at Albacete.

---

[369]

Orwell's Wound

Orwell was shot through the throat by a sniper on 20 May 1937. He discusses the incident in Homage to Catalonia, *pp. 131–3 [VI/137–9]. Eileen sent a telegram from Barcelona at noon on 24 May 1937 to Orwell's parents in Southwold. This read: 'Eric slightly wounded   progress excellent   sends love   no need for anxiety   Eileen.' This reached Southwold just after 2 p.m. Orwell's commandant, George Kopp, wrote a report on his condition on 31 May and 1 June 1937. When this report was lost (see Eileen's letter to her brother, c. 10 June 1937, below), Kopp wrote another, for Dr Laurence O'Shaughnessy, Orwell's brother-in-law, dated 'Barcelona, the 10th. of June 1937' (see below). It differs slightly from the version given in* Orwell Remembered, *158–61. Kopp illustrated his report with a drawing of the bullet's path through Orwell's throat; Bert Govaerts, who uncovered details of Kopp's life, suggests that this shows his training in engineering drawing. Kopp's report is in the British Library, Mss Add. 49384, and is reproduced by kind permission of the Trustees. The slight errors in Kopp's English have been corrected.*

Eric was wounded the 20th of May at 5 a.m. The bullet entered the neck just under the larynx, slightly at the left side of its vertical axis and went out at the dorsal right side of the neck's base. It was a normal 7 mm bore, copper-plated Spanish Mauser bullet, shot from a distance of some 175 yards. At this range, it still had a velocity of some 600 feet per second and a cauterising temperature. Under the impact, Eric fell on his back. The hemorrhaging was insignificant. After dressing at a first aid post some half a mile from the actual line, he was transferred to Barbastro and then to the Hospital of Lérida, where I saw him with Eileen some 50 hours after his having been wounded.

Eric's general state was some sort of excellent; the temperature (taken in the left arm-pit) had never reached 37°C. Eric complained about his right arm aching from the shoulder down to the tip of the middle finger along a humero-cubital line and about a pain, according to himself severe but not unbearable, in the left side some where between the ultimate rib and the spleen. His voice was hoarse and feeble, but covering all the

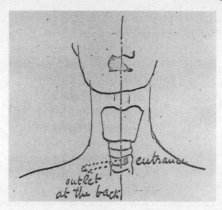

practical purposes of conversational speech. Breathing absolutely regular. Sense of humour untouched.

At the Hospital in Lérida, Eric only received an external treatment of his wound. After a couple of days, the dressing of the entrance wound could be dispensed with. He remained at this Hospital, under care of Dr. Farré, up to the 27th when he was transferred to Tarragona.

Dr. Farré told me on the 22[d] of May that no essential organ had been touched by some sort of unexplainable luck; he admitted that the pain in the arm might be produced by abrasion of one of the arm's main nerves and that the pain in the left side was probably due to hitting the ground when falling from his tremendous height. He told me that there was nothing to fear about the basic wound.

We had Eric ordered to be evacuated from Tarragona to Barcelona and went to fetch him the 29th of May; we found him with a semi-complete aphorisia[1] and a slight fever. The pain in the left side had disappeared in due course. The one in the arm (supposed of nervous origin) subsisted unchanged. The doctor at Tarragona's Hospital had told Eric on that very morning that his larynx was 'broken' and that he would never recover a normal voice. In fact, Eric was able to utter any articulate sound but feebly and with the characteristic, grinding, noise of the brakes of a model T, very antiquated, Ford; his speech was inaudible outside a range of two yards.

Eric reached the sanatorium Maurín in Barcelona on the 29th at 10 p.m., having travelled 60 miles in a saloon-car without any special accommodation. His temperature reached at 11 p.m. 37.8°C (in left arm-pit); he received an aspirin and went immediately to bed, without any meal.

On Sunday, 30th, his voice had improved considerably, his temperature was normal in the morning and his appetite restored. He was able to walk about the place and its park without any exhaustion. I saw him from 11 a.m. to 6 p.m. and found his voice and spirits continuously improving during this period. Eileen was with her husband all the time and states his comportment was absolutely peace-timely.

Today, 30th.[2] Eric travelled by tram and tube, on his own initiative, down to the Centre of Barcelona, where I met him at 11.45 a.m. He explained his escapade by the want of cocktails and decent lunch, which were duly produced by Eileen's tender care (with help of a barman and several waiters).

Eric's temperature had remained normal, the pain in the left side had not reappeared and the pain in the right arm was rather reduced. His voice, according to himself, had improved since yesterday, but Eileen and I don't share this impression, without thinking it was worse. I explain this apparent contradiction by the fact that to reach his present quality of speech costs him less effort than yesterday.

I arranged to have Eric thoroughly examined to-morrow morning by Professor Grau of Barcelona's University and for a subsequent treatment either by some professor, or by another prominent specialist of this town.

I propose to add to this 'bulletin' Professor Grau's opinion with the narrative of the manipulations he will perform on my friend's throat.

Professor Grau examined Eric to day, 1st of June, at 9.30 a.m. at the 'Hospital General de Cataluña'. His diagnostic is:

'incomplete semi-paralysis of the larynx due to abrasion of the right-side larynx dilating nerve.'

He confirmed Dr. Farré's statement that no essential organ had been touched; the bullet went right through, between the trachea and the carotid.

Professor Grau said that electrotherapy was the only thing to be recommended just now and some sort of promise to restore Eric's voice in a long, indefinite, but reasonable time.

He took Eric to Dr. Barraquer, specialist in electric treatments of nervous disturbances and began by having a private talk of some 12 minutes with his colleague. It is unknown if they spoke of Eric's wound or of some other topic. When Eric, Eileen and myself were ushered in Dr. Barraquer's study, Professor Grau explained the case just as if he had never spoken of it before and wanted his friend to investigate any possible nervous lesions outside of the purely laryngic zone out of which he somehow sort of hated to talk.

Dr. Barraquer's additional diagnostic was: 'abrasions of the first right-side spinal rachidean nerve,' which accounts for the pain in the arm. Dr. Barraquer also advocated electrotherapy for both of the nervous lesions and it was agreed upon Eric coming twice a week (on Wed. and Fri.) to have an electrical treatment and once a week (on Fridays) to let Professor Grau look into his throat and hear him saying 'aaaaaah' whilst his tongue is maintained stretched out at full length by the Professor.

Both of the doctors concerned with the case are decent, efficient and fully civilised people, with a lot of similar cases having passed before them since war began; the machinery and installations of the General Catalonian Hospital is complete and modern; most of the nurses are brunettes.

Of course, the doctors have not given any definite opinion upon the duration of the treatment and I felt I could not possibly put any questions about it before they can prove by some sittings the effect of electrotherapy on Eric's nerves. I think that in any case, it would be advisable to let the treatment go at least two weeks and then ask the medical people 'what about having it continued in England?'.

I advocate you writing to Dr. Barraquer (who speaks a fairly good English) a 'colleague's letter' in the reply to which you may be told something more than we, mere mortals, are admitted to hear.[3] Then you would be able to form a reasonable opinion about the case and send Eileen definite instructions which, I am sure she will follow without any reluctance, so high is her admiration for your professional capacities.

With the hope I shall some day have the opportunity of sharing this feeling not only from faith but on experimental evidence, I remain

Yours sincerely

Georges Kopp

1. Kopp meant 'aphasia'.
2. Presumably 31 May.
3. Kopp provided Barrequer's address.

---

[371]

To Cyril Connolly
8 June 1937   Handwritten

Sanatori Maurín,[1] Sania, Barcelona

Dear Cyril,

I wonder if you will be in town during the next few weeks. If you will & would like to meet, you might drop a line to that effect to

at. 24 Crooms Hill

Greenwich S.E.10.

If I can get my discharge papers I ought to be home in about a fortnight. I have been nastily wounded, not really a very bad wound, a bullet through the throat which of course ought to have killed me but has merely given me nervous pains in the right arm & robbed me of most of my voice. The doctors here don't seem certain whether I shall get my voice back or not. Personally I believe I shall, as some days it is much better than others, but in any case I want to get home & be properly treated. I was just reading one of your articles on Spain in a February *New Statesman*. It is a credit to the *New Statesman* that it is the only paper, apart from a few obscure ones such as the *New Leader*, where any but the Communist viewpoint has ever got through. Liston Oak's article[2] recently on the Barcelona troubles was very good & well balanced. I was all through that business & know what lies most of the stuff in the papers was. Thanks also for recently telling the public that I should probably write a book on Spain, as I shall, of course, once this bloody arm is right. I have seen wonderful things & at last really believe in Socialism, which I never did before. On the whole, though I am sorry not to have seen

Madrid, I am glad to have been on a comparatively little-known front among Anarchists & Poum people instead of in the International Brigade, as I should have been if I had come here with C.P. credentials instead of I.L.P. ones. A pity you didn't come up to our position & see me when you were in Aragón. I would have enjoyed giving you tea in a dugout.

Yours

Eric Blair

1. Sanatorium Maurín was run by the POUM. In *Homage to Catalonia*, p. 142 [VI/152], Orwell describes it as being near Tibidabo, 'the queer-shaped mountain that rises abruptly behind Barcelona'. Sarria (not 'Sania' as sometimes recorded) is the name of an old township in the Barcelona area.

2. 'Behind Barcelona's Barricades', by Liston M. Oak, *New Statesman & Nation*, 15 May 1937.

---

[373]

Eileen Blair to Dr Laurence ('Eric') O'Shaughnessy
[c. 10 June 1937]   *Handwritten; undated*

Dear Eric,

Ten days ago George Kopp wrote you an account of the medical investigations & reports on Eric, & I wrote letters to you & Mrs Blair & the aunt. As we wanted you all to get the correspondence quickly we gave them to a man who was crossing into France, to be sent Air Mail from there. Today we hear that he lost the whole packet. So everyone will be feeling bitterly neglected, including me as I had expected a reassuring cable. I've written at least three letters & four postcards each to the three addresses since, but I don't know which have arrived or when. You might ask mother to telephone Mrs Blair & write [to the][1] aunt – or better telephone yourself & give a medical opinion.

Eric is I think much better, though he cannot be brought to admit any improvement. His voice certainly improves very *slowly*, but he uses his arm much more freely though it is still very painful at times. He eats as much as anyone else & can walk about & do any ordinary thing quite effectively for a short time. He is *violently* depressed, which I think encouraging. I have now agreed to spend two or three days on the

Mediterranean (in France) on the way home – probably at Port-Vendres.[2]
In any case we shall probably have to wait somewhere for money. The
discharge is not through but I think we can leave next week, wire you for
money when we arrive at Port-Vendres or other resting place, go on to
Paris & spend there two nights & the day between, & then get the
morning train to England. I do not altogether like this protracted travel,
but no urgent complication seems possible now, & he has an overwhelming desire to follow this programme – anyway it has overwhelmed me.

Give my love to everyone. I now realise I haven't explained that the
enclosed letter from G.K. is a copy of the one that was lost.

Thank you very much for the liniment & the things for Lois, which I
collected today.

Eileen

Did you get £20 from Fenner Brockway?

1. 'to the' is represented by two (or three) indecipherable letters.
2. They spent three days at Banyuls-sur-Mer, about ten kilometres north of the Spanish
border and some five south of Port-Vendres. It was 'the first station up the line' into France,
a 'quiet fishing-town', as Orwell wrote in *Homage to Catalonia*, p. 166–7 [VI/184]. They
continued their journey via Paris, where 'the Exhibition was in full swing, though we
managed to avoid visiting it' (p. 168 [VI/186]).

[374A]

Escape from Spain

*On 23 June 1937, Eileen and Orwell, with John McNair and Stafford
Cottman, boarded the morning train from Barcelona to Paris. Sitting in the
restaurant car, as if they were tourists, they safely crossed into France. Sir
Richard Rees later wrote that the strain of her experience in Barcelona, even
before the May Events, showed clearly on Eileen's face: 'In Eileen Blair I
had seen for the first time the symptoms of a human being living under a
political terror.'[1] The nature of this terror is exemplified by documents
concerning Orwell and Eileen (and also Orwell's colleague, Charles Doran,
1894–1974, see note to Orwell's letter to him of 2 August 1937, below),
prepared for the Tribunal for Espionage and High Treason, Valencia, three
weeks after the Orwells escaped. Orwell's experiences in Spain, exemplified*

by these documents, are significant witnesses to the way Orwell and his comrades, especially those of the POUM, were betrayed by those supposedly fighting with them against Fascism in Spain. It was an experience that Orwell never forgot and coloured his thinking, actions and writing for the rest of his life. Orwell did not know of the existence of these documents though it is clear from Homage to Catalonia *and his letters, articles and reviews that he well understood what had given rise to them.*

The Spanish originals of these documents are in the Archivo Histórico Nacional de España, Madrid. That concerning Orwell was first sent to the editor by Karen Hatherley and a clearer version and the document related to Charles Doran, together with the translations reproduced here, were kindly provided by Robert A. McNeil, Head of Hispanic Collections, Bodleian Library. The editor is very grateful to both. The Spanish version of the Orwell document, with some variants, is included by Victor Alba in his El Proceso del P.O.U.M. *(Barcelona, 1989), the inside back cover of which reproduces a much-overwritten version of the original. The Doran document is not included either in Alba's collection or the* Complete Works. *The trial of the leaders of the POUM took place in Barcelona in October and November 1938 (see letter to Raymond Postgate, 21 October 1938, below). Orwell later corresponded with one of those found guilty, Jordi Arquer (3238, n. 1, XIX/154, and 3651, n. 1, XX/140); see also his letter to Charles Doran, 2 August 1937 (below). Like Orwell and his wife, Doran is also described as 'trotzkista pronunciado'. Among names in the Doran document is Karl Radek (1885–1939?), who had accompanied Lenin in the sealed train in which Lenin returned to Russia just before the October Revolution (see 3649, n. 3, XX/139), and whom it is stated Doran defended. The newspaper cutting in Doran's possession refers to Lt Norman Baillie Stewart ('the prisoner in the Tower'), who had been accused of selling secrets for £90 to German agents through 'a mysterious girl-friend named Marie Louise' (Robert Graves and Alan Hodge,* The Long Week-End, *1940, 267). Curiously, the description 'su misteriosa amiga' also appears in the Spanish document; France, not Germany, is mentioned in the Spanish document. A lengthy afternote to these documents will be found in the* Complete Works, XI/31–7.

BARCELONA 13TH JULY, 1937

Eric Blair and his wife Eileen Blair

It is clear from their correspondence that they are confirmed Trotskyists. They belong to the IRP [*sic*] of England.

ERIC BLAIR was on the ILP Committee functioning in the Lenin Division on the Granja front (HUESCA).

Liaison with the ILP of England (correspondence of D. MOYLE and JOHN MACNAIR).

Among the effects of CHARLES DORAN is found a letter addressed to ERIC B. from JOHN MACNAIR, asking him to write reports for the ILP. –

They must be considered as liaison officers of the ILP with POUM.

They were living in the Hotel Falcon, supported by the POUM Executive Committee.

Credential from the POUM Executive Committee signed by JORGE KOPP (from its character it seems to be a credential in favour of EILEEN B. valid for the events of May. [No closing bracket]

ERIC B. took part in the events of MAY.

Liaison with ALBACETE by means of DAVID WICKES.

Liaison with MOSCOW. –

Eileen B. was on the Huesca front on 13–3–37 (date inscribed on a photograph). She has a credential issued in BARCELONA on 17–3–37. Her husband has a permit to leave the front to go to Barcelona, issued on 14–3–37.

Charles Doran

A man of the ILP, in very close collaboration with the ILP Committee on the Huesca front, within POUM. –

It is clear from his correspondence that he is a confirmed Trotskyist. –

In Spain he had very close contact with the FAI, as well as a firm liaison with the Iberian Communist Youth of POUM. –

Liaison with Albacete. –

In his effects the names KOPP and MACNAIR are frequently found, as is material by BLAIR [*or* as in BLAIR's effects]. –

In Glasgow, Scotland, in December 1936, he wrote a letter in which he defended Trotsky and Karl Radek against the Moscow trial.

Addresses in Spain found in his effects give reason to suppose the existence of co-religionists in Spain. D., as well as Blair and McNair, has written for the ILP. In his effects is found a newspaper extract relating to the trial for espionage in France of an English lieutenant BAILLIESTE NAST and his mysterious girl-friend MARIA LUISA SCHULE (or MARTIN), who both worked for the GESTAPO. –

1. Sir Richard Rees, *George Orwell: Fugitive from the Camp of Victory* (1961), 147. For Burnett Bolloten's application of the word 'terror' to the Spanish experience, see *The Spanish Civil War: Revolution and Counterrevolution* (1991), 570–71.

On 5 July 1937, Victor Gollancz wrote to Orwell to say that, though he could not be sure until he had seen the typescript, he thought it probable that he would not wish to publish Homage to Catalonia, *upon which Orwell was already engaged. Although not a Communist, he felt he should never publish anything 'which could harm the fight against fascism'. He did see the irony of rejecting an account by someone who had been on the spot while he had sat quietly in his office. He hoped Orwell would continue to regard Gollancz as his main publisher. In fact this, and the later rejection of* Animal Farm *(published 1945), led to Orwell's break with Gollancz and his publisher became Martin Secker & Warburg. On the following day, 6 July, Fredric Warburg wrote to Orwell to tell him that two ILP members, John Aplin and Reginald Reynolds (the latter of whom became a good friend), had suggested that Orwell's proposed book 'would not only be of great interest but of considerable political importance'. He asked Orwell to discuss the book with him. On 17 July, Orwell wrote to his agent, Leonard Moore, enclosing 'a sort of rough plan of my book on Spain' which he thought might be of use to Secker's. He was making a more detailed plan and 'no doubt it will be done by Christmas, but I am not going to hurry it'. Orwell told Moore on 6 December that he had finished the rough draft and begun revising and that it should be finished by the middle of January (412). In mid-February, 1938, he supplied Moore with a carbon copy of the typescript (425). On 25 April 1938, Martin Secker & Warburg published 1,500 copies of* Homage to Catalonia. *(See 375, 377; for publication details and some account of reviews of the book, see 438.)*

Homage to Catalonia

A NOTE ON THE TEXT

Orwell's experience in Spain when fighting for the Republicans in the Civil War, and particularly what he saw of the actions of Communists against other political parties fighting Franco, had a profound influence upon his political attitudes, his writing and the publication of his books. Victor Gollancz, who had published Orwell's first five books, rejected Homage to Catalonia, *believing, as did many people on the Left, that everything should be sacrificed in order to preserve a common front against the rise of Fascism. Fredric Warburg agreed to bring out Orwell's book and, in time (and partly as a result of Gollancz's generous impulse), his company, Secker & Warburg, took over the publication of all Orwell's books in Britain. The book's publication on 25 April 1938 created some stir but sales were poor and, although only 1,500 copies were printed, they had not all been sold by the time a second edition was printed for the Uniform Edition on 21 February 1951. The only translation made in Orwell's lifetime was into Italian, published in December 1948, and* Homage to Catalonia *was not published in the United States until February 1952.*

Orwell hoped that, if a second edition were published, it could be revised. He left notes for his Literary Executor indicating what he wanted changed; some four to six months before he died in January 1950 he marked up his copy of Homage to Catalonia *showing what should be amended and sent it to Roger Senhouse, a Director of Secker & Warburg; and he was in correspondence with Madame Yvonne Davet about the changes to be made from as early as the spring of 1938. Senhouse, unfortunately, disregarded Orwell's requests and the Uniform Edition merely reprinted the 1938 text (with additional errors). In France, Madame Davet made her translation even though publication had not been arranged. By 11 September 1938 Orwell had corrected the first six chapters of her work, and corrections to chapters VI–X were returned to her on 19 June 1939. The Second World War then intervened and it was not until 1947 that they could again correspond. Madame Davet's translation was finally published by Gallimard in 1955 and this, unlike any of the editions in English published over a period of nearly half a century, did include many of the changes Orwell required. The most obvious of these was the removal of chapters V and XI from the body of the book, transferring them as appendixes to the end of the book, where Orwell considered it was more appropriate to place historical and political discussion of what otherwise was a personal account of his experiences.*

At various times thought was given to including a preface. Before the Second World War, Madame Davet suggested that Georges Kopp, Orwell's commander in Spain, might be suitable; in 1947 she proposed André Malraux, but Orwell thought that he might find it 'politically rather embarrassing' at that stage of his career – he had acted as General de Gaulle's Minister of Information from November 1945 to January 1946. In the event, only the American edition had a preface, written by Lionel Trilling.

Some of the changes Orwell required can easily be made, although it is sometimes necessary to follow them up with consequential amendments because, for example, chapters V and XI have become appendixes. Some changes specifically required by Orwell present difficult problems and an editor has to do rather more than he would normally regard as appropriate to his task in order to carry them out. Thus, Orwell instructed (referring to the first edition):

Pp. 161–242 [pp. 103–27, 138–69, 190–215]. All through these chapters are constant references to 'Civil Guards'. Should be 'Assault Guards' all the way through. I was misled because the Assault Guards in Catalonia wore a different uniform from those afterwards sent from Valencia, and by the Spaniards referring indifferently to all these formations as 'la guardia'. The remarks on p. 213 [p. 198] lines 14–17 and footnote should be regularised. The undoubted fact that Civil Guards often joined Franco when able to do so makes no reflection on the Assault Guards who were a formation raised since the 2nd Republic. But the general reference to popular hostility to 'la guardia' and this having played its part in the Barcelona business should stand.

Orwell's confusion was shared by many historians. His error was pointed out to him by Geoffrey Gorer on 18 April 1938, but simply replacing 'Assault' for 'Civil' can lead to even worse confusion. On page 121, line 27 Orwell originally wrote: 'It was easy enough to dodge the Assault Guard patrols; the danger was the Civil Guards in the "Moka" . . .' Change 'Civil' to 'Assault' and what was happening is obscured. I have therefore distinguished between the 'local Assault Guards' and 'Valencian Assault Guards' when the sense demands this. In the first edition, Orwell wrote of the 'hated Civil Guards'; changing 'Civil' to 'Assault' here switches the object of hatred. At this point the new edition simply reads 'Assault Guards' (page 116, line 22) but an opportunity was taken a few pages later (page 121, line 11) to reintroduce 'hated' in an appropriate context. Where Orwell wrote of the arrival of Assault Guards from Valencia (page 121, lines 10– 11), 'another formation similar to the Civil Guards', this has been amended to read 'another formation similar to the local Assault Guards and the hated Civil Guards'.

Orwell's list of changes has been drawn on to provide one or two additional footnotes (e.g., those on pages 47 and 99)*. The French edition has a few more explanatory footnotes, evidently the work of the translator though based on information provided by Orwell. These are recorded in the Textual Note to the Complete Works edition, VI/251–61 (Secker & Warburg, 1986). One, subsequently confirmed to the editor in 1984 by Stafford Cottman, Orwell's youngest colleague in Spain, provides a useful gloss on a puzzling reference. Thomas Parker is said to have come 'nearer to being a DSO than he cared about' (page 73, line 11). The French edition explains that DSO parodied 'Distinguished Service Order' and meant 'Dickie Shot Off' (page 79).

This edition, then, endeavours to put into effect Orwell's explicit instructions for the revision of Homage to Catalonia and to make these changes as discreetly as is practicable.

Peter Davison

Answer not a fool according to his folly, lest
thou also be like unto him.
Answer a fool according to his folly, lest he
be wise in his own conceit.

Proverbs, xxvi.4–5

---

* In *Homage to Catalonia* Orwell's own footnotes are those indicated numerically; editorial ones are indicated with asterisks.

I

In the Lenin Barracks in Barcelona, the day before I joined the militia, I saw an Italian militiaman standing in front of the officers' table.

He was a tough-looking youth of twenty-five or -six, with reddish-yellow hair and powerful shoulders. His peaked leather cap was pulled fiercely over one eye. He was standing in profile to me, his chin on his breast, gazing with a puzzled frown at a map which one of the officers had open on the table. Something in his face deeply moved me. It was the face of a man who would commit murder and throw away his life for a friend – the kind of face you would expect in an Anarchist, though as likely as not he was a Communist. There were both candour and ferocity in it; also the pathetic reverence that illiterate people have for their supposed superiors. Obviously he could not make head or tail of the map; obviously he regarded map-reading as a stupendous intellectual feat. I hardly know why, but I have seldom seen anyone – any man, I mean – to whom I have taken such an immediate liking. While they were talking round the table some remark brought it out that I was a foreigner. The Italian raised his head and said quickly:

'*Italiano?*'

I answered in my bad Spanish: '*No, Inglés. Y tú?*'

'*Italiano.*'

As we went out he stepped across the room and gripped my hand very hard. Queer, the affection you can feel for a stranger! It was as though his spirit and mine had momentarily succeeded in bridging the gulf of language and tradition and meeting in utter intimacy. I hoped he liked me as well as I liked him. But I also knew that to retain my first impression of him I must not see him again; and needless to say I never did see him again. One was always making contacts of that kind in Spain.

I mention this Italian militiaman because he has stuck vividly in my memory. With his shabby uniform and fierce pathetic face he typifies for me the special atmosphere of that time. He is bound up with all my memories of that period of the war – the red flags in Barcelona, the gaunt trains full of shabby soldiers creeping to the front, the grey war-stricken towns further up the line, the muddy, ice-cold trenches in the mountains.

This was in late December, 1936, less than seven months ago as I write, and yet it is a period that has already receded into enormous distance. Later events have obliterated it much more completely than they have obliterated 1935, or 1905, for that matter. I had come to Spain with some notion of writing newspaper articles, but I had joined the militia almost immediately, because at that time and in that atmosphere it seemed the only conceivable thing to do. The Anarchists were still in virtual control of Catalonia and the revolution was still in full swing. To anyone who had been there since the beginning it probably seemed even in December or January that the revolutionary period was ending; but when one came straight from England the aspect of Barcelona was something startling and overwhelming. It was the first time that I had ever been in a town where the working class was in the saddle. Practically every building of any size had been seized by the workers and was draped with red flags or with the red and black flag of the Anarchists; every wall was scrawled with the hammer and sickle and with the initials of the revolutionary parties; almost every church had been gutted and its images burnt. Churches here and there were being systematically demolished by gangs of workmen. Every shop and café had an inscription saying that it had been collectivised; even the bootblacks had been collectivised and their boxes painted red and black. Waiters and shop-walkers looked you in the face and treated you as an equal. Servile and even ceremonial forms of speech had temporarily disappeared. Nobody said *'Señor'* or *'Don'* or even *'Usted'*; everyone called everyone else *'Comrade'* and *'Thou'*, and said *'Salud!'* instead of *'Buenos días'*. Almost my first experience was receiving a lecture from an hotel manager for trying to tip a lift-boy. There were no private motor cars, they had all been commandeered, and all the trams and taxis and much of the other transport were painted red and black. The revolutionary posters were everywhere, flaming from the walls in clean reds and blues that made the few remaining advertisements look like daubs of mud. Down the Ramblas, the wide central artery of the town where crowds of people streamed constantly to and fro, the loudspeakers were bellowing revolutionary songs all day and far into the night. And it was the aspect of the crowds that was the queerest thing of all. In outward appearance it was a town in which the wealthy classes had practically ceased to exist. Except for a small number of women and foreigners there were no 'well-dressed' people at all. Practically everyone wore rough working-class clothes, or blue overalls or some variant of the militia uniform. All this was queer and moving. There was much in it that I did not understand, in some ways I did not even like it, but I recognised it immediately as a state of affairs worth fighting for. Also I believed that things were as they appeared, that this was really a workers' State and that the entire bourgeoisie had either fled, been killed, or voluntarily come over to the workers' side; I did not realise that great numbers of well-to-do bourgeois were simply lying low and disguising themselves as proletarians for the time being.

Together with all this there was something of the evil atmosphere of war. The town had a gaunt untidy look, roads and buildings were in poor repair, the streets at night were dimly lit for fear of air-raids, the shops were mostly shabby and half-empty. Meat was scarce and milk practically unobtainable, there was a shortage of coal, sugar, and petrol, and a really serious shortage of bread. Even at this period the bread-queues were often hundreds of yards long. Yet so far as one could judge the people were contented and hopeful. There was no unemployment, and the price of living was still extremely low; you saw very few conspicuously destitute people, and no beggars except the gipsies. Above all, there was a belief in the revolution and the future, a feeling of having suddenly emerged into an era of equality and freedom. Human beings were trying to behave as human beings and not as cogs in the capitalist machine. In the barbers' shops were Anarchist notices (the barbers were mostly Anarchists) solemnly explaining that barbers were no longer slaves. In the streets were coloured posters appealing to prostitutes to stop being prostitutes. To anyone from the hard-boiled, sneering civilisation of the English-speaking races there was something rather pathetic in the literalness with which these idealistic Spaniards took the hackneyed phrases of revolution. At that time revolutionary ballads of the naïvest kind, all about proletarian brotherhood and the wickedness of Mussolini, were being sold on the streets for a few centimes each. I have often seen an illiterate militiaman buy one of these ballads, laboriously spell out the words, and then, when he had got the hang of it, begin singing it to an appropriate tune.

All this time I was at the Lenin Barracks, ostensibly in training for the front. When I joined the militia I had been told that I should be sent to

the front the next day, but in fact I had to wait while a fresh *centuria* was
got ready. The workers' militias, hurriedly raised by the trade unions at
the beginning of the war, had not yet been organised on an ordinary
army basis. The units of command were the 'section', of about thirty men,
the *centuria*, of about a hundred men, and the 'column', which in practice
meant any large number of men. The Lenin Barracks was a block of
splendid stone buildings with a riding-school and enormous cobbled
courtyards; it had been a cavalry barracks and had been captured during
the July fighting. My *centuria* slept in one of the stables, under the stone
mangers where the names of the cavalry chargers were still inscribed. All
the horses had been seized and sent to the front, but the whole place still
smelt of horse-piss and rotten oats. I was at the barracks about a week.
Chiefly I remember the horsy smells, the quavering bugle-calls (all our
buglers were amateurs – I first learned the Spanish bugle-calls by listening
to them outside the Fascist lines), the tramp-tramp of hobnailed boots in
the barrack yard, the long morning parades in the wintry sunshine, the
wild games of football, fifty a side, in the gravelled riding-school. There
were perhaps a thousand men at the barracks, and a score or so of women,
apart from the militiamen's wives who did the cooking. There were still
women serving in the militias, though not very many. In the early battles
they had fought side by side with the men as a matter of course. It is a
thing that seems natural in time of revolution. Ideas were changing
already, however. The militiamen had to be kept out of the riding-school
while the women were drilling there, because they laughed at the women
and put them off. A few months earlier no one would have seen anything
comic in a woman handling a gun.

The whole barracks was in the state of filth and chaos to which the
militia reduced every building they occupied and which seems to be one
of the by-products of revolution. In every corner you came upon piles of
smashed furniture, broken saddles, brass cavalry-helmets, empty sabre-
scabbards, and decaying food. There was frightful wastage of food,
especially bread. From my barrack-room alone a basketful of bread was
thrown away at every meal – a disgraceful thing when the civilian
population was short of it. We ate at long trestle-tables out of permanently
greasy tin pannikins, and drank out of a dreadful thing called a *porrón*. A
porrón is a sort of glass bottle with a pointed spout from which a thin jet

of wine spurts out whenever you tip it up; you can thus drink from a distance, without touching it with your lips, and it can be passed from hand to hand. I went on strike and demanded a drinking-cup as soon as I saw a *porrón* in use. To my eye the things were altogether too like bed-bottles, especially when they were filled with white wine.

By degrees they were issuing the recruits with uniforms, and because this was Spain everything was issued piecemeal, so that it was never quite certain who had received what, and various of the things we most needed, such as belts and cartridge-boxes, were not issued till the last moment, when the train was actually waiting to take us to the front. I have spoken of the militia 'uniform', which probably gives a wrong impression. It was not exactly a uniform. Perhaps a 'multiform' would be the proper name for it. Everyone's clothes followed the same general plan, but they were never quite the same in any two cases. Practically everyone in the army wore corduroy knee-breeches, but there the uniformity ended. Some wore puttees, others corduroy gaiters, others leather leggings or high boots. Everyone wore a zipper jacket, but some of the jackets were of leather, others of wool and of every conceivable colour. The kinds of cap were about as numerous as their wearers. It was usual to adorn the front of your cap with a party badge, and in addition nearly every man wore a red or red and black handkerchief round his throat. A militia column at that time was an extraordinary-looking rabble. But the clothes had to be issued as this or that factory rushed them out, and they were not bad clothes considering the circumstances. The shirts and socks were wretched cotton things, however, quite useless against cold. I hate to think of what the militiamen must have gone through in the earlier months before anything was organised. I remember coming upon a newspaper of only about two months earlier in which one of the POUM leaders, after a visit to the front, said that he would try to see to it that 'every militiaman had a blanket'. A phrase to make you shudder if you have ever slept in a trench.

On my second day at the barracks there began what was comically called 'instruction'. At the beginning there were frightful scenes of chaos. The recruits were mostly boys of sixteen or seventeen from the back streets of Barcelona, full of revolutionary ardour but completely ignorant of the meaning of war. It was impossible even to get them to stand in line. Discipline did not exist; if a man disliked an order he would step out of the ranks and argue fiercely with the officer. The lieutenant who instructed us was a stout, fresh-faced, pleasant young man who had previously been a Regular Army officer, and still looked like one, with his smart carriage and spick-and-span uniform. Curiously enough he was a sincere and ardent Socialist. Even more than the men themselves he insisted upon complete social equality between all ranks. I remember his pained surprise when an ignorant recruit addressed him as *'Señor'*. 'What! *Señor!* Who is that calling me *Señor*? Are we not all comrades?' I doubt whether it made his job any easier. Meanwhile the raw recruits were getting no military training that could be of the slightest use to them. I had been told that foreigners were not obliged to attend 'instruction' (the Spaniards, I noticed, had a pathetic belief that all foreigners knew more of military matters than themselves), but naturally I turned out with the others. I was very anxious to learn how to use a machine-gun; it was a weapon I had never had a chance to handle. To my dismay I found that we were taught nothing about the use of weapons. The so-called instruction was simply parade-ground drill of the most antiquated, stupid kind; right turn, left turn, about turn, marching at attention in column of threes and all the rest of that useless nonsense which I had learned when I was fifteen years old. It was an extraordinary form for the training of a guerrilla army to take. Obviously if you have only a few days in which to train a soldier, you must teach him the things he will most need; how to take cover, how to advance across open ground, how to mount guards and build a parapet – above all, how to use his weapons. Yet this mob of eager children, who were going to be thrown into the front line in a few days' time, were not even taught how to fire a rifle or pull the pin out of a bomb. At the time I did not grasp that this was because there were no weapons to be had. In the POUM militia the shortage of rifles was so desperate that fresh troops reaching the front always had to take their rifles from the troops they relieved in the line. In the whole of the Lenin Barracks there were, I believe, no rifles except those used by the sentries.

After a few days, though still a complete rabble by any ordinary standard, we were considered fit to be seen in public, and in the mornings we were marched out to the public gardens on the hill beyond the Plaza de España. This was the common drill-ground of all the party militias, besides the Carabineros and the first contingents of the newly formed

Popular Army. Up in the public gardens it was a strange and heartening sight. Down every path and alley-way, amid the formal flowerbeds, squads and companies of men marched stiffly to and fro, throwing out their chests and trying desperately to look like soldiers. All of them were unarmed and none completely in uniform, though on most of them the militia uniform was breaking out in patches here and there. The procedure was always very much the same. For three hours we strutted to and fro (the Spanish marching step is very short and rapid), then we halted, broke the ranks and flocked thirstily to a little grocer's shop which was half-way down the hill and was doing a roaring trade in cheap wine. Everyone was very friendly to me. As an Englishman I was something of a curiosity, and the Carabinero officers made much of me and stood me drinks. Meanwhile, whenever I could get our lieutenant into a corner, I was clamouring to be instructed in the use of a machine-gun. I used to drag my Hugo's dictionary out of my pocket and start on him in my villainous Spanish:

　'Yo sé manejar fusil. No sé manejar ametralladora. Quiero aprender ametralladora. Quándo vamos aprender ametralladora?'

The answer was always a harassed smile and a promise that there should be machine-gun instruction *mañana*. Needless to say *mañana* never came. Several days passed and the recruits learned to march in step and spring to attention almost smartly, but if they knew which end of a rifle the bullet came out of, that was all they knew. One day an armed Carabinero strolled up to us when we were halting and allowed us to examine his rifle. It turned out that in the whole of my section no one except myself even knew how to load the rifle, much less how to take aim.

All this time I was having the usual struggles with the Spanish language. Apart from myself there was only one Englishman at the barracks, and nobody even among the officers spoke a word of French. Things were not made easier for me by the fact that when my companions spoke to one another they generally spoke in Catalan. The only way I could get along was to carry everywhere a small dictionary which I whipped out of my pocket in moments of crisis. But I would sooner be a foreigner in Spain than in most countries. How easy it is to make friends in Spain! Within a day or two there was a score of militiamen who called me by my Christian name, showed me the ropes and overwhelmed me with hospitality. I am not writing a book of propaganda and I do not want to idealise the POUM militia. The whole militia-system had serious faults, and the men themselves were a mixed lot, for by this time voluntary recruitment was falling off and many of the best men were already at the front or dead. There was always among us a certain percentage who were completely useless. Boys of fifteen were being brought up for enlistment by their parents, quite openly for the sake of the ten pesetas a day which was the militiaman's wage; also for the sake of the bread which the militia received in plenty and could smuggle home to their parents. But I defy anyone to be thrown as I was among the Spanish working class – I ought perhaps to say the Catalan working class, for apart from a few Aragonese and Andalusians I mixed only with Catalans – and not be struck by their essential decency; above all, their straightforwardness and generosity. A Spaniard's generosity, in the ordinary sense of the word, is at times almost embarrassing. If you ask him for a cigarette he will force the whole packet upon you. And beyond this there is generosity in a deeper sense, a real largeness of spirit, which I have met with again and again in the most unpromising circumstances. Some of the journalists and other foreigners who travelled in Spain during the war have declared that in secret the Spaniards were bitterly jealous of foreign aid. All I can say is that I never observed anything of the kind. I remember that a few days before I left the barracks a group of men returned on leave from the front. They were talking excitedly about their experiences and were full of enthusiasm for some French troops who had been next to them at Huesca. The French were very brave, they said; adding enthusiastically: *'Más valientes que nosotros'* – 'Braver than we are!' Of course I demurred, whereupon they explained that the French knew more of the art of war – were more expert with bombs, machine-guns, and so forth. Yet the remark was significant. An Englishman would cut his hand off sooner than say a thing like that.

Every foreigner who served in the militia spent his first few weeks in learning to love the Spaniards and in being exasperated by certain of their characteristics. In the front line my own exasperation sometimes reached the pitch of fury. The Spaniards are good at many things, but not at making war. All foreigners alike are appalled by their inefficiency, above all their maddening unpunctuality. The one Spanish word that no foreigner can avoid learning is *mañana* – 'to-morrow' (literally, 'the morning'). Whenever it is conceivably possible, the business of today is put off until *mañana*. This is so notorious that even the Spaniards themselves make jokes about it. In Spain nothing, from a meal to a battle, ever happens at the appointed time. As a general rule things happen too late, but just occasionally – just so that you shan't even be able to depend on their happening late – they happen too early. A train which is due to leave at eight will normally leave at any time between nine and ten, but perhaps once a week, thanks to some private whim of the engine-driver, it leaves at half-past seven. Such things can be a little trying. In theory I rather admire the Spaniards for not sharing our Northern time-neurosis; but unfortunately I share it myself.

After endless rumours, *mañanas*, and delays we were suddenly ordered to the front at two hours' notice, when much of our equipment was still unissued. There were terrible tumults in the quartermaster's store; in the end numbers of men had to leave without their full equipment. The barracks had promptly filled with women who seemed to have sprung up from the ground and were helping their menfolk to roll their blankets and pack their kit-bags. It was rather humiliating that I had to be shown how to put on my new leather cartridge-boxes by a Spanish girl, the wife of Williams, the other English militiaman. She was a gentle, dark-eyed, intensely feminine creature who looked as though her life-work was to rock a cradle, but who as a matter of fact had fought bravely in the street-battles of July. At this time she was carrying a baby which was born just ten months after the outbreak of war and had perhaps been begotten behind a barricade.

The train was due to leave at eight, and it was about ten past eight when the harassed, sweating officers managed to marshal us in the barrack square. I remember very vividly the torchlit scene – the uproar and excitement, the red flags flapping in the torchlight, the massed ranks of militiamen with their knapsacks on their backs and their rolled blankets worn bandolier-wise across the shoulder; and the shouting and the clatter of boots and tin pannikins, and then a tremendous and finally successful hissing for silence; and then some political commissar standing beneath a huge rolling red banner and making us a speech in Catalan. Finally they marched us to the station, taking the longest route, three or four miles, so as to show us to the whole town. In the Ramblas they halted us while a borrowed band played some revolutionary tune or other. Once again the conquering-hero stuff – shouting and enthusiasm, red flags and red and black flags everywhere, friendly crowds thronging the pavement to have a look at us, women waving from the windows. How natural it all seemed then; how remote and improbable now! The train was packed so tight with men that there was barely room even on the floor, let alone on the seats. At the last moment Williams's wife came rushing down the platform and gave us a bottle of wine and a foot of that bright red sausage which tastes of soap and gives you diarrhoea. The train crawled out of Catalonia and on to the plateau of Aragón at the normal war-time speed of something under twenty kilometres an hour.

II

Barbastro, though a long way from the front line, looked bleak and chipped. Swarms of militiamen in shabby uniforms wandered up and down the streets, trying to keep warm. On a ruinous wall I came upon a poster dating from the previous year and announcing that 'six handsome bulls' would be killed in the arena on such and such a date. How forlorn its faded colours looked! Where were the handsome bulls and the handsome bullfighters now? It appeared that even in Barcelona there were hardly any bullfights nowadays; for some reason all the best matadors were Fascists.

They sent my company by lorry to Siétamo, then westward to Alcubierre, which was just behind the line fronting Saragossa. Siétamo had been fought over three times before the Anarchists finally took it in October, and parts of it were smashed to pieces by shell-fire and most of the houses pockmarked by rifle-bullets. We were 1,500 feet above sea-level now. It was beastly cold, with dense mists that came swirling up from nowhere. Between Siétamo and Alcubierre the lorry-driver lost his way (this was one of the regular features of the war) and we were wandering for hours in the mist. It was late at night when we reached Alcubierre. Somebody shepherded us through morasses of mud into a mule-stable where we dug ourselves down into the chaff and promptly fell asleep. Chaff is not bad to sleep in when it is clean, not so good as hay but better than straw. It was only in the morning light that I discovered that the chaff was full of breadcrusts, torn newspaper, bones, dead rats, and jagged milk tins.

We were near the front line now, near enough to smell the characteristic smell of war – in my experience a smell of excrement and decaying food. Alcubierre had never been shelled and was in a better state than most of the villages immediately behind the line. Yet I believe that even in peacetime you could not travel in that part of Spain without being struck by the peculiar squalid misery of the Aragonese villages. They are built like fortresses, a mass of mean little houses of mud and stone huddling round the church, and even in spring you see hardly a flower anywhere; the houses have no gardens, only backyards where ragged fowls skate over the beds of mule-dung. It was vile weather, with alternate mist and rain. The narrow earth roads had been churned into a sea of mud, in places two feet deep, through which the lorries struggled with racing wheels and the peasants led their clumsy carts which were pulled by strings of mules, sometimes as many as six in a string, always pulling tandem. The constant come-and-go of troops had reduced the village to a state of unspeakable filth. It did not possess and never had possessed such a thing as a lavatory or a drain of any kind, and there was not a square yard anywhere where you could tread without watching your step. The church had long been used as a latrine; so had all the fields for a quarter of a mile round. I never think of my first two months at war without thinking of wintry stubble fields whose edges are crusted with dung.

Two days passed and no rifles were issued to us. When you had been to the Comité de Guerra and inspected the row of holes in the wall – holes made by rifle-volleys, various Fascists having been executed there – you had seen all the sights that Alcubierre contained. Up in the front line things were obviously quiet; very few wounded were coming in. The chief excitement was the arrival of Fascist deserters, who were brought under guard from the front line. Many of the troops opposite us on this part of the line were not Fascists at all, merely wretched conscripts who had been doing their military service at the time when war broke out and were only too anxious to escape. Occasionally small batches of them took the risk of slipping across to our lines. No doubt more would have done so if their relatives had not been in Fascist territory. These deserters were the first 'real' Fascists I had ever seen. It struck me that they were indistinguishable from ourselves, except that they wore khaki overalls.

They were always ravenously hungry when they arrived – natural enough after a day or two of dodging about in no-man's-land, but it was always triumphantly pointed to as a proof that the Fascist troops were starving. I watched one of them being fed in a peasant's house. It was somehow rather a pitiful sight. A tall boy of twenty, deeply windburnt, with his clothes in rags, crouched over the fire shovelling a pannikinful of stew into himself at desperate speed; and all the while his eyes flitted nervously round the ring of militiamen who stood watching him. I think he still half-believed that we were bloodthirsty 'Reds' and were going to shoot him as soon as he had finished his meal; the armed man who guarded him kept stroking his shoulder and making reassuring noises. On one memorable day fifteen deserters arrived in a single batch. They were led through the village in triumph with a man riding in front of them on a white horse. I managed to take a rather blurry photograph which was stolen from me later.

On our third morning in Alcubierre the rifles arrived. A sergeant with a coarse dark-yellow face was handing them out in the mule-stable. I got a shock of dismay when I saw the thing they gave me. It was a German Mauser dated 1896 – more than forty years old! It was rusty, the bolt was stiff, the wooden barrel-guard was split; one glance down the muzzle showed that it was corroded and past praying for. Most of the rifles were equally bad, some of them even worse, and no attempt was made to give the best weapons to the men who knew how to use them. The best rifle of the lot, only ten years old, was given to a half-witted little beast of fifteen, known to everyone as the *maricón* (Nancy-boy). The sergeant gave us five minutes' 'instruction', which consisted in explaining how you loaded a rifle and how you took the bolt to pieces. Many of the militiamen had never had a gun in their hands before, and very few, I imagine, knew what the sights were for. Cartridges were handed out, fifty to a man, and then the ranks were formed and we strapped our kits on our backs and set out for the front line, about three miles away.

The *centuria*, eighty men and several dogs, wound raggedly up the road. Every militia column had at least one dog attached to it as a mascot. One wretched brute that marched with us had had POUM branded on it in huge letters and slunk along as though conscious that there was something wrong with its appearance. At the head of the column, beside the red flag, Georges Kopp, the stout Belgian *comandante*, was riding a black horse; a little way ahead a youth from the brigand-like militia cavalry pranced to and fro, galloping up every piece of rising ground and posing himself in picturesque attitudes at the summit. The splendid horses of the Spanish cavalry had been captured in large numbers during the revolution and handed over to the militia, who, of course, were busy riding them to death.

The road wound between yellow infertile fields, untouched since last year's harvest. Ahead of us was the low sierra that lies between Alcubierre and Saragossa. We were getting near the front line now, near the bombs, the machine-guns and the mud. In secret I was frightened. I knew the line was quiet at present, but unlike most of the men about me I was old enough to remember the Great War, though not old enough to have fought in it. War, to me, meant roaring projectiles and skipping shards of steel; above all it meant mud, lice, hunger, and cold. It is curious, but I dreaded the cold much more than I dreaded the enemy. The thought of it had been haunting me all the time I was in Barcelona; I had even lain awake at nights thinking of the cold in the trenches, the stand-to's in the grisly dawns, the long hours on sentry-go with a frosted rifle, the icy mud that would slop over my boot-tops. I admit, too, that I felt a kind of horror as I looked at the people I was marching among. You cannot possibly conceive what a rabble we looked. We straggled along with far less cohesion than a flock of sheep; before we had gone two miles the rear of the column was out of sight. And quite half of the so-called men were children – but I mean literally children, of sixteen years old at the very most. Yet they were all happy and excited at the prospect of getting to the front at last. As we neared the line the boys round the red flag in front began to utter shouts of '*Visca POUM!*' '*Fascistas – maricones!*' and so forth – shouts which were meant to be war-like and menacing, but which, from those childish throats, sounded as pathetic as the cries of kittens. It seemed dreadful that the defenders of the Republic should be this mob of ragged children carrying worn-out rifles which they did not know how to use. I remember wondering what would happen if a Fascist aeroplane passed our way – whether the airman would even bother to dive down and give us a burst from his machine-gun. Surely even from the air he could see that we were not real soldiers?

As the road struck into the sierra we branched off to the right and climbed a narrow mule-track that wound round the mountain-side. The hills in that part of Spain are of a queer formation, horseshoe-shaped with flattish tops and very steep sides running down into immense ravines. On the higher slopes nothing grows except stunted shrubs and heath, with the white bones of the limestone sticking out everywhere. The front line here was not a continuous line of trenches, which would have been impossible in such mountainous country; it was simply a chain of fortified posts, always known as 'positions', perched on each hilltop. In the distance you could see our 'position' at the crown of the horseshoe; a ragged barricade of sandbags, a red flag fluttering, the smoke of dug-out fires. A little nearer, and you could smell a sickening sweetish stink that lived in my nostrils for weeks afterwards. Into the cleft immediately behind the position all the refuse of months had been tipped – a deep festering bed of breadcrusts, excrement, and rusty tins.

The company we were relieving were getting their kits together. They had been three months in the line; their uniforms were caked with mud, their boots falling to pieces, their faces mostly bearded. The captain commanding the position, Levinski by name, but known to everyone as Benjamin, and by birth a Polish Jew, but speaking French as his native language, crawled out of his dug-out and greeted us. He was a short youth of about twenty-five, with stiff black hair and a pale eager face which at this period of the war was always very dirty. A few stray bullets were cracking high overhead. The position was a semi-circular enclosure about fifty yards across, with a parapet that was partly sandbags and partly lumps of limestone. There were thirty or forty dug-outs running into the ground like rat-holes. Williams, myself, and Williams's Spanish brother-in-law made a swift dive for the nearest unoccupied dug-out that looked habitable. Somewhere in front an occasional rifle banged, making queer rolling echoes among the stony hills. We had just dumped our kits and were crawling out of the dug-out when there was another bang and one of the children of our company rushed back from the parapet with his face pouring blood. He had fired his rifle and had somehow managed to blow out the bolt; his scalp was torn to ribbons by the splinters of the burst cartridge-case. It was our first casualty, and, characteristically, self-inflicted.

In the afternoon we did our first guard and Benjamin showed us round the position. In front of the parapet there ran a system of narrow trenches hewn out of the rock, with extremely primitive loopholes made of piles of limestone. There were twelve sentries, placed at various points in the trench and behind the inner parapet. In front of the trench was the barbed wire, and then the hill-side slid down into a seemingly bottomless ravine; opposite were naked hills, in places mere cliffs of rock, all grey and wintry, with no life anywhere, not even a bird. I peered cautiously through a loophole, trying to find the Fascist trench.

'Where are the enemy?'

Benjamin waved his hand expansively. 'Over zere.' (Benjamin spoke English – terrible English.)

'But *where?*'

According to my ideas of trench warfare the Fascists would be fifty or a hundred yards away. I could see nothing – seemingly their trenches were very well concealed. Then with a shock of dismay I saw where Benjamin was pointing; on the opposite hill-top, beyond the ravine, seven hundred metres away at the very least, the tiny outline of a parapet and a red-and-yellow flag – the Fascist position. I was indescribably disappointed. We were nowhere near them! At that range our rifles were completely useless. But at this moment there was a shout of excitement. Two Fascists, greyish figurines in the distance, were scrambling up the naked hill-side opposite. Benjamin grabbed the nearest man's rifle, took aim, and pulled the trigger. Click! A dud cartridge; I thought it a bad omen.

The new sentries were no sooner in the trench than they began firing a terrific fusillade at nothing in particular. I could see the Fascists, tiny as ants, dodging to and fro behind their parapet, and sometimes a black dot which was a head would pause for a moment, impudently exposed. It was obviously no use firing. But presently the sentry on my left, leaving his post in the typical Spanish fashion, sidled up to me and began urging me to fire. I tried to explain that at that range and with these rifles you could not hit a man except by accident. But he was only a child, and he kept motioning with his rifle towards one of the dots, grinning as eagerly as a dog that expects a pebble to be thrown. Finally I put my sights up to seven hundred and let fly. The dot disappeared. I hope it went near enough to make him jump. It was the first time in my life that I had fired a gun at a human being.

Now that I had seen the front I was profoundly disgusted. They called this war! And we were hardly even in touch with the enemy! I made no attempt to keep my head below the level of the trench. A little while later, however, a bullet shot past my ear with a vicious crack and banged into the parados behind. Alas! I ducked. All my life I had sworn that I would not duck the first time a bullet passed over me; but the movement appears to be instinctive, and almost everybody does it at least once.

III

In trench warfare five things are important: firewood, food, tobacco, candles and the enemy. In winter on the Saragossa front they were important in that order, with the enemy a bad last. Except at night, when a surprise-attack was always conceivable, nobody bothered about the enemy. They were simply remote black insects whom one occasionally saw hopping to and fro. The real preoccupation of both armies was trying to keep warm.

I ought to say in passing that all the time I was in Spain I saw very little fighting. I was on the Aragón front from January to May, and between January and late March little or nothing happened on that front, except at Teruel. In March there was heavy fighting round Huesca, but I personally played only a minor part in it. Later, in June, there was the disastrous attack on Huesca in which several thousand men were killed in a single day, but I had been wounded and disabled before that happened. The things that one normally thinks of as the horrors of war seldom happened to me. No aeroplane ever dropped a bomb anywhere near me, I do not think a shell ever exploded within fifty yards of me, and I was only in hand-to-hand fighting once (once is once too often, I may say). Of course I was often under heavy machine-gun fire, but usually at longish ranges. Even at Huesca you were generally safe enough if you took reasonable precautions.

Up here, in the hills round Saragossa, it was simply the mingled boredom and discomfort of stationary warfare. A life as uneventful as a city clerk's, and almost as regular. Sentry-go, patrols, digging; digging, patrols, sentry-go. On every hill-top, Fascist or Loyalist, a knot of ragged, dirty men shivering round their flag and trying to keep warm. And all day and night the meaningless bullets wandering across the empty valleys and only by some rare improbable chance getting home on a human body.

Often I used to gaze round the wintry landscape and marvel at the futility of it all. The inconclusiveness of such a kind of war! Earlier, about October, there had been savage fighting for all these hills; then, because the lack of men and arms, especially artillery, made any large-scale operation impossible, each army had dug itself in and settled down on the hill-tops it had won. Over to our right there was a small outpost, also POUM, and on the spur to our left, at seven o'clock of us, a PSUC position faced a taller spur with several small Fascist posts dotted on its peaks. The so-called line zigzagged to and fro in a pattern that would have been quite unintelligible if every position had not flown a flag. The POUM and PSUC flags were red, those of the Anarchists red and black; the Fascists generally flew the monarchist flag (red-yellow-red), but occasionally they flew the flag of the Republic (red-yellow-purple).* The scenery was stupendous, if you could forget that every mountain-top was occupied by troops and was therefore littered with tin cans and crusted with dung. To the right of us the sierra bent south-eastwards and made way for the wide, veined valley that stretched across to Huesca. In the middle of the plain a few tiny cubes sprawled like a throw of dice; this was the town of Robres, which was in Loyalist possession. Often in the mornings the valley was hidden under seas of cloud, out of which the hills rose flat and blue, giving the landscape a strange resemblance to a photographic negative. Beyond Huesca there were more hills of the same formation as our own, streaked with a pattern of snow which altered day by day. In the far distance the monstrous peaks of the Pyrenees, where the snow never melts, seemed to float upon nothing. Even down in the plain everything looked dead and bare. The hills opposite us were grey and wrinkled like the skins of elephants. Almost always the sky was empty

---

* Orwell, in his list of Errata, noted: 'Am not now completely certain that I ever saw Fascists flying the republican flag, though I *think* they sometimes flew it with a small imposed swastika.'

of birds. I do not think I have ever seen a country where there were so few birds. The only birds one saw at any time were a kind of magpie, and the coveys of partridges that startled one at night with their sudden whirring, and, very rarely, the flights of eagles that drifted slowly over, generally followed by rifle-shots which they did not deign to notice.

At night and in misty weather patrols were sent out in the valley between ourselves and the Fascists. The job was not popular, it was too cold and too easy to get lost, and I soon found that I could get leave to go out on patrol as often as I wished. In the huge jagged ravines there were no paths or tracks of any kind; you could only find your way about by making successive journeys and noting fresh landmarks each time. As the bullet flies the nearest Fascist post was seven hundred metres from our own, but it was a mile and a half by the only practicable route. It was rather fun wandering about the dark valleys with the stray bullets flying high overhead like redshanks whistling. Better than night-time were the heavy mists, which often lasted all day and which had a habit of clinging round the hill-tops and leaving the valleys clear. When you were anywhere near the Fascist lines you had to creep at a snail's pace; it was very difficult to move quietly on those hill-sides, among the crackling shrubs and tinkling limestones. It was only at the third or fourth attempt that I managed to find my way to the Fascist lines. The mist was very thick, and I crept up to the barbed wire to listen. I could hear the Fascists talking and singing inside. Then to my alarm I heard several of them coming down the hill towards me. I cowered behind a bush that suddenly seemed very small, and tried to cock my rifle without noise. However, they branched off and did not come within sight of me. Behind the bush where I was hiding I came upon various relics of the earlier fighting – a pile of empty cartridge-cases, a leather cap with a bullet-hole in it, and a red flag, obviously one of our own. I took it back to the position, where it was unsentimentally torn up for cleaning-rags.

I had been made a corporal, or *cabo*, as it was called, as soon as we reached the front, and was in command of a guard of twelve men. It was no sinecure, especially at first. The *centuria* was an untrained mob composed mostly of boys in their teens. Here and there in the militia you came across children as young as eleven or twelve, usually refugees from Fascist territory who had been enlisted as militiamen as the easiest way of providing for them. As a rule they were employed on light work in the rear, but sometimes they managed to worm their way to the front line, where they were a public menace. I remember one little brute throwing a hand-grenade into the dug-out fire 'for a joke'. At Monte Pocero I do not think there was anyone younger than fifteen, but the average age must have been well under twenty. Boys of this age ought never to be used in the front line, because they cannot stand the lack of sleep which is inseparable from trench warfare. At the beginning it was almost impossible to keep our position properly guarded at night. The wretched children of my section could only be roused by dragging them out of their dug-outs feet foremost, and as soon as your back was turned they left their posts and slipped into shelter; or they would even, in spite of the frightful cold, lean up against the wall of the trench and fall fast asleep. Luckily the enemy were very unenterprising. There were nights when it seemed to me that our position could be stormed by twenty Boy Scouts armed with air-guns, or twenty Girl Guides armed with battledores, for that matter.

At this time and until much later the Catalan militias were still on the same basis as they had been at the beginning of the war. In the early days of Franco's revolt the militias had been hurriedly raised by the various trade unions and political parties; each was essentially a political organisation, owing allegiance to its party as much as to the central Government. When the Popular Army, which was a 'non-political' army organised on more or less ordinary lines, was raised at the beginning of 1937, the party militias were theoretically incorporated in it. But for a long time the only changes that occurred were on paper; the new Popular Army troops did not reach the Aragón front in any numbers till June, and until that time the militia-system remained unchanged. The essential point of the system was social equality between officers and men. Everyone from general to private drew the same pay, ate the same food, wore the same clothes, and mingled on terms of complete equality. If you wanted to slap the general commanding the division on the back and ask him for a cigarette, you could do so, and no one thought it curious. In theory at any rate each militia was a democracy and not a hierarchy. It was understood that orders had to be obeyed, but it was also understood that when you gave an order you gave it as comrade to comrade and not as superior to inferior. There were officers and NCOs, but there was no military rank in the ordinary sense; no titles, no badges, no heel-clicking and saluting. They had attempted to produce within the militias a sort of temporary working model of the classless society. Of course there was not perfect equality, but there was a nearer approach to it than I had ever seen or than I would have thought conceivable in time of war.

But I admit that at first sight the state of affairs at the front horrified me. How on earth could the war be won by an army of this type? It was what everyone was saying at the time, and though it was true it was also unreasonable. For in the circumstances the militias could not have been much better than they were. A modern mechanised army does not spring up out of the ground, and if the Government had waited until it had trained troops at its disposal, Franco would never have been resisted. Later it became the fashion to decry the militias, and therefore to pretend that the faults which were due to lack of training and weapons were the result of the equalitarian system. Actually, a newly raised draft of militia was an undisciplined mob not because the officers called the privates 'Comrade' but because raw troops are *always* an undisciplined mob. In practice the democratic 'revolutionary' type of discipline is more reliable than might be expected. In a workers' army discipline is theoretically voluntary. It is based on class-loyalty, whereas the discipline of a bourgeois conscript army is based ultimately on fear. (The Popular Army that replaced the militias was midway between the two types.) In the militias the bullying and abuse that go on in an ordinary army would never have been tolerated for a moment. The normal military punishments existed, but they were only invoked for very serious offences. When a man refused to obey an order you did not immediately get him punished; you first appealed to him in the name of comradeship. Cynical people with no experience of handling men will say instantly that this would never 'work', but as a matter of fact it does 'work' in the long run. The discipline of even the worst drafts of militia visibly improved as time went on. In January the job of keeping a dozen raw recruits up to the mark almost turned my hair grey. In May for a short while I was acting-lieutenant in command of about thirty men, English and Spanish. We had all been under fire for months, and I never had the slightest difficulty in getting an order obeyed or in getting men to volunteer for a dangerous job. 'Revolutionary' discipline depends on political consciousness – on an understanding of *why* orders must be obeyed; it takes time to diffuse this, but it also takes time to drill a man into an automaton on the barrack-square. The journalists who sneered at the militia-system seldom remembered that the militias had to hold the line while the Popular Army was training in the rear. And it is a tribute to the strength of 'revolutionary' discipline that the militias stayed in the field at all. For until about June 1937 there was nothing to keep them there, except class loyalty. Individual deserters could be shot – were shot, occasionally – but if a thousand men had decided to walk out of the line together there was no force to stop them. A conscript army in the same circumstances – with its battle-police removed – would have melted away. Yet the militias held the line, though God knows they won very few victories, and even individual desertions were not common. In four or five months in the POUM militia I only heard of four men deserting, and two of those were fairly certainly spies who had enlisted to obtain information. At the beginning the apparent chaos, the general lack of training, the fact that you often had to argue for five minutes before you could get an order obeyed, appalled and infuriated me. I had British Army ideas, and certainly the Spanish militias were very unlike the British Army. But considering the circumstances they were better troops than one had any right to expect.

Meanwhile, firewood – always firewood. Throughout that period there is probably no entry in my diary that does not mention firewood, or rather the lack of it. We were between two and three thousand feet above sea-level, it was mid-winter and the cold was unspeakable. The temperature was not exceptionally low, on many nights it did not even freeze, and the wintry sun often shone for an hour in the middle of the day; but even if it was not really cold, I assure you that it seemed so. Sometimes there were shrieking winds that tore your cap off and twisted your hair in all directions, sometimes there were mists that poured into the trench like a liquid and seemed to penetrate your bones; frequently it rained, and even a quarter of an hour's rain was enough to make conditions intolerable. The thin skin of earth over the limestone turned promptly into a slippery grease, and as you were always walking on a slope it was impossible to keep your footing. On dark nights I have often fallen half a dozen times in twenty yards; and this was dangerous, because it meant that the lock of one's rifle became jammed with mud. For days together clothes, boots, blankets, and rifles were more or less coated with mud. I had brought as many thick clothes as I could carry, but many of the men were terribly underclad. For the whole garrison, about a hundred men, there were only twelve greatcoats, which had to be handed from sentry to sentry, and most of the men had only one blanket. One icy night I made a list in my diary of the clothes I was wearing. It is of some interest as showing the amount of clothes the human body can carry. I was wearing a thick vest and pants, a flannel shirt, two pullovers, a woollen jacket, a pigskin jacket, corduroy breeches, puttees, thick socks, boots, a stout trench-coat, a muffler, lined leather gloves, and a woollen cap. Nevertheless I was shivering like a jelly. But I admit I am unusually sensitive to cold.

Firewood was the one thing that really mattered. The point about the firewood was that there was practically no firewood to be had. Our miserable mountain had not even at its best much vegetation, and for months it had been ranged over by freezing militiamen, with the result that everything thicker than one's finger had long since been burnt. When we were not eating, sleeping, on guard or on fatigue-duty we were in the valley behind the position, scrounging for fuel. All my memories of that time are memories of scrambling up and down the almost perpendicular slopes, over the jagged limestone that knocked one's boots to pieces, pouncing eagerly on tiny twigs of wood. Three people searching for a couple of hours could collect enough fuel to keep the dug-out fire alight for about an hour. The eagerness of our search for firewood turned us all into botanists. We classified according to their burning qualities every plant that grew on the mountain-side; the various heaths and grasses that were good to start a fire with but burnt out in a few minutes, the wild rosemary and the tiny whin bushes that would burn when the fire was well alight, the stunted oak tree, smaller than a gooseberry bush, that was practically unburnable. There was a kind of dried-up reed that was very good for starting fires with, but these grew only on the hill-top to the left of the position, and you had to go under fire to get them. If the Fascist machine-gunners saw you they gave you a drum of ammunition all to yourself. Generally their aim was high and the bullets sang overhead like birds, but sometimes they crackled and chipped the limestone uncomfortably close, whereupon you flung yourself on your face. You went on gathering reeds, however; nothing mattered in comparison with firewood.

Beside the cold the other discomforts seemed petty. Of course all of us were permanently dirty. Our water, like our food, came on mule-back from Alcubierre, and each man's share worked out at about a quart a day. It was beastly water, hardly more transparent than milk. Theoretically it was for drinking only, but I always stole a pannikinful for washing in the mornings. I used to wash one day and shave the next; there was never enough water for both. The position stank abominably, and outside the little enclosure of the barricade there was excrement everywhere. Some of the militiamen habitually defecated in the trench, a disgusting thing when one had to walk round it in the darkness. But the dirt never worried me. Dirt is a thing people make too much fuss about. It is astonishing how quickly you get used to doing without a handkerchief and to eating out of the tin pannikin in which you also wash. Nor was sleeping in one's clothes any hardship after a day or two. It was of course impossible to take one's clothes and especially one's boots off at night; one had to be ready to turn out instantly in case of an attack. In eighty nights I only took my clothes off three times, though I did occasionally manage to get them off in the daytime. It was too cold for lice as yet, but rats and mice abounded. It is often said that you don't find rats and mice in the same place, but you do when there is enough food for them.

In other ways we were not badly off. The food was good enough and there was plenty of wine. Cigarettes were still being issued at the rate of a packet a day, matches were issued every other day, and there was even an issue of candles. They were very thin candles, like those on a Christmas cake, and were popularly supposed to have been looted from churches. Every dug-out was issued daily with three inches of candle, which would burn for about twenty minutes. At that time it was still possible to buy candles, and I had brought several pounds of them with me. Later on the famine of matches and candles made life a misery. You do not realise the importance of these things until you lack them. In a night-alarm, for instance, when everyone in the dug-out is scrambling for his rifle and treading on everybody else's face, being able to strike a light may make the difference between life and death. Every militiaman possessed a tinder-lighter and several yards of yellow wick. Next to his rifle it was his most important possession. The tinder-lighters had the great advantage that they could be struck in a wind, but they would only smoulder, so that they were no use for lighting a fire. When the match famine was at its worst our only way of producing a flame was to pull the bullet out of a cartridge and touch the cordite off with a tinder-lighter.

It was an extraordinary life that we were living – an extraordinary way to be at war, if you could call it war. The whole militia chafed against the inaction and clamoured constantly to know why we were not allowed to attack. But it was perfectly obvious that there would be no battle for a long while yet, unless the enemy started it. Georges Kopp, on his periodical tours of inspection, was quite frank with us. 'This is not a war,' he used to say, 'it is a comic opera with an occasional death.' As a matter of fact the stagnation on the Aragón front had political causes of which I knew nothing at that time; but the purely military difficulties – quite apart from the lack of reserves of men – were obvious to anybody.

To begin with, there was the nature of the country. The front line, ours and the Fascists', lay in positions of immense natural strength, which as a rule could only be approached from one side. Provided a few trenches have been dug, such places cannot be taken by infantry, except in overwhelming numbers. In our own position or most of those round us a dozen men with two machine-guns could have held off a battalion. Perched on the hill-tops as we were, we should have made lovely marks for artillery; but there was no artillery. Sometimes I used to gaze round the landscape and long – oh, how passionately! – for a couple of batteries of guns. One could have destroyed the enemy positions one after another as easily as smashing nuts with a hammer. But on our side the guns simply did not exist. The Fascists did occasionally manage to bring a gun or two from Saragossa and fire a very few shells, so few that they never even found the range and the shells plunged harmlessly into the empty ravines. Against machine-guns and with-out artillery there are only three things you can do: dig yourself in at a safe distance – four hundred yards, say – advance across the open and be massacred, or make small-scale night-attacks that will not alter the general situation. Practically the alternatives are stagnation or suicide.

And beyond this there was the complete lack of war materials of every description. It needs an effort to realise how badly the militias were armed at this time. Any public school OTC in England is far more like a modern army than we were. The badness of our weapons was so astonishing that it is worth recording in detail.

For this sector of the front the entire artillery consisted of four trench-mortars with *fifteen rounds* for each gun. Of course they were far too precious to be fired and the mortars were kept in Alcubierre. There were machine-guns at the rate of approximately one to fifty men; they were oldish guns, but fairly accurate up to three or four hundred yards. Beyond this we had only rifles, and the majority of the rifles were scrap-iron. There were three types of rifle in use. The first was the long Mauser. These were seldom less than twenty years old, their sights were about as much use as a broken speedometer, and in most of them the rifling was hopelessly corroded; about one rifle in ten was not bad, however. Then there was the short Mauser, or *mousqueton*, really a cavalry weapon. These were more popular than the others because they were lighter to carry and less nuisance in a trench, also because they were comparatively new and looked efficient. Actually they were almost useless. They were made out of reassembled parts, no bolt belonged to its rifle, and three-quarters of them could be counted on to jam after five shots. There were also a few Winchester rifles. These were nice to shoot with, but they were wildly inaccurate, and as their cartridges had no clips they could only be fired one shot at a time. Ammunition was so scarce that each man entering the line was only issued with fifty rounds, and most of it was exceedingly bad. The Spanish-made cartridges were all refills and would jam even the best rifles. The Mexican cartridges were better and were therefore reserved for the machine-guns. Best of all was the German-made ammunition, but as this came only from prisoners and deserters there was not much of it. I always kept a clip of German or Mexican ammunition in my pocket for use in an emergency. But in practice when the emergency came I seldom fired my rifle; I was too frightened of the beastly thing jamming and too anxious to reserve at any rate one round that would go off.

We had no tin hats, no bayonets, hardly any revolvers or pistols, and not more than one bomb between five or ten men. The bomb in use at this time was a frightful object known as the 'FAI bomb', it having been produced by the Anarchists in the early days of the war. It was on the principle of a Mills bomb, but the lever was held down not by a pin but a piece of tape. You broke the tape and then got rid of the bomb with the utmost possible speed. It was said of these bombs that they were 'impartial'; they killed the man they were thrown at and the man who threw them.

There were several other types, even more primitive but probably a little less dangerous – to the thrower, I mean. It was not till late March that I saw a bomb worth throwing.

And apart from weapons there was a shortage of all the minor necessities of war. We had no maps or charts, for instance. Spain has never been fully surveyed, and the only detailed maps of this area were the old military ones, which were almost all in the possession of the Fascists. We had no range-finders, no telescopes, no periscopes, no field-glasses except a few privately-owned pairs, no flares or Very lights, no wire-cutters, no armourers' tools, hardly even any cleaning materials. The Spaniards seemed never to have heard of a pull-through and looked on in surprise when I constructed one. When you wanted your rifle cleaned you took it to the sergeant, who possessed a long brass ramrod which was invariably bent and therefore scratched the rifling. There was not even any gun oil. You greased your rifle with olive oil, when you could get hold of it; at different times I have greased mine with vaseline, with cold cream, and even with bacon-fat. Moreover, there were no lanterns or electric torches – at this time there was not, I believe, such a thing as an electric torch throughout the whole of our sector of the front, and you could not buy one nearer than Barcelona, and only with difficulty even there.

As time went on, and the desultory rifle-fire rattled among the hills, I began to wonder with increasing scepticism whether anything would ever happen to bring a bit of life, or rather a bit of death, into this cock-eyed war. It was pneumonia that we were fighting against, not against men. When the trenches are more than five hundred yards apart no one gets hit except by accident. Of course there were casualties, but the majority of them were self-inflicted. If I remember rightly, the first five men I saw wounded in Spain were all wounded by our own weapons – I don't mean intentionally, but owing to accident or carelessness. Our worn-out rifles were a danger in themselves. Some of them had a nasty trick of going off if the butt was tapped on the ground; I saw a man shoot himself through the hand owing to this. And in the darkness the raw recruits were always firing at one another. One evening when it was barely even dusk a sentry let fly at me from a distance of twenty yards; but he missed me by a yard – goodness knows how many times the Spanish standard of marksmanship has saved my life. Another time I had gone out on patrol in the mist and had carefully warned the guard commander beforehand. But in coming back I stumbled against a bush, the startled sentry called out that the Fascists were coming, and I had the pleasure of hearing the guard commander order everyone to open rapid fire in my direction. Of course I lay down and the bullets went harmlessly over me. Nothing will convince a Spaniard, at least a young Spaniard, that fire-arms are dangerous. Once, rather later than this, I was photographing some machine-gunners with their gun, which was pointed directly towards me.

'Don't fire,' I said half-jokingly as I focused the camera.

'Oh no, we won't fire.'

The next moment there was a frightful roar and a stream of bullets tore past my face so close that my cheek was stung by grains of cordite. It was unintentional, but the machine-gunners considered it a great joke. Yet only a few days earlier they had seen a mule-driver accidentally shot by a political delegate who was playing the fool with an automatic pistol and had put five bullets in the mule-driver's lungs.

The difficult passwords which the army was using at this time were a minor source of danger. They were those tiresome double passwords in which one word has to be answered by another. Usually they were of an elevating and revolutionary nature, such as *Cultura – progreso*, or *Seremos – invencibles*, and it was often impossible to get illiterate sentries to remember these highfalutin' words. One night, I remember, the password was *Cataluña – heroica*, and a moon-faced peasant lad named Jaime Domenech approached me, greatly puzzled, and asked me to explain.

'*Heroica* – what does *heroica* mean?'

I told him that it meant the same as *valiente*. A little while later he was stumbling up the trench in the darkness, and the sentry challenged him:

'*Alto! Cataluña!*'

'*Valiente!*' yelled Jaime, certain that he was saying the right thing.

Bang!

However, the sentry missed him. In this war everyone always did miss everyone else, when it was humanly possible.

IV

When I had been about three weeks in the line a contingent of twenty or thirty men, sent out from England by the ILP, arrived at Alcubierre, and in order to keep the English on this front together Williams and I were sent to join them. Our new position was at Monte Trazo, several miles further west and within sight of Saragossa.

The position was perched on a sort of razor-back of limestone with dug-outs driven horizontally into the cliff like sand-martins' nests. They went into the ground for prodigious distances, and inside they were pitch dark and so low that you could not even kneel in them, let alone stand. On the peaks to the left of us there were two more POUM positions, one of them an object of fascination to every man in the line, because there were three militiawomen there who did the cooking. These women were not exactly beautiful, but it was found necessary to put the position out of bounds to men of other companies. Five hundred yards to our right there was a PSUC post at the bend of the Alcubierre road. It was just here that the road changed hands. At night you could watch the lamps of our supply-lorries winding out from Alcubierre and, simultaneously, those of the Fascists coming from Saragossa. You could see Saragossa itself, a thin string of lights like the lighted port-holes of a ship, twelve miles south-westward. The Government troops had gazed at it from that distance since August 1936, and they are gazing at it still.

There were about thirty of ourselves, including one Spaniard (Ramón, Williams's brother-in-law), and there were a dozen Spanish machine-gunners. Apart from the one or two inevitable nuisances – for, as everyone knows, war attracts riff-raff – the English were an exceptionally good crowd, both physically and mentally. Perhaps the best of the bunch was Bob Smillie – the grandson of the famous miners' leader – who afterwards died such an evil and meaningless death in Valencia. It says a lot for the Spanish character that the English and the Spaniards always got on well together, in spite of the language difficulty. All Spaniards, we discovered, knew two English expressions. One was 'OK, baby,' the other was a word used by the Barcelona whores in their dealings with English sailors, and I am afraid the compositors would not print it.

Once again there was nothing happening all along the line: only the random crack of bullets and, very rarely, the crash of a Fascist mortar that sent everyone running to the top trench to see which hill the shells were bursting on. The enemy was somewhat closer to us here, perhaps three or four hundred yards away. Their nearest position was exactly opposite ours, with a machine-gun nest whose loopholes constantly tempted one to waste cartridges. The Fascists seldom bothered with rifle-shots, but sent bursts of accurate machine-gun fire at anyone who exposed himself. Nevertheless it was ten days or more before we had our first casualty. The troops opposite us were Spaniards, but according to the deserters there were a few German NCOs among them. At some time in the past there had also been Moors there – poor devils, how they must have felt the cold! – for out in no-man's-land there was a dead Moor who was one of the sights of the locality. A mile or two to the left of us the line ceased to be continuous and there was a tract of country, lower-lying and thickly wooded, which belonged neither to the Fascists nor ourselves. Both we and they used to make daylight patrols there. It was not bad fun in a Boy Scoutish way, though I never saw a Fascist patrol nearer than several hundred yards. By a lot of crawling on your belly you could work your way partly through the Fascist lines and could even see the farm-house flying the monarchist flag, which was the local Fascist headquarters. Occasionally we gave it a rifle-volley and then slipped into cover before the machine-guns could locate us. I hope we broke a few windows, but it was a good eight hundred metres away, and with our rifles you could not make sure of hitting even a house at that range.

The weather was mostly clear and cold; sometimes sunny at midday, but always cold. Here and there in the soil of the hill-sides you found the green beaks of wild crocuses or irises poking through; evidently spring was coming, but coming very slowly. The nights were colder than ever. Coming off guard in the small hours we used to rake together what was left of the cook-house fire and then stand in the red-hot embers. It was bad for your boots, but it was very good for your feet. But there were mornings when the sight of the dawn among the mountain-tops made it almost worthwhile to be out of bed at godless hours. I hate mountains, even from a spectacular point of view. But sometimes the dawn breaking behind the hill-tops in our rear, the first narrow streaks of gold, like swords slitting the darkness, and then the growing light and the seas of carmine cloud stretching away into inconceivable distances, were worth watching even when you had been up all night, when your legs were numb from the knees down and you were sullenly reflecting that there was no hope of food for another three hours. I saw the dawn oftener during this campaign than during the rest of my life put together – or during the part that is to come, I hope.

We were short-handed here, which meant longer guards and more fatigues. I was beginning to suffer a little from the lack of sleep which is inevitable even in the quietest kind of war. Apart from guard-duties and patrols there were constant night-alarms and stand-to's, and in any case you can't sleep properly in a beastly hole in the ground with your feet aching with the cold. In my first three or four months in the line I do not suppose I had more than a dozen periods of twenty-four hours that were completely without sleep; on the other hand I certainly did not have a dozen nights of full sleep. Twenty or thirty hours' sleep in a week was quite a normal amount. The effects of this were not so bad as might be expected; one grew very stupid, and the job of climbing up and down the hills grew harder instead of easier, but one felt well and one was constantly hungry – heavens, how hungry! All food seemed good, even the eternal haricot beans which everyone in Spain finally learned to hate the sight of. Our water, what there was of it, came from miles away, on the backs of mules or little persecuted donkeys. For some reason the Aragón peasants treated their mules well but their donkeys abominably. If a donkey refused to go it was quite usual to kick him in the testicles. The issue of candles had ceased, and matches were running short. The Spaniards taught us how to make olive oil lamps out of a condensed milk tin, a cartridge-clip, and a bit of rag. When you had any olive oil, which was not often, these things would burn with a smoky flicker, about a quarter candle-power, just enough to find your rifle by.

There seemed no hope of any real fighting. When we left Monte Pocero I had counted my cartridges and found that in nearly three weeks I had fired just three shots at the enemy. They say it takes a thousand bullets to kill a man, and at this rate it would be twenty years before I killed my first Fascist. At Monte Trazo the lines were closer and one fired oftener, but I am reasonably certain that I never hit anyone. As a matter of fact,

on this front and at this period of the war the real weapon was not the
rifle but the megaphone. Being unable to kill your enemy you shouted at
him instead. This method of warfare is so extraordinary that it needs
explaining.

Wherever the lines were within hailing distance of one another there
was always a good deal of shouting from trench to trench. From ourselves:
'Fascistas – maricones!' From the Fascists: *'Viva España! Viva Franco!'* – or,
when they knew that there were English opposite them: 'Go home, you
English! We don't want foreigners here!' On the Government side, in the
party militias, the shouting of propaganda to undermine the enemy morale
had been developed into a regular technique. In every suitable position
men, usually machine-gunners, were told off for shouting-duty and provided with megaphones. Generally they shouted a set-piece, full of revolutionary sentiments which explained to the Fascist soldiers that they were
merely the hirelings of international capitalism, that they were fighting
against their own class, etc. etc., and urged them to come over to our side.
This was repeated over and over by relays of men; sometimes it continued
almost the whole night. There is very little doubt that it had its effect;
everyone agreed that the trickle of Fascist deserters was partly caused by
it. If one comes to think of it, when some poor devil of a sentry –
very likely a Socialist or Anarchist trade union member who has been
conscripted against his will – is freezing at his post, the slogan 'Don't
fight against your own class!' ringing again and again through the darkness
is bound to make an impression on him. It might make just the difference
between deserting and not deserting. Of course such a proceeding does
not fit in with the English conception of war. I admit I was amazed and
scandalised when I first saw it done. The idea of trying to convert your
enemy instead of shooting him! I now think that from any point of view
it was a legitimate manoeuvre. In ordinary trench warfare, when there is
no artillery, it is extremely difficult to inflict casualties on the enemy
without receiving an equal number yourself. If you can immobilise a
certain number of men by making them desert, so much the better;
deserters are actually more useful to you than corpses, because they can
give information. But at the beginning it dismayed all of us; it made us
feel that the Spaniards were not taking this war of theirs sufficiently
seriously. The man who did the shouting at the PSUC post down on our

right was an artist at the job. Sometimes, instead of shouting revolutionary slogans he simply told the Fascists how much better we were fed than they were. His account of the Government rations was apt to be a little imaginative. 'Buttered toast!' – you could hear his voice echoing across the lonely valley – 'We're just sitting down to buttered toast over here! Lovely slices of buttered toast!' I do not doubt that, like the rest of us, he had not seen butter for weeks or months past, but in the icy night the news of buttered toast probably set many a Fascist mouth watering. It even made mine water, though I knew he was lying.

One day in February we saw a Fascist aeroplane approaching. As usual, a machine-gun was dragged into the open and its barrel cocked up, and everyone lay on his back to get a good aim. Our isolated positions were not worth bombing, and as a rule the few Fascist aeroplanes that passed our way circled round to avoid machine-gun fire. This time the aeroplane came straight over, too high up to be worth shooting at, and out of it came tumbling not bombs but white glittering things that turned over and over in the air. A few fluttered down into the position. They were copies of a Fascist newspaper, the *Heraldo de Aragón*, announcing the fall of Málaga.

That night the Fascists made a sort of abortive attack. I was just getting down into kip, half dead with sleep, when there was a heavy stream of bullets overhead and someone shouted into the dug-out: 'They're attacking!' I grabbed my rifle and slithered up to my post, which was at the top of the position, beside the machine-gun. There was utter darkness and diabolical noise. The fire of, I think, five machine-guns was pouring upon us, and there was a series of heavy crashes caused by the Fascists flinging bombs over their own parapet in the most idiotic manner. It was intensely dark. Down in the valley to the left of us I could see the greenish flash of rifles where a small party of Fascists, probably a patrol, were chipping in. The bullets were flying round us in the darkness, crack-zip-crack. A few shells came whistling over, but they fell nowhere near us and (as usual in this war) most of them failed to explode. I had a bad moment when yet another machine-gun opened fire from the hill-top in our rear – actually a gun that had been brought up to support us, but at the time it looked as though we were surrounded. Presently our own machine-gun jammed, as it always did jam with those vile cartridges, and the ramrod was lost in the impenetrable darkness. Apparently there was nothing that one could do except stand still and be shot at. The Spanish machine-gunners disdained to take cover, in fact exposed themselves deliberately, so I had to do likewise. Petty though it was, the whole experience was very interesting. It was the first time that I had been properly speaking under fire, and to my humiliation I found that I was horribly frightened. You always, I notice, feel the same when you are under heavy fire – not so much afraid of being hit as afraid because you don't know *where* you will be hit. You are wondering all the while just where the bullet will nip you, and it gives your whole body a most unpleasant sensitiveness.

After an hour or two the firing slowed down and died away. Meanwhile we had had only one casualty. The Fascists had advanced a couple of machine-guns into no-man's-land, but they had kept at a safe distance and made no attempt to storm our parapet. They were in fact not attacking, merely wasting cartridges and making a cheerful noise to celebrate the fall of Málaga. The chief importance of the affair was that it taught me to read the war news in the papers with a more disbelieving eye. A day or two later the newspapers and the radio published reports of a tremendous attack with cavalry and tanks (up a perpendicular hill-side!) which had been beaten off by the heroic English.

When the Fascists told us that Málaga had fallen we set it down as a lie, but next day there were more convincing rumours, and it must have been a day or two later that it was admitted officially. By degrees the whole disgraceful story leaked out – how the town had been evacuated without firing a shot, and how the fury of the Italians had fallen not upon the troops, who were gone, but upon the wretched civilian population, some of whom were pursued and machine-gunned for a hundred miles. The news sent a sort of chill all along the line, for, whatever the truth may have been, every man in the militia believed that the loss of Málaga was due to treachery. It was the first talk I had heard of treachery or divided aims. It set up in my mind the first vague doubt about this war in which, hitherto, the rights and wrongs had seemed so beautifully simple.

In mid-February we left Monte Trazo and were sent, together with all the POUM troops in this sector, to make a part of the army besieging Huesca. It was a fifty-mile lorry journey across the wintry plain, where the clipped vines were not yet budding and the blades of the winter barley were just poking through the lumpy soil. Four kilometres from our new trenches Huesca glittered small and clear like a city of dolls' houses. Months earlier, when Siétamo was taken, the general commanding the Government troops had said gaily: 'Tomorrow we'll have coffee in Huesca.' It turned out that he was mistaken. There had been bloody attacks, but the town did not fall, and 'Tomorrow we'll have coffee in Huesca' had become a standing joke throughout the army. If I ever go back to Spain I shall make a point of having a cup of coffee in Huesca.

v

On the eastern side of Huesca, until late March, nothing happened – almost literally nothing. We were twelve hundred metres from the enemy. When the Fascists were driven back into Huesca the Republican Army troops who held this part of the line had not been over-zealous in their advance, so that the line formed a kind of pocket. Later it would have to be advanced – a ticklish job under fire – but for the present the enemy might as well have been non-existent; our sole preoccupation was keeping warm and getting enough to eat.

Meanwhile, the daily – more particularly nightly – round, the common task. Sentry-go, patrols, digging; mud, rain, shrieking winds, and occasional snow. It was not till well into April that the nights grew noticeably warmer. Up here on the plateau the March days were mostly like an English March, with bright blue skies and nagging winds. The winter barley was a foot high, crimson buds were forming on the cherry trees (the line here ran through deserted orchards and vegetable gardens), and if you searched the ditches you could find violets and a kind of wild hyacinth like a poor specimen of a bluebell. Immediately behind the line there ran a wonderful, green, bubbling stream, the first transparent water I had seen since coming to the front. One day I set my teeth and crawled into the river to have my first bath in six weeks. It was what you might call a brief bath, for the water was mainly snow-water and not much above freezing-point.

Meanwhile nothing happened, nothing ever happened. The English had got into the habit of saying that this wasn't a war, it was a bloody pantomime. We were hardly under direct fire from the Fascists. The only danger was from stray bullets, which, as the lines curved forward on either side, came from several directions. All the casualties at this time were from strays. Arthur Clinton got a mysterious bullet that smashed his left shoulder and disabled his arm, permanently, I am afraid. There was a little shell-fire, but it was extraordinarily ineffectual. The scream and crash of the shells was actually looked upon as a mild diversion. The Fascists never dropped their shells on our parapet. A few hundred yards behind us there was a country house, called La Granja, with big farm-buildings, which was used as a store, headquarters, and cook-house for this sector of the line. It was this that the Fascist gunners were trying for, but they were five or six kilometres away and they never aimed well enough to do more than smash the windows and chip the walls. You were only in danger if you happened to be coming up the road when the firing started, and the shells plunged into the fields on either side of you. One learned almost immediately the mysterious art of knowing by the sound of a shell how close it will fall. The shells the Fascists were firing at this period were wretchedly bad. Although they were 150 mm they only made a crater about six feet wide by four deep, and at least one in four failed to explode. There were the usual romantic tales of sabotage in the Fascist factories and unexploded shells in which, instead of the charge, there was found a scrap of paper saying 'Red Front', but I never saw one. The truth was that the shells were hopelessly old; someone picked up a brass fuse-cap stamped with the date, and it was 1917. The Fascist guns were of the same make and calibre as our own, and the unexploded shells were often reconditioned and fired back. There was said to be one old shell with a nickname of its own which travelled daily to and fro, never exploding.

At night small patrols used to be sent into no-man's-land to lie in ditches near the Fascist lines and listen for sounds (bugle-calls, motor-horns, and so forth) that indicated activity in Huesca. There was a constant come-and-go of Fascist troops, and the numbers could be checked to some extent from listeners' reports. We always had special orders to report the ringing of church bells. It seemed that the Fascists always heard mass before going into action. In among the fields and orchards there were deserted mud-walled huts which it was safe to explore with a lighted match when you had plugged up the windows. Sometimes you came on valuable pieces of loot such as a hatchet or a Fascist water-bottle (better than ours and greatly sought after). You could explore in the daytime as well, but mostly it had to be done crawling on all fours. It was queer to creep about in those empty, fertile fields where everything had been arrested just at the harvest-moment. Last year's crops had never been touched. The unpruned vines were snaking across the ground, the cobs on the standing maize had gone as hard as stone, the mangels and sugar-beets were hypertrophied into huge woody lumps. How the peasants must have cursed both armies! Sometimes parties of men went spud-gathering in no-man's-land. About a mile to the right of us, where the lines were closer together, there was a patch of potatoes that was frequented both by the Fascists and ourselves. We went there in the daytime, they only at night, as it was commanded by our machine-guns. One night to our annoyance they turned out *en masse* and cleared up the whole patch. We discovered another patch further on, where there was practically no cover and you had to lift the potatoes lying on your belly – a fatiguing job. If their machine-gunners spotted you, you had to flatten yourself out like a rat when it squirms under a door, with the bullets cutting up the clods a few yards behind you. It seemed worth it at the time. Potatoes were getting very scarce. If you got a sackful you could take them down to the cook-house and swap them for a water-bottleful of coffee.

And still nothing happened, nothing ever looked like happening. 'When are we going to attack? Why don't we attack?' were the questions you heard night and day from Spaniard and Englishman alike. When you think what fighting means it is queer that soldiers want to fight, and yet undoubtedly they do. In stationary warfare there are three things that all soldiers long for: a battle, more cigarettes, and a week's leave. We were somewhat better armed now than before. Each man had a hundred and fifty rounds of ammunition instead of fifty, and by degrees we were being issued with bayonets, steel helmets, and a few bombs. There were constant rumours of forthcoming battles, which I have since thought were deliberately circulated to keep up the spirits of the troops. It did not need much military knowledge to see that there would be no major action on this side of Huesca, at any rate for the time being. The strategic point was the road to Jaca, over on the other side. Later, when the Anarchists made their attacks on the Jaca road, our job was to make 'holding attacks' and force the Fascists to divert troops from the other side.

During all this time, about six weeks, there was only one action on our part of the front. This was when our Shock Troopers attacked the Manicomio, a disused lunatic asylum which the Fascists had converted into a fortress. There were several hundred refugee Germans serving with the POUM. They were organised in a special battalion called the Battallon de Choque, and from a military point of view they were on quite a different level from the rest of the militia – indeed, were more like soldiers than anyone I saw in Spain, except the Assault Guards and some of the International Column. The attack was mucked up, as usual. How many operations in this war, on the Government side, were *not* mucked up, I wonder? The Shock Troops took the Manicomio by storm, but the troops, of I forget which militia, who were to support them by seizing the neighbouring hill that commanded the Manicomio, were badly let down. The captain who led them was one of those Regular Army officers of doubtful loyalty whom the Government persisted in employing. Either from fright or treachery he warned the Fascists by flinging a bomb when they were two hundred yards away. I am glad to say his men shot him dead on the spot. But the surprise-attack was no surprise, and the militiamen were mown down by heavy fire and driven off the hill, and at nightfall the Shock Troops had to abandon the Manicomio. Through the night the ambulances filed down the abominable road to Siétamo, killing the badly wounded with their joltings.

All of us were lousy by this time; though still cold it was warm enough for that. I have had a big experience of body vermin of various kinds, and for sheer beastliness the louse beats everything I have encountered. Other insects, mosquitoes for instance, make you suffer more, but at least they aren't *resident* vermin. The human louse somewhat resembles a tiny lobster, and he lives chiefly in your trousers. Short of burning all your clothes there is no known way of getting rid of him. Down the seams of your trousers he lays his glittering white eggs, like tiny grains of rice, which hatch out and breed families of their own at horrible speed. I think the pacifists might find it helpful to illustrate their pamphlets with enlarged photographs of lice. Glory of war, indeed! In war *all* soldiers are lousy, at least when it is warm enough. The men who fought at Verdun, at Waterloo, at Flodden, at Senlac, at Thermopylae – every one of them had lice crawling over his testicles. We kept the brutes down to some extent by burning out the eggs and by bathing as often as we could face it. Nothing short of lice could have driven me into that ice-cold river.

Everything was running short – boots, clothes, tobacco, soap, candles, matches, olive oil. Our uniforms were dropping to pieces, and many of the men had no boots, only rope-soled sandals. You came on piles of worn-out boots everywhere. Once we kept a dug-out fire burning for two days mainly with boots, which are not bad fuel. By this time my wife was in Barcelona and used to send me tea, chocolate, and even cigars when such things were procurable; but even in Barcelona everything was running short, especially tobacco. The tea was a godsend, though we had no milk and seldom any sugar. Parcels were constantly being sent from England to men in the contingent, but they never arrived; food, clothes, cigarettes – everything was either refused by the Post Office or seized in France. Curiously enough, the only firm that succeeded in sending packets of tea – even, on one memorable occasion, a tin of biscuits – to my wife was the Army and Navy Stores. Poor old Army and Navy! They did their duty nobly, but perhaps they might have felt happier if the stuff had been going to Franco's side of the barricade. The shortage of tobacco was the worst of all. At the beginning we had been issued with a packet of cigarettes a day, then it got down to eight cigarettes a day, then to five. Finally there were ten deadly days when there was no issue of tobacco at all. For the first time, in Spain, I saw something that you see every day in London – people picking up fag-ends.

Towards the end of March I got a poisoned hand that had to be lanced and put in a sling. I had to go into hospital, but it was not worth sending me to Siétamo for such a petty injury, so I stayed in the so-called hospital at Monflorite, which was merely a casualty clearing station. I was there ten days, part of the time in bed. The *practicantes* (hospital assistants) stole practically every valuable object I possessed, including my camera and all my photographs. At the front everyone stole, it was the inevitable effect of shortage, but the hospital people were always the worst. Later, in the hospital at Barcelona, an American who had come to join the International Column on a ship that was torpedoed by an Italian submarine, told me how he was carried ashore wounded, and how, even as they lifted him into the ambulance, the stretcher-bearers pinched his wrist-watch.

While my arm was in the sling I spent several blissful days wandering about the countryside. Monflorite was the usual huddle of mud and stone houses, with narrow tortuous alleys that had been churned by lorries till they looked like the craters of the moon. The church had been badly knocked about but was used as a military store. In the whole neighbourhood there were only two farm-houses of any size, Torre Lorenzo and Torre Fabián, and only two really large buildings, obviously the houses of the landowners who had once lorded it over the countryside; you could see their wealth reflected in the miserable huts of the peasants. Just behind the river, close to the front line, there was an enormous flour-mill with a country-house attached to it. It seemed shameful to see the huge costly machines rusting useless and the wooden flour-chutes torn down for firewood. Later on, to get firewood for the troops further back, parties of men were sent in lorries to wreck the place systematically. They used to smash the floor-boards of a room by bursting a hand-grenade in it. La Granja, our store and cook-house, had possibly at one time been a convent. It had huge courtyards and out-houses, covering an acre or more, with stabling for thirty or forty horses. The country-houses in that part of Spain are of no interest architecturally, but their farm-buildings, of lime-washed stone with round arches and magnificent roof-beams, are noble places, built on a plan that has probably not altered for centuries. Sometimes it gave you a sneaking sympathy with the Fascist ex-owners to see the way the militia treated the buildings they had seized. In La Granja every room that was not in use had been turned into a latrine – a frightful shambles of smashed furniture and excrement. The little church that adjoined it, its walls perforated by shell-holes, had its floor inches deep in dung. In the great courtyard where the cooks ladled out the rations the litter of rusty tins, mud, mule dung, and decaying food was revolting. It gave point to the old army song:

> *There are rats, rats,*
> *Rats as big as cats,*
> *In the quartermaster's store!*

The ones at La Granja itself really were as big as cats, or nearly; great bloated brutes that waddled over the beds of muck, too impudent even to run away unless you shot at them.

Spring was really here at last. The blue in the sky was softer, the air grew suddenly balmy. The frogs were mating noisily in the ditches. Round the drinking-pool that served for the village mules I found exquisite green frogs the size of a penny, so brilliant that the young grass looked dull beside them. Peasant lads went out with buckets hunting for snails, which they roasted alive on sheets of tin. As soon as the weather improved the peasants had turned out for the spring ploughing. It is typical of the utter vagueness in which the Spanish agrarian revolution is wrapped that I could not even discover for certain whether the land here was col-lectivised or whether the peasants had simply divided it up among themselves. I fancy that in theory it was collectivised, this being POUM and Anarchist territory. At any rate the landowners were gone, the fields were being cultivated, and people seemed satisfied. The friendliness of the peasants towards ourselves never ceased to astonish me. To some of the older ones the war must have seemed meaningless, visibly it produced a shortage of everything and a dismal dull life for everybody, and at the best of times peasants hate having troops quartered upon them. Yet they were invariably friendly – I suppose reflecting that, however intolerable we might be in other ways, we did stand between them and their one-time landlords. Civil war is a queer thing. Huesca was not five miles away, it was these people's market town, all of them had relatives there, every week of their lives they had gone there to sell their poultry and vegetables. And now for eight months an impenetrable barrier of barbed wire and machine-guns had lain between. Occasionally it slipped their memory. Once I was talking to an old woman who was carrying one of those tiny iron lamps in which the Spaniards burn olive oil. 'Where can I buy a lamp like that?' I said. 'In Huesca,' she said without thinking, and then we both laughed. The village girls were splendid vivid creatures with coal-black hair, a swinging walk, and a straightforward, man-to-man demeanour which was probably a by-product of the revolution.

Men in ragged blue shirts and black corduroy breeches, with broad-brimmed straw hats, were ploughing the fields behind teams of mules with rhythmically flopping ears. Their ploughs were wretched things, only stirring the soil, not cutting anything we should regard as a furrow. All the agricultural implements were pitifully antiquated, everything being governed by the expensiveness of metal. A broken ploughshare, for instance, was patched, and then patched again, till sometimes it was mainly patches. Rakes and pitchforks were made of wood. Spades, among a people who seldom possessed boots, were unknown; they did their digging with a clumsy hoe like those used in India. There was a kind of harrow that took one straight back to the later Stone Age. It was made of boards joined together, to about the size of a kitchen table; in the boards hundreds of holes were morticed, and into each hole was jammed a piece of flint which had been chipped into shape exactly as men used to chip them ten thousand years ago. I remember my feeling almost of horror when I first came upon one of these things in a derelict hut in no-man's-land. I had to puzzle over it for a long while before grasping that it was a harrow. It made me sick to think of the work that must go into the making of such a thing, and the poverty that was obliged to use flint in place of steel. I have felt more kindly towards industrialism ever since. But in the village there were two up-to-date farm tractors, no doubt seized from some big landowner's estate.

Once or twice I wandered out to the little walled graveyard that stood a mile or so from the village. The dead from the front were normally sent to Siétamo; these were the village dead. It was queerly different from an English graveyard. No reverence for the dead here! Everything overgrown with bushes and coarse grass, human bones littered everywhere. But the really surprising thing was the almost complete lack of religious inscriptions on the gravestones, though they all dated from before the revolution. Only once, I think, I saw the 'Pray for the soul of so-and-so' which is usual on Catholic graves. Most of the inscriptions were purely secular, with ludicrous poems about the virtues of the deceased. On perhaps one grave in four or five there was a small cross or a perfunctory reference to Heaven; this had usually been chipped off by some industrious atheist with a chisel.

It struck me that the people in this part of Spain must be genuinely without religious feeling – religious feeling, I mean, in the orthodox sense. It is curious that all the time I was in Spain I never once saw a person cross himself; yet you would think such a movement would become instinctive, revolution or no revolution. Obviously the Spanish Church will come back (as the saying goes, night and the Jesuits always return), but there is no doubt that at the outbreak of the revolution it collapsed and was smashed up to an extent that would be unthinkable even for the moribund C of E in like circumstances. To the Spanish people, at any rate in Catalonia and Aragón, the Church was a racket pure and simple. And possibly Christian belief was replaced to some extent by Anarchism, whose influence is widely spread and which undoubtedly has a religious tinge.

It was the day I came back from hospital that we advanced the line to what was really its proper position, about a thousand yards forward, along the little stream that lay a couple of hundred yards in front of the Fascist line. This operation ought to have been carried out months earlier. The point of doing it now was that the Anarchists were attacking on the Jaca road, and to advance on this side made them divert troops to face us.

We were sixty or seventy hours without sleep, and my memories go down into a sort of blur, or rather a series of pictures. Listening-duty in no-man's-land, a hundred yards from the Casa Francesa, a fortified farm-house which was part of the Fascist line. Seven hours lying in a horrible marsh, in reedy-smelling water into which one's body subsided gradually deeper and deeper: the reedy smell, the numbing cold, the stars immovable in the black sky, the harsh croaking of the frogs. Though this was April it was the coldest night that I remember in Spain. Only a hundred yards behind us the working-parties were hard at it, but there was utter silence except for the chorus of the frogs. Just once during the night I heard a sound – the familiar noise of a sandbag being flattened with a spade. It is queer how, just now and again, Spaniards can carry out a brilliant feat of organisation. The whole move was beautifully planned. In seven hours six hundred men constructed twelve hundred metres of trench and parapet, at distances of from a hundred and fifty to three hundred yards from the Fascist line, and all so silently that the Fascists heard nothing, and during the night there was only one casualty. There were more next day, of course. Every man had his job assigned to him, even to the cook-house orderlies who suddenly arrived when the work was done with buckets of wine laced with brandy.

And then the dawn coming up and the Fascists suddenly discovering that we were there. The square white block of the Casa Francesa, though it was two hundred yards away, seemed to tower over us, and the machine-guns in its sand-bagged upper windows seemed to be pointing straight down into the trench. We all stood gaping at it, wondering why the Fascists didn't see us. Then a vicious swirl of bullets, and everyone had flung himself on his knees and was frantically digging, deepening the trench and scooping out small shelters in the side. My arm was still in bandages, I could not dig, and I spent most of that day reading a detective story – *The Missing Moneylender* its name was. I don't remember the plot of it, but I remember very clearly the feeling of sitting there reading it; the dampish clay of the trench bottom underneath me, the constant shifting of my legs out of the way as men hurried stooping down the trench, the crack-crack-crack of bullets a foot or two overhead. Thomas Parker got a bullet through the top of his thigh, which, as he said, was nearer to being a DSO than he cared about. Casualties were happening all along the line, but nothing to what there would have been if they had caught us on the move during the night. A deserter told us afterwards that five Fascist sentries were shot for negligence. Even now they could have massacred us if they had had the initiative to bring up a few mortars. It was an awkward job getting the wounded down the narrow, crowded trench. I saw one poor devil, his breeches dark with blood, flung out of his stretcher and gasping in agony. One had to carry wounded men a long distance, a mile or more, for even when a road existed the ambulances never came very near the front line. If they came too near the Fascists had a habit of shelling them – justifiably, for in modern war no one scruples to use an ambulance for carrying ammunition.

And then, next night, waiting at Torre Fabián for an attack that was called off at the last moment by wireless. In the barn where we waited the floor was a thin layer of chaff over deep beds of bones, human bones and cows' bones mixed up, and the place was alive with rats. The filthy brutes came swarming out of the ground on every side. If there is one thing I hate more than another it is a rat running over me in the darkness. However, I had the satisfaction of catching one of them a good punch that sent him flying.

And then waiting fifty or sixty yards from the Fascist parapet for the order to attack. A long line of men crouching in an irrigation ditch with their bayonets peeping over the edge and the whites of their eyes shining through the darkness. Kopp and Benjamin squatting behind us with a man who had a wireless receiving-box strapped to his shoulders. On the western horizon rosy gun-flashes followed at intervals of several seconds by enormous explosions. And then a pip-pip-pip noise from the wireless and the whispered order that we were to get out of it while the going was good. We did so, but not quickly enough. Twelve wretched children of the JCI (the Youth League of the POUM, corresponding to the JSU of the PSUC) who had been posted only about forty yards from the Fascist parapet, were caught by the dawn and unable to escape. All day they had to lie there, with only tufts of grass for cover, the Fascists shooting at them every time they moved. By nightfall seven were dead, then the other five managed to creep away in the darkness.

And then, for many mornings to follow, the sound of the Anarchist attacks on the other side of Huesca. Always the same sound. Suddenly, at some time in the small hours, the opening crash of several score bombs bursting simultaneously – even from miles away a diabolical, rending crash – and then the unbroken roar of massed rifles and machine-guns, a heavy rolling sound curiously similar to the roll of drums. By degrees the firing would spread all round the lines that encircled Huesca, and we would stumble out into the trench to lean sleepily against the parapet while a ragged meaningless fire swept overhead.

In the day-time the guns thundered fitfully. Torre Fabián, now our cook-house, was shelled and partially destroyed. It is curious that when you are watching artillery-fire from a safe distance you always want the gunner to hit his mark, even though the mark contains your dinner and some of your comrades. The Fascists were shooting well that morning; perhaps there were German gunners on the job. They bracketed neatly on Torre Fabián. One shell beyond it, one shell short of it, then whizz-BOOM! Burst rafters leaping upwards and a sheet of uralite skimming down the air like a flicked playing-card. The next shell took off the corner of a building as neatly as a giant might do it with a knife. But the cooks produced dinner on time – a memorable feat.

As the days went on the unseen but audible guns began each to assume a distinct personality. There were the two batteries of Russian 75-mm guns which fired from close in our rear and which somehow evoked in my mind the picture of a fat man hitting a golf-ball. These were the first Russian guns I had seen – or heard, rather. They had a low trajectory and a very high velocity, so that you heard the cartridge explosion, the whizz and the shell-burst almost simultaneously. Behind Monflorite were two very heavy guns which fired a few times a day, with a deep, muffled roar that was like the baying of distant chained-up monsters. Up at Mount Aragón, the medieval fortress which the Government troops had stormed last year (the first time in its history, it was said), and which guarded one of the approaches to Huesca, there was a heavy gun which must have dated well back into the nineteenth century. Its great shells whistled over so slowly that you felt certain you could run beside them and keep up with them. A shell from this gun sounded like nothing so much as a man riding along on a bicycle and whistling. The trench-mortars, small though they were, made the most evil sound of all. Their shells are really a kind of winged torpedo, shaped like the darts thrown in public-houses and about the size of a quart bottle; they go off with a devilish metallic crash, as of some monstrous globe of brittle steel being shattered on an anvil. Sometimes our aeroplanes flew over and let loose the aerial torpedoes whose tremendous echoing roar makes the earth tremble even at two miles' distance. The shell-bursts from the Fascist anti-aircraft guns dotted the sky like cloudlets in a bad water-colour, but I never saw them get within a thousand yards of an aeroplane. When an aeroplane swoops down and uses its machine-gun the sound, from below, is like the fluttering of wings.

On our part of the line not much was happening. Two hundred yards to the right of us, where the Fascists were on higher ground, their snipers picked off a few of our comrades. Two hundred yards to the left, at the bridge over the stream, a sort of duel was going on between the Fascist mortars and the men who were building a concrete barricade across the bridge. The evil little shells whizzed over, zwing-crash! zwing-crash!, making a doubly diabolical noise when they landed on the asphalt road. A hundred yards away you could stand in perfect safety and watch the columns of earth and black smoke leaping into the air like magic trees. The poor devils round the bridge spent much of the day-time cowering in the little man-holes they had scooped in the side of the trench. But there were less casualties than might have been expected, and the barricade rose steadily, a wall of concrete two feet thick with embrasures for two machine-guns and a small field-gun. The concrete was being reinforced with old bedsteads, which apparently was the only iron that could be found for the purpose.

VI

One afternoon Benjamin told us that he wanted fifteen volunteers. The attack on the Fascist redoubt which had been called off on the previous occasion was to be carried out tonight. I oiled my ten Mexican cartridges, dirtied my bayonet (the things give your position away if they flash too much), and packed up a hunk of bread, three inches of red sausage, and a cigar which my wife had sent from Barcelona and which I had been hoarding for a long time. Bombs were served out, three to a man. The Spanish Government had at last succeeded in producing a decent bomb. It was on the principle of a Mills bomb, but with two pins instead of one. After you had pulled the pins out there was an interval of seven seconds before the bomb exploded. Its chief disadvantage was that one pin was very stiff and the other very loose, so that you had the choice of leaving both pins in place and being unable to pull the stiff one out in a moment of emergency, or pulling out the stiff one beforehand and being in a constant stew lest the thing should explode in your pocket. But it was a handy little bomb to throw.

A little before midnight Benjamin led the fifteen of us down to Torre Fabián. Ever since evening the rain had been pelting down. The irrigation ditches were brimming over, and every time you stumbled into one you were in water up to your waist. In the pitch darkness and sheeting rain in the farm-yard a dim mass of men was waiting. Kopp addressed us, first in Spanish, then in English, and explained the plan of attack. The Fascist line here made an L-bend and the parapet we were to attack lay on rising ground at the corner of the L. About thirty of us, half English and half Spanish, under the command of Jorge Roca, our battalion commander (a battalion in the militia was about four hundred men), and Benjamin, were to creep up and cut the Fascist wire. Jorge would fling the first bomb as a signal, then the rest of us were to send in a rain of bombs, drive the Fascists out of the parapet and seize it before they could rally. Simultaneously seventy Shock Troopers were to assault the next Fascist 'position', which lay two hundred yards to the right of the other, joined to it by a communication-trench. To prevent us from shooting each other in the darkness white armlets would be worn. At this moment a messenger arrived to say that there were no white armlets. Out of the darkness a plaintive voice suggested: 'Couldn't we arrange for the Fascists to wear white armlets instead?'

There was an hour or two to put in. The barn over the mule stable was so wrecked by shell-fire that you could not move about in it without a light. Half the floor had been torn away by a plunging shell and there was a twenty-foot drop onto the stones beneath. Someone found a pick and levered a burst plank out of the floor, and in a few minutes we had got a fire alight and our drenched clothes were steaming. Someone else produced a pack of cards. A rumour – one of those mysterious rumours that are endemic in war – flew round that hot coffee with brandy in it was about to be served out. We filed eagerly down the almost-collapsing staircase and wandered round the dark yard, enquiring where the coffee was to be found. Alas! there was no coffee. Instead, they called us together, ranged us into single file, and then Jorge and Benjamin set off rapidly into the darkness, the rest of us following.

It was still raining and intensely dark, but the wind had dropped. The mud was unspeakable. The paths through the beet-fields were simply a succession of lumps, as slippery as a greasy pole, with huge pools everywhere. Long before we got to the place where we were to leave our own parapet everyone had fallen several times and our rifles were coated with mud. At the parapet a small knot of men, our reserves, were waiting, and the doctor and a row of stretchers. We filed through the gap in the parapet and waded through another irrigation ditch. Splash-gurgle! Once again in water up to your waist, with the filthy, slimy mud oozing over your boot-tops. On the grass outside Jorge waited till we were all through. Then, bent almost double, he began creeping slowly forward. The Fascist parapet was about a hundred and fifty yards away. Our one chance of getting there was to move without noise.

I was in front with Jorge and Benjamin. Bent double, but with faces raised, we crept into the almost utter darkness at a pace that grew slower at every step. The rain beat lightly in our faces. When I glanced back I could see the men who were nearest to me, a bunch of humped shapes like huge black mushrooms gliding slowly forward. But every time I raised my head Benjamin, close beside me, whispered fiercely in my ear: 'To keep ze head down! To keep ze head down!' I could have told him that he needn't worry. I knew by experiment that on a dark night you can never see a man at twenty paces. It was far more important to go quietly. If they once heard us we were done for. They had only to spray the darkness with their machine-gun and there was nothing for it but to run or be massacred.

But on the sodden ground it was almost impossible to move quietly. Do what you would your feet stuck to the mud, and every step you took was slop-slop, slop-slop. And the devil of it was that the wind had dropped, and in spite of the rain it was a very quiet night. Sounds would carry a long way. There was a dreadful moment when I kicked against a tin and thought every Fascist within miles must have heard it. But no, not a sound, no answering shot, no movement in the Fascist lines. We crept onwards, always more slowly. I cannot convey to you the depth of my desire to get there. Just to get within bombing distance before they heard us! At such a time you have not even any fear, only a tremendous hopeless longing to get over the intervening ground. I have felt exactly the same thing when stalking a wild animal; the same agonised desire to get within range, the same dreamlike certainty that it is impossible. And how the distance stretched out! I knew the ground well, it was barely a hundred and fifty yards, and yet it seemed more like a mile. When you are creeping at that pace you are aware as an ant might be of the enormous variations in the ground; the splendid patch of smooth grass here, the evil patch of sticky mud there, the tall rustling reeds that have got to be avoided, the heap of stones that almost makes you give up hope because it seems impossible to get over it without noise.

We had been creeping forward for such an age that I began to think we had gone the wrong way. Then in the darkness thin parallel lines of something blacker were faintly visible. It was the outer wire (the Fascists had two lines of wire). Jorge knelt down, fumbled in his pocket. He had our only pair of wire-cutters. Snip, snip. The trailing stuff was lifted delicately aside. We waited for the men at the back to close up. They seemed to be making a frightful noise. It might be fifty yards to the Fascist parapet now. Still onwards, bent double. A stealthy step, lowering your foot as gently as a cat approaching a mousehole; then a pause to listen; then another step. Once I raised my head; in silence Benjamin put his hand behind my neck and pulled it violently down. I knew that the inner wire was barely twenty yards from the parapet. It seemed to me inconceivable that thirty men could get there unheard. Our breathing was enough to give us away. Yet somehow we did get there. The Fascist parapet was visible now, a dim black mound, looming high above us. Once again Jorge knelt and fumbled. Snip, snip. There was no way of cutting the stuff silently.

So that was the inner wire. We crawled through it on all fours and rather more rapidly. If we had time to deploy now all was well. Jorge and Benjamin crawled across to the right. But the men behind, who were spread out, had to form into single file to get through the narrow gap in the wire, and just at this moment there was a flash and a bang from the Fascist parapet. The sentry had heard us at last. Jorge poised himself on one knee and swung his arm like a bowler. Crash! His bomb burst somewhere over the parapet. At once, far more promptly than one would have thought possible, a roar of fire, ten or twenty rifles, burst out from the Fascist parapet. They had been waiting for us after all. Momentarily you could see every sandbag in the lurid light. Men too far back were flinging their bombs and some of them were falling short of the parapet. Every loophole seemed to be spouting jets of flame. It is always hateful to be shot at in the dark – every rifle-flash seems to be pointed straight at yourself – but it was the bombs that were the worst. You cannot conceive the horror of these things till you have seen one burst close to you and in darkness; in the daytime there is only the crash of the explosion, in the darkness there is the blinding red glare as well. I had flung myself down at the first volley. All this while I was lying on my side in the greasy mud, wrestling savagely with the pin of a bomb. The damned thing *would* not come out. Finally I realised that I was twisting it in the wrong direction. I got the pin out, rose to my knees, hurled the bomb, and threw myself down again. The bomb burst over to the right, outside the parapet; fright had spoiled my aim. Just at this moment another bomb burst right in front of me, so close that I could feel the heat of the explosion. I flattened myself out and dug my face into the mud so hard that I hurt my neck and thought that I was wounded. Through the din I heard an English voice behind me say quietly: 'I'm hit.' The bomb had, in fact, wounded several people round about me without touching myself. I rose to my knees and flung my second bomb. I forget where that one went.

The Fascists were firing, our people behind were firing, and I was very conscious of being in the middle. I felt the blast of a shot and realised that a man was firing from immediately behind me. I stood up and shouted at him: 'Don't shoot at me, you bloody fool!' At this moment I saw that Benjamin, ten or fifteen yards to my right, was motioning to me with his arm. I ran across to him. It meant crossing the line of spouting loop-holes, and as I went I clapped my left hand over my cheek; an idiotic gesture – as though one's hand could stop a bullet! – but I had a horror of being hit in the face. Benjamin was kneeling on one knee with a pleased, devilish sort of expression on his face and firing carefully at the rifle-flashes with his automatic pistol. Jorge had dropped wounded at the first volley and was somewhere out of sight. I knelt beside Benjamin, pulled the pin out of my third bomb and flung it. Ah! No doubt about it that time. The bomb crashed inside the parapet, at the corner, just by the machine-gun nest.

The Fascist fire seemed to have slackened very suddenly. Benjamin leapt to his feet and shouted: 'Forward! Charge!' We dashed up the short steep slope on which the parapet stood. I say 'dashed'; 'lumbered' would be a better word; the fact is that you can't move fast when you are sodden and mudded from head to foot and weighted down with a heavy rifle and bayonet and a hundred and fifty cartridges. I took it for granted that there would be a Fascist waiting for me at the top. If he fired at that range he could not miss me, and yet somehow I never expected him to fire, only to try for me with his bayonet. I seemed to feel in advance the sensation of our bayonets crossing, and I wondered whether his arm would be stronger than mine. However, there was no Fascist waiting. With a vague feeling of relief I found that it was a low parapet and the sandbags gave a good foothold. As a rule they are difficult to get over. Everything inside was smashed to pieces, beams flung all over the place, and great shards of uralite littered everywhere. Our bombs had wrecked all the huts and dug-outs. And still there was not a soul visible. I thought they would be lurking somewhere underground, and shouted in English (I could not think of any Spanish at the moment): 'Come on out of it! Surrender!' No answer. Then a man, a shadowy figure in the half-light, skipped over the roof of one of the ruined huts and dashed away to the left. I started after him, prodding my bayonet ineffectually into the darkness. As I rounded the corner of the hut I saw a man – I don't know whether or not it was the same man as I had seen before – fleeing up the communication-trench that led to the other Fascist position. I must have been very close to him, for I could see him clearly. He was bareheaded and seemed to have nothing on except a blanket which he was clutching round his shoulders. If I had fired I could have blown him to pieces. But for fear of shooting one another we had been ordered to use only bayonets once we were inside the parapet, and in any case I never even thought of firing. Instead, my mind leapt backwards twenty years, to our boxing instructor at school, showing me in vivid pantomime how he had bayoneted a Turk at the Dardanelles. I gripped my rifle by the small of the butt and lunged at the man's back. He was just out of my reach. Another lunge: still out of reach. And for a little distance we proceeded like this, he rushing up the trench and I after him on the ground above, prodding at his shoulder-blades and never quite getting there – a comic memory for me to look back upon, though I suppose it seemed less comic to him.

Of course, he knew the ground better than I and had soon slipped away from me. When I came back the position was full of shouting men. The noise of firing had lessened somewhat. The Fascists were still pouring a heavy fire at us from three sides, but it was coming from a greater distance. We had driven them back for the time being. I remember saying in an oracular manner: 'We can hold this place for half an hour, not more.' I don't know why I picked on half an hour. Looking over the right-hand parapet you could see innumerable greenish rifle-flashes stabbing the darkness; but they were a long way back, a hundred or two hundred yards. Our job now was to search the position and loot anything that was worth looting. Benjamin and some others were already scrabbling among the ruins of a big hut or dug-out in the middle of the position. Benjamin staggered excitedly through the ruined roof, tugging at the rope handle of an ammunition box.

'Comrades! Ammunition! Plenty ammunition here!'

'We don't want ammunition,' said a voice, 'we want rifles.'

This was true. Half our rifles were jammed with mud and unusable. They could be cleaned, but it is dangerous to take the bolt out of a rifle in the darkness; you put it down somewhere and then you lose it. I had a tiny electric torch which my wife had managed to buy in Barcelona, otherwise we had no light of any description between us. A few men with good rifles began a desultory fire at the flashes in the distance. No one dared fire too rapidly; even the best of the rifles were liable to jam if they got too hot. There were about sixteen of us inside the parapet, including one or two who were wounded. A number of wounded, English and Spanish, were lying outside. Patrick O'Hara, a Belfast Irishman who had had some training in first-aid, went to and fro with packets of bandages, binding up the wounded men and, of course, being shot at every time he returned to the parapet, in spite of his indignant shouts of 'POUM!'

We began searching the position. There were several dead men lying about, but I did not stop to examine them. The thing I was after was the machine-gun. All the while when we were lying outside I had been wondering vaguely why the gun did not fire. I flashed my torch inside the machine-gun nest. A bitter disappointment! The gun was not there. Its tripod was there, and various boxes of ammunition and spare parts, but the gun was gone. They must have unscrewed it and carried it off at the first alarm. No doubt they were acting under orders, but it was a stupid and cowardly thing to do, for if they had kept the gun in place they could have slaughtered the whole lot of us. We were furious. We had set our hearts on capturing a machine-gun.

We poked here and there but did not find anything of much value. There were quantities of Fascist bombs lying about – a rather inferior type of bomb, which you touched off by pulling a string – and I put a couple of them in my pocket as souvenirs. It was impossible not to be struck by the bare misery of the Fascist dug-outs. The litter of spare clothes, books, food, petty personal belongings that you saw in our own dug-outs was completely absent; these poor unpaid conscripts seemed to own nothing except blankets and a few soggy hunks of bread. Up at the far end there was a small dug-out which was partly above ground and had a tiny window. We flashed the torch through the window and instantly raised a cheer. A cylindrical object in a leather case, four feet high and six inches in diameter, was leaning against the wall. Obviously the machine-gun barrel. We dashed round and got in at the doorway, to find that the thing in the leather case was not a machine-gun but something which, in our weapon-starved army, was even more precious. It was an enormous telescope, probably of at least sixty or seventy magnifications, with a folding tripod. Such telescopes simply did not exist on our side of the line and they were desperately needed. We brought it out in triumph and leaned it against the parapet, to be carried off later.

At this moment someone shouted that the Fascists were closing in. Certainly the din of firing had grown very much louder. But it was obvious that the Fascists would not counter-attack from the right, which meant crossing no-man's-land and assaulting their own parapet. If they had any sense at all they would come at us from inside the line. I went round to the other side of the dug-outs. The position was roughly horseshoe-shaped, with the dug-outs in the middle, so that we had another parapet covering us on the left. A heavy fire was coming from that direction, but it did not matter greatly. The danger-spot was straight in front, where there was no protection at all. A stream of bullets was passing just overhead. They must be coming from the other Fascist position further up the line; evidently the Shock Troopers had not captured it after all. But this time the noise was deafening. It was the unbroken, drum-like roar of massed rifles which I was used to hearing from a little distance; this was the first time I had been in the middle of it. And by now, of course, the firing had spread along the line for miles around. Douglas Thompson, with a wounded arm dangling useless at his side, was leaning against the parapet and firing one-handed at the flashes. Someone whose rifle had jammed was loading for him.

There were four or five of us round this side. It was obvious what we must do. We must drag the sandbags from the front parapet and make a barricade across the unprotected side. And we had got to be quick. The fire was high at present, but they might lower it at any moment; by the flashes all round I could see that we had a hundred or two hundred men against us. We began wrenching the sandbags loose, carrying them twenty yards forward and dumping them into a rough heap. It was a vile job. They were big sandbags, weighing a hundredweight each, and it took every ounce of your strength to prise them loose; and then the rotten sacking split and the damp earth cascaded all over you, down your neck and up your sleeves. I remember feeling a deep horror at everything: the chaos, the darkness, the frightful din, the slithering to and fro in the mud, the struggles with the bursting sandbags – all the time encumbered with my rifle, which I dared not put down for fear of losing it. I even shouted to someone as we staggered along with a bag between us: 'This is war! Isn't it bloody?' Suddenly a succession of tall figures came leaping over the front parapet. As they came nearer we saw that they wore the uniform of the Shock Troopers, and we cheered, thinking they were reinforcements. However, there were only four of them, three Germans and a Spaniard. We heard afterwards what had happened to the Shock Troopers. They did not know the ground and in the darkness had been led to the wrong place, where they were caught on the Fascist wire and numbers of them were shot down. These were four who had got lost, luckily for themselves. The Germans did not speak a word of English, French, or Spanish. With difficulty and much gesticulation we explained what we were doing and got them to help us in building the barricade.

The Fascists had brought up a machine-gun now. You could see it spitting like a squib a hundred or two hundred yards away; the bullets came over us with a steady, frosty crackle. Before long we had flung enough sandbags into place to make a low breastwork behind which the few men who were on this side of the position could lie down and fire. I was kneeling behind them. A mortar-shell whizzed over and crashed somewhere in no-man's-land. That was another danger, but it would take them some minutes to find our range. Now that we had finished wrestling with those beastly sandbags it was not bad fun in a way; the noise, the darkness, the flashes approaching, our own men blazing back at the flashes. One even had time to think a little. I remember wondering whether I was frightened, and deciding that I was not. Outside, where I was probably in less danger, I had been half sick with fright. Suddenly there was another shout that the Fascists were closing in. There was no doubt about it this time, the rifle-flashes were much nearer. I saw a flash hardly twenty yards away. Obviously they were working their way up the communication-trench. At twenty yards they were within easy bombing range; there were eight or nine of us bunched together and a single well-placed bomb would blow us all to fragments. Bob Smillie, the blood running down his face from a small wound, sprang to his knee and flung a bomb. We cowered, waiting for the crash. The fuse fizzled red as it sailed through the air, but the bomb failed to explode. (At least a quarter of these bombs were duds.) I had no bombs left except the Fascist ones and I was not certain how these worked. I shouted to the others to know if anyone had a bomb to spare. Douglas Moyle felt in his pocket and passed one across. I flung it and threw myself on my face. By one of those strokes of luck that happen about once in a year I had managed to drop the bomb almost exactly where the rifle had flashed. There was the roar of the explosion and then, instantly, a diabolical outcry of screams and groans. We had got one of them, anyway; I don't know whether he was killed, but certainly he was badly hurt. Poor wretch, poor wretch! I felt a vague sorrow as I heard him screaming. But at the same instant, in the dim light of the rifle-flashes, I saw or thought I saw a figure standing near the place where the rifle had flashed. I threw up my rifle and let fly. Another scream, but I think it was still the effect of the bomb. Several more bombs were thrown. The next rifle-flashes we saw were a long way off, a hundred yards or more. So we had driven them back, temporarily at least.

Everyone began cursing and saying why the hell didn't they send us some supports. With a sub-machine-gun or twenty men with clean rifles we could hold this place against a battalion. At this moment Paddy Donovan, who was second-in-command to Benjamin and had been sent back for orders, climbed over the front parapet.

'Hi! Come on out of it! All men to retire at once!'

'What?'

'Retire! Get out of it!'

'Why?'

'Orders. Back to our own lines double-quick.'

People were already climbing over the front parapet. Several of them were struggling with a heavy ammunition box. My mind flew to the telescope which I had left leaning against the parapet on the other side of the position. But at this moment I saw that the four Shock Troopers, acting I suppose on some mysterious orders they had received beforehand, had begun running up the communication-trench. It led to the other Fascist position and – if they got there – to certain death. They were disappearing into the darkness. I ran after them, trying to think of the Spanish for 'retire'; finally I shouted, '*Atrás! Atrás!*', which perhaps conveyed the right meaning. The Spaniard understood it and brought the others back. Paddy was waiting at the parapet.

'Come on, hurry up.'

'But the telescope!'

'Bugger the telescope! Benjamin's waiting outside.'

We climbed out. Paddy held the wire aside for me. As soon as we got away from the shelter of the Fascist parapet we were under a devilish fire that seemed to be coming at us from every direction. Part of it, I do not doubt, came from our own side, for everyone was firing all along the line. Whichever way we turned a fresh stream of bullets swept past; we were driven this way and that in the darkness like a flock of sheep. It did not make it any easier that we were dragging a captured box of ammunition – one of those boxes that hold 1750 rounds and weigh about a hundred-weight – besides a box of bombs and several Fascist rifles. In a few minutes, although the distance from parapet to parapet was not two hundred yards and most of us knew the ground, we were completely lost. We found ourselves slithering about in a muddy field, knowing nothing except that bullets were coming from both sides. There was no moon to go by, but the sky was growing a little lighter. Our lines lay east of Huesca; I wanted to stay where we were till the first crack of dawn showed us which was east and which was west; but the others were against it. We slithered onwards, changing our direction several times and taking it in turns to haul at the ammunition-box. At last we saw the low flat line of a parapet looming in front of us. It might be ours or it might be the Fascists'; nobody had the dimmest idea which way we were going. Benjamin crawled on his belly through some tall whitish weeds till he was about twenty yards from the parapet and tried a challenge. A shout of 'POUM!' answered him. We jumped to our feet, found our way along the parapet, slopped once more through the irrigation ditch – splash-gurgle! – and were in safety.

Kopp was waiting inside the parapet with a few Spaniards. The doctor and the stretchers were gone. It appeared that all the wounded had been got in except Jorge and one of our own men, Hiddlestone by name, who were missing. Kopp was pacing up and down, very pale. Even the fat folds at the back of his neck were pale; he was paying no attention to the bullets that streamed over the low parapet and cracked close to his head. Most of us were squatting behind the parapet for cover. Kopp was muttering. *Jorge! Coño! Jorge!* And then in English. 'If Jorge is gone it is terreeble, terreeble!' Jorge was his personal friend and one of his best officers. Suddenly he turned to us and asked for five volunteers, two English and three Spanish, to go and look for the missing men. Moyle and I volunteered with three Spaniards.

As we got outside the Spaniards murmured that it was getting dangerously light. This was true enough; the sky was dimly blue. There was a tremendous noise of excited voices coming from the Fascist redoubt. Evidently they had reoccupied the place in much greater force than before. We were sixty or seventy yards from the parapet when they must have seen or heard us, for they sent over a heavy burst of fire which made us drop on our faces. One of them flung a bomb over the parapet – a sure sign of panic. We were lying in the grass, waiting for an opportunity to move on, when we either heard or thought we heard – I have no doubt it was pure imagination, but it seemed real enough at the time – that the Fascist voices were much closer. They had left the parapet and were coming after us. 'Run!' I yelled to Moyle, and jumped to my feet. And heavens, how I ran! I had thought earlier in the night that you can't run when you are sodden from head to foot and weighted down with a rifle and cartridges; I learned now you can *always* run when you think you have fifty or a hundred armed men after you. But if I could run fast, others could run faster. In my flight something that might have been a shower of meteors sped past me. It was the three Spaniards, who had been in front. They were back to our own parapet before they stopped and I could catch up with them. The truth was that our nerves were all to pieces. I knew, however, that in a half-light one man is invisible where five are clearly visible, so I went back alone. I managed to get to the outer wire and searched the ground as well as I could, which was not very well, for I had to lie on my belly. There was no sign of Jorge or Hiddlestone, so I crept back. We learned afterwards that both Jorge and Hiddlestone had been taken to the dressing-station earlier. Jorge was lightly wounded through the shoulder. Hiddlestone had received a dreadful wound – a bullet which travelled right up his left arm, breaking the bone in several places; as he lay helpless on the ground a bomb had burst near him and torn various other parts of his body. He recovered, I am glad to say. Later he told me that he had worked his way some distance lying on his back, then had clutched hold of a wounded Spaniard and they had helped one another in.

It was getting light now. Along the line for miles around a ragged meaningless fire was thundering, like the rain that goes on raining after a storm. I remember the desolate look of everything, the morasses of mud, the weeping poplar trees, the yellow water in the trench-bottoms; and men's exhausted faces, unshaven, streaked with mud and blackened to the eyes with smoke. When I got back to my dug-out the three men I shared it with were already fast asleep. They had flung themselves down with all their equipment on and their muddy rifles clutched against them. Everything was sodden, inside the dug-out as well as outside. By long searching I managed to collect enough chips of dry wood to make a tiny fire. Then I smoked the cigar which I had been hoarding and which, surprisingly enough, had not got broken during the night.

Afterwards we learned that the action had been a success, as such things go. It was merely a raid to make the Fascists divert troops from the other side of Huesca, where the Anarchists were attacking again. I had judged that the Fascists had thrown a hundred or two hundred men into the counter-attack, but a deserter told us later on that it was six hundred. I dare say he was lying – deserters, for obvious reasons, often try to curry favour. It was a great pity about the telescope. The thought of losing that beautiful bit of loot worries me even now.

VII

The days grew hotter and even the nights grew tolerably warm. On a bullet-chipped tree in front of our parapet thick clusters of cherries were forming. Bathing in the river ceased to be an agony and became almost a pleasure. Wild roses with pink blooms the size of saucers straggled over the shell-holes round Torre Fabián. Behind the line you met peasants wearing wild roses over their ears. In the evenings they used to go out with green nets, hunting quails. You spread the net over the tops of the grasses and then lay down and made a noise like a female quail. Any male quail that was within hearing then came running towards you, and when he was underneath the net you threw a stone to scare him, whereupon he sprang into the air and was entangled in the net. Apparently only male quails were caught, which struck me as unfair.

There was a section of Andalusians next to us in the line now. I do not know quite how they got to this front. The current explanation was that they had run away from Málaga so fast that they had forgotten to stop at Valencia; but this, of course, came from the Catalans, who professed to look down on the Andalusians as a race of semi-savages. Certainly the Andalusians were very ignorant. Few if any of them could read, and they seemed not even to know the one thing that everybody knows in Spain – which political party they belonged to. They thought they were Anarchists, but were not quite certain; perhaps they were Communists. They were gnarled, rustic-looking men, shepherds or labourers from the olive groves, perhaps, with faces deeply stained by the ferocious suns of further south. They were very useful to us, for they had an extraordinary dexterity at rolling the dried-up Spanish tobacco into cigarettes. The issue of cigarettes had ceased, but in Monflorite it was occasionally possible to buy packets of the cheapest kind of tobacco, which in appearance and texture was very like chopped chaff. Its flavour was not bad, but it was so dry that even when you had succeeded in making a cigarette the tobacco promptly fell out and left an empty cylinder. The Andalusians, however, could roll admirable cigarettes and had a special technique for tucking the ends in.

Two Englishmen were laid low by sunstroke. My salient memories of that time are the heat of the midday sun, and working half-naked with sandbags punishing one's shoulders which were already flayed by the sun; and the lousiness of our clothes and boots, which were literally dropping to pieces; and the struggles with the mule which brought our rations and which did not mind rifle-fire but took to flight when shrapnel burst in the air; and the mosquitoes (just beginning to be active) and the rats, which were a public nuisance and would even devour leather belts and cartridge-pouches. Nothing was happening except an occasional casualty from a sniper's bullet and the sporadic artillery-fire and air-raids on Huesca. Now that the trees were in full leaf we had constructed snipers' platforms, like *machans*, in the poplar trees that fringed the line. On the other side of Huesca the attacks were petering out. The Anarchists had had heavy losses and had not succeeded in completely cutting the Jaca road. They had managed to establish themselves close enough on either side to bring the road itself under machine-gun fire and make it impassable for traffic; but the gap was a kilometre wide and the Fascists had constructed a sunken road, a sort of enormous trench, along which a certain number of lorries could come and go. Deserters reported that in Huesca there were plenty of munitions and very little food. But the town was evidently not going to fall. Probably it would have been impossible to take it with the fifteen thousand ill-armed men who were available. Later, in June, the Government brought troops from the Madrid front and concentrated thirty thousand men on Huesca, with an enormous quantity of aeroplanes, but still the town did not fall.

When we went on leave I had been a hundred and fifteen days in the line, and at the time this period seemed to me to have been one of the most futile of my whole life. I had joined the militia in order to fight against Fascism, and as yet I had scarcely fought at all, had merely existed as a sort of passive object, doing nothing in return for my rations except to suffer from cold and lack of sleep. Perhaps that is the fate of most soldiers in most wars. But now that I can see this period in perspective I do not altogether regret it. I wish, indeed, that I could have served the Spanish Government a little more effectively; but from a personal point of view – from the point of view of my own development – those first three or four months that I spent in the line were less futile than I then thought. They formed a kind of interregnum in my life, quite different from anything that had gone before and perhaps from anything that is to come, and they taught me things that I could not have learned in any other way.

The essential point is that all this time I had been isolated – for at the front one was almost completely isolated from the outside world: even of what was happening in Barcelona one had only a dim conception – among people who could roughly but not too inaccurately be described as revolutionaries. This was the result of the militia-system, which on the Aragón front was not radically altered till about June 1937. The workers' militias, based on the trade unions and each composed of people of approximately the same political opinions, had the effect of canalising into one place all the most revolutionary sentiment in the country. I had dropped more or less by chance into the only community of any size in Western Europe where political consciousness and disbelief in capitalism were more normal than their opposites. Up here in Aragón one was among tens of thousands of people, mainly though not entirely of working-class origin, all living at the same level and mingling on terms of equality. In theory it was perfect equality, and even in practice it was not far from it. There is a sense in which it would be true to say that one was experiencing a foretaste of Socialism, by which I mean that the prevailing mental atmosphere was that of Socialism. Many of the normal motives of civilised life – snobbishness, money-grubbing, fear of the boss, etc. – had simply ceased to exist. The ordinary class-division of society had disappeared to an extent that is almost unthinkable in the money-tainted air of England; there was no one there except the peasants and ourselves, and no one owned anyone else as his master. Of course such a state of affairs could not last. It was simply a temporary and local phase in an enormous game that is being played over the whole surface of the earth. But it lasted long enough to have its effect upon anyone who experienced it. However much one cursed at the time, one realised afterwards that one had been in contact with something strange and valuable. One had been in a community where hope was more normal than apathy or cynicism, where the word 'comrade' stood for comradeship and not, as in most countries, for humbug. One had breathed the air of equality. I am well aware that it is now the fashion to deny that Socialism has anything to do with equality. In every country in the world a huge tribe of party-hacks and sleek little professors are busy 'proving' that Socialism means no more than a planned state-capitalism with the grab-motive left intact. But fortunately there also exists a vision of Socialism quite different from this. The thing that attracts ordinary men to Socialism and makes them willing to risk their skins for it, the 'mystique' of Socialism, is the idea of equality; to the vast majority of people Socialism means a classless society, or it means nothing at all. And it was here that those few months in the militia were valuable to me. For the Spanish militias, while they lasted, were a sort of microcosm of a classless society. In that community where no one was on the make, where there was a shortage of everything but no privilege and no boot-licking, one got, perhaps, a crude forecast of what the opening stages of Socialism might be like. And, after all, instead of disillusioning me it deeply attracted me. The effect was to make my desire to see Socialism established much more actual than it had been before. Partly, perhaps, this was due to the good luck of being among Spaniards, who, with their innate decency and their ever-present Anarchist tinge, would make even the opening stages of Socialism tolerable if they had the chance.

Of course at the time I was hardly conscious of the changes that were occurring in my own mind. Like everyone about me I was chiefly conscious of boredom, heat, cold, dirt, lice, privation, and occasional danger. It is quite different now. This period which then seemed so futile and eventless is now of great importance to me. It is so different from the rest of my life that already it has taken on the magic quality which, as a rule, belongs only to memories that are years old. It was beastly while it was happening, but it is a good patch for my mind to browse upon. I wish I could convey to you the atmosphere of that time. I hope I have done so, a little, in the earlier chapters of this book. It is all bound up in my mind with the winter cold, the ragged uniforms of militiamen, the oval Spanish faces, the Morse-like tapping of machine-guns, the smells of urine and rotting bread, the tinny taste of bean-stews wolfed hurriedly out of unclean pannikins.

The whole period stays by me with curious vividness. In my memory I live over incidents that might seem too petty to be worth recalling. I am in the dug-out at Monte Pocero again, on the ledge of limestone that serves as a bed, and young Ramón is snoring with his nose flattened between my shoulder-blades. I am stumbling up the mucky trench, through the mist that swirls round me like cold steam. I am half-way up a crack in the mountain-side, struggling to keep my balance and to tug a root of wild rosemary out of the ground. High overhead some meaningless bullets are singing.

I am lying hidden among small fir-trees on the low ground west of Monte Trazo, with Kopp and Bob Edwards and three Spaniards. Up the naked grey hill to the right of us a string of Fascists are climbing like ants. Close in front a bugle-call rings out from the Fascist lines. Kopp catches my eye and, with a schoolboy gesture, thumbs his nose at the sound.

I am in the mucky yard at La Granja, among the mob of men who are struggling with their tin pannikins round the cauldron of stew. The fat and harassed cook is warding them off with the ladle. At a table nearby a bearded man with a huge automatic pistol strapped to his belt is hewing loaves of bread into five pieces. Behind me a Cockney voice (Bill Chambers, with whom I quarrelled bitterly and who was afterwards killed outside Huesca) is singing:

> *There are rats, rats,*
> *Rats as big as cats,*
> *In the . . .*

A shell comes screaming over. Children of fifteen fling themselves on their faces. The cook dodges behind the cauldron. Everyone rises with a sheepish expression as the shell plunges and booms a hundred yards away.

I am walking up and down the line of sentries, under the dark boughs of the poplars. In the flooded ditch outside the rats are paddling about, making as much noise as otters. As the yellow dawn comes up behind us, the Andalusian sentry, muffled in his cloak, begins singing. Across no-man's-land, a hundred or two hundred yards away, you can hear the Fascist sentry also singing.

On 25 April, after the usual *mañanas*, another section relieved us and we handed over our rifles, packed our kits and marched back to Monflorite. I was not sorry to leave the line. The lice were multiplying in my trousers far faster than I could massacre them, and for a month past I had had no socks and my boots had very little sole left, so that I was walking more or less barefoot. I wanted a hot bath, clean clothes and a night between sheets more passionately than it is possible to want anything when one has been living a normal civilised life. We slept a few hours in a barn in Monflorite, jumped a lorry in the small hours, caught the five o'clock train at Barbastro and – having the luck to connect with a fast train at Lérida – were in Barcelona by three o'clock in the afternoon of the 26th. And after that the trouble began.

VIII

From Mandalay, in Upper Burma, you can travel by train to Maymyo, the principal hill-station of the province, on the edge of the Shan plateau. It is rather a queer experience. You start off in the typical atmosphere of an eastern city – the scorching sunlight, the dusty palms, the smells of fish and spices and garlic, the squashy tropical fruits, the swarming dark-faced human beings – and because you are so used to it you carry this atmosphere intact, so to speak, in your railway carriage. Mentally you are still in Mandalay when the train stops at Maymyo, four thousand feet above sea-level. But in stepping out of the carriage you step into a different hemisphere. Suddenly you are breathing cool sweet air that might be that of England, and all round you are green grass, bracken, fir-trees, and hill-women with pink cheeks selling baskets of strawberries.

Getting back to Barcelona, after three and a half months at the front, reminded me of this. There was the same abrupt and startling change of atmosphere. In the train, all the way to Barcelona, the atmosphere of the front persisted; the dirt, the noise, the discomfort, the ragged clothes, the feeling of privation, comradeship and equality. The train, already full of militiamen when it left Barbastro, was invaded by more and more peasants at every station on the line; peasants with bundles of vegetables, with terrified fowls which they carried head-downwards, with sacks which looped and writhed all over the floor and were discovered to be full of live rabbits – finally with a quite considerable flock of sheep which were driven into the compartments and wedged into every empty space. The militiamen shouted revolutionary songs which drowned the rattle of the train and kissed their hands or waved red and black handkerchiefs to every pretty girl along the line. Bottles of wine and of anís, the filthy Aragonese liqueur, travelled from hand to hand. With the Spanish goat-skin water-bottles you can squirt a jet of wine right across a railway carriage into your friend's mouth, which saves a lot of trouble. Next to me a black-eyed boy of fifteen was recounting sensational and, I do not doubt, completely untrue stories of his own exploits at the front to two old leather-faced peasants who listened open-mouthed. Presently the peasants undid their bundles and gave us some sticky dark-red wine. Everyone was profoundly happy, more happy than I can convey. But when the train had rolled through Sabadell and into Barcelona, we stepped into an atmosphere that was scarcely less alien and hostile to us and our kind than if this had been Paris or London.

Everyone who has made two visits, at intervals of months, to Barcelona during the war has remarked upon the extraordinary changes that took place in it. And curiously enough, whether they went there first in August and again in January, or, like myself, first in December and again in April, the thing they said was always the same: that the revolutionary atmosphere had vanished. No doubt to anyone who had been there in August, when the blood was scarcely dry in the streets and militia were quartered in the smart hotels, Barcelona in December would have seemed bourgeois; to me, fresh from England, it was liker to a workers' city than anything I had conceived possible. Now the tide had rolled back. Once again it was an ordinary city, a little pinched and chipped by war, but with no outward sign of working-class predominance.

The change in the aspect of the crowds was startling. The militia uniform and the blue overalls had almost disappeared; everyone seemed to be wearing the smart summer suits in which Spanish tailors specialise. Fat prosperous men, elegant women, and sleek cars were everywhere. (It appeared that there were still no private cars; nevertheless, anyone who 'was anyone' seemed able to command a car.) The officers of the new Popular Army, a type that had scarcely existed when I left Barcelona, swarmed in surprising numbers. The Popular Army was officered at the rate of one officer to ten men. A certain number of these officers had served in the militia and been brought back from the front for technical instruction, but the majority were young men who had gone to the School of War in preference to joining the militia. Their relation to their men was not quite the same as in a bourgeois army, but there was a definite social difference, expressed by the difference of pay and uniform. The men wore a kind of coarse brown overalls, the officers wore an elegant khaki uniform with a tight waist, like a British Army officer's uniform, only a little more so. I do not suppose that more than one in twenty of them had yet been to the front, but all of them had automatic pistols strapped to their belts; we, at the front, could not get pistols for love or money. As we made our way up the street I noticed that people were staring at our dirty exteriors. Of course, like all men who have been several months in the line, we were a dreadful sight. I was conscious of looking like a scarecrow. My leather jacket was in tatters, my woollen cap had lost its shape and slid perpetually over one eye, my boots consisted of very little beyond splayed-out uppers. All of us were in more or less the same state, and in addition we were dirty and unshaven, so it was no wonder that the people stared. But it dismayed me a little, and brought it home to me that some queer things had been happening in the last three months.

During the next few days I discovered by innumerable signs that my first impression had not been wrong. A deep change had come over the town. There were two facts that were the keynote of all else. One was that the people – the civil population – had lost much of their interest in the war; the other was that the normal division of society into rich and poor, upper class and lower class, was reasserting itself.

The general indifference to the war was surprising and rather disgusting. It horrified people who came to Barcelona from Madrid or even from Valencia. Partly it was due to the remoteness of Barcelona from the actual fighting; I noticed the same thing a month later in Tarragona, where the ordinary life of a smart seaside town was continuing almost undisturbed. But it was significant that all over Spain voluntary enlistment had dwindled from about January onwards. In Catalonia, in February, there had been a wave of enthusiasm over the first big drive for the Popular Army, but it had not led to any great increase in recruiting. The war was only six months old or thereabouts when the Spanish Government had to resort to conscription, which would be natural in a foreign war, but seems anomalous in a civil war. Undoubtedly it was bound up with the dis-appointment of the revolutionary hopes with which the war had started. The trade union members who formed themselves into militias and chased the Fascists back to Saragossa in the first few weeks of war had done so largely because they believed themselves to be fighting for working-class control; but it was becoming more and more obvious that working-class control was a lost cause, and the common people, especially the town proletariat, who have to fill the ranks in any war, civil or foreign, could not be blamed for a certain apathy. Nobody wanted to lose the war, but the majority were chiefly anxious for it to be over. You noticed this wherever you went. Everywhere you met with the same perfunctory remark: 'This war – terrible, isn't it? When is it going to end?' Politically conscious people were far more aware of the internecine struggle between Anarchist and Communist than of the fight against Franco. To the mass of the people the food-shortage was the most important thing. 'The front' had come to be thought of as a mythical far-off place to which young men disappeared and either did not return or returned after three or four months with vast sums of money in their pockets. (A militiaman usually received his back pay when he went on leave.) Wounded men, even when they were hopping about on crutches, did not receive any special consideration. To be in the militia was no longer fashionable. The shops, always the barometers of public taste, showed this clearly. When I first reached Barcelona the shops, poor and shabby though they were, had specialised in militiamen's equipment. Forage-caps, zipper jackets, Sam Browne belts, hunting-knives, water-bottles, revolver-holsters were displayed in every window. Now the shops were markedly smarter, but the war had been thrust into the background. As I discovered later, when buying my kit before going back to the front, certain things that one badly needed at the front were very difficult to procure.

Meanwhile there was going on a systematic propaganda against the party militias and in favour of the Popular Army. The position here was rather curious. Since February the entire armed forces had theoretically been incorporated in the Popular Army, and the militias were, on paper, reconstructed along Popular Army lines, with differential pay-rates, gazetted rank, etc. etc. The divisions were made up of 'mixed brigades', which were supposed to consist partly of Popular Army troops and partly of militia. But the only changes that had actually taken place were changes of name. The POUM troops, for instance, previously called the Lenin Division, were now known as the 29th Division. Until June very few Popular Army troops reached the Aragón front, and in consequence the militias were able to retain their separate structure and their special character. But on every wall the Government agents had stencilled: 'We need a Popular Army,' and over the radio and in the Communist Press there was a ceaseless and sometimes very malignant gibing against the militias, who were described as ill-trained, undisciplined, etc. etc.; the Popular Army was always described as 'heroic'. From much of this propaganda you would have derived the impression that there was something disgraceful in having gone to the front voluntarily and something praiseworthy in waiting to be conscripted. For the time being, however, the militias were holding the line while the Popular Army was training in the rear, and this fact had to be advertised as little as possible. Drafts of militia returning to the front were no longer marched through the streets with drums beating and flags flying. They were smuggled away by train or lorry at five o'clock in the morning. A few drafts of the Popular Army were now beginning to leave for the front, and these, as before, were marched ceremoniously through the streets; but even they, owing to the general waning of interest in the war, met with comparatively little enthusiasm. The fact that the militia troops were also, on paper, Popular Army troops, was skilfully used in the Press propaganda. Any credit that happened to be going was automatically handed to the Popular Army, while all blame was reserved for the militias. It sometimes happened that the same troops were praised in one capacity and blamed in the other.

But besides all this there was the startling change in the social atmosphere – a thing difficult to conceive unless you have actually experienced it. When I first reached Barcelona I had thought it a town where class distinctions and great differences of wealth hardly existed. Certainly that was what it looked like. 'Smart' clothes were an abnormality, nobody cringed or took tips, waiters and flower-women and bootblacks looked you in the eye and called you 'comrade'. I had not grasped that this was mainly a mixture of hope and camouflage. The working class believed in a revolution that had been begun but never consolidated, and the bourgeoisie were scared and temporarily disguising themselves as workers. In the first months of revolution there must have been many thousands of people who deliberately put on overalls and shouted revolutionary slogans as a way of saving their skins. Now things were returning to normal. The smart restaurants and hotels were full of rich people wolfing expensive meals, while for the working-class population food-prices had jumped enormously without any corresponding rise in wages. Apart from the expensiveness of everything, there were recurrent shortages of this and that, which, of course, always hit the poor rather than the rich. The restaurants and hotels seemed to have little difficulty in getting whatever they wanted, but in the working-class quarters the queues for bread, olive oil, and other necessaries were hundreds of yards long. Previously in Barcelona I had been struck by the absence of beggars; now there were quantities of them. Outside the delicatessen shops at the top of the Ramblas gangs of barefooted children were always waiting to swarm round anyone who came out and clamour for scraps of food. The 'revolutionary' forms of speech were dropping out of use. Strangers seldom addressed you as *tú* and *camarada* nowadays; it was usually *señor* and *Usted*. *Buenos días* was beginning to replace *salud*. The waiters were back in their boiled shirts and the shop-walkers were cringing in the familiar manner. My wife and I went into a hosiery shop on the Ramblas to buy some stockings. The shopman bowed and rubbed his hands as they do not do even in England nowadays, though they used to do it twenty or thirty years ago. In a furtive indirect way the practice of tipping was coming back. The workers' patrols had been ordered to dissolve and the pre-war police forces were back on the streets. One result of this was that the cabaret shows and high-class brothels, many of which had been closed by the workers' patrols, had promptly re-opened.[1] A small but significant instance of the way in which everything was now orientated in favour of the wealthier classes could be seen in the tobacco shortage. For the mass of the people the shortage of tobacco was so desperate that cigarettes filled with sliced liquorice-root were being sold in the streets. I tried some of these once. (A lot of people tried them once.) Franco held the Canaries, where all the Spanish tobacco is grown; consequently the only stocks of tobacco left on the Government side were those that had been in existence before the war. These were running so low that the tobacconists' shops only opened once a week; after waiting for a couple of hours in a queue you might, if you were lucky, get a three-quarter-ounce packet of tobacco. Theoretically the Government would not allow tobacco to be purchased from abroad, because this meant reducing the gold-reserves, which had got to be kept for arms and other necessities. Actually there was a steady supply of smuggled foreign cigarettes of the more expensive kinds, Lucky Strikes and so forth, which gave a grand opportunity for profiteering. You could buy the smuggled cigarettes openly in the smart hotels and hardly less openly in the streets, provided that you could pay ten pesetas (a militiaman's daily wage) for a packet. The smuggling was for the benefit of wealthy people, and was therefore connived at. If you had enough money there was nothing that you could not get in any quantity, with the possible exception of bread, which was rationed fairly strictly. This open contrast of wealth and poverty would have been impossible a few months earlier, when the working class still were or seemed to be in control. But

[1] The workers' patrols are said to have closed 75 per cent of the brothels.

[In his list of Errata, Orwell noted: 'I have no good evidence that prostitution decreased 75% in the early days of the war, and I believe the Anarchists went on the principle of "collectivising" the brothels, not suppressing them. But there was a drive against prostitution (posters etc.) and it is a fact that the smart brothel and naked cabaret shows were shut in the early months of the war and open again when the war was about a year old.' The French-language text retains the original footnote without comment. *Ed.*]

it would not be fair to attribute it solely to the shift of political power. Partly it was a result of the safety of life in Barcelona, where there was little to remind one of the war except an occasional air-raid. Everyone who had been in Madrid said that it was completely different there. In Madrid the common danger forced people of almost all kinds into some sense of comradeship. A fat man eating quails while children are begging for bread is a disgusting sight, but you are less likely to see it when you are within sound of the guns.

A day or two after the street-fighting I remember passing through one of the fashionable streets and coming upon a confectioner's shop with a window full of pastries and bon-bons of the most elegant kinds, at staggering prices. It was the kind of shop you see in Bond Street or the Rue de la Paix. And I remember feeling a vague horror and amazement that money could still be wasted upon such things in a hungry war-stricken country. But God forbid that I should pretend to any personal superiority. After several months of discomfort I had a ravenous desire for decent food and wine, cocktails, American cigarettes, and so forth, and I admit to having wallowed in every luxury that I had money to buy. During that first week, before the street-fighting began, I had several preoccupations which interacted upon one another in a curious way. In the first place, as I have said, I was busy making myself as comfortable as I could. Secondly, thanks to over-eating and over-drinking, I was slightly out of health all that week. I would feel a little unwell, go to bed for half a day, get up and eat another excessive meal, and then feel ill again. At the same time I was making secret negotiations to buy a revolver. I badly wanted a revolver – in trench-fighting much more useful than a rifle – and they were very difficult to get hold of. The Government issued them to policemen and Popular Army officers, but refused to issue them to the militia; you had to buy, illegally, from the secret stores of the Anarchists. After a lot of fuss and nuisance an Anarchist friend managed to procure me a tiny .26-inch automatic pistol, a wretched weapon, useless at more than five yards, but better than nothing. And besides all this I was making preliminary arrangements to leave the POUM militia and enter some other unit that would ensure my being sent to the Madrid front.

I had told everyone for a long time past that I was going to leave the

POUM. As far as my purely personal preferences went I would have liked to join the Anarchists. If one became a member of the CNT it was possible to enter the FAI militia, but I was told that the FAI were likelier to send me to Teruel than to Madrid. If I wanted to go to Madrid I must join the International Column, which meant getting a recommendation from a member of the Communist Party. I sought out a Communist friend, attached to the Spanish Medical Aid, and explained my case to him. He seemed very anxious to recruit me and asked me, if possible, to persuade some of the other ILP Englishmen to come with me. If I had been in better health I should probably have agreed there and then. It is hard to say now what difference this would have made. Quite possibly I should have been sent to Albacete before the Barcelona fighting started; in which case, not having seen the fighting at close quarters, I might have accepted the official version of it as truthful. On the other hand, if I had been in Barcelona during the fighting, under Communist orders but still with a sense of personal loyalty to my comrades in the POUM, my position would have been impossible. But I had another week's leave due to me and I was very anxious to get my health back before returning to the line. Also – the kind of detail that is always deciding one's destiny – I had to wait while the bootmakers made me a new pair of marching boots. (The entire Spanish army had failed to produce a pair of boots big enough to fit me.) I told my Communist friend that I would make definite arrangements later. Meanwhile I wanted a rest. I even had a notion that we – my wife and I – might go to the seaside for two or three days. What an idea! The political atmosphere ought to have warned me that that was not the kind of thing one could do nowadays.

For under the surface-aspect of the town, under the luxury and growing poverty, under the seeming gaiety of the streets, with their flower-stalls, their many-coloured flags, their propaganda-posters, and thronging crowds, there was an unmistakable and horrible feeling of political rivalry and hatred. People of all shades of opinion were saying forebodingly: 'There's going to be trouble before long.' The danger was quite simple and intelligible. It was the antagonism between those who wished the revolution to go forward and those who wished to check or prevent it – ultimately, between Anarchists and Communists. Politically there was now no power in Catalonia except the PSUC and their Liberal allies. But over against this there was the uncertain strength of the CNT, less well-armed and less sure of what they wanted than their adversaries, but powerful because of their numbers and their predominance in various key industries. Given this alignment of forces there was bound to be trouble. From the point of view of the PSUC-controlled Generalidad, the first necessity, to make their position secure, was to get the weapons out of the CNT workers' hands. As I have pointed out earlier,* the move to break up the party militias was at bottom a manoeuvre towards this end. At the same time the pre-war armed police forces, Civil Guards, and so forth, had been brought back into use and were being heavily reinforced and armed. This could mean only one thing. The Civil Guards, in particular, were a gendarmerie of the ordinary continental type, who for nearly a century past had acted as the bodyguards of the possessing class. Meanwhile a decree had been issued that all arms held by private persons were to be surrendered. Naturally this order had not been obeyed; it was clear that the Anarchists' weapons could only be taken from them by force. Throughout this time there were rumours, always vague and contradictory owing to newspaper censorship, of minor clashes that were occurring all over Catalonia. In various places the armed police forces had made attacks on Anarchist strongholds. At Puigcerdá, on the French frontier, a band of Carabineros were sent to seize the Customs Office, previously controlled by Anarchists, and Antonio Martín, a well-known Anarchist, was killed. Similar incidents had occurred at Figueras and, I think, at Tarragona. In Barcelona there had been a series of more or less unofficial brawls in the working-class suburbs. CNT and UGT members had been murdering one another for some time past; on several occasions the murders were followed by huge, provocative funerals which were quite deliberately intended to stir up political hatred. A short time earlier a CNT member had been murdered, and the CNT had turned out in hundreds of thousands to follow the cortège. At the end of April, just after I got to Barcelona, Roldán Cortada, a prominent member of the UGT, was murdered, presumably by someone in the CNT. The Government ordered all shops to close and staged an enormous funeral procession, largely of Popular Army troops, which took two hours to pass a given point. From the hotel

---

* See Appendix I, originally placed between Sections IV and V.

window I watched it without enthusiasm. It was obvious that the so-called funeral was merely a display of strength; a little more of this kind of thing and there might be bloodshed. The same night my wife and I were woken by a fusillade of shots from the Plaza de Cataluña, a hundred or two hundred yards away. We learned next day that it was a CNT man being bumped off, presumably by someone in the UGT. It was of course distinctly possible that all these murders were committed by *agents provocateurs*. One can gauge the attitude of the foreign capitalist Press towards the Communist-Anarchist feud by the fact that Roldán Cortada's murder was given wide publicity, while the answering murder was carefully unmentioned.

The 1st of May was approaching, and there was talk of a monster demonstration in which both the CNT and the UGT were to take part. The CNT leaders, more moderate than many of their followers, had long been working for a reconciliation with the UGT; indeed the keynote of their policy was to try and form the two blocks of unions into one huge coalition. The idea was that the CNT and the UGT should march together and display their solidarity. But at the last moment the demonstration was called off. It was perfectly clear that it would only lead to rioting. So nothing happened on 1 May. It was a queer state of affairs. Barcelona, the so-called revolutionary city, was probably the only city in non-Fascist Europe that had no celebrations that day. But I admit I was rather relieved. The ILP contingent was expected to march in the POUM section of the procession, and everyone expected trouble. The last thing I wished for was to be mixed up in some meaningless street-fight. To be marching up the street behind red flags inscribed with elevating slogans, and then to be bumped off from an upper window by some total stranger with a sub-machine-gun – that is not my idea of a useful way to die.

IX

About midday on 3 May a friend crossing the lounge of the hotel said casually: 'There's been some kind of trouble at the Telephone Exchange, I hear.' For some reason I paid no attention to it at the time.

That afternoon, between three and four, I was half-way down the Ramblas when I heard several rifle-shots behind me. I turned round and saw some youths, with rifles in their hands and the red and black handkerchiefs of the Anarchists round their throats, edging up a side-street that ran off the Ramblas northward. They were evidently exchanging shots with someone in a tall octagonal tower – a church, I think – that commanded the side-street. I thought instantly: 'It's started!' But I thought it without any very great feeling of surprise – for days past everyone had been expecting 'it' to start at any moment. I realised that I must get back to the hotel at once and see if my wife was all right. But the knot of Anarchists round the opening of the side-street were motioning the people back and shouting to them not to cross the line of fire. More shots rang out. The bullets from the tower were flying across the street and a crowd of panic-stricken people was rushing down the Ramblas, away from the firing; up and down the street you could hear snap-snap-snap as the shop-keepers slammed the steel shutters over their windows. I saw two Popular Army officers retreating cautiously from tree to tree with their hands on their revolvers. In front of me the crowd was surging into the Metro station in the middle of the Ramblas to take cover. I immediately decided not to follow them. It might mean being trapped underground for hours.

At this moment an American doctor who had been with us at the front ran up to me and grabbed me by the arm. He was greatly excited.

'Come on, we must get down to the Hotel Falcón.' (The Hotel Falcón was a sort of boarding-house maintained by the POUM and used chiefly by militiamen on leave.) 'The POUM chaps will be meeting there. The trouble's starting. We must hang together.'

'But what the devil is it all about?' I said.

The doctor was hauling me along by the arm. He was too excited to give a very clear statement. It appeared that he had been in the Plaza de Cataluña when several lorry-loads of armed Assault Guards* had driven up to the Telephone Exchange, which was operated mainly by CNT workers, and made a sudden assault upon it. Then some Anarchists had arrived and there had been a general affray. I gathered that the 'trouble' earlier in the day had been a demand by the Government to hand over the Telephone Exchange, which, of course, was refused.

* See note, p. 198.

As we moved down the street a lorry raced past us from the opposite direction. It was full of Anarchists with rifles in their hands. In front a ragged youth was lying on a pile of mattresses behind a light machine-gun. When we got to the Hotel Falcón, which was at the bottom of the Ramblas, a crowd of people was seething in the entrance-hall; there was great confusion, nobody seemed to know what we were expected to do, and nobody was armed except the handful of Shock Troopers who usually acted as guards for the building. I went across to the Comité Local of the POUM, which was almost opposite. Upstairs, in the room where militiamen normally went to draw their pay, another crowd was seething. A tall, pale, rather handsome man of about thirty, in civilian clothes, was trying to restore order and handing out belts and cartridge-boxes from a pile in the corner. There seemed to be no rifles as yet. The doctor had disappeared – I believe there had already been casualties and a call for doctors – but another Englishman had arrived. Presently, from an inner office, the tall man and some others began bringing out armfuls of rifles and handing them round. The other Englishman and myself, as foreigners, were slightly under suspicion and at first nobody would give us a rifle. Then a militiaman whom I had known at the front arrived and recognised me, after which we were given rifles and a few clips of cartridges, somewhat grudgingly.

There was a sound of firing in the distance and the streets were completely empty of people. Everyone said that it was impossible to go up the Ramblas. The Assault Guards had seized buildings in commanding positions and were letting fly at everyone who passed. I would have risked it and gone back to the hotel, but there was a vague idea floating round that the Comité Local was likely to be attacked at any moment and we had better stand by. All over the building, on the stairs and on the pavement outside, small knots of people were standing and talking excitedly. No one seemed to have a very clear idea of what was happening. All I could gather was that the Assault Guards had attacked the Telephone Exchange and seized various strategic spots that commanded other buildings belonging to the workers. There was a general impression that the Assault Guards were 'after' the CNT and the working class generally. It was noticeable that, at this stage, no one seemed to put the blame on the Government. The poorer classes in Barcelona looked upon the Assault

Guards as something rather resembling the Black and Tans, and it seemed to be taken for granted that they had started this attack on their own initiative. Once I had heard how things stood I felt easier in my mind. The issue was clear enough. On one side the CNT, on the other side the police. I have no particular love for the idealised 'worker' as he appears in the bourgeois Communist's mind, but when I see an actual flesh-and-blood worker in conflict with his natural enemy, the policeman, I do not have to ask myself which side I am on.

A long time passed and nothing seemed to be happening at our end of the town. It did not occur to me that I could ring up the hotel and find out whether my wife was all right; I took it for granted that the Telephone Exchange would have stopped working – though, as a matter of fact, it was only out of action for a couple of hours. There seemed to be about three hundred people in the two buildings. Predominantly they were people of the poorest class, from the back-streets down by the quays; there was a number of women among them, some of them carrying babies, and a crowd of little ragged boys. I fancy that many of them had no notion what was happening and had simply fled into the POUM buildings for protection. There was also a number of militiamen on leave, and a sprinkling of foreigners. As far as I could estimate, there were only about sixty rifles between the lot of us. The office upstairs was ceaselessly besieged by a crowd of people who were demanding rifles and being told that there were none left. The younger militia boys, who seemed to regard the whole affair as a kind of picnic, were prowling round and trying to wheedle or steal rifles from anyone who had them. It was not long before one of them got my rifle away from me by a clever dodge and immediately made himself scarce. So I was unarmed again, except for my tiny automatic pistol, for which I had only one clip of cartridges.

It grew dark, I was getting hungry, and seemingly there was no food in the Falcón. My friend and I slipped out to his hotel, which was not far away, to get some dinner. The streets were utterly dark and silent, not a soul stirring, steel shutters drawn over all the shop windows, but no barricades built yet. There was a great fuss before they would let us into the hotel, which was locked and barred. When we got back I learned that the Telephone Exchange was working and went to the telephone in the office upstairs to ring up my wife. Characteristically, there was no telephone directory in the building, and I did not know the number of the Hotel Continental; after searching from room to room for about an hour I came upon a guidebook which gave me the number. I could not make contact with my wife, but I managed to get hold of John McNair, the ILP representative in Barcelona. He told me that all was well, nobody had been shot, and asked me if we were all right at the Comité Local. I said that we should be all right if we had some cigarettes. I only meant this as a joke; nevertheless half an hour later McNair appeared with two packets of Lucky Strike. He had braved the pitch-dark streets, roamed by Anarchist patrols who had twice stopped him at the pistol's point and examined his papers. I shall not forget this small act of heroism. We were very glad of the cigarettes.

They had placed armed guards at most of the windows, and in the street below a little group of Shock Troopers were stopping and questioning the few passers-by. An Anarchist patrol car drove up, bristling with weapons. Beside the driver a beautiful dark-haired girl of about eighteen was nursing a sub-machine-gun across her knees. I spent a long time wandering about the building, a great rambling place of which it was impossible to learn the geography. Everywhere was the usual litter, the broken furniture and torn paper that seem to be the inevitable products of revolution. All over the place people were sleeping; on a broken sofa in a passage two poor women from the quayside were peacefully snoring. The place had been a cabaret-theatre before the POUM took it over. There were raised stages in several of the rooms; on one of them was a desolate grand piano. Finally I discovered what I was looking for – the armoury. I did not know how this affair was going to turn out, and I badly wanted a weapon. I had heard it said so often that all the rival parties, PSUC, POUM, and CNT–FAI alike, were hoarding arms in Barcelona, that I could not believe that two of the principal POUM buildings contained only the fifty or sixty rifles that I had seen. The room which acted as an armoury was unguarded and had a flimsy door; another Englishman and myself had no difficulty in prising it open. When we got inside we found that what they had told us was true – there *were* no more weapons. All we found there were about two dozen small-bore rifles of an obsolete pattern and a few shot-guns, with no cartridges for any of them. I went up to the office and asked if they had any spare pistol ammunition; they had none.

There were a few boxes of bombs, however, which one of the Anarchist patrol cars had brought us. I put a couple in one of my cartridge-boxes. They were a crude type of bomb, ignited by rubbing a sort of match at the top and very liable to go off of their own accord.

People were sprawling asleep all over the floor. In one room a baby was crying, crying ceaselessly. Though this was May the night was getting cold. On one of the cabaret-stages the curtains were still up, so I ripped a curtain down with my knife, rolled myself up in it and had a few hours' sleep. My sleep was disturbed, I remember, by the thought of those beastly bombs, which might blow me into the air if I rolled on them too vigorously. At three in the morning the tall handsome man who seemed to be in command woke me up, gave me a rifle and put me on guard at one of the windows. He told me that Salas, the Chief of Police responsible for the attack on the Telephone Exchange, had been placed under arrest. (Actually, as we learned later, he had only been deprived of his post. Nevertheless the news confirmed the general impression that the Assault Guards had acted without orders.) As soon as it was dawn the people downstairs began building two barricades, one outside the Comité Local and the other outside the Hotel Falcón. The Barcelona streets are paved with square cobbles, easily built up into a wall, and under the cobbles is a kind of shingle that is good for filling sandbags. The building of those barricades was a strange and wonderful sight; I would have given something to be able to photograph it. With the kind of passionate energy that Spaniards display when they have definitely decided to begin upon any job of work, long lines of men, women, and quite small children were tearing up the cobblestones, hauling them along in a hand-cart that had been found somewhere, and staggering to and fro under heavy sacks of sand. In the doorway of the Comité Local a German-Jewish girl, in a pair of militiaman's trousers whose knee-buttons just reached her ankles, was watching with a smile. In a couple of hours the barricades were head-high, with riflemen posted at the loopholes, and behind one barricade a fire was burning and men were frying eggs.

They had taken my rifle away again, and there seemed to be nothing that one could usefully do. Another Englishman and myself decided to go back to the Hotel Continental. There was a lot of firing in the distance, but seemingly none in the Ramblas. On the way up we looked in at the food-market. A very few stalls had opened; they were besieged by a crowd of people from the working-class quarters south of the Ramblas. Just as we got there, there was a heavy crash of rifle-fire outside, some panes of glass in the roof were shivered, and the crowd went flying for the back exits. A few stalls remained open, however; we managed to get a cup of coffee each and buy a wedge of goat's-milk cheese which I tucked in beside my bombs. A few days later I was very glad of that cheese.

At the street-corner where I had seen the Anarchists begin firing the day before a barricade was now standing. The man behind it (I was on the other side of the street) shouted to me to be careful. The Assault Guards in the church tower were firing indiscriminately at everyone who passed. I paused and then crossed the opening at a run; sure enough, a bullet cracked past me, uncomfortably close. When I neared the POUM Executive Building, still on the other side of the road, there were fresh shouts of warning from some Shock Troopers standing in the doorway – shouts which, at the moment, I did not understand. There were trees and a newspaper kiosk between myself and the building (streets of this type in Spain have a broad walk running down the middle), and I could not see what they were pointing at. I went up to the Continental, made sure that all was well, washed my face and then went back to the POUM Executive Building (it was about a hundred yards down the street) to ask for orders. By this time the roar of rifle and machine-gun fire from various directions was almost comparable to the din of a battle. I had just found Kopp and was asking him what we were supposed to do when there was a series of appalling crashes down below. The din was so loud that I made sure someone must be firing at us with a field-gun. Actually it was only hand-grenades, which make double their usual noise when they burst among stone buildings.

Kopp glanced out of the window, cocked his stick behind his back, said: 'Let us investigate,' and strolled down the stairs in his usual unconcerned manner, I following. Just inside the doorway a group of Shock Troopers were bowling bombs down the pavement as though playing skittles. The bombs were bursting twenty yards away with a frightful, ear-splitting crash which was mixed up with the banging of rifles. Half across the street, from behind the newspaper kiosk, a head – it was the head of an American militiaman whom I knew well – was sticking up, for all the world like a coconut at a fair. It was only afterwards that I grasped what was really happening. Next door to the POUM building there was a café with an hotel above it, called the Café Moka. The day before twenty or thirty armed Assault Guards had entered the café and then, when the fighting started, had suddenly seized the building and barricaded themselves in. Presumably they had been ordered to seize the café as a preliminary to attacking the POUM offices later. Early in the morning they had attempted to come out, shots had been exchanged and one Shock Trooper was badly wounded and an Assault Guard killed. The Assault Guards had fled back into the café, but when the American came down the street they had opened fire on him, though he was not armed. The American had flung himself behind the kiosk for cover, and the Shock Troopers were flinging bombs at the Assault Guards to drive them indoors again.

Kopp took in the scene at a glance, pushed his way forward and hauled back a red-haired German Shock Trooper who was just drawing the pin out of a bomb with his teeth. He shouted to everyone to stand back from the doorway, and told us in several languages that we had got to avoid bloodshed. Then he stepped out onto the pavement and, in sight of the Assault Guards, ostentatiously took off his pistol and laid it on the ground. Two Spanish militia officers did the same, and the three of them walked slowly up to the doorway where the Assault Guards were huddling. It was a thing I would not have done for twenty pounds. They were walking, unarmed, up to men who were frightened out of their wits and had loaded guns in their hands. An Assault Guard, in shirt-sleeves and livid with fright, came out of the door to parley with Kopp. He kept pointing in an agitated manner at two unexploded bombs that were lying on the pavement. Kopp came back and told us we had better touch the bombs off. Lying there, they were a danger to anyone who passed. A Shock Trooper fired his rifle at one of the bombs and burst it, then fired at the other and missed. I asked him to give me his rifle, knelt down and let fly at the second bomb. I also missed it, I am sorry to say. This was the only shot I fired during the disturbances. The pavement was covered with broken glass from the sign over the Café Moka, and two cars that were parked outside, one of them Kopp's official car, had been riddled with bullets and their windscreens smashed by bursting bombs.

Kopp took me upstairs again and explained the situation. We had got to defend the POUM buildings if they were attacked, but the POUM leaders had sent instructions that we were to stand on the defensive and not open fire if we could possibly avoid it. Immediately opposite there was a cinematograph, called the Poliorama, with a museum above it, and at the top, high above the general level of the roofs, a small observatory with twin domes. The domes commanded the street, and a few men posted up there with rifles could prevent any attack on the POUM buildings. The caretakers at the cinema were CNT members and would let us come and go. As for the Assault Guards in the Café Moka, there would be no trouble with them; they did not want to fight and would be only too glad to live and let live. Kopp repeated that our orders were not to fire unless we were fired on ourselves or our buildings attacked. I gathered, though he did not say so, that the POUM leaders were furious at being dragged into this affair, but felt that they had got to stand by the CNT.

They had already placed guards in the observatory. The next three days and nights I spent continuously on the roof of the Poliorama, except for brief intervals when I slipped across to the hotel for meals. I was in no danger, I suffered from nothing worse than hunger and boredom, yet it was one of the most unbearable periods of my whole life. I think few experiences could be more sickening, more disillusioning or, finally, more nerve-racking than those evil days of street warfare.

I used to sit on the roof marvelling at the folly of it all. From the little windows in the observatory you could see for miles around – vista after vista of tall slender buildings, glass domes and fantastic curly roofs with brilliant green and copper tiles; over to eastward the glittering pale blue sea – the first glimpse of the sea that I had had since coming to Spain. And the whole huge town of a million people was locked in a sort of violent inertia, a nightmare of noise without movement. The sunlit streets were quite empty. Nothing was happening except the streaming of bullets from barricades and sandbagged windows. Not a vehicle was stirring in the streets; here and there along the Ramblas the trams stood motionless where their drivers had jumped out of them when the fighting started. And all the while the devilish noise, echoing from thousands of stone buildings, went on and on and on, like a tropical rainstorm. Crack-crack, rattle-rattle, roar – sometimes it died away to a few shots, sometimes it quickened to a deafening fusillade, but it never stopped while daylight lasted, and punctually next dawn it started again.

What the devil was happening, who was fighting whom and who was winning, was at first very difficult to discover. The people of Barcelona are so used to street-fighting and so familiar with the local geography that they know by a kind of instinct which political party will hold which streets and which buildings. A foreigner is at a hopeless disadvantage. Looking out from the observatory, I could grasp that the Ramblas, which is one of the principal streets of the town, formed a dividing line. To the right of the Ramblas the working-class quarters were solidly Anarchist; to the left a confused fight was going on among the tortuous by-streets, but on that side the PSUC and the Assault Guards were more or less in control. Up at our end of the Ramblas, round the Plaza de Cataluña, the position was so complicated that it would have been quite unintelligible if every building had not flown a party flag. The principal landmark here was the Hotel Colón, the headquarters of the PSUC, dominating the Plaza de Cataluña. In a window near the last O but one in the huge 'Hotel Colón' that sprawled across its face they had a machine-gun that could sweep the square with deadly effect. A hundred yards to the right of us, down the Ramblas, the JSU, the youth league of the PSUC (corresponding to the Young Communist League in England), were holding a big department store whose sandbagged side-windows fronted our observatory. They had hauled down their red flag and hoisted the Catalan national flag. On the Telephone Exchange, the starting-point of all the trouble, the Catalan national flag and the Anarchist flag were flying side by side. Some kind of temporary compromise had been arrived at there, the exchange was working uninterruptedly and there was no firing from the building.

In our position it was strangely peaceful. The Assault Guards in the Café Moka had drawn down the steel curtains and piled up the café furniture to make a barricade. Later half a dozen of them came onto the roof, opposite to ourselves, and built another barricade of mattresses, over which they hung a Catalan national flag. But it was obvious that they had no wish to start a fight. Kopp had made a definite agreement with them: if they did not fire at us we would not fire at them. He had grown quite friendly with the Assault Guards by this time, and had been to visit them several times in the Café Moka. Naturally they had looted everything drinkable the café possessed, and they made Kopp a present of fifteen bottles of beer. In return Kopp had actually given them one of our rifles to make up for one they had somehow lost on the previous day. Nevertheless, it was a queer feeling sitting on that roof. Sometimes I was merely bored with the whole affair, paid no attention to the hellish noise, and spent hours reading a succession of Penguin Library books which, luckily, I had bought a few days earlier; sometimes I was very conscious of the armed men watching me fifty yards away. It was a little like being in the trenches again; several times I caught myself, from force of habit, speaking of the Assault Guards as 'the Fascists'. There were generally about six of us up there. We placed a man on guard in each of the observatory towers, and the rest of us sat on the lead roof below, where there was no cover except a stone palisade. I was well aware that at any moment the Assault Guards might receive telephone orders to open fire. They had agreed to give us warning before doing so, but there was no certainty that they would keep to their agreement. Only once, however, did trouble look like starting. One of the Assault Guards opposite knelt down and began firing across the barricade. I was on guard in the observatory at the time. I trained my rifle on him and shouted across:

'Hi! Don't you shoot at us!'

'What?'

'Don't you fire at us or we'll fire back!'

'No, no! I wasn't firing at you. Look – down there!'

He motioned with his rifle towards the side-street that ran past the bottom of our building. Sure enough, a youth in blue overalls, with a rifle in his hand, was dodging round the corner. Evidently he had just taken a shot at the Assault Guards on the roof.

'I was firing at him. He fired first.' (I believe this was true.) 'We don't want to shoot you. We're only workers, the same as you are.'

He made the anti-Fascist salute, which I returned. I shouted across:

'Have you got any more beer left?'

'No, it's all gone.'

The same day, for no apparent reason, a man in the JSU building further down the street suddenly raised his rifle and let fly at me when I was leaning out of the window. Perhaps I made a tempting mark. I did not fire back. Though he was only a hundred yards away the bullet went so wide that it did not even hit the roof of the observatory. As usual, Spanish standards of marksmanship had saved me. I was fired at several times from this building.

The devilish racket of firing went on and on. But so far as I could see, and from all I heard, the fighting was defensive on both sides. People simply remained in their buildings or behind their barricades and blazed away at the people opposite. About half a mile away from us there was a street where some of the main offices of the CNT and the UGT were almost exactly facing one another; from that direction the volume of noise was terrific. I passed down that street the day after the fighting was over and the panes of the shop-windows were like sieves. (Most of the shop-keepers in Barcelona had their windows criss-crossed with strips of paper, so that when a bullet hit a pane it did not shiver to pieces.) Sometimes the rattle of rifle and machine-gun fire was punctuated by the crash of hand-grenades. And at long intervals, perhaps a dozen times in all, there were tremendously heavy explosions which at the time I could not account for; they sounded like aerial bombs, but that was impossible, for there were no aeroplanes about. I was told afterwards – quite possibly it was true – that *agents provocateurs* were touching off masses of explosive in order to increase the general noise and panic. There was, however, no artillery-fire. I was listening for this, for if the guns began to fire it would mean that the affair was becoming serious (artillery is the determining factor in street warfare). Afterwards there were wild tales in the newspapers about batteries of guns firing in the streets, but no one was able to point to a building that had been hit by a shell. In any case the sound of gunfire is unmistakable if one is used to it.

Almost from the start food was running short. With difficulty and under cover of darkness (for the Assault Guards were constantly sniping into the Ramblas) food was brought from the Hotel Falcón for the fifteen or twenty militiamen who were in the POUM Executive Building, but there was barely enough to go round, and as many of us as possible went to the Hotel Continental for our meals. The Continental had been 'collectivised' by the Generalidad and not, like most of the hotels, by the CNT or UGT, and it was regarded as neutral ground. No sooner had the fighting started than the hotel filled to the brim with a most extraordinary collection of people. There were foreign journalists, political suspects of every shade, an American airman in the service of the Government, various Communist agents, including a fat, sinister-looking Russian, said to be an agent of the Ogpu, who was nicknamed Charlie Chan and wore attached to his waistband a revolver and a neat little bomb, some families of well-to-do Spaniards who looked like Fascist sympathisers, two or three wounded men from the International Column, a gang of lorry drivers from some huge French lorries which had been carrying a load of oranges back to France and had been held up by the fighting, and a number of Popular Army officers. The Popular Army, as a body, remained neutral throughout the fighting, though a few soldiers slipped away from the barracks and took part as individuals; on the Tuesday morning I had seen a couple of them at the POUM barricades. At the beginning, before the food-shortage became acute and the newspapers began stirring up hatred, there was a tendency to regard the whole affair as a joke. This was the kind of thing that happened every year in Barcelona, people were saying. George Tioli, an Italian journalist, a great friend of ours, came in with his trousers drenched with blood. He had gone out to see what was happening and had been binding up a wounded man on the pavement when someone playfully tossed a hand-grenade at him, fortunately not wounding him seriously. I remember his remarking that the Barcelona paving-stones ought to be numbered; it would save such a lot of trouble in building and demolishing barricades. And I remember a couple of men from the International Column sitting in my room at the hotel when I came in tired, hungry, and dirty after a night on guard. Their attitude was completely neutral. If they had been good party-men they would, I suppose, have urged me to change sides, or even have pinioned me and taken away the bombs of which my pockets were full; instead they merely commiserated with me for having to spend my leave in doing guard-duty on a roof. The general attitude was: 'This is only a dust-up between the Anarchists and the police – it doesn't mean anything.' In spite of the extent of the fighting and the number of casualties I believe this was nearer the truth than the official version which represented the affair as a planned rising.

It was about Wednesday (5 May) that a change seemed to come over things. The shuttered streets looked ghastly. A very few pedestrians, forced abroad for one reason or another, crept to and fro, flourishing white handkerchiefs, and at a spot in the middle of the Ramblas that was safe from bullets some men were crying newspapers to the empty street. On Tuesday *Solidaridad Obrera*, the Anarchist paper, had described the attack on the Telephone Exchange as a 'monstrous provocation' (or words to that effect), but on Wednesday it changed its tune and began imploring everyone to go back to work. The Anarchist leaders were broadcasting the same message. The office of *La Batalla*, the POUM paper, which was not defended, had been raided and seized by the Assault Guards at about the same time as the Telephone Exchange, but the paper was being printed, and a few copies distributed, from another address. It urged everyone to remain at the barricades. People were divided in their minds and wondering uneasily how the devil this was going to end. I doubt whether anyone left the barricades as yet, but everyone was sick of the meaningless fighting, which could obviously lead to no real decision, because no one wanted this to develop into a full-sized civil war which might mean losing the war against Franco. I heard this fear expressed on all sides. So far as one could gather from what people were saying at the time the CNT rank and file wanted, and had wanted from the beginning, only two things: the handing back of the Telephone Exchange and the disarming of the Assault Guards. If the Generalidad had promised to do these two things, and also promised to put an end to the food profiteering, there is little doubt that the barricades would have been down in two hours. But it was obvious that the Generalidad was not going to give in. Ugly rumours were flying round. It was said that the Valencia Government was sending six thousand men to occupy Barcelona, and that five thousand Anarchist and POUM troops had left the Aragón front to oppose them. Only the first of these rumours was true. Watching from the observatory tower we saw the low grey shapes of warships closing in upon the harbour. Douglas Moyle, who had been a sailor, said that they looked like British destroyers. As a matter of fact they *were* British destroyers, though we did not learn this till afterwards.

That evening we heard that on the Plaza de España four hundred Assault Guards had surrendered and handed their arms to the Anarchists; also the news was vaguely filtering through that in the suburbs (mainly working-class quarters) the CNT were in control. It looked as though we were winning. But the same evening Kopp sent for me and, with a grave face, told me that according to information he had just received the Government was about to outlaw the POUM and declare a state of war upon it. The news gave me a shock. It was the first glimpse I had had of the interpretation that was likely to be put upon this affair later on. I dimly foresaw that when the fighting ended the entire blame would be laid upon the POUM, which was the weakest party and therefore the most suitable scapegoat. And meanwhile our local neutrality was at an end. If the Government declared war upon us we had no choice but to defend ourselves, and here at the Executive building we could be certain that the Assault Guards next door would get orders to attack us. Our only chance was to attack them first. Kopp was waiting for orders on the telephone; if we heard definitely that the POUM was outlawed we must make preparations at once to seize the Café Moka.

I remember the long, nightmarish evening that we spent in fortifying the building. We locked the steel curtains across the front entrance and behind them built a barricade of slabs of stone left behind by the workmen who had been making some alterations. We went over our stock of weapons. Counting the six rifles that were on the roof of the Poliorama opposite, we had twenty-one rifles, one of them defective, about fifty rounds of ammunition for each rifle, and a few dozen bombs; otherwise nothing except a few pistols and revolvers. About a dozen men, mostly Germans, had volunteered for the attack on the Café Moka, if it came off. We should attack from the roof, of course, some time in the small hours, and take them by surprise; they were more numerous, but our morale was better, and no doubt we could storm the place, though people were bound to be killed in doing so. We had no food in the building except a few slabs of chocolate, and the rumour had gone round that 'they' were going to cut off the water supply. (Nobody knew who 'they' were. It might be the Government that controlled the water-works, or it might be the CNT – nobody knew.) We spent a long time filling up every basin in the lavatories, every bucket we could lay hands on, and, finally, the fifteen beer bottles, now empty, which the Assault Guards had given to Kopp.

I was in a ghastly frame of mind and dog-tired after about sixty hours without much sleep. It was now late into the night. People were sleeping all over the floor behind the barricade downstairs. Upstairs there was a small room, with a sofa in it, which we intended to use as a dressing-station, though, needless to say, we discovered that there was neither iodine nor bandages in the building. My wife had come down from the hotel in case a nurse should be needed. I lay down on the sofa, feeling that I would like half an hour's rest before the attack on the 'Moka', in which I should presumably be killed. I remember the intolerable discomfort caused by my pistol, which was strapped to my belt and sticking into the small of my back. And the next thing I remember is waking up with a jerk to find my wife standing beside me. It was broad daylight, nothing had happened, the Government had not declared war on the POUM, the water had not been cut off, and except for the sporadic firing in the streets everything was normal. My wife said that she had not had the heart to wake me and had slept in an arm-chair in one of the front rooms.

That afternoon there was a kind of armistice. The firing died away and with surprising suddenness the streets filled with people. A few shops began to pull up their shutters, and the market was packed with a huge crowd clamouring for food, though the stalls were almost empty. It was noticeable, however, that the trams did not start running. The Assault Guards were still behind their barricades in the 'Moka'; on neither side were the fortified buildings evacuated. Everyone was rushing round and trying to buy food. And on every side you heard the same anxious questions: 'Do you think it's stopped? Do you think it's going to start again?' 'It' – the fighting – was now thought of as some kind of natural calamity, like a hurricane or an earthquake, which was happening to us all alike and which we had no power of stopping. And sure enough, almost immediately – I suppose there must really have been several hours' truce, but they seemed more like minutes than hours – a sudden crash of rifle-fire, like a June cloud-burst, sent everyone scurrying; the steel shutters snapped into place, the streets emptied like magic, the barricades were manned, and 'it' had started again.

I went back to my post on the roof with a feeling of concentrated disgust and fury. When you are taking part in events like these you are, I suppose, in a small way, making history, and you ought by rights to feel like an historical character. But you never do, because at such times the physical details always outweigh everything else. Throughout the fighting

I never made the correct 'analysis' of the situation that was so glibly made by journalists hundreds of miles away. What I was chiefly thinking about was not the rights and wrongs of the miserable internecine scrap, but simply the discomfort and boredom of sitting day and night on that intolerable roof, and the hunger which was growing worse and worse – for none of us had had a proper meal since Monday. It was in my mind all the while that I should have to go back to the front as soon as this business was over. It was infuriating. I had been a hundred and fifteen days in the line and had come back to Barcelona ravenous for a bit of rest and comfort; and instead I had to spend my time sitting on a roof opposite Assault Guards as bored as myself, who periodically waved to me and assured me that they were 'workers' (meaning that they hoped I would not shoot them), but who would certainly open fire if they got the order to do so. If this was history it did not feel like it. It was more like a bad period at the front, when men were short and we had to do abnormal hours of guard-duty; instead of being heroic one just had to stay at one's post, bored, dropping with sleep and completely uninterested as to what it was all about.

Inside the hotel, among the heterogeneous mob who for the most part had not dared to put their noses out of doors, a horrible atmosphere of suspicion had grown up. Various people were infected with spy mania and were creeping round whispering that everyone else was a spy of the Communists, or the Trotskyists, or the Anarchists, or what-not. The fat Russian agent was cornering all the foreign refugees in turn and explaining plausibly that this whole affair was an Anarchist plot. I watched him with some interest, for it was the first time that I had seen a person whose profession was telling lies – unless one counts journalists. There was something repulsive in the parody of smart hotel life that was still going on behind shuttered windows amid the rattle of rifle-fire. The front dining-room had been abandoned after a bullet came through the window and chipped a pillar, and the guests were crowded into a darkish room at the back, where there were never quite enough tables to go round. The waiters were reduced in numbers – some of them were CNT members and had joined in the general strike – and had dropped their boiled shirts for the time being, but meals were still being served with a pretence of ceremony. There was, however, practically nothing to eat. On that

Thursday night the principal dish at dinner was *one* sardine each. The hotel had had no bread for days, and even the wine was running so low that we were drinking older and older wines at higher and higher prices. This shortage of food went on for several days after the fighting was over. Three days running, I remember, my wife and I breakfasted off a little piece of goat's-milk cheese with no bread and nothing to drink. The only thing that was plentiful was oranges. The French lorry drivers brought quantities of their oranges into the hotel. They were a tough-looking bunch; they had with them some flashy Spanish girls and a huge porter in a black blouse. At any other time the little snob of an hotel manager would have done his best to make them uncomfortable, in fact would have refused to have them on the premises, but at present they were popular because, unlike the rest of us, they had a private store of bread which everyone was trying to cadge from them.

I spent that final night on the roof, and the next day it did really look as though the fighting was coming to an end. I do not think there was much firing that day – the Friday. No one seemed to know for certain whether the troops from Valencia were really coming; they arrived that evening, as a matter of fact. The Government was broadcasting half-soothing, half-threatening messages, asking everyone to go home and saying that after a certain hour anyone found carrying arms would be arrested. Not much attention was paid to the Government's broadcasts, but everywhere the people were fading away from the barricades. I have no doubt that it was mainly the food shortage that was responsible. From every side you heard the same remark: 'We have no more food, we must go back to work.' On the other hand the Assault Guards, who could count on getting their rations so long as there was any food in the town, were able to stay at their posts. By the afternoon the streets were almost normal, though the deserted barricades were still standing; the Ramblas were thronged with people, the shops nearly all open, and – most reassuring of all – the trams that had stood so long in frozen blocks jerked into motion and began running. The Assault Guards were still holding the Café Moka and had not taken down their barricades, but some of them brought chairs out and sat on the pavement with their rifles across their knees. I winked at one of them as I went past and got a not unfriendly grin; he recognised me, of course. Over the Telephone Exchange the

Anarchist flag had been hauled down and only the Catalan flag was flying. That meant that the workers were definitely beaten; I realised – though, owing to my political ignorance, not so clearly as I ought to have done – that when the Government felt more sure of itself there would be reprisals. But at the time I was not interested in that aspect of things. All I felt was a profound relief that the devilish din of firing was over, and that one could buy some food and have a bit of rest and peace before going back to the front.

It must have been late that evening that the troops from Valencia first appeared in the streets. They were Assault Guards, another formation similar to the local Assault Guards, the hated Civil Guards and the Carabineros (i.e. a formation intended primarily for police work), and the picked troops of the Republic. Quite suddenly they seemed to spring up out of the ground; you saw them everywhere patrolling the streets in groups of ten – tall men in grey or blue uniforms, with long rifles slung over their shoulders, and a sub-machine-gun to each group. Meanwhile there was a delicate job to be done. The six rifles which we had used for the guard in the observatory towers were still lying there, and by hook or by crook we had got to get them back to the POUM building. It was only a question of getting them across the street. They were part of the regular armoury of the building, but to bring them into the street was to contravene the Government's order, and if we were caught with them in our hands we should certainly be arrested – worse, the rifles would be confiscated. With only twenty-one rifles in the building we could not afford to lose six of them. After a lot of discussion as to the best method, a red-haired Spanish boy and myself began to smuggle them out. It was easy enough to dodge the Valencian Assault Guard patrols; the danger was the local Assault Guards in the 'Moka', who were well aware that we had rifles in the observatory and might give the show away if they saw us carrying them across. Each of us partially undressed and slung a rifle over the left shoulder, the butt under the armpit, the barrel down the trouser-leg. It was unfortunate that they were long Mausers. Even a man as tall as I am cannot wear a long Mauser down his trouser-leg without discomfort. It was an intolerable job getting down the corkscrew staircase of the observatory with a completely rigid left leg. Once in the street, we found that the only way to move was with extreme slowness, so slowly that you did not have to bend your knees. Outside the picture-house I saw a group of people staring at me with great interest as I crept along at tortoise-speed. I have often wondered what they thought was the matter with me. Wounded in the war, perhaps. However, all the rifles were smuggled across without incident.

Next day the Valencian Assault Guards were everywhere, walking the streets like conquerors. There was no doubt that the Government was simply making a display of force in order to overawe a population which it already knew would not resist; if there had been any real fear of further outbreaks the Valencian Assault Guards would have been kept in barracks and not scattered through the streets in small bands. They were splendid troops, much the best I had seen in Spain, and, though I suppose they were in a sense 'the enemy', I could not help liking the look of them. But it was with a sort of amazement that I watched them strolling to and fro. I was used to the ragged, scarcely-armed militia on the Aragón front, and I had not known that the Republic possessed troops like these. It was not only that they were picked men physically, it was their weapons that most astonished me. All of them were armed with brand-new rifles of the type known as 'the Russian rifle' (these rifles were sent to Spain by the USSR, but were, I believe, manufactured in America). I examined one of them. It was a far from perfect rifle, but vastly better than the dreadful old blunderbusses we had at the front. The Valencian Assault Guards had one sub-machine-gun between ten men and an automatic pistol each; we at the front had approximately one machine-gun between fifty men, and as for pistols and revolvers, you could only procure them illegally. As a matter of fact, though I had not noticed it till now, it was the same everywhere. The Assault Guards and Carabineros, who were not intended for the front at all, were better armed and far better clad than ourselves. I suspect it is the same in all wars – always the same contrast between the sleek police in the rear and the ragged soldiers in the line. On the whole the Valencian Assault Guards got on very well with the population after the first day or two. On the first day there was a certain amount of trouble because some of them – acting on instructions, I suppose – began behaving in a provocative manner. Bands of them boarded trams, searched the passengers, and, if they had CNT membership cards in their pockets, tore them up and stamped on them. This led to scuffles with armed Anarchists, and one or two people were killed. Very soon, however, the Valencian Assault Guards dropped their conquering air and relations became more friendly. It was noticeable that most of them had picked up a girl after a day or two.

The Barcelona fighting had given the Valencia Government the long-wanted excuse to assume fuller control of Catalonia. The workers' militias were to be broken up and redistributed among the Popular Army. The Spanish Republican flag was flying all over Barcelona – the first time I had seen it, I think, except over a Fascist trench.* In the working-class quarters the barricades were being pulled down, rather fragmentarily, for it is a lot easier to build a barricade than to put the stones back. Outside the PSUC buildings the barricades were allowed to remain standing, and indeed many were standing as late as June. The Assault Guards were still occupying strategic points. Huge seizures of arms were being made from CNT strongholds, though I have no doubt a good many escaped seizure. *La Batalla* was still appearing, but it was censored until the front page was almost completely blank. The PSUC papers were uncensored and were publishing inflammatory articles demanding the suppression of the POUM. The POUM was declared to be a disguised Fascist organisation, and a cartoon representing the POUM as a figure slipping off a mask marked with the hammer and sickle and revealing a hideous, maniacal face marked with the swastika, was being circulated all over the town by PSUC agents. Evidently the official version of the Barcelona fighting was already fixed upon: it was to be represented as a 'fifth column' Fascist rising engineered solely by the POUM.

In the hotel the horrible atmosphere of suspicion and hostility had grown worse now that the fighting was over. In the face of the accusations that were being flung about it was impossible to remain neutral. The posts were working again, the foreign Communist papers were beginning to arrive, and their accounts of the fighting were not only violently partisan but, of course, wildly inaccurate as to facts. I think some of the Communists on the spot, who had seen what was actually happening, were dismayed by the interpretation that was being put upon events, but naturally they had to stick to their own side. Our Communist friend approached me

* See note, p. 47.

once again and asked me whether I would not transfer into the International Column.

I was rather surprised. 'Your papers are saying I'm a Fascist,' I said. 'Surely I should be politically suspect, coming from the POUM.'

'Oh, that doesn't matter. After all, you were only acting under orders.'

I had to tell him that after this affair I could not join any Communist-controlled unit. Sooner or later it might mean being used against the Spanish working class. One could not tell when this kind of thing would break out again, and if I had to use my rifle at all in such an affair I would use it on the side of the working class and not against them. He was very decent about it. But from now on the whole atmosphere was changed. You could not, as before, 'agree to differ' and have drinks with a man who was supposedly your political opponent. There were some ugly wrangles in the hotel lounge. Meanwhile the jails were already full and overflowing. After the fighting was over the Anarchists had, of course, released their prisoners, but the Assault Guards had not released theirs, and most of them were thrown into prison and kept there without trial, in many cases for months on end. As usual, completely innocent people were being arrested owing to police bungling. I mentioned earlier that Douglas Thompson was wounded about the beginning of April. Afterwards we had lost touch with him, as usually happened when a man was wounded, for wounded men were frequently moved from one hospital to another. Actually he was at Tarragona hospital and was sent back to Barcelona about the time when the fighting started. On the Tuesday morning I met him in the street, considerably bewildered by the firing that was going on all round. He asked the question everyone was asking:

'What the devil is this all about?'

I explained as well as I could. Thompson said promptly:

'I'm going to keep out of this. My arm's still bad. I shall go back to my hotel and stay there.'

He went back to his hotel, but unfortunately (how important it is in street-fighting to understand the local geography!) it was an hotel in a part of the town controlled by the Assault Guards. The place was raided and Thompson was arrested, flung into jail, and kept for eight days in a cell so full of people that nobody had room to lie down. There were many similar cases. Numerous foreigners with doubtful political records were on the run, with the police on their track and in constant fear of denunciation. It was worst for the Italians and Germans, who had no passports and were generally wanted by the secret police in their own countries. If they were arrested they were liable to be deported to France, which might mean being sent back to Italy or Germany, where God knew what horrors were awaiting them. One or two foreign women hurriedly regularised their position by 'marrying' Spaniards. A German girl who had no papers at all dodged the police by posing for several days as a man's mistress. I remember the look of shame and misery on the poor girl's face when I accidentally bumped into her coming out of the man's bedroom. Of course she was not his mistress, but no doubt she thought I thought she was. You had all the while a hateful feeling that someone hitherto your friend might be denouncing you to the secret police. The long nightmare of the fighting, the noise, the lack of food and sleep, the mingled strain and boredom of sitting on the roof and wondering whether in another minute I should be shot myself or be obliged to shoot somebody else had put my nerves on edge. I had got to the point when every time a door banged I grabbed for my pistol. On the Saturday morning there was an uproar of shots outside and everyone cried out: 'It's starting again!' I ran into the street to find that it was only some Valencian Assault Guards shooting a mad dog. No one who was in Barcelona then, or for months later, will forget the horrible atmosphere produced by fear, suspicion, hatred, censored newspapers, crammed jails, enormous food queues and prowling gangs of armed men.

I have tried to give some idea of what it felt like to be in the middle of the Barcelona fighting; yet I do not suppose I have succeeded in conveying much of the strangeness of that time. One of the things that stick in my mind when I look back is the casual contacts one made at the time, the sudden glimpses of non-combatants to whom the whole thing was simply a meaningless uproar. I remember the fashionably-dressed woman I saw strolling down the Ramblas, with a shopping-basket over her arm and leading a white poodle, while the rifles cracked and roared a street or two away. It is conceivable that she was deaf. And the man I saw rushing across the completely empty Plaza de Cataluña, brandishing a white handkerchief in each hand. And the large party of people all dressed in black who kept trying for about an hour to cross the Plaza de Cataluña and always failing. Every time they emerged from the side-street at the corner the PSUC machine-gunners in the Hotel Colón opened fire and drove them back – I don't know why, for they were obviously unarmed. I have since thought that they may have been a funeral party. And the little man who acted as caretaker at the museum over the Poliorama and who seemed to regard the whole affair as a social occasion. He was so pleased to have the English visiting him – the English were so *simpático*, he said. He hoped we would all come and see him again when the trouble was over; as a matter of fact I did go and see him. And the other little man, sheltering in a doorway, who jerked his head in a pleased manner towards the hell of firing on the Plaza de Cataluña and said (as though remarking that it was a fine morning): 'So we've got the nineteenth of July back again!' And the people in the shoe-shop who were making my marching-boots. I went there before the fighting, after it was over, and, for a very few minutes, during the brief armistice on 5 May. It was an expensive shop, and the shop-people were UGT and may have been PSUC members – at any rate they were politically on the other side and they knew that I was serving with the POUM. Yet their attitude was completely indifferent. 'Such a pity, this kind of thing, isn't it? And so bad for business. What a pity it doesn't stop! As though there wasn't enough of that kind of thing at the front!' etc. etc. There must have been quantities of people, perhaps a majority of the inhabitants of Barcelona, who regarded the whole affair without a flicker of interest, or with no more interest than they would have felt in an air-raid.

In this chapter I have described only my personal experiences. In *Appendix II* I discuss as best I can the larger issues – what actually happened and with what results, what were the rights and wrongs of the affair, and who if anyone was responsible. So much political capital has been made out of the Barcelona fighting that it is important to try and get a balanced view of it. An immense amount, enough to fill many books, has already been written on the subject, and I do not suppose I should exaggerate if I said that nine-tenths of it is untruthful. Nearly all the newspaper accounts published at the time were manufactured by journalists at a distance, and were not only inaccurate in their facts but intentionally misleading. As usual, only one side of the question has been allowed to get to the wider public. Like everyone who was in Barcelona at the time, I saw only what was happening in my immediate neighbourhood, but I saw and heard quite enough to be able to contradict many of the lies that have been circulated.

X

It must have been three days after the Barcelona fighting ended that we returned to the front. After the fighting – more particularly after the slanging-match in the newspapers – it was difficult to think about this war in quite the same naïvely idealistic manner as before. I suppose there is no one who spent more than a few weeks in Spain without being in some degree disillusioned. My mind went back to the newspaper correspondent whom I had met my first day in Barcelona, and who said to me: 'This war is a racket the same as any other.' The remark had shocked me deeply, and at that time (December) I did not believe it was true; it was not true even now, in May; but it was becoming truer. The fact is that every war suffers a kind of progressive degradation with every month that it continues, because such things as individual liberty and a truthful press are simply not compatible with military efficiency.

One could begin now to make some kind of guess at what was likely to happen. It was easy to see that the Caballero Government would fall and be replaced by a more Right-wing Government with a stronger Communist influence (this happened a week or two later), which would set itself to break the power of the trade unions once and for all. And afterwards, when Franco was beaten – and putting aside the huge problems raised by the reorganisation of Spain – the prospect was not rosy. As for the newspaper talk about this being a 'war for democracy', it was plain eyewash. No one in his senses supposed that there was any hope of democracy, even as we understand it in England or France, in a country so divided and exhausted as Spain would be when the war was over. It would have to be a dictatorship, and it was clear that the chance of a working-class dictatorship had passed. That meant that the general movement would be in the direction of some kind of Fascism. Fascism called, no doubt, by some politer name, and – because this was Spain – more human and less efficient than the German or Italian varieties. The only alternatives were an infinitely worse dictatorship by Franco, or (always a possibility) that the war would end with Spain divided up, either by actual frontiers or into economic zones.

Whichever way you took it it was a depressing outlook. But it did not follow that the Government was not worth fighting for as against the more naked and developed Fascism of Franco and Hitler. Whatever faults the post-war Government might have, Franco's régime would certainly be worse. To the workers – the town proletariat – it might in the end make very little difference who won, but Spain is primarily an agricultural country and the peasants would almost certainly benefit by a Government victory. Some at least of the seized lands would remain in their possession, in which case there would also be a distribution of land in the territory that had been Franco's, and the virtual serfdom that had existed in some parts of Spain was not likely to be restored. The Government in control at the end of the war would at any rate be anti-clerical and anti-feudal. It would keep the Church in check, at least for the time being, and would modernise the country – build roads, for instance, and promote education and public health; a certain amount had been done in this direction even during the war. Franco, on the other hand, in so far as he was not merely the puppet of Italy and Germany, was tied to the big feudal landlords and stood for a stuffy clerico-military reaction. The Popular Front might be a swindle, but Franco was an anachronism. Only millionaires or romantics could want him to win.

Moreover, there was the question of the international prestige of Fascism, which for a year or two past had been haunting me like a nightmare. Since 1930 the Fascists had won all the victories; it was time they got a beating, it hardly mattered from whom. If we could drive Franco and his foreign mercenaries into the sea it might make an immense improvement in the world situation, even if Spain itself emerged with a stifling dictatorship and all its best men in jail. For that alone the war would have been worth winning.

This was how I saw things at the time. I may say that I now think much more highly of the Negrín Government than I did when it came into office. It has kept up the difficult fight with splendid courage, and it has shown more political tolerance than anyone expected. But I still believe that – unless Spain splits up, with unpredictable consequences – the tendency of the post-war Government is bound to be Fascistic. Once again I let this opinion stand, and take the chance that time will do to me what it does to most prophets.

We had just reached the front when we heard that Bob Smillie, on his way back to England, had been arrested at the frontier, taken down to Valencia and thrown into jail. Smillie had been in Spain since the previous October. He had worked for several months at the POUM office and had then joined the militia when the other ILP members arrived, on the understanding that he was to do three months at the front before going back to England to take part in a propaganda tour. It was some time before we could discover what he had been arrested for. He was being kept *incommunicado*, so that not even a lawyer could see him. In Spain there is – at any rate in practice – no habeas corpus, and you can be kept in jail for months at a stretch without even being charged, let alone tried. Finally we learned from a released prisoner that Smillie had been arrested for 'carrying arms'. The 'arms', as I happened to know, were two hand-grenades of the primitive type used at the beginning of the war, which he had been taking home to show off at his lectures, along with shell splinters and other souvenirs. The charges and fuses had been removed from them – they were mere cylinders of steel and completely harmless. It was obvious that this was only a pretext and that he had been arrested because of his known connection with the POUM. The Barcelona fighting had only just ended and the authorities were, at that moment, extremely anxious not to let anyone out of Spain who was in a position to contradict the official version. As a result people were liable to be arrested at the frontier on more or less frivolous pretexts. Very possibly the intention, at the beginning, was only to detain Smillie for a few days. But the trouble is that, in Spain, once you are in jail you generally stay there, with or without trial.

We were still at Huesca, but they had placed us further to the right, opposite the Fascist redoubt which we had temporarily captured a few weeks earlier. I was now acting as *teniente* – corresponding to second-lieutenant in the British Army, I suppose – in command of about thirty men, English and Spanish. They had sent my name in for a regular commission; whether I should get it was uncertain. Previously the militia officers had refused to accept regular commissions, which meant extra pay and conflicted with the equalitarian ideas of the militia, but they were now obliged to do so. Benjamin had already been gazetted captain and Kopp was in process of being gazetted major. The Government could not, of course, dispense with the militia officers, but it was not confirming any of them in a higher rank than major, presumably in order to keep the higher commands for Regular Army officers and the new officers from the School of War. As a result, in our division, the 29th, and no doubt in many others, you had the queer temporary situation of the divisional commander, the brigade commanders and the battalion commanders all being majors.

There was not much happening at the front. The battle round the Jaca road had died away and did not begin again till mid-June. In our position the chief trouble was the snipers. The Fascist trenches were more than a hundred and fifty yards away, but they were on higher ground and were on two sides of us, our line forming a right-angle salient. The corner of the salient was a dangerous spot; there had always been a toll of sniper casualties there. From time to time the Fascists let fly at us with a rifle-grenade or some similar weapon. It made a ghastly crash – unnerving, because you could not hear it coming in time to dodge – but was not really dangerous; the hole it blew in the ground was no bigger than a wash-tub. The nights were pleasantly warm, the days blazing hot, the mosquitoes were becoming a nuisance, and in spite of the clean clothes we had brought from Barcelona we were almost immediately lousy. Out in the deserted orchards in no-man's-land the cherries were whitening on the trees. For two days there were torrential rains, the dug-outs flooded and the parapet sank a foot; after that there were more days of digging out the sticky clay with the wretched Spanish spades which have no handles and bend like tin spoons.

They had promised us a trench-mortar for the company; I was looking forward to it greatly. At nights we patrolled as usual – more dangerous than it used to be, because the Fascist trenches were better manned and they had grown more alert; they had scattered tin cans just outside their wire and used to open up with the machine-guns when they heard a clank. In the daytime we sniped from no-man's-land. By crawling a hundred yards you could get to a ditch, hidden by tall grasses, which commanded a gap in the Fascist parapet. We had set up a rifle-rest in the ditch. If you waited long enough you generally saw a khaki-clad figure slip hurriedly across the gap. I had several shots. I don't know whether I hit anyone – it is most unlikely; I am a very poor shot with a rifle. But it was rather fun, the Fascists did not know where the shots were coming from, and I made sure I would get one of them sooner or later. However, the dog it was that died – a Fascist sniper got me instead. I had been about ten days at the front when it happened. The whole experience of being hit by a bullet is very interesting and I think it is worth describing in detail.

It was at the corner of the parapet, at five o'clock in the morning. This was always a dangerous time, because we had the dawn at our backs, and if you stuck your head above the parapet it was clearly outlined against the sky. I was talking to the sentries preparatory to changing the guard. Suddenly, in the very middle of saying something, I felt – it is very hard to describe what I felt, though I remember it with the utmost vividness.

Roughly speaking it was the sensation of being *at the centre* of an explosion. There seemed to be a loud bang and a blinding flash of light all round me, and I felt a tremendous shock – no pain, only a violent shock, such as you get from an electric terminal; with it a sense of utter weakness, a feeling of being stricken and shrivelled up to nothing. The sandbags in front of me receded into immense distance. I fancy you would feel much the same if you were struck by lightning. I knew immediately that I was hit, but because of the seeming bang and flash I thought it was a rifle nearby that had gone off accidentally and shot me. All this happened in a space of time much less than a second. The next moment my knees crumpled up and I was falling, my head hitting the ground with a violent bang which, to my relief, did not hurt. I had a numb, dazed feeling, a consciousness of being very badly hurt, but no pain in the ordinary sense.

The American sentry I had been talking to had started forward. 'Gosh! Are you hit?' People gathered round. There was the usual fuss – 'Lift him up! Where's he hit? Get his shirt open!' etc. etc. The American called for a knife to cut my shirt open. I knew that there was one in my pocket and tried to get it out, but discovered that my right arm was paralysed. Not being in pain, I felt a vague satisfaction. This ought to please my wife, I thought; she had always wanted me to be wounded, which would save me from being killed when the great battle came. It was only now that it occurred to me to wonder where I was hit, and how badly; I could feel nothing, but I was conscious that the bullet had struck me somewhere in the front of the body. When I tried to speak I found that I had no voice, only a faint squeak, but at the second attempt I managed to ask where I was hit. In the throat, they said. Harry Webb, our stretcher-bearer, had brought a bandage and one of the little bottles of alcohol they gave us for field-dressings. As they lifted me up a lot of blood poured out of my mouth, and I heard a Spaniard behind me say that the bullet had gone clean through my neck. I felt the alcohol, which at ordinary times would sting like the devil, splash onto the wound as a pleasant coolness.

They laid me down again while somebody fetched a stretcher. As soon as I knew that the bullet had gone clean through my neck I took it for granted that I was done for. I had never heard of a man or an animal getting a bullet through the middle of the neck and surviving it. The blood was dribbling out of the corner of my mouth. 'The artery's gone,' I thought. I wondered how long you last when your carotid artery is cut; not many minutes, presumably. Everything was very blurry. There must have been about two minutes during which I assumed that I was killed. And that too was interesting – I mean it is interesting to know what your thoughts would be at such a time. My first thought, conventionally enough, was for my wife. My second was a violent resentment at having to leave this world which, when all is said and done, suits me so well. I had time to feel this very vividly. The stupid mischance infuriated me. The meaninglessness of it! To be bumped off, not even in battle, but in this stale corner of the trenches, thanks to a moment's carelessness! I thought, too, of the man who had shot me – wondered what he was like, whether he was a Spaniard or a foreigner, whether he knew he had got me, and so forth. I could not feel any resentment against him. I reflected that as he was a Fascist I would have killed him if I could, but that if he had been taken prisoner and brought before me at this moment I would merely have congratulated him on his good shooting. It may be, though, that if you were really dying your thoughts would be quite different.

They had just got me onto the stretcher when my paralysed right arm came to life and began hurting damnably. At the time I imagined that I must have broken it in falling; but the pain reassured me, for I knew that your sensations do not become more acute when you are dying. I began to feel more normal and to be sorry for the four poor devils who were sweating and slithering with the stretcher on their shoulders. It was a mile and a half to the ambulance, and vile going, over lumpy, slippery tracks. I knew what a sweat it was, having helped to carry a wounded man down a day or two earlier. The leaves of the silver poplars which, in places, fringed our trenches brushed against my face; I thought what a good thing it was to be alive in a world where silver poplars grow. But all the while the pain in my arm was diabolical, making me swear and then try not to swear, because every time I breathed too hard the blood bubbled out of my mouth.

The doctor re-bandaged the wound, gave me a shot of morphia, and sent me off to Siétamo. The hospitals at Siétamo were hurriedly constructed wooden huts where the wounded were, as a rule, only kept for a few hours before being sent on to Barbastro or Lérida. I was dopey from morphia but still in great pain, practically unable to move and swallowing blood constantly. It was typical of Spanish hospital methods that while I was in this state the untrained nurse tried to force the regulation hospital meal – a huge meal of soup, eggs, greasy stew and so forth – down my throat and seemed surprised when I would not take it. I asked for a cigarette, but this was one of the periods of tobacco famine and there was not a cigarette in the place. Presently two comrades who had got permission to leave the line for a few hours appeared at my bedside.

'Hullo! You're alive, are you? Good. We want your watch and your revolver and your electric torch. And your knife, if you've got one.'

They made off with all my portable possessions. This always happened when a man was wounded – everything he possessed was promptly divided up; quite rightly, for watches, revolvers, and so forth were precious at the front and if they went down the line in a wounded man's kit they were certain to be stolen somewhere on the way.

By the evening enough sick and wounded had trickled in to make up a few ambulance-loads, and they sent us on to Barbastro. What a journey! It used to be said that in this war you got well if you were wounded in the extremities, but always died of a wound in the abdomen. I now realised why. No one who was liable to bleed internally could have survived those miles of jolting over metal roads that had been smashed to pieces by heavy lorries and never repaired since the war began. Bang, bump, wallop! It took me back to my early childhood and a dreadful thing called the Wiggle-Woggle at the White City Exhibition. They had forgotten to tie us into the stretchers. I had enough strength in my left arm to hang on, but one poor wretch was spilt onto the floor and suffered God knows what agonies. Another, a walking case who was sitting in the corner of the ambulance, vomited all over the place. The hospital in Barbastro was very crowded, the beds so close together that they were almost touching. Next morning they loaded a number of us onto the hospital train and sent us down to Lérida.

I was five or six days in Lérida. It was a big hospital, with sick, wounded, and ordinary civilian patients more or less jumbled up together. Some of the men in my ward had frightful wounds. In the next bed to me there was a youth with black hair who was suffering from some disease or other and was being given medicine that made his urine as green as emerald. His bed-bottle was one of the sights of the ward. An English-speaking Dutch Communist, having heard that there was an Englishman in the hospital, befriended me and brought me English newspapers. He had been terribly wounded in the October fighting, and had somehow managed to settle down at Lérida hospital and had married one of the nurses. Thanks to his wound, one of his legs had shrivelled till it was no thicker than my arm. Two militiamen on leave, whom I had met my first week at the front, came in to see a wounded friend and recognised me. They were kids of about eighteen. They stood awkwardly beside my bed, trying to think of something to say, and then, as a way of demonstrating that they were sorry I was wounded, suddenly took all the tobacco out of their pockets, gave it to me, and fled before I could give it back. How typically Spanish! I discovered afterwards that you could not buy tobacco anywhere in the town and what they had given me was a week's ration.

After a few days I was able to get up and walk about with my arm in a sling. For some reason it hurt much more when it hung down. I also had, for the time being, a good deal of internal pain from the damage I had done myself in falling, and my voice had disappeared almost completely, but I never had a moment's pain from the bullet wound itself. It seems this is usually the case. The tremendous shock of a bullet prevents sensation locally; a splinter of shell or bomb, which is jagged and usually hits you less hard, would probably hurt like the devil. There was a pleasant garden in the hospital grounds, and in it was a pool with goldfishes and some small dark grey fish – bleak, I think. I used to sit watching them for hours. The way things were done at Lérida gave me an insight into the hospital system on the Aragón front – whether it was the same on other fronts I do not know. In some ways the hospitals were very good. The doctors were able men and there seemed to be no shortage of drugs and equipment. But there were two bad faults on account of which, I have no doubt, hundreds or thousands of men have died who might have been saved.

One was the fact that all the hospitals anywhere near the front line were used more or less as casualty clearing-stations. The result was that you got no treatment there unless you were too badly wounded to be moved. In theory most of the wounded were sent straight to Barcelona or Tarragona, but owing to the lack of transport they were often a week or ten days in getting there. They were kept hanging about at Siétamo, Barbastro, Monzón, Lérida, and other places, and meanwhile they were getting no treatment except an occasional clean bandage, sometimes not even that. Men with dreadful shell wounds, smashed bones and so forth, were swathed in a sort of casing made of bandages and plaster of Paris; a description of the wound was written in pencil on the outside, and as a rule the casing was not removed till the man reached Barcelona or Tarragona ten days later. It was almost impossible to get one's wound examined on the way; the few doctors could not cope with the work, and they simply walked hurriedly past your bed, saying: 'Yes, yes, they'll attend to you at Barcelona.' There were always rumours that the hospital train was leaving for Barcelona *mañana*. The other fault was the lack of competent nurses. Apparently there was no supply of trained nurses in Spain, perhaps because before the war this work was done chiefly by nuns. I have no complaint against the Spanish nurses, they always treated me with the greatest kindness, but there is no doubt that they were terribly ignorant. All of them knew how to take a temperature, and some of them knew how to tie a bandage, but that was about all. The result was that men who were too ill to fend for themselves were often shamefully neglected. The nurses would let a man remain constipated for a week on end, and they seldom washed those who were too weak to wash themselves. I remember one poor devil with a smashed arm telling me that he had been three weeks without having his face washed. Even beds were left unmade for days together. The food in all the hospitals was very good

– too good, indeed. Even more in Spain than elsewhere it seemed to be the tradition to stuff sick people with heavy food. At Lérida the meals were terrific. Breakfast, at about six in the morning, consisted of soup, an omelette, stew, bread, white wine, and coffee, and lunch was even larger – this at a time when most of the civil population was seriously underfed. Spaniards seem not to recognise such a thing as a light diet. They give the same food to sick people as to well ones – always the same rich, greasy cookery, with everything sodden in olive oil.

One morning it was announced that the men in my ward were to be sent down to Barcelona today. I managed to send a wire to my wife, telling her that I was coming, and presently they packed us into buses and took us down to the station. It was only when the train was actually starting that the hospital orderly who travelled with us casually let fall that we were not going to Barcelona after all, but to Tarragona. I suppose the engine-driver had changed his mind. 'Just like Spain!' I thought. But it was very Spanish, too, that they agreed to hold up the train while I sent another wire, and more Spanish still that the wire never got there.

They had put us into ordinary third-class carriages with wooden seats, and many of the men were badly wounded and had only got out of bed for the first time that morning. Before long, what with the heat and the jolting, half of them were in a state of collapse and several vomited on the floor. The hospital orderly threaded his way among the corpse-like forms that sprawled everywhere, carrying a large goatskin bottle full of water which he squirted into this mouth or that. It was beastly water; I remember the taste of it still. We got into Tarragona as the sun was getting low. The line runs along the shore a stone's throw from the sea. As our train drew into the station a troop-train full of men from the International Column was drawing out, and a knot of people on the bridge were waving to them. It was a very long train, packed to bursting-point with men, with field-guns lashed on the open trucks and more men clustering round the guns. I remember with peculiar vividness the spectacle of that train passing in the yellow evening light; window after window full of dark, smiling faces, the long tilted barrels of the guns, the scarlet scarves fluttering – all this gliding slowly past us against a turquoise-coloured sea.

'*Estranjeros* – foreigners,' said someone. 'They're Italians.'

Obviously they were Italians. No other people could have grouped themselves so picturesquely or returned the salutes of the crowd with so much grace – a grace that was none the less because about half the men on the train were drinking out of up-ended wine bottles. We heard afterwards that these were some of the troops who won the great victory at Guadalajara in March; they had been on leave and were being transferred to the Aragón front. Most of them, I am afraid, were killed at Huesca only a few weeks later. The men who were well enough to stand had moved across the carriage to cheer the Italians as they went past. A crutch waved out of the window; bandaged forearms made the Red Salute. It was like an allegorical picture of war; the trainload of fresh men gliding proudly up the line, the maimed men sliding slowly down, and all the while the guns on the open trucks making one's heart leap as guns always do, and reviving that pernicious feeling, so difficult to get rid of, that war *is* glorious after all.

The hospital at Tarragona was a very big one and full of wounded from all fronts. What wounds one saw there! They had a way of treating certain wounds which I suppose was in accordance with the latest medical practice, but which was peculiarly horrible to look at. This was to leave the wound completely open and unbandaged, but protected from flies by a net of butter-muslin, stretched over wires. Under the muslin you would see the red jelly of a half-healed wound. There was one man wounded in the face and throat who had his head inside a sort of spherical helmet of butter-muslin; his mouth was closed up and he breathed through a little tube that was fixed between his lips. Poor devil, he looked so lonely, wandering to and fro, looking at you through his muslin cage and unable to speak. I was three or four days at Tarragona. My strength was coming back, and one day, by going slowly, I managed to walk down as far as the beach. It was queer to see the seaside life going on almost as usual; the smart cafés along the promenade and the plump local bourgeoisie bathing and sunning themselves in deck-chairs as though there had not been a war within a thousand miles. Nevertheless, as it happened, I saw a bather drowned, which one would have thought impossible in that shallow and tepid sea.

Finally, eight or nine days after leaving the front, I had my wound examined. In the surgery where newly-arrived cases were examined, doctors with huge pairs of shears were hacking away the breast-plates of plaster in which men with smashed ribs, collar-bones and so forth had been cased at the dressing-stations behind the line; out of the neck-hole of the huge clumsy breast-plate you would see protruding an anxious, dirty face, scrubby with a week's beard. The doctor, a brisk, handsome man of about thirty, sat me down in a chair, grasped my tongue with a piece of rough gauze, pulled it out as far as it would go, thrust a dentist's mirror down my throat and told me to say 'Eh!' After doing this till my tongue was bleeding and my eyes running with water, he told me that one vocal cord was paralysed.

'When shall I get my voice back?' I said.

'Your voice? Oh, you'll never get your voice back,' he said cheerfully.

However, he was wrong, as it turned out. For about two months I could not speak much above a whisper, but after that my voice became normal rather suddenly, the other vocal cord having 'compensated'. The pain in my arm was due to the bullet having pierced a bunch of nerves at the back of the neck. It was a shooting pain like neuralgia, and it went on hurting continuously for about a month, especially at night, so that I did not get much sleep. The fingers of my right hand were also semi-paralysed. Even now, five months afterwards, my forefinger is still numb – a queer effect for a neck wound to have.

The wound was a curiosity in a small way and various doctors examined it with much clicking of tongues and *'Qué suerte! Qué suerte!'* One of them told me with an air of authority that the bullet had missed the artery by 'about a millimetre'. I don't know how he knew. No one I met at this time – doctors, nurses, *practicantes*, or fellow-patients – failed to assure me that a man who is hit through the neck and survives it is the luckiest creature alive. I could not help thinking that it would be even luckier not to be hit at all.

XI

In Barcelona, during all those last weeks I spent there, there was a peculiar evil feeling in the air – an atmosphere of suspicion, fear, uncertainty, and veiled hatred. The May fighting had left ineradicable after-effects behind it. With the fall of the Caballero Government the Communists had come definitely into power, the charge of internal order had been handed over to Communist ministers, and no one doubted that they would smash their political rivals as soon as they got a quarter of a chance. Nothing was happening as yet, I myself had not even any mental picture of what was going to happen; and yet there was a perpetual vague sense of danger, a consciousness of some evil thing that was impending. However little you were actually conspiring, the atmosphere forced you to feel like a conspirator. You seemed to spend all your time holding whispered conversations in corners of cafés and wondering whether that person at the next table was a police spy.

Sinister rumours of all kinds were flying round, thanks to the press censorship. One was that the Negrín-Prieto Government was planning to compromise the war. At the time I was inclined to believe this, for the Fascists were closing in on Bilbao and the Government was visibly doing nothing to save it. Basque flags were displayed all over the town, girls rattled collecting-boxes in the cafés, and there were the usual broadcasts about 'heroic defenders', but the Basques were getting no real assistance. It was tempting to believe that the Government was playing a double game. Later events have proved that I was quite wrong here, but it seems probable that Bilbao could have been saved if a little more energy had been shown. An offensive on the Aragón front, even an unsuccessful one, would have forced Franco to divert part of his army; as it was the Government did not begin any offensive action till it was far too late – indeed, till about the time when Bilbao fell. The CNT was distributing in huge numbers a leaflet saying: 'Be on your guard!' and hinting that 'a certain Party' (meaning the Communists) was plotting a *coup d'état*. There was also a widespread fear that Catalonia was going to be invaded. Earlier, when we went back to the front, I had seen the powerful defences that were being constructed scores of miles behind the front line, and fresh bomb-proof shelters were being dug all over Barcelona. There were frequent scares of air-raids and sea-raids; more often than not these were false alarms, but every time the sirens blew the lights all over the town blacked out for hours on end and timid people dived for the cellars. Police spies were everywhere. The jails were still crammed with prisoners left over from the May fighting, and others – always, of course, Anarchist and POUM adherents – were disappearing into jail by ones and twos. So far as one could discover, no one was ever tried or even charged – not even charged with anything so definite as 'Trotskyism'; you were simply flung into jail and kept there, usually *incommunicado*. Bob Smillie was still in jail in Valencia. We could discover nothing except that neither the ILP representative on the spot nor the lawyer who had been engaged, was permitted to see him. Foreigners from the International Column and other militias were getting into jail in larger and larger numbers. Usually they were arrested as deserters. It was typical of the general situation that nobody now knew for certain whether a militiaman was a volunteer or a regular soldier. A few months earlier anyone enlisting in the militia had been told that he was a volunteer and could, if he wished, get his discharge papers at any time when he was due for leave. Now it appeared that the Government had changed its mind, a militiaman was a regular soldier and counted as a deserter if he tried to go home. But even about this no one seemed certain. At some parts of the front the authorities were still issuing discharges. At the frontier these were sometimes recognised, sometimes not; if not, you were promptly thrown into jail. Later the number of foreign 'deserters' in jail swelled into hundreds, but most of them were repatriated when a fuss was made in their own countries.

Bands of armed Valencian Assault Guards roamed everywhere in the streets, the local Assault Guards were still holding cafés and other buildings in strategic spots, and many of the PSUC buildings were still sandbagged and barricaded. At various points in the town there were posts manned by local Assault Guards or Carabineros who stopped passers-by and demanded their papers. Everyone warned me not to show my POUM militiaman's card but merely to show my passport and my hospital ticket. Even to be known to have served in the POUM militia was vaguely dangerous. POUM militiamen who were wounded or on leave were penalised in petty ways – it was made difficult for them to draw their pay, for instance. *La Batalla* was still appearing, but it was censored almost out of existence, and *Solidaridad* and the other Anarchist papers were also heavily censored. There was a new rule that censored portions of a newspaper must not be left blank but filled up with other matter; as a result it was often impossible to tell when something had been cut out.

The food shortage, which had fluctuated throughout the war, was in one of its bad stages. Bread was scarce and the cheaper sorts were being adulterated with rice; the bread the soldiers were getting in the barracks was dreadful stuff like putty. Milk and sugar were very scarce and tobacco almost non-existent, except for the expensive smuggled cigarettes. There was an acute shortage of olive oil, which Spaniards use for half a dozen different purposes. The queues of women waiting to buy olive oil were controlled by mounted Assault Guards who sometimes amused themselves by backing their horses into the queue and trying to make them tread on the women's toes. A minor annoyance of the time was the lack of small change. The silver had been withdrawn and as yet no new coinage had been issued, so that there was nothing between the ten-centime piece and the note for two and a half pesetas, and all notes below ten pesetas were very scarce.[1] For the poorest people this meant an aggravation of the food shortage. A woman with only a ten-peseta note in her possession might wait for hours in a queue outside the grocery and then be unable to buy anything after all because the grocer had no change and she could not afford to spend the whole note.

It is not easy to convey the nightmare atmosphere of that time – the peculiar uneasiness produced by rumours that were always changing, by censored newspapers and the constant presence of armed men. It is not easy to convey it because, at the moment, the thing essential to such an atmosphere does not exist in England. In England political intolerance is not yet taken for granted. There is political persecution in a petty way; if I were a coalminer I would not care to be known to the boss as a Communist; but the 'good party man', the gangster-gramophone of continental politics, is still a rarity, and the notion of 'liquidating' or 'eliminating' everyone who happens to disagree with you does not yet seem natural. It seemed only too natural in Barcelona. The 'Stalinists' were in the saddle, and therefore it was a matter of course that every 'Trotskyist' was in danger. The thing everyone feared was a thing which, after all, did not happen – a fresh outbreak of street-fighting, which, as before, would be blamed on the POUM and the Anarchists. There were times when I caught my ears listening for the first shots. It was as though some huge evil intelligence were brooding over the town. Everyone noticed it and remarked upon it. And it was queer how everyone expressed it in almost the same words: 'The atmosphere of this place – it's horrible.

[1] The purchasing value of the peseta was about fourpence [about 1.7p in decimal currency].

Like being in a lunatic asylum.' But perhaps I ought not to say *everyone*. Some of the English visitors who flitted briefly through Spain, from hotel to hotel, seem not to have noticed that there was anything wrong with the general atmosphere. The Duchess of Atholl writes, I notice (*Sunday Express*, 17 October 1937):

I was in Valencia, Madrid, and Barcelona . . . perfect order prevailed in all three towns without any display of force. All the hotels in which I stayed were not only 'normal' and 'decent', but extremely comfortable, in spite of the shortage of butter and coffee.

It is a peculiarity of English travellers that they do not really believe in the existence of anything outside the smart hotels. I hope they found some butter for the Duchess of Atholl.

I was at the Sanatorium Maurín, one of the sanatoria run by the POUM. It was in the suburbs near Tibidabo, the queer-shaped mountain that rises abruptly behind Barcelona and is traditionally supposed to have been the hill from which Satan showed Jesus the countries of the earth (hence its name). The house had previously belonged to some wealthy bourgeois and had been seized at the time of the revolution. Most of the men there had either been invalided out of the line or had some wound that had permanently disabled them – amputated limbs, and so forth. There were several other Englishmen there: Williams, with a damaged leg, and Stafford Cottman, a boy of eighteen, who had been sent back from the trenches with suspected tuberculosis, and Arthur Clinton, whose smashed left arm was still strapped onto one of those huge wire contraptions, nicknamed aeroplanes, which the Spanish hospitals were using. My wife was still staying at the Hotel Continental, and I generally came into Barcelona in the daytime. In the morning I used to attend the General Hospital for electrical treatment of my arm. It was a queer business – a series of prickly electric shocks that made the various sets of muscles jerk up and down – but it seemed to do some good; the use of my fingers came back and the pain grew somewhat less. Both of us had decided that the best thing we could do was to go back to England as soon as possible. I was extremely weak, my voice was gone, seemingly for good, and the doctors told me that at best it would be several months before I was fit to fight. I had got to start earning some money sooner or later, and there did not seem much sense in staying in Spain and eating food that was needed for other people. But my motives were mainly selfish. I had an overwhelming desire to get away from it all; away from the horrible atmosphere of political suspicion and hatred, from streets thronged by armed men, from air-raids, trenches, machine-guns, screaming trams, milkless tea, oil cookery, and shortage of cigarettes – from almost everything that I had learnt to associate with Spain.

The doctors at the General Hospital had certified me medically unfit, but to get my discharge I had to see a medical board at one of the hospitals near the front and then go to Siétamo to get my papers stamped at the POUM militia headquarters. Kopp had just come back from the front, full of jubilation. He had just been in action and said that Huesca was going to be taken at last. The Government had brought troops from the Madrid front and were concentrating thirty thousand men, with aeroplanes in huge numbers. The Italians I had seen going up the line from Tarragona had attacked on the Jaca road but had had heavy casualties and lost two tanks. However, the town was bound to fall, Kopp said. (Alas! It didn't. The attack was a frightful mess-up and led to nothing except an orgy of lying in the newspapers.) Meanwhile Kopp had to go down to Valencia for an interview at the Ministry of War. He had a letter from General Pozas, now commanding the Army of the East – the usual letter, describing Kopp as a 'person of all confidence' and recommending him for a special appointment in the engineering section (Kopp had been an engineer in civil life). He left for Valencia the same day as I left for Siétamo – 15 June.

It was five days before I got back to Barcelona. A lorry-load of us reached Siétamo about midnight, and as soon as we got to the POUM headquarters they lined us up and began handing out rifles and cartridges, before even taking our names. It seemed that the attack was beginning and they were likely to call for reserves at any moment. I had my hospital ticket in my pocket, but I could not very well refuse to go with the others. I kipped down on the ground, with a cartridge-box for a pillow, in a mood of deep dismay. Being wounded had spoiled my nerve for the time being – I believe this usually happens – and the prospect of being under fire frightened me horribly. However, there was a bit of *mañana*, as usual, we were not called out after all, and next morning I produced my hospital ticket and went in search of my discharge. It meant a series of confused, tiresome journeys. As usual they bandied one to and fro from hospital to hospital – Siétamo, Barbastro, Monzón, then back to Siétamo to get my discharge stamped, then down the line again via Barbastro and Lérida – and the convergence of troops on Huesca had monopolised all the transport and disorganised everything. I remember sleeping in queer places – once in a hospital bed, but once in a ditch, once on a very narrow bench which I fell off in the middle of the night, and once in a sort of municipal lodging-house in Barbastro. As soon as you got away from the railroad there was no way of travelling except by jumping chance lorries. You had to wait by the roadside for hours, sometimes three or four hours at a stretch, with knots of disconsolate peasants who carried bundles full of ducks and rabbits, waving to lorry after lorry. When finally you struck a lorry that was not chock full of men, loaves of bread or ammunition-boxes the bumping over the vile roads walloped you to pulp. No horse has ever thrown me so high as those lorries used to throw me. The only way of travelling was to crowd all together and cling to one another. To my humiliation I found that I was still too weak to climb onto a lorry without being helped.

I slept a night at Monzón Hospital, where I went to see my medical board. In the next bed to me there was an Assault Guard, wounded over the left eye. He was friendly and gave me cigarettes. I said: 'In Barcelona we should have been shooting one another,' and we laughed over this. It was queer how the general spirit seemed to change when you got anywhere near the front line. All or nearly all of the vicious hatreds of the political parties evaporated. During all the time I was at the front I never once remember any PSUC adherent showing me hostility because I was POUM. That kind of thing belonged in Barcelona or in places even remoter from the war. There were a lot of Assault Guards in Siétamo. They had been sent on from Barcelona to take part in the attack on Huesca. The Assault Guards were a corps not intended primarily for the front, and many of them had not been under fire before. Down in Barcelona they were lords of the street, but up here they were *quintos* (rookies) and palled up with militia children of fifteen who had been in the line for months.

At Monzón Hospital the doctor did the usual tongue-pulling and mirror-thrusting business, assured me in the same cheerful manner as the others that I should never have a voice again, and signed my certificate. While I waited to be examined there was going on inside the surgery some dreadful operation without anaesthetics – why without anaesthetics I do not know. It went on and on, scream after scream, and when I went in there were chairs flung about and on the floor were pools of blood and urine.

The details of that final journey stand out in my mind with strange clarity. I was in a different mood, a more observing mood, than I had been in for months past. I had got my discharge, stamped with the seal of the 29th Division, and the doctor's certificate in which I was 'declared useless'. I was free to go back to England; consequently I felt able, almost for the first time, to look at Spain. I had a day to put in at Barbastro, for there was only one train a day. Previously I had seen Barbastro in brief glimpses, and it had seemed to me simply a part of the war – a grey, muddy, cold place, full of roaring lorries and shabby troops. It seemed queerly different now. Wandering through it I became aware of pleasant tortuous streets, old stone bridges, wine shops with great oozy barrels as tall as a man, and intriguing semi-subterranean shops where men were making cartwheels, daggers, wooden spoons and goatskin water-bottles. I watched a man making a skin bottle and discovered with great interest, what I had never known before, that they are made with the fur inside and the fur is not removed, so that you are really drinking distilled goat's hair. I had drunk out of them for months without knowing this. And at the back of the town there was a shallow jade-green river, and rising out of it a perpendicular cliff of rock, with houses built into the rock, so that from your bedroom window you could spit straight into the water a hundred feet below. Innumerable doves lived in the holes in the cliff. And in Lérida there were old crumbling buildings upon whose cornices thousands upon thousands of swallows had built their nests, so that at a little distance the crusted pattern of nests was like some florid moulding of the rococo period. It was queer how for nearly six months past I had had no eyes for such things. With my discharge papers in my pocket I felt like a human being again, and also a little like a tourist. For almost the first time I felt that I was really in Spain, in a country that I had longed all my life to visit. In the quiet back streets of Lérida and Barbastro I seemed to catch a momentary glimpse, a sort of far-off rumour of the Spain that dwells in everyone's imagination. White sierras, goatherds, dungeons of the Inquisition, Moorish palaces, black winding trains of mules, grey olive trees and groves of lemons, girls in black mantillas, the wines of Málaga and Alicante, cathedrals, cardinals, bullfights, gypsies, serenades – in short, Spain. Of all Europe it was the country that had had most hold upon my imagination. It seemed a pity that when at last I had managed to come here I had seen only this north-eastern corner, in the middle of a confused war and for the most part in winter.

It was late when I got back to Barcelona, and there were no taxis. It was no use trying to get to the Sanatorium Maurín, which was right outside the town, so I made for the Hotel Continental, stopping for dinner on the way. I remember the conversation I had with a very fatherly waiter about the oak jugs, bound with copper, in which they served the wine. I said I would like to buy a set of them to take back to England. The waiter was sympathetic. Yes, beautiful, were they not? But impossible to buy nowadays. Nobody was manufacturing them any longer – nobody was manufacturing anything. This war – such a pity! We agreed that the war was a pity. Once again I felt like a tourist. The waiter asked me gently, had I liked Spain; would I come back to Spain? Oh, yes, I should come back to Spain. The peaceful quality of this conversation sticks in my memory, because of what happened immediately afterwards.

When I got to the hotel my wife was sitting in the lounge. She got up and came towards me in what struck me as a very unconcerned manner; then she put an arm round my neck and, with a sweet smile for the benefit of the other people in the lounge, hissed in my ear:

'*Get out!*'

'What?'

'Get out of here *at once!*'

'What?'

'Don't keep standing here! You must get outside quickly!'

'What? Why? What do you mean?'

She had me by the arm and was already leading me towards the stairs. Half-way down we met a Frenchman – I am not going to give his name, for though he had no connection with the POUM he was a good friend to us all during the trouble. He looked at me with a concerned face.

'Listen! You mustn't come in here. Get out quickly and hide yourself before they ring up the police.'

And behold! at the bottom of the stairs one of the hotel staff, who was a POUM member (unknown to the management, I fancy), slipped furtively out of the lift and told me in broken English to get out. Even now I did not grasp what had happened.

'What the devil is all this about?' I said as soon as we were on the pavement.

'Haven't you *heard?*'

'No. Heard what? I've heard nothing.'

'The POUM's been suppressed. They've seized all the buildings. Practically everyone's in prison. And they say they're shooting people already.'

So that was it. We had to have somewhere to talk. All the big cafés on the Ramblas were thronged with police, but we found a quiet café in a side-street. My wife explained to me what had happened while I was away.

On 15 June the police had suddenly arrested Andrés Nin in his office, and the same evening had raided the Hotel Falcón and arrested all the people in it, mostly militiamen on leave. The place was converted immediately into a prison, and in a very little while it was filled to the brim with prisoners of all kinds. Next day the POUM was declared an illegal organisation and all its offices, book-stalls, sanatoria, Red Aid centres and so forth were seized. Meanwhile the police were arresting everyone they could lay hands on who was known to have any connection with the POUM. Within a day or two all or almost all of the forty members of the Executive Committee were in prison. Possibly one or two had escaped into hiding, but the police were adopting the trick (extensively used on both sides in this war) of seizing a man's wife as a hostage if he disappeared. There was no way of discovering how many people had been arrested. My wife had heard that it was about four hundred in Barcelona alone. I have since thought that even at that time the number must have been greater. And the most fantastic people had been arrested. In some cases the police had even gone to the length of dragging wounded militiamen out of the hospitals.

It was all profoundly dismaying. What the devil was it all about? I could understand their suppressing the POUM, but what were they arresting people for? For nothing, so far as one could discover. Apparently the suppression of the POUM had a retrospective effect; the POUM was now illegal, and therefore one was breaking the law by having previously belonged to it. As usual, none of the arrested people had been charged. Meanwhile, however, the Valencia Communist papers were flaming with the story of a huge 'Fascist plot', radio communication with the enemy, documents signed in invisible ink, etc. etc. I shall deal with this story in greater detail in *Appendix II*. The significant thing was that it was appearing only in the Valencia papers; I think I am right in saying that there was not a single word about it, or about the suppression of the POUM, in any Barcelona papers, Communist, Anarchist, or Republican. We first learned the precise nature of the charges against the POUM leaders not from any Spanish paper but from the English papers that reached Barcelona a day or two later. What we could not know at this time was that the Government was not responsible for the charge of treachery and espionage, and that members of the Government were later to repudiate it. We only vaguely knew that the POUM leaders, and presumably all the rest of us, were accused of being in Fascist pay. And already the rumours were flying round that people were being secretly shot in jail. There was a lot of exaggeration about this, but it certainly happened in some cases, and there is not much doubt that it happened in the case of Nin. After his arrest Nin was transferred to Valencia and thence to Madrid, and as early as 21 June the rumour reached Barcelona that he had been shot. Later the rumour took a more definite shape: Nin had been shot in prison by the secret police and his body dumped into the street. This story came from several sources, including Federica Montseny, an ex-member of the Government. From that day to this Nin has never been heard of alive again. When, later, the Government were questioned by delegates from various countries, they shilly-shallied and would say only that Nin had disappeared and they knew nothing of his whereabouts. Some of the newspapers produced a tale that he had escaped to Fascist territory. No evidence was given in support of it, and Irujo, the Minister of Justice, later declared that the Espagne news-agency had falsified his official *communiqué*.[1] In any case it is most unlikely that a political prisoner of Nin's importance would be allowed to escape. Unless at some future time

[1] See the reports of the Maxton delegation [in Appendix II].

he is produced alive, I think we must take it that he was murdered in prison.

The tale of arrests went on and on, extending over months, until the number of political prisoners, not counting Fascists, swelled into thousands. One noticeable thing was the autonomy of the lower ranks of the police. Many of the arrests were admittedly illegal, and various people whose release had been ordered by the Chief of Police were re-arrested at the jail gate and carried off to 'secret prisons'. A typical case is that of Kurt Landau and his wife. They were arrested about 17 June, and Landau immediately 'disappeared'. Five months later his wife was still in jail, untried and without news of her husband. She declared a hunger-strike, after which the Minister of Justice sent word to assure her that her husband was dead. Shortly afterwards she was released, to be almost immediately re-arrested and flung into prison again. And it was noticeable that the police, at any rate at first, seemed completely indifferent as to any effect their actions might have upon the war. They were quite ready to arrest military officers in important posts without getting permission beforehand. About the end of June José Rovira, the general commanding the 29th Division, was arrested somewhere near the front line by a party of police who had been sent from Barcelona. His men sent a delegation to protest at the Ministry of War. It was found that neither the Ministry of War, nor Ortega, the Chief of Police, had even been informed of Rovira's arrest. In the whole business the detail that most sticks in my throat, though perhaps it is not of great importance, is that all news of what was happening was kept from the troops at the front. As you will have seen, neither I nor anyone else at the front had heard anything about the suppression of the POUM. All the POUM militia headquarters, Red Aid centres and so forth were functioning as usual, and as late as 20 June and as far down the line as Lérida, only about 100 miles from Barcelona, no one had heard what was happening. All word of it was kept out of the Barcelona papers (the Valencia papers, which were running the spy stories, did not reach the Aragón front), and no doubt one reason for arresting all the POUM militiamen on leave in Barcelona was to prevent them from getting back to the front with the news. The draft with which I had gone up the line on 15 June must have been about the last to go. I am still puzzled to know how the thing was kept secret, for the supply lorries and so forth were still passing to and fro; but there is no doubt that it *was* kept secret, and, as I have since learned from a number of others, the men in the front line heard nothing till several days later. The motive for all this is clear enough. The attack on Huesca was beginning, the POUM militia was still a separate unit, and it was probably feared that if the men knew what was happening they would refuse to fight. Actually nothing of the kind happened when the news arrived. In the intervening days there must have been numbers of men who were killed without ever learning that the newspapers in the rear were calling them Fascists. This kind of thing is a little difficult to forgive. I know it was the usual policy to keep bad news from the troops, and perhaps as a rule that is justified. But it is a different matter to send men into battle and not even tell them that behind their backs their party is being suppressed, their leaders accused of treachery, and their friends and relatives thrown into prison.

My wife began telling me what had happened to our various friends. Some of the English and other foreigners had got across the frontier. Williams and Stafford Cottman had not been arrested when the Sanatorium Maurín was raided, and were in hiding somewhere. So was John McNair, who had been in France and had re-entered Spain after the POUM was declared illegal – a rash thing to do, but he had not cared to stay in safety while his comrades were in danger. For the rest it was simply a chronicle of 'They've got so and so' and 'They've got so and so.' They seemed to have 'got' nearly everyone. It took me aback to hear that they had also 'got' Georges Kopp.

'What! Kopp? I thought he was in Valencia.'

It appeared that Kopp had come back to Barcelona; he had a letter from the Ministry of War to the colonel commanding the engineering operations on the eastern front. He knew that the POUM had been suppressed, of course, but probably it did not occur to him that the police could be such fools as to arrest him when he was on his way to the front on an urgent military mission. He had come round to the Hotel Continental to fetch his kit-bags; my wife had been out at the time, and the hotel people had managed to detain him with some lying story while they rang up the police. I admit I was angry when I heard of Kopp's arrest. He was my personal friend, I had served under him for months, I had been under fire with him, and I knew his history. He was a man who had sacrificed everything – family, nationality, livelihood – simply to come to Spain and fight against Fascism. By leaving Belgium without permission and joining a foreign army while he was on the Belgian Army reserve, and, earlier, by helping to manufacture munitions illegally for the Spanish Government, he had piled up years of imprisonment for himself if he should ever return to his own country. He had been in the line since October 1936, had worked his way up from militiaman to major, had been in action I do not know how many times, and had been wounded once. During the May trouble, as I had seen for myself, he had prevented fighting locally and probably saved ten or twenty lives. And all they could do in return was to fling him into jail. It is waste of time to be angry, but the stupid malignity of this kind of thing does try one's patience.

Meanwhile they had not 'got' my wife. Although she had remained at the Continental the police had made no move to arrest her. It was fairly obvious that she was being used as a decoy duck. A couple of nights earlier, however, in the small hours of the morning, six of the plain-clothes police had invaded our room at the hotel and searched it. They had seized every scrap of paper we possessed, except, fortunately, our passports and cheque-book. They had taken my diaries, all our books, all the press-cuttings that had been piling up for months past (I have often wondered what use those press-cuttings were to them), all my war souvenirs, and all our letters. (Incidentally, they took away a number of letters I had received from readers. Some of them had not been answered, and of course I have not the addresses. If anyone who wrote to me about my last book, and who did not get an answer, happens to read these lines, will he please accept this as an apology?) I learned afterwards that the police had also seized various belongings that I had left at the Sanatorium Maurín. They even carried off a bundle of my dirty linen. Perhaps they thought it had messages written on it in invisible ink.

It was obvious that it would be safer for my wife to stay at the hotel, at any rate for the time being. If she tried to disappear they would be after her immediately. As for myself, I should have to go straight into hiding. The prospect revolted me. In spite of the innumerable arrests it was almost impossible for me to believe that I was in any danger. The whole thing seemed too meaningless. It was the same refusal to take this idiotic onslaught seriously that had led Kopp into jail. I kept saying, but why should anyone want to arrest me? What had I done? I was not even a party member of the POUM. Certainly I had carried arms during the May fighting, but so had (at a guess) forty or fifty thousand people. Besides, I was badly in need of a proper night's sleep. I wanted to risk it and go back to the hotel. My wife would not hear of it. Patiently she explained the state of affairs. It did not matter what I had done or not done. This was not a round-up of criminals; it was merely a reign of terror. I was not guilty of any definite act, but I was guilty of 'Trotskyism'. The fact that I had served in the POUM militia was quite enough to get me into prison. It was no use hanging on to the English notion that you are safe so long as you keep the law. Practically the law was what the police chose to make it. The only thing to do was to lie low and conceal the fact that I had anything to do with the POUM. We went through the papers in my pockets. My wife made me tear up my militiaman's card, which had 'POUM' on it in big letters, also a photo of a group of militiamen with a POUM flag in the background; that was the kind of thing that got you arrested nowadays. I had to keep my discharge papers, however. Even these were a danger, for they bore the seal of the 29th Division, and the police would probably know that the 29th Division was the POUM; but without them I could be arrested as a deserter.

The thing we had got to think of now was getting out of Spain. There was no sense in staying here with the certainty of imprisonment sooner or later. As a matter of fact both of us would greatly have liked to stay, just to see what happened. But I foresaw that Spanish prisons would be lousy places (actually they were a lot worse than I imagined), once in prison you never knew when you would get out, and I was in wretched health, apart from the pain in my arm. We arranged to meet next day at the British Consulate, where Cottman and McNair were also coming. It would probably take a couple of days to get our passports in order. Before leaving Spain you had to have your passport stamped in three separate places – by the Chief of Police, by the French Consul and by the Catalan immigration authorities. The Chief of Police was the danger, of course. But perhaps the British Consul could fix things up without letting it be known that we had anything to do with the POUM. Obviously there must be a list of foreign 'Trotskyist' suspects, and very likely our names were on it, but with luck we might get to the frontier before the list.

There was sure to be a lot of muddle and *mañana*. Fortunately this was Spain and not Germany. The Spanish secret police had some of the spirit of the Gestapo, but not much of its competence.

So we parted. My wife went back to the hotel and I wandered off into the darkness to find somewhere to sleep. I remember feeling sulky and bored. I had so wanted a night in bed! There was nowhere I could go, no house where I could take refuge. The POUM had practically no underground organisation. No doubt the leaders had always realised that the party was likely to be suppressed, but they had never expected a wholesale witch-hunt of this description. They had expected it so little, indeed, that they were actually continuing the alterations to the POUM buildings (among other things they were constructing a cinema in the Executive Building, which had previously been a bank) up to the very day when the POUM was suppressed. Consequently the rendezvous and hiding-places which every revolutionary party ought to possess as a matter of course did not exist. Goodness knows how many people – people whose homes had been raided by the police – were sleeping in the streets that night. I had had five days of tiresome journeys, sleeping in impossible places, my arm was hurting damnably, and now these fools were chasing me to and fro and I had got to sleep on the ground again. That was about as far as my thoughts went. I did not make any of the correct political reflections. I never do when things are happening. It seems to be always the case when I get mixed up in war or politics – I am conscious of nothing save physical discomfort and a deep desire for this damned nonsense to be over. Afterwards I can see the significance of events, but while they are happening I merely want to be out of them – an ignoble trait, perhaps.

I walked a long way and fetched up somewhere near the General Hospital. I wanted a place where I could lie down without some nosing policeman finding me and demanding my papers. I tried an air-raid shelter, but it was newly dug and dripping with damp. Then I came upon the ruins of a church that had been gutted and burnt in the revolution. It was a mere shell, four roofless walls surrounding piles of rubble. In the half-darkness I poked about and found a kind of hollow where I could lie down. Lumps of broken masonry are not good to lie on, but fortunately it was a warm night and I managed to get several hours' sleep.

XII

The worst of being wanted by the police in a town like Barcelona is that everything opens so late. When you sleep out of doors you always wake about dawn, and none of the Barcelona cafés opens much before nine. It was hours before I could get a cup of coffee or a shave. It seemed queer, in the barber's shop, to see the Anarchist notice still on the wall, explaining that tips were prohibited. 'The Revolution has struck off our chains,' the notice said. I felt like telling the barbers that their chains would soon be back again if they didn't look out.

I wandered back to the centre of the town. Over the POUM buildings the red flags had been torn down, Republican flags were floating in their place, and knots of armed Assault Guards were lounging in the doorways. At the Red Aid centre on the corner of the Plaza de Cataluña the police had amused themselves by smashing most of the windows. The POUM bookstalls had been emptied of books and the notice-board further down the Ramblas had been plastered with an anti-POUM cartoon – the one representing the mask and the Fascist face beneath. Down at the bottom of the Ramblas, near the quay, I came upon a queer sight; a row of militiamen, still ragged and muddy from the front, sprawling exhaustedly on the chairs placed there for the bootblacks. I knew who they were – indeed, I recognised one of them. They were POUM militiamen who had come down the line on the previous day to find that the POUM had been suppressed, and had had to spend the night in the streets because their homes had been raided. Any POUM militiaman who returned to Barcelona at this time had the choice of going straight into hiding or into jail – not a pleasant reception after three or four months in the line.

It was a queer situation that we were in. At night one was a hunted fugitive, but in the daytime one could live an almost normal life. Every house known to harbour POUM supporters was – or at any rate was likely to be – under observation, and it was impossible to go to a hotel or boarding-house, because it had been decreed that on the arrival of a stranger the hotel-keeper must inform the police immediately. Practically this meant spending the night out of doors. In the daytime, on the other hand, in a town the size of Barcelona, you were fairly safe. The streets were thronged by local and Valencian Assault Guards, Carabineros and ordinary police, besides God knows how many spies in plain clothes; still, they could not stop everyone who passed, and if you looked normal you might escape notice. The thing to do was to avoid hanging round POUM buildings and going to cafés and restaurants where the waiters knew you by sight. I spent a long time that day, and the next, in having a bath at one of the public baths. This struck me as a good way of putting in the time and keeping out of sight. Unfortunately the same idea occurred to a lot of people, and a few days later – after I left Barcelona – the police raided one of the public baths and arrested a number of 'Trotskyists' in a state of nature.

Half-way up the Ramblas I ran into one of the wounded men from the Sanatorium Maurín. We exchanged the sort of invisible wink that people were exchanging at that time, and managed in an unobtrusive way to meet in a café further up the street. He had escaped arrest when the Maurín was raided, but, like the others, had been driven into the street. He was in shirt-sleeves – had had to flee without his jacket – and had no money. He described to me how one of the Assault Guards had torn the large coloured portrait of Maurín from the wall and kicked it to pieces. Maurín (one of the founders of the POUM) was a prisoner in the hands of the Fascists and at that time was believed to have been shot by them.

I met my wife at the British Consulate at ten o'clock. McNair and Cottman turned up shortly afterwards. The first thing they told me was that Bob Smillie was dead. He had died in prison at Valencia – of what, nobody knew for certain. He had been buried immediately, and the ILP representative on the spot, David Murray, had been refused permission to see his body.

Of course I assumed at once that Smillie had been shot. It was what everyone believed at the time, but I have since thought that I may have been wrong. Later the cause of his death was given out as appendicitis, and we heard afterwards from another prisoner who had been released that Smillie had certainly been ill in prison. So perhaps the appendicitis story was true. The refusal to let Murray see his body may have been due to pure spite. I must say this, however, Bob Smillie was only twenty-two years old and physically he was one of the toughest people I have met. He was, I think, the only person I knew, English or Spanish, who went three months in the trenches without a day's illness. People so tough as that do not usually die of appendicitis if they are properly looked after. But when you saw what the Spanish jails were like – the makeshift jails used for political prisoners – you realised how much chance there was of a sick man getting proper attention. The jails were places that could only be described as dungeons. In England you would have to go back to the eighteenth century to find anything comparable. People were penned together in small rooms where there was barely space for them to lie down, and often they were kept in cellars and other dark places. This was not as a temporary measure – there were cases of people being kept four and five months almost without sight of daylight. And they were fed on a filthy and insufficient diet of two plates of soup and two pieces of bread a day. (Some months later, however, the food seems to have improved a little.) I am not exaggerating; ask any political suspect who was imprisoned in Spain. I have had accounts of the Spanish jails from a number of separate sources, and they agree with one another too well to be dis-believed; besides, I had a few glimpses into one Spanish jail myself. Another English friend who was imprisoned later writes that his experi-ences in jail 'make Smillie's case easier to understand'. Smillie's death is not a thing I can easily forgive. Here was this brave and gifted boy, who had thrown up his career at Glasgow University in order to come and fight against Fascism, and who, as I saw for myself, had done his job at the front with faultless courage and willingness; and all they could find to do with him was to fling him into jail and let him die like a neglected animal. I know that in the middle of a huge and bloody war it is no use making too much fuss over an individual death. One aeroplane bomb in a crowded street causes more suffering than quite a lot of political persecution. But what angers one about a death like this is its utter pointlessness. To be killed in battle – yes, that is what one expects; but to be flung into jail, not even for any imaginary offence, but simply owing to dull blind spite, and then left to die in solitude – that is a different matter. I fail to see how this kind of thing – and it is not as though Smillie's case were exceptional – brought victory any nearer.

My wife and I visited Kopp that afternoon. You were allowed to visit prisoners who were not *incommunicado*, though it was not safe to do so more than once or twice. The police watched the people who came and went, and if you visited the jails too often you stamped yourself as a friend of 'Trotskyists' and probably ended in jail yourself. This had already happened to a number of people.

Kopp was not *incommunicado* and we got a permit to see him without difficulty. As they led us through the steel doors into the jail, a Spanish militiaman whom I had known at the front was being led out between two Assault Guards. His eye met mine; again the ghostly wink. And the first person we saw inside was an American militiaman who had left for home a few days earlier; his papers were in good order, but they had arrested him at the frontier all the same, probably because he was still wearing corduroy breeches and was therefore identifiable as a militiaman. We walked past one another as though we had been total strangers. That was dreadful. I had known him for months, had shared a dug-out with him, he had helped to carry me down the line when I was wounded; but it was the only thing one could do. The blue-clad guards were snooping everywhere. It would be fatal to recognise too many people.

The so-called jail was really the ground floor of a shop. Into two rooms each measuring about twenty feet square, close on a hundred people were penned. The place had the real eighteenth-century Newgate Calendar appearance, with its frowzy dirt, its huddle of human bodies, its lack of furniture – just the bare stone floor, one bench and a few ragged blankets – and its murky light, for the corrugated steel shutters had been drawn over the windows. On the grimy walls revolutionary slogans – *'Visca POUM!' 'Viva la Revolución!'* and so forth – had been scrawled. The place had been used as a dump for political prisoners for months past. There was a deafening racket of voices. This was the visiting hour, and the place was so packed with people that it was difficult to move. Nearly all of them were of the poorest of the working-class population. You saw women undoing pitiful packets of food which they had brought for their imprisoned men-folk. There were several of the wounded men from the Sanatorium Maurín among the prisoners. Two of them had amputated legs; one of them had been brought to prison without his crutch and was hopping about on one foot. There was also a boy of not more than twelve; they were even arresting children, apparently. The place had the beastly stench that you always get when crowds of people are penned together without proper sanitary arrangements.

Kopp elbowed his way through the crowd to meet us. His plump fresh-coloured face looked much as usual, and in that filthy place he had kept his uniform neat and had even contrived to shave. There was another officer in the uniform of the Popular Army among the prisoners. He and Kopp saluted as they struggled past one another; the gesture was pathetic, somehow. Kopp seemed in excellent spirits. 'Well, I suppose we shall all be shot,' he said cheerfully. The word 'shot' gave me a sort of inward shudder. A bullet had entered my own body recently and the feeling of it was fresh in my memory; it is not nice to think of that happening to anyone you know well. At that time I took it for granted that all the principal people in the POUM, and Kopp among them, *would* be shot. The first rumour of Nin's death had just filtered through, and we knew that the POUM were being accused of treachery and espionage. Everything pointed to a huge frame-up trial followed by a massacre of leading 'Trotskyists'. It is a terrible thing to see your friend in jail and to know yourself impotent to help him. For there was nothing that one could do; useless even to appeal to the Belgian authorities, for Kopp had broken the law of his own country by coming here. I had to leave most of the talking to my wife; with my squeaking voice I could not make myself heard in the din. Kopp was telling us about the friends he had made among the other prisoners, about the guards, some of whom were good fellows, but some of whom abused and beat the more timid prisoners, and about the food, which was 'pig-wash'. Fortunately we had thought to bring a packet of food, also cigarettes. Then Kopp began telling us about the papers that had been taken from him when he was arrested. Among them was his letter from the Ministry of War, addressed to the colonel commanding engineering operations in the Army of the East. The police had seized it and refused to give it back; it was said to be lying in the Chief of Police's office. It might make a very great difference if it were recovered.

I saw instantly how important this might be. An official letter of that kind, bearing the recommendation of the Ministry of War and of General Pozas, would establish Kopp's bona fides. But the trouble was to prove that the letter existed; if it were opened in the Chief of Police's office one could be sure that some nark or other would destroy it. There was only one person who might possibly be able to get it back, and that was the officer to whom it was addressed. Kopp had already thought of this, and he had written a letter which he wanted me to smuggle out of the jail and post. But it was obviously quicker and surer to go in person. I left my wife with Kopp, rushed out and, after a long search, found a taxi. I knew that time was everything. It was now about half-past five, the colonel would probably leave his office at six, and by tomorrow the letter might be God knew where – destroyed, perhaps, or lost somewhere in the chaos of documents that was presumably piling up as suspect after suspect was arrested. The colonel's office was at the War Department, down by the quay. As I hurried up the steps the Assault Guard on duty at the door barred the way with his long bayonet and demanded 'papers'. I waved my discharge ticket at him; evidently he could not read, and he let me pass, impressed by the vague mystery of 'papers'. Inside, the place was a huge complicated warren running round a central courtyard, with hundreds of offices on each floor; and, as this was Spain, nobody had the vaguest idea where the office I was looking for was. I kept repeating: *'El coronel—, jefe de ingenieros, Ejército del Este!'* People smiled and shrugged their shoulders gracefully. Everyone who had an opinion sent me in a different direction; up these stairs, down those, along interminable passages which turned out to be blind alleys. And time was slipping away. I had the strangest sensation of being in a nightmare: the rushing up and down flights of stairs, the mysterious people coming and going, the glimpses through open doors of chaotic offices with papers strewn everywhere and typewriters clicking; and time slipping away and a life perhaps in the balance.

However, I got there in time, and slightly to my surprise I was granted a hearing. I did not see Colonel —, but his aide-de-camp or secretary, a little slip of an officer in smart uniform, with large and squinting eyes, came out to interview me in the ante-room. I began to pour forth my story. I had come on behalf of my superior officer, Major Jorge Kopp, who was on an urgent mission to the front and had been arrested by mistake. The letter to Colonel — was of a confidential nature and should be recovered without delay. I had served with Kopp for months, he was an officer of the highest character, obviously his arrest was a mistake, the police had confused him with someone else, etc. etc. etc. I kept piling it on about the urgency of Kopp's mission to the front, knowing that this was the strongest point. But it must have sounded a strange tale, in my villainous Spanish which relapsed into French at every crisis. The worst was that my voice gave out almost at once and it was only by violent straining that I could produce a sort of croak. I was in dread that it would disappear altogether and the little officer would grow tired of trying to listen to me. I have often wondered what he thought was wrong with my voice – whether he thought I was drunk or merely suffering from a guilty conscience.

However, he heard me patiently, nodded his head a great number of times and gave a guarded assent to what I said. Yes, it sounded as though there might have been a mistake. Clearly the matter should be looked into. *Mañana* —. I protested. Not *mañana!* The matter was urgent; Kopp was due at the front already. Again the officer seemed to agree. Then came the question I was dreading:

'This Major Kopp – what force was he serving in?'

The terrible word had to come out: 'In the POUM militia.'

'POUM!'

I wish I could convey to you the shocked alarm in his voice. You have got to remember how the POUM was regarded at that moment. The spy-scare was at its height; probably all good Republicans did believe for a day or two that the POUM was a huge spying organisation in German pay. To have to say such a thing to an officer in the Popular Army was like going into the Cavalry Club immediately after the Red Letter scare and announcing yourself a Communist. His dark eyes moved obliquely across my face. Another long pause, then he said slowly:

'And you say you were with him at the front. Then you were serving in the POUM militia yourself?'

'Yes.'

He turned and dived into the colonel's room. I could hear an agitated conversation. 'It's all up,' I thought. We should never get Kopp's letter back. Moreover I had had to confess that I was in the POUM myself, and no doubt they would ring up the police and get me arrested, just to add another Trotskyist to the bag. Presently, however, the officer reappeared, fitting on his cap, and sternly signed to me to follow. We were going to the Chief of Police's office. It was a long way, twenty minutes' walk. The little officer marched stiffly in front with a military step. We did not exchange a single word the whole way. When we got to the Chief of Police's office a crowd of the most dreadful-looking scoundrels, obviously police narks, informers, and spies of every kind, were hanging about outside the door. The little officer went in; there was a long, heated conversation. You could hear voices furiously raised; you pictured violent gestures, shruggings of the shoulders, bangings on the table. Evidently the police were refusing to give the letter up. At last, however, the officer emerged, flushed, but carrying a large official envelope. It was Kopp's letter. We had won a tiny victory – which, as it turned out, made not the slightest difference. The letter was duly delivered, but Kopp's military superiors were quite unable to get him out of jail.

The officer promised me that the letter should be delivered. But what about Kopp? I said. Could we not get him released? He shrugged his shoulders. That was another matter. They did not know what Kopp had been arrested for. He could only tell me that the proper inquiries would be made. There was no more to be said; it was time to part. Both of us bowed slightly. And then there happened a strange and moving thing. The little officer hesitated a moment, then stepped across and shook hands with me.

I do not know if I can bring home to you how deeply that action touched me. It sounds a small thing, but it was not. You have got to realise what was the feeling of the time – the horrible atmosphere of suspicion and hatred, the lies and rumours circulating everywhere, the posters screaming from the hoardings that I and everyone like me was a Fascist spy. And you have got to remember that we were standing outside the Chief of Police's office, in front of that filthy gang of tale-bearers and *agents provocateurs*, any one of whom might know that I was 'wanted' by the police. It was like publicly shaking hands with a German during the Great War. I suppose he had decided in some way that I was not really a Fascist spy; still, it was good of him to shake hands.

I record this, trivial though it may sound, because it is somehow typical of Spain – of the flashes of magnanimity that you get from Spaniards in the worst of circumstances. I have the most evil memories of Spain, but I have very few bad memories of Spaniards. I only twice remember even being seriously angry with a Spaniard, and on each occasion, when I look back, I believe I was in the wrong myself. They have, there is no doubt, a generosity, a species of nobility, that do not really belong to the twentieth century. It is this that makes one hope that in Spain even Fascism may take a comparatively loose and bearable form. Few Spaniards possess the damnable efficiency and consistency that a modern totalitarian state needs. There had been a queer little illustration of this fact a few nights earlier, when the police had searched my wife's room. As a matter of fact that search was a very interesting business, and I wish I had seen it, though perhaps it is as well that I did not, for I might not have kept my temper.

The police conducted the search in the recognised Ogpu or Gestapo style. In the small hours of the morning there was a pounding on the door, and six men marched in, switched on the light and immediately took up various positions about the room, obviously agreed upon beforehand. They then searched both rooms (there was a bathroom attached) with inconceivable thoroughness. They sounded the walls, took up the mats, examined the floor, felt the curtains, probed under the bath and the radiator, emptied every drawer and suitcase and felt every garment and held it up to the light. They impounded all papers, including the contents of the waste-paper basket, and all our books into the bargain. They were thrown into ecstasies of suspicion by finding that we possessed a French translation of Hitler's *Mein Kampf*. If that had been the only book they found our doom would have been sealed. It is obvious that a person who reads *Mein Kampf* must be a Fascist. The next moment, however, they came upon a copy of Stalin's pamphlet, *Ways of Liquidating Trotskyists and other Double Dealers*, which reassured them somewhat. In one drawer there was a number of packets of cigarette papers. They picked each packet to pieces and examined each paper separately, in case there should be messages written on them. Altogether they were on the job for nearly two hours. Yet all this time they *never searched the bed*. My wife was lying in bed all the while; obviously there might have been half a dozen sub-machine-guns under the mattress, not to mention a library of Trotskyist documents under the pillow. Yet the detectives made no move to touch the bed, never even looked underneath it. I cannot believe that this is a regular feature of the Ogpu routine. One must remember that the police were almost entirely under Communist control, and these men were probably Communist Party members themselves. But they were also

Spaniards, and to turn a woman out of bed was a little too much for them. This part of the job was silently dropped, making the whole search meaningless.

That night McNair, Cottman, and I slept in some long grass at the edge of a derelict building-lot. It was a cold night for the time of year and no one slept much. I remember the long dismal hours of loitering about before one could get a cup of coffee. For the first time since I had been in Barcelona I went to have a look at the cathedral – a modern cathedral, and one of the most hideous buildings in the world. It had four crenellated spires exactly the shape of hock bottles. Unlike most of the churches in Barcelona it was not damaged during the revolution – it was spared because of its 'artistic value', people said. I think the Anarchists showed bad taste in not blowing it up when they had the chance, though they did hang a red and black banner between its spires. That afternoon my wife and I went to see Kopp for the last time. There was nothing that we could do for him, absolutely nothing, except to say good-bye and leave money with Spanish friends who would take him food and cigarettes. A little while later, however, after we had left Barcelona, he was placed *incommunicado* and not even food could be sent to him. That night, walking down the Ramblas, we passed the Café Moka, which the Assault Guards were still holding in force. On an impulse I went in and spoke to two of them who were leaning against the counter with their rifles slung over their shoulders. I asked them if they knew which of their comrades had been on duty here at the time of the May fighting. They did not know, and, with the usual Spanish vagueness, did not know how one could find out. I said that my friend Jorge Kopp was in prison and would perhaps be put on trial for something in connection with the May fighting; that the men who were on duty here would know that he had stopped the fighting and saved some of their lives; they ought to come forward and give evidence to that effect. One of the men I was talking to was a dull, heavy-looking man who kept shaking his head because he could not hear my voice in the din of the traffic. But the other was different. He said he had heard of Kopp's action from some of his comrades; Kopp was *buen chico* (a good fellow). But even at the time I knew that it was all useless. If Kopp were ever tried, it would be, as in all such trials, with faked evidence. If he has been shot (and I am afraid it is quite likely), that will be his epitaph: the *buen chico* of the poor Assault Guard who was part of a dirty system but had remained enough of a human being to know a decent action when he saw one.

It was an extraordinary, insane existence that we were leading. By night we were criminals, but by day we were prosperous English visitors – that was our pose, anyway. Even after a night in the open, a shave, a bath and a shoe-shine do wonders with your appearance. The safest thing at present was to look as bourgeois as possible. We frequented the fashionable residential quarter of the town, where our faces were not known, went to expensive restaurants and were very English with the waiters. For the first time in my life I took to writing things on walls. The passageways of several smart restaurants had *'Visca POUM!'* scrawled on them as large as I could write it. All the while, though I was technically in hiding, I could not feel myself in danger. The whole thing seemed too absurd. I had the ineradicable English belief that 'they' cannot arrest you unless you have broken the law. It is a most dangerous belief to have during a political pogrom. There was a warrant out for McNair's arrest, and the chances were that the rest of us were on the list as well. The arrests, raids, searchings were continuing without pause; practically everyone we knew, except those who were still at the front, was in jail by this time. The police were even boarding the French ships that periodically took off refugees and seizing suspected 'Trotskyists'.

Thanks to the kindness of the British Consul, who must have had a very trying time during that week, we had managed to get our passports into order. The sooner we left the better. There was a train that was due to leave for Port Bou at half-past seven in the evening and might normally be expected to leave at about half-past eight. We arranged that my wife should order a taxi beforehand and then pack her bags, pay her bill and leave the hotel at the last possible moment. If she gave the hotel-people too much notice they would be sure to send for the police. I got down to the station at about seven to find that the train had already gone – it had left at ten to seven. The engine-driver had changed his mind, as usual. Fortunately we managed to warn my wife in time. There was another train early the following morning. McNair, Cottman, and I had dinner at a little restaurant near the station and by cautious questioning discovered that the restaurant-keeper was a CNT member and friendly. He let us a three-bedded room and forgot to warn the police. It was the first time in five nights that I had been able to sleep with my clothes off.

Next morning my wife slipped out of the hotel successfully. The train was about an hour late in starting. I filled in the time by writing a long letter to the Ministry of War, telling them about Kopp's case – that without a doubt he had been arrested by mistake, that he was urgently needed at the front, that countless people would testify that he was innocent of any offence, etc. etc. etc. I wonder if anyone read that letter, written on pages torn out of a note-book in wobbly handwriting (my fingers were still partly paralysed) and still more wobbly Spanish. At any rate, neither this letter nor anything else took effect. As I write, six months after the event, Kopp (if he has not been shot) is still in jail, untried and uncharged. At the beginning we had two or three letters from him, smuggled out by released prisoners and posted in France. They all told the same story – imprisonment in filthy dark dens, bad and insufficient food, serious illness due to the conditions of imprisonment, and refusal of medical attention. I have had all this confirmed from several other sources, English and French. More recently he disappeared into one of the 'secret prisons' with which it seems impossible to make any kind of communication. His case is the case of scores or hundreds of foreigners and no one knows how many thousands of Spaniards.

In the end we crossed the frontier without incident. The train had a first class and a dining-car, the first I had seen in Spain. Until recently there had been only one class on the trains in Catalonia. Two detectives came round the train taking the names of foreigners, but when they saw us in the dining-car they seemed satisfied that we were respectable. It was queer how everything had changed. Only six months ago, when the Anarchists still reigned, it was looking like a proletarian that made you respectable. On the way down from Perpignan to Cerbères a French commercial traveller in my carriage had said to me in all solemnity: 'You mustn't go into Spain looking like that. Take off that collar and tie. They'll tear them off you in Barcelona.' He was exaggerating, but it showed how Catalonia was regarded. And at the frontier the Anarchist guards had turned back a smartly-dressed Frenchman and his wife, solely – I think – because they looked too bourgeois. Now it was the other way about; to look bourgeois was the one salvation. At the passport office they looked us up in the card-index of suspects, but thanks to the inefficiency of the police our names were not listed, not even McNair's. We were searched from head to foot, but we possessed nothing incriminating, except my discharge-papers, and the carabineros who searched me did not know that the 29th Division was the POUM. So we slipped through the barrier, and after just six months I was on French soil again. My only souvenirs of Spain were a goatskin waterbottle and one of those tiny iron lamps in which the Aragón peasants burn olive-oil – lamps almost exactly the shape of the terra-cotta lamps that the Romans used two thousand years ago – which I had picked up in some ruined hut, and which had somehow got stuck in my luggage.

After all, it turned out that we had come away none too soon. The very first newspaper we saw announced McNair's arrest for espionage. The Spanish authorities had been a little premature in announcing this. Fortunately, 'Trotskyism' is not extraditable.

I wonder what is the appropriate first action when you come from a country at war and set foot on peaceful soil. Mine was to rush to the tobacco-kiosk and buy as many cigars and cigarettes as I could stuff into my pockets. Then we all went to the buffet and had a cup of tea, the first tea with fresh milk in it that we had had for many months. It was several days before I could get used to the idea that you could buy cigarettes whenever you wanted them. I always half-expected to see the tobacconists' doors barred and the forbidding notice *'No hay tabaco'* in the window.

McNair and Cottman were going on to Paris. My wife and I got off the train at Banyuls, the first station up the line, feeling that we would like a rest. We were not too well received in Banyuls when they discovered that we had come from Barcelona. Quite a number of times I was involved in the same conversation: 'You come from Spain? Which side were you fighting on? The Government? Oh!' – and then a marked coolness. The little town seemed solidly pro-Franco, no doubt because of the various Spanish Fascist refugees who had arrived there from time to time. The waiter at the café I frequented was a pro-Franco Spaniard and used to give me lowering glances as he served me with an aperitif. It was otherwise in Perpignan, which was stiff with Government partisans and where all the different factions were caballing against one another almost as in

Barcelona. There was one café where the word 'POUM' immediately procured you French friends and smiles from the waiter.

I think we stayed three days in Banyuls. It was a strangely restless time. In this quiet fishing-town, remote from bombs, machine-guns, food-queues, propaganda, and intrigue, we ought to have felt profoundly relieved and thankful. We felt nothing of the kind. The things we had seen in Spain did not recede and fall into proportion now that we were away from them; instead they rushed back upon us and were far more vivid than before. We thought, talked, dreamed incessantly of Spain. For months past we had been telling ourselves that 'when we get out of Spain' we would go somewhere beside the Mediterranean and be quiet for a little while and perhaps do a little fishing; but now that we were here it was merely a bore and a disappointment. It was chilly weather, a persistent wind blew off the sea, the water was dull and choppy, round the harbour's edge a scum of ashes, corks, and fish-guts bobbed against the stones. It sounds like lunacy, but the thing that both of us wanted was to be back in Spain. Though it could have done no good to anybody, might indeed have done serious harm, both of us wished that we had stayed to be imprisoned along with the others. I suppose I have failed to convey more than a little of what those months in Spain mean to me. I have recorded some of the outward events, but I cannot record the feeling they have left me with. It is all mixed up with sights, smells, and sounds that cannot be conveyed in writing: the smell of the trenches, the mountain dawns stretching away into inconceivable distances, the frosty crackle of bullets, the roar and glare of bombs; the clear cold light of the Barcelona mornings, and the stamp of boots in the barrack yard, back in December when people still believed in the revolution; and the food-queues and the red and black flags and the faces of Spanish militiamen; above all the faces of militiamen – men whom I knew in the line and who are now scattered Lord knows where, some killed in battle, some maimed, some in prison – most of them, I hope, still safe and sound. Good luck to them all; I hope they win their war and drive all the foreigners out of Spain, Germans, Russians and Italians alike. This war, in which I played so ineffectual a part, has left me with memories that are mostly evil, and yet I do not wish that I had missed it. When you have had a glimpse of such a disaster as this – and however it ends the Spanish war will turn out to have been an appalling disaster, quite apart from the slaughter and physical suffering – the result is not necessarily disillusionment and cynicism. Curiously enough the whole experience has left me with not less but more belief in the decency of human beings. And I hope the account I have given is not too misleading. I believe that on such an issue as this no one is or can be completely truthful. It is difficult to be certain about anything except what you have seen with your own eyes, and consciously or unconsciously everyone writes as a partisan. In case I have not said this somewhere earlier in the book I will say it now: beware of my partisanship, my mistakes of fact and the distortion inevitably caused by my having seen only one corner of events. And beware of exactly the same things when you read any other book on this period of the Spanish war.

Because of the feeling that we ought to be doing something, though actually there was nothing we could do, we left Banyuls earlier than we had intended. With every mile that you went northward France grew greener and softer. Away from the mountain and the vine, back to the meadow and the elm. When I had passed through Paris on my way to Spain it had seemed to be decayed and gloomy, very different from the Paris I had known eight years earlier, when living was cheap and Hitler was not heard of. Half the cafés I used to know were shut for lack of custom, and everyone was obsessed with the high cost of living and the fear of war. Now, after poor Spain, even Paris seemed gay and prosperous. And the Exhibition was in full swing, though we managed to avoid visiting it.

And then England – southern England, probably the sleekest landscape in the world. It is difficult when you pass that way, especially when you are peacefully recovering from sea-sickness with the plush cushions of a boat-train carriage underneath you, to believe that anything is really happening anywhere. Earthquakes in Japan, famines in China, revolutions in Mexico? Don't worry, the milk will be on the doorstep tomorrow morning, the *New Statesman* will come out on Friday. The industrial towns were far away, a smudge of smoke and misery hidden by the curve of the earth's surface. Down here it was still the England I had known in my childhood: the railway-cuttings smothered in wild flowers, the deep meadows where the great shining horses browse and meditate, the slow-moving streams bordered by willows, the green bosoms of the elms, the larkspurs in the cottage gardens; and then the huge peaceful wilderness of outer London, the barges on the miry river, the familiar streets, the posters telling of cricket matches and Royal weddings, the men in bowler hats, the pigeons in Trafalgar Square, the red buses, the blue policemen – all sleeping the deep, deep sleep of England, from which I sometimes fear that we shall never wake till we are jerked out of it by the roar of bombs.

THE END

APPENDIX I

[Formerly Chapter V of First Edition, placed between Chapters IV and V of this edition. Placed here at Orwell's request.]

At the beginning I had ignored the political side of the war, and it was only about this time that it began to force itself upon my attention. If you are not interested in the horrors of party politics, please skip; I am trying to keep the political parts of this narrative in separate chapters for precisely that purpose. But at the same time it would be quite impossible to write about the Spanish war from a purely military angle. It was above all things a political war. No event in it, at any rate during the first year, is intelligible unless one has some grasp of the inter-party struggle that was going on behind the Government lines.

When I came to Spain, and for some time afterwards, I was not only uninterested in the political situation but unaware of it. I knew there was a war on, but I had no notion what kind of a war. If you had asked me why I had joined the militia I should have answered: 'To fight against Fascism,' and if you had asked me what I was fighting *for*, I should have answered: 'Common decency.' I had accepted the *News Chronicle–New Statesman* version of the war as the defence of civilisation against a maniacal outbreak by an army of Colonel Blimps in the pay of Hitler. The revolutionary atmosphere of Barcelona had attracted me deeply, but I had made no attempt to understand it. As for the kaleidoscope of political parties and trade unions, with their tiresome names – PSUC, POUM, FAI, CNT, UGT, JCI, JSU, AIT – they merely exasperated me. It looked at first sight as though Spain were suffering from a plague of initials. I knew that I was serving in something called the POUM. (I had only joined the POUM militia rather than any other because I happened to arrive in Barcelona with ILP papers), but I did not realise that there were serious differences between the political parties. At Monte Pocero, when they pointed to the position on our left and said: 'Those are the Socialists' (meaning the PSUC), I was puzzled and said: 'Aren't we all Socialists?' I thought it idiotic that people fighting for their lives should *have* separate parties; my attitude always was, 'Why can't we drop all this political nonsense and get on with the war?' This of course was the correct 'anti-Fascist' attitude which had been carefully disseminated by the English newspapers, largely in order to prevent people from grasping the real nature of the struggle. But in Spain, especially in Catalonia, it was an attitude that no one could or did keep up indefinitely. Everyone, however unwillingly, took sides sooner or later. For even if one cared nothing for the political parties and their conflicting 'lines', it was too obvious that one's own destiny was involved. As a militiaman one was a soldier against Franco, but one was also a pawn in an enormous struggle that was being fought out between two political theories. When I scrounged for firewood on the mountain-side and wondered whether this was really a war or whether the *News Chronicle* had made it up, when I dodged the Communist machine-guns in the Barcelona riots, when I finally fled from Spain with the police one jump behind me – all these things happened to me in that particular way because I was serving in the POUM militia and not in the PSUC. So great is the difference between two sets of initials!

To understand the alignment on the Government side one has got to remember how the war started. When the fighting broke out on 18 July it is probable that every anti-Fascist in Europe felt a thrill of hope. For here at last, apparently, was democracy standing up to Fascism. For years past the so-called democratic countries had been surrendering to Fascism at every step. The Japanese had been allowed to do as they liked in Manchuria. Hitler had walked into power and proceeded to massacre political opponents of all shades. Mussolini had bombed the Abyssinians while fifty-three nations (I think it was fifty-three) made pious noises 'off'. But when Franco tried to overthrow a mildly Left-wing Government the Spanish people, against all expectation, had risen against him. It seemed – possibly it was – the turning of the tide.

But there were several points that escaped general notice. To begin with, Franco was not strictly comparable with Hitler or Mussolini. His rising was a military mutiny backed up by the aristocracy and the Church, and in the main, especially at the beginning, it was an attempt not so much to impose Fascism as to restore feudalism. This meant that Franco had against him not only the working class but also various sections of the liberal bourgeoisie – the very people who are the supporters of Fascism when it appears in a more modern form. More important than this was the fact that the Spanish working class did not, as we might conceivably do in England, resist Franco in the name of 'democracy' and the *status quo*; their resistance was accompanied by – one might almost say it consisted of – a definite revolutionary outbreak. Land was seized by the peasants; many factories and most of the transport were seized by the trade unions; churches were wrecked and the priests driven out or killed. The *Daily Mail*, amid the cheers of the Catholic clergy, was able to represent Franco as a patriot delivering his country from hordes of fiendish 'Reds'.

For the first few months of the war Franco's real opponent was not so much the Government as the trade unions. As soon as the rising broke out the organised town workers replied by calling a general strike and then by demanding – and, after a struggle, getting – arms from the public arsenals. If they had not acted spontaneously and more or less independently it is quite conceivable that Franco would never have been resisted. There can, of course, be no certainty about this, but there is at least reason for thinking it. The Government had made little or no attempt to forestall the rising, which had been foreseen for a long time past, and when the trouble started its attitude was weak and hesitant, so much so, indeed, that Spain had three premiers in a single day.[1] Moreover, the one step that could save the immediate situation, the arming of the workers, was only taken unwillingly and in response to violent popular clamour. However, the arms were distributed, and in the big towns of Eastern Spain the Fascists were defeated by a huge effort, mainly of the working class, aided by some of the armed forces (Assault Guards, etc.) who had remained loyal. It was the kind of effort that could probably only be made by people who were fighting with a revolutionary intention – i.e. believed that they were fighting for something better than the *status quo*. In the

---

[1] Quiroga, Barrio, and Giral. The first two refused to distribute arms to the trade unions.

various centres of revolt it is thought that three thousand people died in the streets in a single day. Men and women armed only with sticks of dynamite rushed across the open squares and stormed stone buildings held by trained soldiers with machine-guns. Machine-gun nests that the Fascists had placed at strategic spots were smashed by rushing taxis at them at sixty miles an hour. Even if one had heard nothing of the seizure of the land by the peasants, the setting up of local soviets, etc., it would be hard to believe that the Anarchists and Socialists who were the backbone of the resistance were doing this kind of thing for the preservation of capitalist democracy, which especially in the Anarchist view was no more than a centralised swindling machine.

Meanwhile the workers had weapons in their hands, and at this stage they refrained from giving them up. (Even a year later it was computed that the Anarcho-Syndicalists in Catalonia possessed 30,000 rifles.) The estates of the big pro-Fascist landlords were in many places seized by the peasants. Along with the collectivisation of industry and transport there was an attempt to set up the rough beginnings of a workers' government by means of local committees, workers' patrols to replace the old pro-capitalist police forces, workers' militias based on the trade unions, and so forth. Of course the process was not uniform, and it went further in Catalonia than elsewhere. There were areas where the institutions of local government remained almost untouched, and others where they existed side by side with revolutionary committees. In a few places independent Anarchist communes were set up, and some of them remained in being till about a year later, when they were forcibly suppressed by the Government. In Catalonia, for the first few months, most of the actual power was in the hands of the Anarcho-Syndicalists, who controlled most of the key industries. The thing that had happened in Spain was, in fact, not merely a civil war, but the beginning of a revolution. It is this fact that the anti-Fascist press outside Spain has made it its special business to obscure. The issue has been narrowed down to 'Fascism versus democracy' and the revolutionary aspect concealed as much as possible. In England, where the Press is more centralised and the public more easily deceived than elsewhere, only two versions of the Spanish war have had any publicity to speak of: the Right-wing version of Christian patriots versus Bolsheviks dripping with blood, and the Left-wing version of gentlemanly republicans quelling a military revolt. The central issue has been successfully covered up.

There were several reasons for this. To begin with, appalling lies about atrocities were being circulated by the pro-Fascist press, and well-meaning propagandists undoubtedly thought that they were aiding the Spanish Government by denying that Spain had 'gone Red'. But the main reason was this: that, except for the small revolutionary groups which exist in all countries, the whole world was determined upon preventing revolution in Spain. In particular the Communist Party, with Soviet Russia behind it, had thrown its whole weight against revolution. It was the Communist thesis that revolution at this stage would be fatal and that what was to be aimed at in Spain was not workers' control, but bourgeois democracy. It hardly needs pointing out why 'liberal' capitalist opinion took the same line. Foreign capital was heavily invested in Spain. The Barcelona Traction Company, for instance, represented ten millions of British capital; and meanwhile the trade unions had seized all the transport in Catalonia. If the revolution went forward there would be no compensation, or very little; if the capitalist republic prevailed, foreign investments would be safe. And since the revolution had got to be crushed, it greatly simplified things to pretend that no revolution had happened. In this way the real significance of every event could be covered up; every shift of power from the trade unions to the central Government could be represented as a necessary step in military reorganisation. The situation produced was curious in the extreme. Outside Spain few people grasped that there was a revolution; inside Spain nobody doubted it. Even the PSUC newspapers, Communist-controlled and more or less committed to an anti-revolutionary policy, talked about 'our glorious revolution'. And meanwhile the Communist press in foreign countries was shouting that there was no sign of revolution anywhere; the seizure of factories, setting up of workers' committees, etc., had not happened – or, alternatively, had happened, but 'had no political significance'. According to the *Daily Worker* (6 August 1936) those who said that the Spanish people were fighting for social revolution, or for anything other than bourgeois democracy, were 'downright lying scoundrels'. On the other hand, Juan López, a member of the Valencia Government, declared in February 1937 that 'the Spanish people are shedding their blood, not for the democratic

Republic and its paper Constitution, but for . . . a revolution.' So it would appear that the downright lying scoundrels included members of the Government for which we were bidden to fight. Some of the foreign anti-Fascist papers even descended to the pitiful lie of pretending that churches were only attacked when they were used as Fascist fortresses. Actually churches were pillaged everywhere and as a matter of course, because it was perfectly well understood that the Spanish Church was part of the capitalist racket. In six months in Spain I only saw two undamaged churches, and until about July 1937 no churches were allowed to reopen and hold services, except for one or two Protestant churches in Madrid.

But, after all, it was only the beginning of a revolution, not the complete thing. Even when the workers, certainly in Catalonia and possibly elsewhere, had the power to do so, they did not overthrow or completely replace the Government. Obviously they could not do so when Franco was hammering at the gate and sections of the middle class were on their side. The country was in a transitional state that was capable either of developing in the direction of Socialism or of reverting to an ordinary capitalist republic. The peasants had most of the land, and they were likely to keep it, unless Franco won; all large industries had been collectivised, but whether they remained collectivised, or whether capitalism was reintroduced, would depend finally upon which group gained control. At the beginning both the central Government and the Generalidad de Cataluña (the semi-autonomous Catalan Government) could definitely be said to represent the working class. The Government was headed by Caballero, a Left-wing Socialist, and contained ministers representing the UGT (Socialist trade unions) and the CNT (Syndicalist unions controlled by the Anarchists). The Catalan Generalidad was for a while virtually superseded by an anti-Fascist Defence Committee[1] consisting mainly of delegates from the trade unions. Later the Defence Committee was dissolved and the Generalidad was reconstituted so as to represent the unions

---

[1] Comité Central de Milicias Antifascistas. Delegates were chosen in proportion to the membership of their organisations. Nine delegates represented the trade unions, three the Catalan Liberal parties, and two the various Marxist parties (POUM, Communists, and others).

and the various Left-wing parties. But every subsequent reshuffling of the Government was a move towards the Right. First the POUM was expelled from the Generalidad; six months later Caballero was replaced by the Right-wing Socialist Negrín; shortly afterwards the CNT was eliminated from the Government; then the UGT; then the CNT was turned out of the Generalidad; finally, a year after the outbreak of war and revolution, there remained a Government composed entirely of Right-wing Socialists, Liberals, and Communists.

The general swing to the Right dates from about October–November 1936, when the USSR began to supply arms to the Government and power began to pass from the Anarchists to the Communists. Except Russia and Mexico no country had had the decency to come to the rescue of the Government, and Mexico, for obvious reasons, could not supply arms in large quantities. Consequently the Russians were in a position to dictate terms. There is very little doubt that these terms were, in substance, 'Prevent revolution or you get no weapons,' and that the first move against the revolutionary elements, the expulsion of the POUM from the Catalan Generalidad, was done under orders from the USSR. It has been denied that any direct pressure was exerted by the Russian Government, but the point is not of great importance, for the Communist parties of all countries can be taken as carrying out Russian policy, and it is not denied that the Communist Party was the chief mover first against the POUM, later against the Anarchists and against Caballero's section of the Socialists, and, in general, against a revolutionary policy. Once the USSR had intervened the triumph of the Communist Party was assured. To begin with, gratitude to Russia for the arms and the fact that the Communist Party, especially since the arrival of the International Brigades, looked capable of winning the war, immensely raised the Communist prestige. Secondly, the Russian arms were supplied via the Communist Party and the parties allied to them, who saw to it that as few as possible got to their political opponents.[1] Thirdly, by proclaiming a non-revolutionary

---

[1] This was why there were so few Russian arms on the Aragón front, where the troops were predominantly Anarchist. Until April 1937 the only Russian weapon I saw – with the exception of some aeroplanes which may or may not have been Russian – was a solitary sub-machine-gun.

policy the Communists were able to gather in all those whom the extremists had scared. It was easy, for instance, to rally the wealthier peasants against the collectivisation policy of the Anarchists. There was an enormous growth in the membership of the party, and the influx was largely from the middle class – shopkeepers, officials, army officers, well-to-do peasants, etc. etc. The war was essentially a triangular struggle. The fight against Franco had to continue, but the simultaneous aim of the Government was to recover such power as remained in the hands of the trade unions. It was done by a series of small moves – a policy of pin-pricks, as somebody called it – and on the whole very cleverly. There was no general and obvious counter-revolutionary move, and until May 1937 it was scarcely necessary to use force. The workers could always be brought to heel by an argument that is almost too obvious to need stating: 'Unless you do this, that and the other we shall lose the war.' In every case, needless to say, it appeared that the thing demanded by military necessity was the surrender of something that the workers had won for themselves in 1936. But the argument could hardly fail, because to lose the war was the last thing that the revolutionary parties wanted; if the war was lost democracy and revolution, Socialism and Anarchism, became meaningless words. The Anarchists, the only revolutionary party that was big enough to matter, were obliged to give way on point after point. The process of collectivisation was checked, the local committees were got rid of, the workers' patrols were abolished and the pre-war police forces, largely reinforced and very heavily armed, were restored, and various key industries which had been under the control of the trade unions were taken over by the Government (the seizure of the Barcelona Telephone Exchange, which led to the May fighting, was one incident in this process); finally, most important of all, the workers' militias, based on the trade unions, were gradually broken up and redistributed among the new Popular Army, a 'non-political' army on semi-bourgeois lines, with a differential pay rate, a privileged officer-caste, etc. etc. In the special circumstances this was the really decisive step; it happened later in Catalonia than elsewhere because it was there that the revolutionary parties were strongest. Obviously the only guarantee that the workers could have of retaining their winnings was to keep some of the armed forces under their own control. As usual, the breaking-up of the militias was done in the name of military efficiency; and no one denied that a thorough military reorganisation was needed. It would, however, have been quite possible to reorganise the militias and make them more efficient while keeping them under direct control of the trade unions; the main purpose of the change was to make sure that the Anarchists did not possess an army of their own. Moreover, the democratic spirit of the militias made them breeding-grounds for revolutionary ideas. The Communists were well aware of this, and inveighed ceaselessly and bitterly against the POUM and Anarchist principle of equal pay for all ranks. A general 'bourgeoisification', a deliberate destruction of the equalitarian spirit of the first few months of the revolution, was taking place. All happened so swiftly that people making successive visits to Spain at intervals of a few months have declared that they seemed scarcely to be visiting the same country; what had seemed on the surface and for a brief instant to be a workers' State was changing before one's eyes into an ordinary bourgeois republic with the normal division into rich and poor. By the autumn of 1937 the 'Socialist' Negrín was declaring in public speeches that 'we respect private property,' and members of the Cortes who at the beginning of the war had had to fly the country because of their suspected Fascist sympathies were returning to Spain.

The whole process is easy to understand if one remembers that it proceeds from the temporary alliance that Fascism, in certain forms, forces upon the bourgeois and the worker. This alliance, known as the Popular Front, is in essential an alliance of enemies, and it seems probable that it must always end by one partner swallowing the other. The only unexpected feature in the Spanish situation – and outside Spain it has caused an immense amount of misunderstanding – is that among the parties on the Government side the Communists stood not upon the extreme Left, but upon the extreme Right. In reality this should cause no surprise, because the tactics of the Communist Party elsewhere, especially in France, have made it clear that official Communism must be regarded, at any rate for the time being, as an anti-revolutionary force. The whole of Comintern policy is now subordinated (excusably, considering the world situation) to the defence of the USSR, which depends upon a system of military alliances. In particular, the USSR is in alliance with France, a capitalist-imperialist country. The alliance is of little use to Russia unless French capitalism is strong, therefore Communist policy in France has got to be anti-revolutionary. This means not only that French Communists now march behind the tricolour and sing the Marseillaise, but, what is more important, that they have had to drop all effective agitation in the French colonies. It is less than three years since Thorez, the Secretary of the French Communist Party, was declaring that the French workers would never be bamboozled into fighting against their German comrades;[1] he is now one of the loudest-lunged patriots in France. The clue to the behaviour of the Communist Party in any country is the military relation of that country, actual or potential, towards the USSR. In England, for instance, the position is still uncertain, hence the English Communist Party is still hostile to the National Government, and, ostensibly, opposed to re-armament. If, however, Great Britain enters into an alliance or military understanding with the USSR, the English Communist, like the French Communist, will have no choice but to become a good patriot and imperialist; there are premonitory signs of this already. In Spain the Communist 'line' was undoubtedly influenced by the fact that France, Russia's ally, would strongly object to a revolutionary neighbour and would raise heaven and earth to prevent the liberation of Spanish Morocco. The *Daily Mail*, with its tales of red revolution financed by Moscow, was even more wildly wrong than usual. In reality it was the Communists above all others who prevented revolution in Spain. Later, when the Right-wing forces were in full control, the Communists showed themselves willing to go a great deal further than the Liberals in hunting down the revolutionary leaders.[2]

I have tried to sketch the general course of the Spanish revolution during its first year, because this makes it easier to understand the situation at any given moment. But I do not want to suggest that in February I held all of the opinions that are implied in what I have said above. To begin with, the things that most enlightened me had not yet happened, and in any case my sympathies were in some ways different from what they are

[1] In the Chamber of Deputies, March 1935.
[2] For the best account of the interplay between the parties on the Government side, see Franz Borkenau's *The Spanish Cockpit*. This is by a long way the ablest book that has yet appeared on the Spanish war.

now. This was partly because the political side of the war bored me and I naturally reacted against the viewpoint of which I heard most – i.e. the POUM–ILP viewpoint. The Englishmen I was among were mostly ILP members, with a few CP members among them, and most of them were much better educated politically than myself. For weeks on end, during the dull period when nothing was happening round Huesca, I found myself in the middle of a political discussion that practically never ended. In the draughty evil-smelling barn of the farm-house where we were billeted, in the stuffy blackness of dug-outs, behind the parapet in the freezing midnight hours, the conflicting party 'lines' were debated over and over. Among the Spaniards it was the same, and most of the newspapers we saw made the inter-party feud their chief feature. One would have had to be deaf or an imbecile not to pick up some idea of what the various parties stood for.

From the point of view of political theory there were only three parties that mattered, the PSUC, the POUM, and the CNT–FAI, loosely described as the Anarchists. I take the PSUC first, as being the most important; it was the party that finally triumphed, and even at this time it was visibly in the ascendant.

It is necessary to explain that when one speaks of the PSUC 'line' one really means the Communist Party 'line'. The PSUC (Partido Socialista Unificado de Cataluña) was the Socialist Party of Catalonia; it had been formed at the beginning of the war by the fusion of various Marxist parties, including the Catalan Communist Party, but it was now entirely under Communist control and was affiliated to the Third International. Elsewhere in Spain no formal unification between Socialists and Communists had taken place, but the Communist viewpoint and the Right-wing Socialist viewpoint could everywhere be regarded as identical. Roughly speaking, the PSUC was the political organ of the UGT (Unión General de Trabajadores), the Socialist trade unions. The membership of these unions throughout Spain now numbered about a million and a half. They contained many sections of the manual workers, but since the outbreak of war they had also been swollen by a large influx of middle-class members, for in the early 'revolutionary' days people of all kinds had found it useful to join either the UGT or the CNT. The two blocks of unions overlapped, but of the two the CNT was more definitely a working-class organisation. The PSUC was therefore a party partly of the workers and partly of the small bourgeoisie – the shopkeepers, the officials, and the wealthier peasants.

The PSUC 'line', which was preached in the Communist and pro-Communist press throughout the world, was approximately this:

'At present nothing matters except winning the war; without victory in the war all else is meaningless. Therefore this is not the moment to talk of pressing forward with the revolution. We can't afford to alienate the peasants by forcing collectivisation upon them, and we can't afford to frighten away the middle classes who are fighting on our side. Above all for the sake of efficiency we must do away with revolutionary chaos. We must have a strong central government in place of local committees, and we must have a properly trained and fully militarised army under a unified command. Clinging on to fragments of workers' control and parroting revolutionary phrases is worse than useless; it is not merely obstructive, but even counter-revolutionary, because it leads to divisions which can be used against us by the Fascists. At this stage we are not fighting for the dictatorship of the proletariat, we are fighting for parliamentary democracy. Whoever tries to turn the civil war into a social revolution is playing into the hands of the Fascists and is in effect, if not in intention, a traitor.'

The POUM 'line' differed from this on every point except, of course, the importance of winning the war. The POUM (Partido Obrero de Unificación Marxista) was one of those dissident Communist parties which have appeared in many countries in the last few years as a result of the opposition to 'Stalinism'; i.e. to the change, real or apparent, in Communist policy. It was made up partly of ex-Communists and partly of an earlier party, the Workers' and Peasants' Bloc. Numerically it was a small party,[1] with not much influence outside Catalonia, and chiefly important because it contained an unusually high proportion of politically conscious members. In Catalonia its chief stronghold was Lérida. It did not represent

---

[1] The figures for the POUM membership are given as: July 1936, 10,000; December 1936, 70,000; June 1937, 40,000. But these are from POUM sources; a hostile estimate would probably divide them by four. The only thing one can say with any certainty about the membership of the Spanish political parties is that every party overestimates its own numbers.

any block of trade unions. The POUM militiamen were mostly CNT members, but the actual party-members generally belonged to the UGT. It was, however, only in the CNT that the POUM had any influence. The POUM 'line' was approximately this:

'It is nonsense to talk of opposing Fascism by bourgeois "democracy". Bourgeois "democracy" is only another name for capitalism, and so is Fascism; to fight against Fascism on behalf of "democracy" is to fight against one form of capitalism on behalf of a second which is liable to turn into the first at any moment. The only real alternative to Fascism is workers' control. If you set up any less goal than this, you will either hand the victory to Franco, or, at best, let in Fascism by the back door. Meanwhile the workers must cling to every scrap of what they have won; if they yield anything to the semi-bourgeois Government they can depend upon being cheated. The workers' militias and police-forces must be preserved in their present form and every effort to "bourgeoisify" them must be resisted. If the workers do not control the armed forces, the armed forces will control the workers. The war and the revolution are inseparable.'

The Anarchist viewpoint is less easily defined. In any case the loose term 'Anarchists' is used to cover a multitude of people of very varying opinions. The huge block of unions making up the CNT (Confederación Nacional del Trabajo), with round about two million members in all, had for its political organ the FAI (Federación Anarquista Ibérica), an actual Anarchist organisation. But even the members of the FAI, though always tinged, as perhaps most Spaniards are, with the Anarchist philosophy, were not necessarily Anarchists in the purest sense. Especially since the beginning of the war they had moved more in the direction of ordinary Socialism, because circumstances had forced them to take part in centralised administration and even to break all their principles by entering the Government. Nevertheless they differed fundamentally from the Communists in so much that, like the POUM, they aimed at workers' control and not a parliamentary democracy. They accepted the POUM slogan: 'The war and the revolution are inseparable,' though they were less dogmatic about it. Roughly speaking, the CNT–FAI stood for: (1) Direct control over industry by the workers engaged in each industry, e.g. transport, the textile factories, etc.; (2) Government by local committees and resistance to all forms of centralised authoritarianism; (3) Uncompromising hostility to the bourgeoisie and the Church. The last point, though the least precise, was the most important. The Anarchists were the opposite of the majority of so-called revolutionaries in so much that though their principles were rather vague their hatred of privilege and injustice was perfectly genuine. Philosophically, Communism and Anarchism are poles apart. Practically – i.e. in the form of society aimed at – the difference is mainly one of emphasis, but it is quite irreconcilable. The Communist's emphasis is always on centralism and efficiency, the Anarchist's on liberty and equality. Anarchism is deeply rooted in Spain and is likely to outlive Communism when the Russian influence is withdrawn. During the first two months of the war it was the Anarchists more than anyone else who had saved the situation, and much later than this the Anarchist militia, in spite of their indiscipline, were notoriously the best fighters among the purely Spanish forces. From about February 1937 onwards the Anarchists and the POUM could to some extent be lumped together. If the Anarchists, the POUM and the Left wing of the Socialists had had the sense to combine at the start and press a realistic policy, the history of the war might have been different. But in the early period, when the revolutionary parties seemed to have the game in their hands, this was impossible. Between the Anarchists and the Socialists there were ancient jealousies, the POUM, as Marxists, were sceptical of Anarchism, while from the pure Anarchist standpoint the 'Trotskyism' of the POUM was not much preferable to the 'Stalinism' of the Communists. Nevertheless the Communist tactics tended to drive the two parties together. When the POUM joined in the disastrous fighting in Barcelona in May, it was mainly from an instinct to stand by the CNT, and later, when the POUM was suppressed, the Anarchists were the only people who dared to raise a voice in its defence.

So, roughly speaking, the alignment of forces was this. On the one side the CNT–FAI, the POUM, and a section of the Socialists, standing for workers' control: on the other side the Right-wing Socialists, Liberals, and Communists, standing for centralised government and a militarised army.

It is easy to see why, at this time, I preferred the Communist viewpoint to that of the POUM. The Communists had a definite practical policy, an obviously better policy from the point of view of the common sense which looks only a few months ahead. And certainly the day-to-day policy of the POUM, their propaganda and so forth, was unspeakably bad; it must have been so, or they would have been able to attract a bigger mass-following. What clinched everything was that the Communists – so it seemed to me – were getting on with the war while we and the Anarchists were standing still. This was the general feeling at the time. The Communists had gained power and a vast increase of membership partly by appealing to the middle classes against the revolutionaries, but partly also because they were the only people who looked capable of winning the war. The Russian arms and the magnificent defence of Madrid by troops mainly under Communist control had made the Communists the heroes of Spain. As someone put it, every Russian aeroplane that flew over our heads was Communist propaganda. The revolutionary purism of the POUM, though I saw its logic, seemed to me rather futile. After all, the one thing that mattered was to win the war.

Meanwhile there was the diabolical inter-party feud that was going on in the newspapers, in pamphlets, on posters, in books – everywhere. At this time the newspapers I saw most often were the POUM papers, *La Battalla* and *Adelante*, and their ceaseless carping against the 'counter-revolutionary' PSUC struck me as priggish and tiresome. Later, when I studied the PSUC and Communist press more closely, I realised that the POUM were almost blameless compared with their adversaries. Apart from anything else, they had much smaller opportunities. Unlike the Communists, they had no footing in any press outside their own country, and inside Spain they were at an immense disadvantage because the press censorship was mainly under Communist control, which meant that the POUM papers were liable to be suppressed or fined if they said anything damaging. It is also fair to the POUM to say that though they might preach endless sermons on revolution and quote Lenin *ad nauseam*, they did not usually indulge in personal libel. Also they kept their polemics mainly to newspaper articles. Their large coloured posters, designed for a wider public (posters are important in Spain, with its large illiterate population), did not attack rival parties, but were simply anti-Fascist or abstractly revolutionary; so were the songs the militiamen sang. The Communist attacks were quite a different matter. I shall have to deal with some of these later in this book. Here I can only give a brief indication of the Communist line of attack.

On the surface the quarrel between the Communists and the POUM was one of tactics. The POUM was for immediate revolution, the Communist not. So far so good; there was much to be said on both sides. Further, the Communists contended that the POUM propaganda divided and weakened the Government forces and thus endangered the war; again, though finally I do not agree, a good case could be made out for this. But here the peculiarity of Communist tactics came in. Tentatively at first, then more loudly, they began to assert that the POUM was splitting the Government forces not by bad judgment but by deliberate design. The POUM was declared to be no more than a gang of disguised Fascists, in the pay of Franco and Hitler, who were pressing a pseudo-revolutionary policy as a way of aiding the Fascist cause. The POUM was a 'Trotskyist' organisation and 'Franco's Fifth Column'. This implied that scores of thousands of working-class people, including eight or ten thousand soldiers who were freezing in the front-line trenches and hundreds of foreigners who had come to Spain to fight against Fascism, often sacrificing their livelihood and their nationality by doing so, were simply traitors in the pay of the enemy. And this story was spread all over Spain by means of posters, etc., and repeated over and over in the Communist and pro-Communist press of the whole world. I could fill half a dozen books with quotations if I chose to collect them.

This, then, was what they were saying about us: we were Trotskyists, Fascists, traitors, murderers, cowards, spies, and so forth. I admit it was not pleasant, especially when one thought of some of the people who were responsible for it. It is not a nice thing to see a Spanish boy of fifteen carried down the line on a stretcher, with a dazed white face looking out from among the blankets, and to think of the sleek persons in London and Paris who are writing pamphlets to prove that this boy is a Fascist in disguise. One of the most horrible features of war is that all the war-propaganda, all the screaming and lies and hatred, comes invariably from people who are not fighting. The PSUC militiamen whom I knew in the line, the Communists from the International Brigade whom I met from time to time, never called me a Trotskyist or a traitor; they left that kind of thing to the journalists in the rear. The people who wrote pamphlets against us and vilified us in the newspapers all remained safe at home, or at worst in the newspaper offices of Valencia, hundreds of miles from the bullets and the mud. And apart from the libels of the inter-party feud, all the usual war-stuff, the tub-thumping, the heroics, the vilification of the enemy – all these were done, as usual, by people who were not fighting and who in many cases would have run a hundred miles sooner than fight. One of the dreariest effects of this war has been to teach me that the Left-wing press is every bit as spurious and dishonest as that of the Right.[1] I do earnestly feel that on our side – the Government side – this war was different from ordinary, imperialistic wars; but from the nature of the war-propaganda you would never have guessed it. The fighting had barely started when the newspapers of the Right and Left dived simultaneously into the same cesspool of abuse. We all remember the *Daily Mail*'s poster: 'REDS CRUCIFY NUNS,' while to the *Daily Worker* Franco's Foreign Legion was 'composed of murderers, white-slavers, dope-fiends and the offal of every European country'. As late as October 1937 the *New Statesman* was treating us to tales of Fascist barricades made of the bodies of living children (a most unhandy thing to make barricades with), and Mr Arthur Bryant was declaring that 'the sawing-off of a Conservative tradesman's legs' was 'a commonplace' in Loyalist Spain. The people who write that kind of stuff never fight; possibly they believe that to write it is a substitute for fighting. It is the same in all wars; the soldiers do the fighting, the journalists do the shouting, and no true patriot ever gets near a front-line trench, except on the briefest of propaganda-tours. Sometimes it is a comfort to me to think that the aeroplane is altering the conditions of war. Perhaps when the next great war comes we may see that sight unprecedented in all history, a jingo with a bullet-hole in him.

As far as the journalistic part of it went, this war was a racket like all other wars. But there was this difference, that whereas the journalists usually reserve their most murderous invective for the enemy, in this case,

---

[1] I should like to make an exception of the *Manchester Guardian*. In connection with this book I have had to go through the files of a good many English papers. Of our larger papers, the *Manchester Guardian* is the only one that leaves me with an increased respect for its honesty.

as time went on, the Communists and the POUM came to write more bitterly about one another than about the Fascists. Nevertheless at the time I could not bring myself to take it very seriously. The inter-party feud was annoying and even disgusting, but it appeared to me as a domestic squabble. I did not believe that it would alter anything or that there was any really irreconcilable difference of policy. I grasped that the Communists and Liberals had set their faces against allowing the revolution to go forward; I did not grasp that they might be capable of swinging it *back*.

There was a good reason for this. All this time I was at the front, and at the front the social and political atmosphere did not change. I had left Barcelona in early January and I did not go on leave till late April; and all this time – indeed, till later – in the strip of Aragón controlled by Anarchist and POUM troops, the same conditions persisted, at least outwardly. The revolutionary atmosphere remained as I had first known it. General and private, peasant and militiaman, still met as equals; everyone drew the same pay, wore the same clothes, ate the same food and called everyone else 'thou' and 'comrade'; there was no boss-class, no menial-class, no beggars, no prostitutes, no lawyers, no priests, no boot-licking, no cap-touching. I was breathing the air of equality, and I was simple enough to imagine that it existed all over Spain. I did not realise that more or less by chance I was isolated among the most revolutionary section of the Spanish working class.

So, when my more politically educated comrades told me that one could not take a purely military attitude towards the war, and that the choice lay between revolution and Fascism, I was inclined to laugh at them. On the whole I accepted the Communist viewpoint, which boiled down to saying: 'We can't talk of revolution till we've won the war,' and not the POUM viewpoint, which boiled down to saying: 'We must go forward or we shall go back.' When later on I decided that the POUM were right, or at any rate righter than the Communists, it was not altogether upon a point of theory. On paper the Communist case was a good one; the trouble was that their actual behaviour made it difficult to believe that they were advancing it in good faith. The often-repeated slogan: 'The war first and the revolution afterwards,' though devoutly believed in by the average PSUC militiaman, who honestly thought that the revolution could continue when the war had been won, was eyewash. The thing for which the Communists were working was not to postpone the Spanish revolution till a more suitable time, but to make sure that it never happened. This became more and more obvious as time went on, as power was twisted more and more out of working-class hands, and as more and more revolutionaries of every shade were flung into jail. Every move was made in the name of military necessity, because this pretext was, so to speak, ready-made, but the effect was to drive the workers back from an advantageous position and into a position in which, when the war was over, they would find it impossible to resist the reintroduction of capitalism. Please notice that I am saying nothing against the rank-and-file Communist, least of all against the thousands of Communists who died heroically round Madrid. But those were not the men who were directing party policy. As for the people higher up, it is inconceivable that they were not acting with their eyes open.

But, finally, the war was worth winning even if the revolution was lost. And in the end I came to doubt whether, in the long run, the Communist policy made for victory. Very few people seem to have reflected that a different policy might be appropriate at different periods of the war. The Anarchists probably saved the situation in the first two months, but they were incapable of organising resistance beyond a certain point; the Communists probably saved the situation in October–December, but to win the war outright was a different matter. In England the Communist war-policy has been accepted without question, because very few criticisms of it have been allowed to get into print and because its general line – do away with revolutionary chaos, speed up production, militarise the army – sounds realistic and efficient. It is worth pointing out its inherent weakness.

In order to check every revolutionary tendency and make the war as much like an ordinary war as possible, it became necessary to throw away the strategic opportunities that actually existed. I have described how we were armed, or not armed, on the Aragón front. There is very little doubt that arms were deliberately withheld lest too many of them should get into the hands of the Anarchists, who would afterwards use them for a revolutionary purpose; consequently the big Aragón offensive which would have made Franco draw back from Bilbao, and possibly from

Madrid, never happened. But this was comparatively a small matter. What was more important was that once the war had been narrowed down to a 'war for democracy' it became impossible to make any large-scale appeal for working-class aid abroad. If we face facts we must admit that the working class of the world has regarded the Spanish war with detachment. Tens of thousands of individuals came to fight, but the tens of millions behind them remained apathetic. During the first year of the war the entire British public is thought to have subscribed to various 'aid Spain' funds about a quarter of a million pounds – probably less than half of what they spend in a single week on going to the pictures. The way in which the working class in the democratic countries could really have helped her Spanish comrades was by industrial action – strikes and boycotts. No such thing ever even began to happen. The Labour and Communist leaders everywhere declared that it was unthinkable; and no doubt they were right, so long as they were also shouting at the tops of their voices that 'red' Spain was not 'red'. Since 1914–1918 'war for democracy' has had a sinister sound. For years past the Communists themselves had been teaching the militant workers in all countries that 'democracy' was a polite name for capitalism. To say first 'Democracy is a swindle', and then 'Fight for democracy!' is not good tactics. If, with the huge prestige of Soviet Russia behind them, they had appealed to the workers of the world in the name not of 'democratic Spain', but of 'revolutionary Spain', it is hard to believe that they would not have got a response.

But what was most important of all, with a non-revolutionary policy it was difficult, if not impossible, to strike at Franco's rear. By the summer of 1937 Franco was controlling a larger population than the Government – much larger, if one counts in the colonies – with about the same number of troops. As everyone knows, with a hostile population at your back it is impossible to keep an army in the field without an equally large army to guard your communications, suppress sabotage, etc. Obviously, therefore, there was no real popular movement in Franco's rear. It was inconceivable that the people in his territory, at any rate the town-workers and the poorer peasants, liked or wanted Franco, but with every swing to the Right the Government's superiority became less apparent. What clinches everything is the case of Morocco. Why was there no rising in Morocco?

Franco was trying to set up an infamous dictatorship, and the Moors actually preferred him to the Popular Front Government! The palpable truth is that no attempt was made to foment a rising in Morocco, because to do so would have meant putting a revolutionary construction on the war. The first necessity, to convince the Moors of the Government's good faith, would have been to proclaim Morocco liberated. And we can imagine how pleased the French would have been by that! The best strategic opportunity of the war was flung away in the vain hope of placating French and British capitalism. The whole tendency of the Communist policy was to reduce the war to an ordinary, non-revolutionary war in which the Government was heavily handicapped. For a war of that kind has got to be won by mechanical means, i.e. ultimately, by limitless supplies of weapons; and the Government's chief donor of weapons, the USSR, was at a great disadvantage, geographically, compared with Italy and Germany. Perhaps the POUM and Anarchist slogan: 'The war and the revolution are inseparable,' was less visionary than it sounds.

I have given my reasons for thinking that the Communist anti-revolutionary policy was mistaken, but so far as its effect upon the war goes I do not hope that my judgment is right. A thousand times I hope that it is wrong. I would wish to see this war won by any means whatever. And of course we cannot tell yet what may happen. The Government may swing to the Left again, the Moors may revolt of their own accord, England may decide to buy Italy out, the war may be won by straight-forward military means – there is no knowing. I let the above opinions stand, and time will show how far I am right or wrong.

But in February 1937 I did not see things quite in this light. I was sick of the inaction of the Aragón front and chiefly conscious that I had not done my fair share of the fighting. I used to think of the recruiting poster in Barcelona which demanded accusingly of passers-by: 'What have *you* done for democracy?' and feel that I could only answer. 'I have drawn my rations.' When I joined the militia I had promised myself to kill one Fascist – after all, if each of us killed one they would soon be extinct – and I had killed nobody yet, had hardly had the chance to do so. And of course I wanted to go to Madrid. Everyone in the army, whatever his political opinions, always wanted to go to Madrid. This would probably mean exchanging into the International Column, for the POUM had now very few troops at Madrid and the Anarchists not so many as formerly.

For the present, of course, one had to stay in the line, but I told everyone that when we went on leave I should, if possible, exchange into the International Column, which meant putting myself under Communist control. Various people tried to dissuade me, but no one attempted to interfere. It is fair to say that there was very little heresy-hunting in the POUM, perhaps not enough, considering their special circumstances; short of being a pro-Fascist no one was penalised for holding the wrong political opinions. I spent much of my time in the militia in bitterly criticising the POUM 'line', but I never got into trouble for it. There was not even any pressure upon one to become a political member of the party, though I think the majority of the militiamen did so. I myself never joined the party – for which afterwards, when the POUM was suppressed, I was rather sorry.

APPENDIX II

[Formerly Chapter XI of the First Edition, placed between Chapters IX and X of this edition at Orwell's request, preceded by the final paragraph of Chapter X of the First Edition (Chapter IX of this edition)]

If you are not interested in political controversy and the mob of parties and sub-parties with their confusing names (rather like the names of the generals in a Chinese war), please skip. It is a horrible thing to have to enter into the details of inter-party polemics; it is like diving into a cesspool. But it is necessary to try and establish the truth, so far as it is possible. This squalid brawl in a distant city is more important than might appear at first sight.

It will never be possible to get a completely accurate and unbiased account of the Barcelona fighting, because the necessary records do not exist. Future historians will have nothing to go upon except a mass of accusations and party propaganda. I myself have little data beyond what I saw with my own eyes and what I have learned from other eye-witnesses whom I believe to be reliable. I can, however, contradict some of the more flagrant lies and help to get the affair into some kind of perspective.

First of all, what actually happened?

For some time past there had been tension throughout Catalonia. Earlier in this book I have given some account of the struggle between Communists and Anarchists. By May 1937 things had reached a point at which some kind of violent outbreak could be regarded as inevitable. The immediate cause of friction was the Government's order to surrender all private weapons, coinciding with the decision to build up a heavily-armed 'non-political' police-force from which trade union members were to be excluded. The meaning of this was obvious to everyone; and it was also obvious that the next move would be the taking over of some of the key industries controlled by the CNT. In addition there was a certain amount of resentment among the working classes because of the growing contrast of wealth and poverty and a general vague feeling that the revolution had been sabotaged. Many people were agreeably surprised when there was no rioting on 1 May. On 3 May the Government decided to take over the Telephone Exchange, which had been operated since the beginning of the war mainly by CNT workers; it was alleged that it was badly run and that official calls were being tapped. Salas, the Chief of Police (who may or may not have been exceeding his orders), sent three lorry-loads of armed Assault Guards to seize the building, while the streets outside were cleared by armed police in civilian clothes. At about the same time bands of Assault Guards seized various other buildings in strategic spots. Whatever the real intention may have been, there was a widespread belief that this was the signal for a general attack on the CNT by the Assault Guards and the PSUC (Communists and Socialists). The word flew round the town that the workers' buildings were being attacked, armed Anarchists appeared on the streets, work ceased, and fighting broke out immediately. That night and the next morning barricades were built all over the town, and there was no break in the fighting until the morning of 6 May. The fighting was, however, mainly defensive on both sides. Buildings were besieged, but, so far as I know, none were stormed, and there was no use of artillery. Roughly speaking, the CNT–FAI–POUM forces held the working-class suburbs, and the armed police-forces and the PSUC held the central and official portion of the town. On 6 May there was an armistice, but fighting soon broke out again, probably because of premature attempts by Assault Guards to disarm CNT workers. Next morning, however, the people began to leave the barricades of their own accord. Up till, roughly, the night of 5 May the CNT had had the better of it, and large numbers of Assault Guards had surrendered. But there was no generally accepted leadership and no fixed plan – indeed, so far as one could judge, no plan at all except a vague determination to resist the Assault Guards. The official leaders of the CNT had joined with those of the UGT in imploring everyone to go back to work; above all, food was running short. In such circumstances nobody was sure enough of the issue to go on fighting. By the afternoon of 7 May conditions were almost normal. That evening six thousand Assault Guards, sent by sea from Valencia, arrived and took control of the town. The Government issued an order for the surrender of all arms except those held by the regular forces, and during the next few days large numbers of arms were seized. The casualties during the fighting were officially given out as four hundred killed and about a thousand wounded. Four hundred killed is possibly an exaggeration, but as there is no way of verifying this we must accept it as accurate.

Secondly, as to the after-effects of the fighting. Obviously it is imposs-ible to say with any certainty what these were. There is no evidence that the outbreak had any direct effect upon the course of the war, though obviously it must have had if it had continued even a few days longer. It was made the excuse for bringing Catalonia under the direct control of Valencia, for hastening the break-up of the militias, and for the suppression of the POUM, and no doubt it also had its share in bringing down the Caballero Government. But we may take it as certain that these things would have happened in any case. The real question is whether the CNT workers who came into the street gained or lost by showing fight on this occasion. It is pure guesswork, but my own opinion is that they gained more than they lost. The seizure of the Barcelona Telephone Exchange was simply one incident in a long process. Since the previous year direct power had been gradually manoeuvred out of the hands of the syndicates, and the general movement was away from working-class control and towards centralised control, leading on to State capitalism or, possibly, towards the reintroduction of private capitalism. The fact that at this point there was resistance probably slowed the process down. A year after the outbreak of war the Catalan workers had lost much of their power, but their position was still comparatively favourable. It might have been much less so if they had made it clear that they would lie down under no matter what provocation. There are occasions when it pays better to fight and be beaten than not to fight at all.

Thirdly, what purpose, if any, lay behind the outbreak? Was it any kind of *coup d'état* or revolutionary attempt? Did it definitely aim at overthrowing the Government? Was it preconcerted at all?

My own opinion is that the fighting was only preconcerted in the sense that everyone expected it. There were no signs of any very definite plan on either side. On the Anarchist side the action was almost certainly spontaneous, for it was an affair mainly of the rank and file. The people came into the streets and their political leaders followed reluctantly, or did not follow at all. The only people who even *talked* in a revolutionary strain were the Friends of Durruti, a small extremist group within the FAI, and the POUM. But once again they were following and not leading. The Friends of Durruti distributed some kind of revolutionary leaflet, but this did not appear until 5 May and cannot be said to have started the fighting, which had started of its own accord two days earlier. The official leaders of the CNT disowned the whole affair from the start. There were a number of reasons for this. To begin with, the fact that the CNT was still represented in the Government and the Generalidad ensured that its leaders would be more conservative than their followers. Secondly, the main object of the CNT leaders was to form an alliance with the UGT, and the fighting was bound to widen the split between CNT and UGT, at any rate for the time being. Thirdly – though this was not generally known at the time – the Anarchist leaders feared that if things went beyond a certain point and the workers took possession of the town, as they were perhaps in a position to do on 5 May, there would be foreign intervention. A British cruiser and two British destroyers had closed in upon the harbour, and no doubt there were other warships not far away. The English newspapers gave it out that these ships were proceeding to Barcelona 'to protect British interests', but in fact they made no move to do so; that is, they did not land any men or take off any refugees. There can be no certainty about this, but it was at least inherently likely that the British Government, which had not raised a finger to save the Spanish Government from Franco, would intervene quickly enough to save it from its own working class.

The POUM leaders did not disown the affair, in fact they encouraged their followers to remain at the barricades and even gave their approval (in *La Batalla*, 6 May) to the extremist leaflet issued by the Friends of Durruti. (There is great uncertainty about this leaflet, of which no one now seems able to produce a copy. In some of the foreign papers it was described as an 'inflammatory poster' which was 'plastered' all over the town. There was certainly no such poster. From comparison of various reports I should say that the leaflet called for (i) The formation of a revolutionary council (junta). (ii) The shooting of those responsible for the attack on the Telephone Exchange. (iii) The disarming of the Assault Guards. There is also some uncertainty as to how far *La Batalla* expressed agreement with the leaflet. I myself did not see the leaflet or *La Batalla* of that date. The only handbill I saw during the fighting was one issued by the tiny group of Trotskyists ('Bolshevik-Leninists') on 4 May. This merely said: 'Everyone to the barricades – general strike of all industries except war industries.' In other words, it merely demanded what was happening already.) But in reality the attitude of the POUM leaders was hesitating. They had never been in favour of insurrection until the war against Franco was won; on the other hand the workers had come into the streets, and the POUM leaders took the rather pedantic Marxist line that when the workers are on the streets it is the duty of the revolutionary parties to be with them. Hence, in spite of uttering revolutionary slogans about the 'reawakening of the spirit of 19 July', and so forth, they did their best to limit the workers' action to the defensive. They never, for instance, ordered an attack on any building; they merely ordered their followers to remain on guard and, as I mentioned in Chapter IX, not to fire when it could be avoided. *La Batalla* also issued instructions that no troops were to leave the front.[1] As far as one can estimate it, I should say that the responsibility of the POUM amounts to having urged everyone to remain at the barricades, and probably to having persuaded a certain number to remain there longer than they would otherwise have done. Those who were in personal touch with the POUM leaders at the time (I myself was not) have told me that they were in reality dismayed by the whole business,

---

[1] A recent number of *Inprecor* states the exact opposite – that *La Batalla* ordered the POUM troops to leave the front! The point can easily be settled by referring to *La Batalla* of the date named.

but felt that they had got to associate themselves with it. Afterwards, of course, political capital was made out of it in the usual manner. Gorkin, one of the POUM leaders, even spoke later of 'the glorious days of May'. From the propaganda point of view this may have been the right line; certainly the POUM rose somewhat in numbers during the brief period before its suppression. Tactically it was probably a mistake to give countenance to the leaflet of the Friends of Durruti, which was a very small organisation and normally hostile to the POUM. Considering the general excitement and the things that were being said on both sides, the leaflet did not in effect mean much more than 'Stay at the barricades,' but by seeming to approve of it while *Solidaridad Obrera*, the Anarchist paper, repudiated it, the POUM leaders made it easy for the Communist press to say afterwards that the fighting was a kind of insurrection engineered solely by the POUM. However, we may be certain that the Communist press would have said this in any case. It was nothing compared with the accusations that were made both before and afterwards on less evidence. The CNT leaders did not gain much by their more cautious attitude; they were praised for their loyalty but were levered out of both the Government and the Generalidad as soon as the opportunity arose.

So far as one could judge from what people were saying at the time, there was no real revolutionary intention anywhere. The people behind the barricades were ordinary CNT workers, probably with a sprinkling of UGT workers among them, and what they were attempting was not to overthrow the Government but to resist what they regarded, rightly or wrongly, as an attack by the police. Their action was essentially defensive, and I doubt whether it should be described, as it was in nearly all the foreign newspapers, as a 'rising'. A rising implies aggressive action and a definite plan. More exactly it was a riot – a very bloody riot, because both sides had fire-arms in their hands and were willing to use them.

But what about the intentions on the other side? If it was not an Anarchist *coup d'état*, was it perhaps a Communist *coup d'état* – a planned effort to smash the power of the CNT at one blow?

I do not believe it was, though certain things might lead one to suspect it. It is significant that something very similar (seizure of the Telephone Exchange by armed police acting under orders from Barcelona) happened in Tarragona two days later. And in Barcelona the raid on the Telephone

Exchange was not an isolated act. In various parts of the town bands of local Assault Guards and PSUC adherents seized buildings in strategic spots, if not actually before the fighting started, at any rate with surprising promptitude. But what one has got to remember is that these things were happening in Spain and not in England. Barcelona is a town with a long history of street-fighting. In such places things happen quickly, the factions are ready-made, everyone knows the local geography, and when the guns begin to shoot people take their places almost as in a fire-drill. Presumably those responsible for the seizure of the Telephone Exchange expected trouble – though not on the scale that actually happened – and had made ready to meet it. But it does not follow that they were planning a general attack on the CNT. There are two reasons why I do not believe that either side had made preparations for large-scale fighting:

(i) Neither side had brought troops to Barcelona beforehand. The fighting was only between those who were in Barcelona already, mainly civilians and police.

(ii) The food ran short almost immediately. Anyone who has served in Spain knows that the one operation of war that Spaniards perform really well is that of feeding their troops. It is most unlikely that if either side had contemplated a week or two of street-fighting and a general strike they would not have stored food beforehand.

Finally, as to the rights and wrongs of the affair.

A tremendous dust was kicked up in the foreign anti-Fascist press, but, as usual, only one side of the case has had anything like a hearing. As a result the Barcelona fighting has been represented as an insurrection by disloyal Anarchists and Trotskyists who were 'stabbing the Spanish Government in the back', and so forth. The issue was not quite so simple as that. Undoubtedly when you are at war with a deadly enemy it is better not to begin fighting among yourselves; but it is worth remembering that it takes two to make a quarrel and that people do not begin building barricades unless they have received something that they regard as a provocation.

The trouble sprang naturally out of the Government's order to the Anarchists to surrender their arms. In the English press this was translated into English terms and took this form: that arms were desperately needed on the Aragón front and could not be sent there because the unpatriotic

Anarchists were holding them back. To put it like this is to ignore the conditions actually existing in Spain. Everyone knew that both the Anarchists and the PSUC were hoarding arms, and when the fighting broke out in Barcelona this was made clearer still; both sides produced arms in abundance. The Anarchists were well aware that even if they surrendered their arms, the PSUC, politically the main power in Catalonia, would still retain theirs; and this in fact was what happened after the fighting was over. Meanwhile, actually visible on the streets, there were quantities of arms which would have been very welcome at the front, but which were being retained for the 'non-political' police-forces in the rear. And underneath this there was the irreconcilable difference between Communists and Anarchists, which was bound to lead to some kind of struggle sooner or later. Since the beginning of the war the Spanish Communist Party had grown enormously in numbers and captured most of the political power, and there had come into Spain thousands of foreign Communists, many of whom were openly expressing their intention of 'liquidating' Anarchism as soon as the war against Franco was won. In the circumstances one could hardly expect the Anarchists to hand over the weapons which they had got possession of in the summer of 1936.

The seizure of the Telephone Exchange was simply the match that fired an already existing bomb. It is perhaps just conceivable that those responsible imagined that it would not lead to trouble. Companys, the Catalan President, is said to have declared laughingly a few days earlier that the Anarchists would put up with anything.[1] But certainly it was not a wise action. For months past there had been a long series of armed clashes between Communists and Anarchists in various parts of Spain. Catalonia and especially Barcelona was in a state of tension that had already led to street affrays, assassinations, and so forth. Suddenly the news ran round the city that armed men were attacking the buildings that the workers had captured in the July fighting and to which they attached great sentimental importance. One must remember that the Civil Guards were not loved by the working-class population. For generations past *la guardia* had been simply an appendage of the landlord and the boss, and the Civil Guards were doubly hated because they were suspected, quite

[1] *New Statesman*, 14 May.

justly, of being of very doubtful loyalty against the Fascists.[1] It is probable that the emotion that brought people into the streets in the first few hours was much the same emotion as had led them to resist the rebel generals at the beginning of the war. Of course it is arguable that the CNT workers ought to have handed over the Telephone Exchange without protest. One's opinion here will be governed by one's attitude on the question of centralised government and working-class control. More relevantly it may be said: 'Yes, very likely the CNT had a case. But, after all, there was a war on, and they had no business to start a fight behind the lines.' Here I agree entirely. Any internal disorder was likely to aid Franco. But what actually precipitated the fighting? The Government may or may not have had the right to seize the Telephone Exchange; the point is that in the actual circumstances it was bound to lead to a fight. It was a provocative action, a gesture which said in effect, and presumably was meant to say: 'Your power is at an end – we are taking over.' It was not common sense to expect anything but resistance. If one keeps a sense of proportion one must realise that the fault was not – could not be, in a matter of this kind – entirely on one side. The reason why a one-sided version has been accepted is simply that the Spanish revolutionary parties have no footing in the foreign press. In the English press, in particular, you would have to search for a long time before finding any favourable reference, at any period of the war, to the Spanish Anarchists. They have been systematically denigrated, and, as I know by my own experience, it is almost impossible to get anyone to print anything in their defence.

I have tried to write objectively about the Barcelona fighting, though,

---

[1] At the outbreak of war the Civil Guards had everywhere sided with the stronger party. On several occasions later in the war, e.g. at Santander, the local Civil Guards went over to the Fascists in a body.

[Orwell originally mistook the Assault Guards in Barcelona for Civil Guards and thought only the troops brought from Valencia were Assault Guards. In his list of Errata he asked that 'Civil' be replaced by 'Assault' in the original chapters X and XI (now XI and *Appendix II*). But he also wished it made plain that the Civil Guards were hated. Fulfilling his wishes presents some textual problems. Details of how these have been resolved are given in A Note on the Text. Suffice here to note that on this occasion 'Civil' is retained; elsewhere, if there could be confusion, what he first called Civil Guards are referred to as 'local' Assault Guards and those brought into Barcelona are referred to as 'Valencian' Assault Guards. *Ed.*]

obviously, no one can be completely objective on a question of this kind. One is practically obliged to take sides, and it must be clear enough which side I am on. Again, I must inevitably have made mistakes of fact, not only here but in other parts of this narrative. It is very difficult to write accurately about the Spanish war, because of the lack of non-propagandist documents. I warn everyone against my bias, and I warn everyone against my mistakes. Still, I have done my best to be honest. But it will be seen that the account I have given is completely different from that which appeared in the foreign and especially the Communist press. It is necessary to examine the Communist version, because it was published all over the world, has been supplemented at short intervals ever since, and is probably the most widely accepted one.

In the Communist and pro-Communist press the entire blame for the Barcelona fighting was laid upon the POUM. The affair was represented not as a spontaneous outbreak, but as a deliberate, planned insurrection against the Government, engineered solely by the POUM with the aid of a few misguided 'uncontrollables'. More than this, it was definitely a Fascist plot, carried out under Fascist orders with the idea of starting civil war in the rear and thus paralysing the Government. The POUM was 'Franco's Fifth Column' – a 'Trotskyist' organisation working in league with the Fascists. According to the *Daily Worker* (11 May):

The German and Italian agents, who poured into Barcelona ostensibly to 'prepare' the notorious 'Congress of the Fourth International', had one big task. It was this:

They were – in co-operation with the local Trotskyists – to prepare a situation of disorder and bloodshed, in which it would be possible for the Germans and Italians to declare that they were 'unable to exercise naval control of the Catalan coasts effectively because of the disorder prevailing in Barcelona' and were, therefore, 'unable to do otherwise than land forces in Barcelona.'

In other words, what was being prepared was a situation in which the German and Italian Governments could land troops or marines quite openly on the Catalan coasts, declaring that they were doing so 'in order to preserve order' . . .

The instrument for all this lay ready to hand for the Germans and Italians in the shape of the Trotskyist organisation known as the POUM.

The POUM, acting in co-operation with well-known criminal elements, and with certain other deluded persons in the Anarchist organisations, planned, organised and led the attack in the rear-guard, accurately timed to coincide with the attack on the front at Bilbao, etc. etc.

Later in the article the Barcelona fighting becomes 'the POUM attack', and in another article in the same issue it is stated that there is 'no doubt that it is at the door of the POUM that the responsibility for the bloodshed in Catalonia must be laid'. *Inprecor* (29 May) states that those who erected the barricades in Barcelona were 'only members of the POUM organised from that party for this purpose'.

I could quote a great deal more, but this is clear enough. The POUM was wholly responsible and the POUM was acting under Fascist orders. In a moment I will give some more extracts from the accounts that appeared in the Communist press; it will be seen that they are so self-contradictory as to be completely worthless. But before doing so it is worth pointing to several *a priori* reasons why this version of the May fighting as a Fascist rising engineered by the POUM is next door to incredible.

(i) The POUM had not the numbers or influence to provoke disorders of this magnitude. Still less had it the power to call a general strike. It was a political organisation with no very definite footing in the trade unions, and it would have been hardly more capable of producing a strike throughout Barcelona than (say) the English Communist Party would be of producing a general strike throughout Glasgow. As I said earlier, the attitude of the POUM leaders may have helped to prolong the fighting to some extent; but they could not have originated it even if they had wanted to.

(ii) The alleged Fascist plot rests on bare assertion and all the evidence points in the other direction. We are told that the plan was for the German and Italian Governments to land troops in Catalonia; but no German or Italian troopships approached the coast. As to the 'Congress of the Fourth International' and the 'German and Italian agents', they are pure myth. So far as I know there had not even been any talk of a Congress of the Fourth International. There were vague plans for a Congress of the POUM and its brother-parties (English ILP, German SAP, etc. etc.); this had been tentatively fixed for some time in July – two months later – and not a single delegate had yet arrived. The 'German and Italian agents' have no existence outside the pages of the *Daily Worker*. Anyone who crossed the frontier at that time knows that it was not so easy to 'pour' into Spain, or out of it, for that matter.

(iii) Nothing happened either at Lérida, the chief stronghold of the POUM, or at the front. It is obvious that if the POUM leaders had wanted to aid the Fascists they would have ordered their militia to walk out of the line and let the Fascists through. But nothing of the kind was done or suggested. Nor were any extra men brought out of the line beforehand, though it would have been easy enough to smuggle, say, a thousand or two thousand men back to Barcelona on various pretexts. And there was no attempt even at indirect sabotage of the front. The transport of food, munitions, and so forth continued as usual; I verified this by inquiry afterwards. Above all, a planned rising of the kind suggested would have needed months of preparation, subversive propaganda among the militia, and so forth. But there was no sign or rumour of any such thing. The fact that the militia at the front played no part in the 'rising' should be conclusive. If the POUM were really planning a *coup d'état* it is inconceivable that they would not have used the ten thousand or so armed men who were the only striking force they had.

It will be clear enough from this that the Communist thesis of a POUM 'rising' under Fascist orders rests on less than no evidence. I will add a few more extracts from the Communist press. The Communist accounts of the opening incident, the raid on the Telephone Exchange, are illuminating; they agree in nothing except in putting the blame on the other side. It is noticeable that in the English Communist papers the blame is put first upon the Anarchists and only later upon the POUM. There is a fairly obvious reason for this. Not everyone in England has heard of 'Trotskyism', whereas every English-speaking person shudders at the name of 'Anarchist'. Let it once be known that 'Anarchists' are implicated, and the right atmosphere of prejudice is established; after that the blame can safely be transferred to the 'Trotskyists'. The *Daily Worker* begins thus (6 May):

A minority gang of Anarchists on Monday and Tuesday seized and attempted to hold the telephone and telegram buildings, and started firing into the street.

There is nothing like starting off with a reversal of roles. The local Assault Guards attack a building held by the CNT; so, the CNT are represented as attacking their own building – attacking themselves, in fact. On the other hand, the *Daily Worker* of 11 May states:

The Left Catalan Minister of Public Security, Ayguadé, and the United Socialist General Commissar of Public Order, Rodrique Salas, sent the armed republican police into the Telefónica building to disarm the employees there, most of them members of CNT unions.

This does not seem to agree very well with the first statement; nevertheless the *Daily Worker* contains no admission that the first statement was wrong. The *Daily Worker* of 11 May states that the leaflets of the Friends of Durruti, which were disowned by the CNT, appeared on 4 May and 5 May, during the fighting. *Inprecor* (22 May) states that they appeared on 3 May, *before* the fighting, and adds that 'in view of these facts' (the appearance of various leaflets):

The police, led by the Prefect of Police in person, occupied the central telephone exchange in the afternoon of May 3rd. The police were shot at while discharging their duty. This was the signal for the provocateurs to begin shooting affrays all over the city.

And here is *Inprecor* for 29 May:

At three o'clock in the afternoon the Commissar for Public Security, Comrade Salas, went to the Telephone Exchange, which on the previous night had been occupied by 50 members of the POUM and various uncontrollable elements.

This seems rather curious. The occupation of the Telephone Exchange by 50 POUM members is what one might call a picturesque circumstance, and one would have expected somebody to notice it at the time. Yet it appears that it was only discovered three or four weeks later. In another issue of *Inprecor* the 50 POUM members become 50 POUM militiamen. It would be difficult to pack together more contradictions than are contained in these few short passages. At one moment the CNT are attacking the Telephone Exchange, the next they are being attacked there; a leaflet appears before the seizure of the Telephone Exchange and is the cause of it, or, alternatively, appears afterwards and is the result of it; the people in the Telephone Exchange are alternatively CNT members and POUM members – and so on. And in a still later issue of the *Daily Worker*

(3 June) Mr J. R. Campbell informs us that the Government only seized the Telephone Exchange because the barricades were already erected!

For reasons of space I have taken only the reports of one incident, but the same discrepancies run all through the accounts in the Communist press. In addition there are various statements which are obviously pure fabrication. Here for instance is something quoted by the *Daily Worker* (7 May) and said to have been issued by the Spanish Embassy in Paris:

A significant feature of the uprising has been that the old monarchist flag was flown from the balcony of various houses in Barcelona, doubtless in the belief that those who took part in the rising had become masters of the situation.

The *Daily Worker* very probably reprinted this statement in good faith, but those responsible for it at the Spanish Embassy must have been quite deliberately lying. Any Spaniard would understand the internal situation better than that. A monarchist flag in Barcelona! It was the one thing that could have united the warring factions in a moment. Even the Communists on the spot were obliged to smile when they read about it. It is the same with the reports in the various Communist papers upon the arms supposed to have been used by the POUM during the 'rising'. They would be credible only if one knew nothing whatever of the facts. In the *Daily Worker* of 17 May Mr Frank Pitcairn states:

There were actually all sorts of arms used by them in the outrage. There were the arms which they have been stealing for months past, and hidden, and there were arms such as tanks, which they stole from the barracks just at the beginning of the rising. It is clear that scores of machine-guns and several thousand rifles are still in their possession.

Inprecor (29 May) also states:

On May 3rd the POUM had at its disposal some dozens of machine-guns and several thousand rifles . . .On the Plaza d'España the Trotskyists brought into action batteries of '75' guns which were destined for the front in Aragón and which the militia had carefully concealed on their premises.

Mr Pitcairn does not tell us how and when it became clear that the POUM possessed scores of machine-guns and several thousand rifles. I have given an estimate of the arms which were at three of the principal

POUM buildings – about eighty rifles, a few bombs, and no machine-guns; i.e. about sufficient for the armed guards which, at that time, all the political parties placed on their buildings. It seems strange that afterwards, when the POUM was suppressed and all its buildings seized, these thousands of weapons never came to light; especially the tanks and field-guns, which are not the kind of thing that can be hidden up the chimney. But what is revealing in the two statements above is the complete ignorance they display of the local circumstances. According to Mr Pitcairn the POUM stole tanks 'from the barracks'. He does not tell us which barracks. The POUM militiamen who were in Barcelona (now comparatively few, as direct recruitment to the party militias had ceased) shared the Lenin Barracks with a considerably larger number of Popular Army troops. Mr Pitcairn is asking us to believe, therefore, that the POUM stole tanks with the connivance of the Popular Army. It is the same with the 'premises' on which the 75-mm guns were concealed. There is no mention of where these 'premises' were. Those batteries of guns, firing on the Plaza de España, appeared in many newspaper reports, but I think we can say with certainty that they never existed. As I mentioned earlier, I heard no artillery-fire during the fighting, though the Plaza de España was only a mile or so away. A few days later I examined the Plaza de España and could find no buildings that showed marks of shell-fire. And an eye-witness who was in that neighbourhood throughout the fighting declares that no guns ever appeared there. (Incidentally, the tale of the stolen guns may have originated with Antonov-Ovseenko, the Russian Consul-General. He, at any rate, communicated it to a well-known English journalist, who afterwards repeated it in good faith in a weekly paper. Antonov-Ovseenko has since been 'purged'. How this would affect his credibility I do not know.) The truth is, of course, that these tales about tanks, field-guns, and so forth have only been invented because otherwise it is difficult to reconcile the scale of the Barcelona fighting with the POUM's small numbers. It was necessary to claim that the POUM was wholly responsible for the fighting; it was also necessary to claim that it was an insignificant party with no following and 'numbered only a few thousand members', according to *Inprecor*. The only hope of making both statements credible was to pretend that the POUM had all the weapons of a modern mechanised army.

It is impossible to read through the reports in the Communist Press without realising that they are consciously aimed at a public ignorant of the facts and have no other purpose than to work up prejudice. Hence, for instance, such statements as Mr Pitcairn's in the *Daily Worker* of 11 May that the 'rising' was suppressed by the Popular Army. The idea here is to give outsiders the impression that all Catalonia was solid against the 'Trotskyists'. But the Popular Army remained neutral throughout the fighting; everyone in Barcelona knew this, and it is difficult to believe that Mr Pitcarn did not know it too. Or again, the juggling in the Communist Press with the figures for killed and wounded, with the object of exaggerating the scale of the disorders. Díaz, General Secretary of the Spanish Communist Party, widely quoted in the Communist Press, gave the numbers as 900 dead and 2500 wounded. The Catalan Minister of Propaganda, who was hardly likely to underestimate, gave the numbers as 400 killed and 1000 wounded. The Communist Party doubles the bid and adds a few more hundreds for luck.

The foreign capitalist newspapers, in general, laid the blame for the fighting upon the Anarchists, but there were a few that followed the Communist line. One of these was the English *News Chronicle*, whose correspondent, Mr John Langdon-Davies, was in Barcelona at the time. I quote portions of his article here:

A TROTSKYIST REVOLT

. . . This has not been an Anarchist uprising. It is a frustrated *putsch* of the 'Trotskyist' POUM, working through their controlled organisations, 'Friends of Durruti' and Libertarian Youth . . . The tragedy began on Monday afternoon when the Government sent armed police into the Telephone Building, to disarm the workers there, mostly CNT men. Grave irregularities in the service had been a scandal for some time. A large crowd gathered in the Plaza de Cataluña outside, while the CNT men resisted, retreating floor by floor to the top of the building . . . The incident was very obscure, but word went round that the Government was out against the Anarchists. The streets filled with armed men . . . By nightfall every workers' centre and Government building was barricaded, and at ten o'clock the first volleys were fired and the first ambulances began ringing their way through the streets. By dawn all Barcelona was under fire . . . As the day wore on and the dead mounted to over a hundred, one could make a guess at what was happening. The Anarchist CNT and Socialist UGT were not technically 'out in the street'. So long as they remained behind the barricades they were merely watchfully waiting, an attitude which included the right to shoot at anything armed in the open street . . . (the) general bursts were invariably aggravated by *pacos* – hidden solitary men, usually Fascists, shooting from roof-tops at nothing in particular, but doing all they could to add to the general panic . . .By Wednesday evening, however, it began to be clear who was behind the revolt. All the walls had been plastered with an inflammatory poster calling for an immediate revolution and for the shooting of Republican and Socialist leaders. It was signed by the 'Friends of Durruti'. On Thursday morning the Anarchist daily denied all knowledge or sympathy with it, but *La Batalla*, the POUM paper, reprinted the document with the highest praise. Barcelona, the first city of Spain, was plunged into bloodshed by *agents provocateurs* using this subversive organisation.

This does not agree very completely with the Communist versions I have quoted above, but it will be seen that even as it stands it is self-contradictory. First the affair is described as 'a Trotskyist revolt', then it is shown to have resulted from a raid on the Telephone building and the general belief that the Government was 'out against' the Anarchists. The city is barricaded and both CNT and UGT are behind the barricades; two days afterwards the inflammatory poster (actually a leaflet) appears, and this is declared by implication to have started the whole business – effect preceding cause. But there is a piece of very serious misrepresentation here. Mr Langdon-Davies describes the Friends of Durruti and Libertarian Youth as 'controlled organisations' of the POUM. Both were Anarchist organisations and had no connection with the POUM. The Libertarian Youth was the youth league of the Anarchists, corresponding to the JSU of the PSUC, etc. The Friends of Durruti was a small organisation within the FAI, and was in general bitterly hostile to the POUM. So far as I can discover, there was no one who was a member of both. It would be about equally true to say that the Socialist League is a 'controlled organisation' of the English Liberal Party. Was Mr Langdon-Davies unaware of this? If he was, he should have written with more caution about this very complex subject.

I am not attacking Mr Langdon-Davies's good faith; but admittedly he left Barcelona as soon as the fighting was over, i.e. at the moment when he could have begun serious inquiries, and throughout his report there are clear signs that he has accepted the official version of a 'Trotskyist revolt' without sufficient verification. This is obvious even in the extract I have quoted. 'By nightfall' the barricades are built, and 'at ten o'clock' the first volleys are fired. These are not the words of an eye-witness. From this you would gather that it is usual to wait for your enemy to build a barricade before beginning to shoot at him. The impression given is that some hours elapsed between the building of the barricades and the firing of the first volleys; whereas – naturally – it was the other way about. I and many others saw the first volleys fired early in the afternoon. Again, there are the solitary men, 'usually Fascists', who are shooting from the roof-tops. Mr Langdon-Davies does not explain how he knew that these men were Fascists. Presumably he did not climb onto the roofs and ask them. He is simply repeating what he has been told and, as it fits in with the official version, is not questioning it. As a matter of fact, he indicates one probable source of much of his information by an incautious reference to the Minister of Propaganda at the beginning of his article. Foreign journalists in Spain were hopelessly at the mercy of the Ministry of Propaganda, though one would think that the very name of this ministry would be a sufficient warning. The Minister of Propaganda was, of course, about as likely to give an objective account of the Barcelona trouble as (say) the late Lord Carson would have been to give an objective account of the Dublin rising of 1916.

I have given reasons for thinking that the Communist version of the Barcelona fighting cannot be taken seriously. In addition I must say something about the general charge that the POUM was a secret Fascist organisation in the pay of Franco and Hitler.

This charge was repeated over and over in the Communist Press, especially from the beginning of 1937 onwards. It was part of the world-wide drive of the official Communist Party against 'Trotskyism', of which the POUM was supposed to be representative in Spain. 'Trotskyism', according to *Frente Rojo* (the Valencia Communist paper), 'is not a political doctrine. Trotskyism is an official capitalist organisation, a Fascist terrorist band occupied in crime and sabotage against the people.' The POUM was a 'Trotskyist' organisation in league with the Fascists and part of 'Franco's Fifth Column.' What was noticeable from the start was that no evidence was produced in support of this accusation; the thing was simply asserted with an air of authority. And the attack was made with the maximum of personal libel and with complete irresponsibility as to any effects it might have upon the war. Compared with the job of libelling the POUM, many Communist writers appear to have considered the betrayal of military secrets unimportant. In a February number of the *Daily Worker*, for instance, a writer (Winifred Bates) is allowed to state that the POUM had only half as many troops on its section of the front as it pretended. This was not true, but presumably the writer believed it to be true. She and the *Daily Worker* were perfectly willing, therefore, to hand to the enemy one of the most important pieces of information that can be handed through the columns of a newspaper. In the *New Republic* Mr Ralph Bates stated that the POUM troops were 'playing football with the Fascists in no-man's-land' at a time when, as a matter of fact, the POUM troops were suffering heavy casualties and a number of my personal friends were killed and wounded. Again, there was the malignant cartoon which was widely circulated, first in Madrid and later in Barcelona, representing the POUM as slipping off a mask marked with the hammer and sickle and revealing a face marked with the swastika. Had the Government not been virtually under Communist control it would never have permitted a thing of this kind to be circulated in wartime. It was a deliberate blow at the morale not only of the POUM militia, but of any others who happened to be near them; for it is not encouraging to be told that the troops next to you in the line are traitors. As a matter of fact, I doubt whether the abuse that was heaped upon them from the rear actually had the effect of demoralising the POUM militia. But certainly it was calculated to do so, and those responsible for it must be held to have put political spite before anti-Fascist unity.

The accusation against the POUM amounted to this: that a body of some scores of thousands of people, almost entirely working class, besides numerous foreign helpers and sympathisers, mostly refugees from Fascist countries, and thousands of militia, was simply a vast spying organisation in Fascist pay. The thing was opposed to common sense, and the past history of the POUM was enough to make it incredible. All the POUM leaders had revolutionary histories behind them. Some of them had been mixed up in the 1934 revolt, and most of them had been imprisoned for Socialist activities under the Lerroux Government or the monarchy. In 1936 its then leader, Joaquín Maurín, was one of the deputies who gave warning in the Cortes of Franco's impending revolt. Some time after the outbreak of war he was taken prisoner by the Fascists while trying to organise resistance in Franco's rear. When the revolt broke out the POUM played a conspicuous part in resisting it, and in Madrid, in particular, many of its members were killed in the street-fighting. It was one of the first bodies to form columns of militia in Catalonia and Madrid. It seems almost impossible to explain these as the actions of a party in Fascist pay. A party in Fascist pay would simply have joined in on the other side.

Nor was there any sign of pro-Fascist activities during the war. It was arguable – though finally I do not agree – that by pressing for a more revolutionary policy the POUM divided the Government forces and thus aided the Fascists; I think any Government of reformist type would be justified in regarding a party like the POUM as a nuisance. But this is a very different matter from direct treachery. There is no way of explaining why, if the POUM was really a Fascist body, its militia remained loyal. Here were eight or ten thousand men holding important parts of the line during the intolerable conditions of the winter of 1936–37. Many of them were in the trenches four or five months at a stretch. It is difficult to see why they did not simply walk out of the line or go over to the enemy. It was always in their power to do so, and at times the effect might have been decisive. Yet they continued to fight, and it was shortly after the POUM was suppressed as a political party, when the event was fresh in everyone's mind, that the militia – not yet redistributed among the Popular Army – took part in the murderous attack to the east of Huesca when several thousand men were killed in one or two days. At the very least one would have expected fraternisation with the enemy and a constant trickle of deserters. But, as I have pointed out earlier, the number of desertions was exceptionally small. Again, one would have expected pro-Fascist propaganda, 'defeatism' and so forth. Yet there was no sign of any such thing. Obviously there must have been Fascist spies and *agents provocateurs* in the POUM; they exist in all Left-wing parties; but there is no evidence that there were more of them there than elsewhere.

It is true that some of the attacks in the Communist Press said, rather grudgingly, that only the POUM leaders were in Fascist pay, and not the rank and file. But this was merely an attempt to detach the rank and file from their leaders. The nature of the accusation implied that ordinary members, militiamen, and so forth, were all in the plot together; for it was obvious that if Nin, Gorkin, and the others were really in Fascist pay, it was more likely to be known to their followers, who were in contact with them, than to journalists in London, Paris, and New York. And in any case, when the POUM was suppressed the Communist-controlled secret police acted on the assumption that all were guilty alike and arrested everyone connected with the POUM whom they could lay hands on, including even wounded men, hospital nurses, wives of POUM members and, in some cases, even children.

Finally, on 15–16 June, the POUM was suppressed and declared an illegal organisation. This was one of the first acts of the Negrín Government which came into office in May. When the Executive Committee of the POUM had been thrown into jail, the Communist Press produced what purported to be the discovery of an enormous Fascist plot. For a while the Communist Press of the whole world was flaming with this kind of thing (*Daily Worker*, 21 June, summarising various Spanish Communist papers):

SPANISH TROTSKYISTS PLOT WITH FRANCO

Following the arrest of a large number of leading Trotskyists in Barcelona and elsewhere . . . there became known, over the week-end, details of one of the most ghastly pieces of espionage ever known in wartime, and the ugliest revelation of Trotskyist treachery to date . . .Documents in the possession of the police, together with the full confession of no less than 200 persons under arrest, prove, etc. etc.

What these revelations 'proved' was that the POUM leaders were transmitting military secrets to General Franco by radio, were in touch with Berlin and were acting in collaboration with the secret Fascist organisation in Madrid. In addition there were sensational details about secret messages in invisible ink, a mysterious document signed with the letter N (standing for Nin), and so on and so forth.

But the final upshot was this: six months after the event, as I write, most of the POUM leaders are still in jail, but they have never been brought to trial, and the charges of communicating with Franco by radio, etc., have never even been formulated. Had they really been guilty of espionage they would have been tried and shot in a week, as so many Fascist spies had been previously. But not a scrap of evidence was ever produced except the unsupported statements in the Communist press. As for the two hundred 'full confessions', which, if they had existed, would have been enough to convict anybody, they have never been heard of again. They were, in fact, two hundred efforts of somebody's imagination.

More than this, most of the members of the Spanish Government have disclaimed all belief in the charges against the POUM. Recently the cabinet decided by five to two in favour of releasing anti-Fascist political prisoners; the two dissentients being the Communist ministers. In August an international delegation headed by James Maxton, MP, went to Spain to inquire into the charges against the POUM and the disappearance of Andrés Nin. Prieto, the Minister of National Defence, Irujo, the Minister of Justice, Zugazagoitia, Minister of the Interior, Ortega y Gasset, the Procureur-General, Prat García, and others all repudiated any belief in the POUM leaders being guilty of espionage. Irujo added that he had been through the dossier of the case, that none of the so-called pieces of evidence would bear examination, and that the document supposed to have been signed by Nin was 'valueless' – i.e. a forgery. Prieto considered the POUM leaders to be responsible for the May fighting in Barcelona, but dismissed the idea of their being Fascist spies. 'What is most grave,' he added, 'is that the arrest of the POUM leaders was not decided upon by the Government, and the police carried out these arrests on their own authority. Those responsible are not the heads of the police, but their entourage, which has been infiltrated by the Communists according to their usual custom.' He cited other cases of illegal arrests by the police. Irujo likewise declared that the police had become 'quasi-independent' and were in reality under the control of foreign Communist elements. Prieto hinted fairly broadly to the delegation that the Government could not afford to offend the Communist Party while the Russians were supplying arms. When another delegation, headed by John McGovern, MP, went to Spain in December, they got much the same answers as before, and Zugazagoitia, the Minister of the Interior, repeated Prieto's hint in even plainer terms. 'We have received aid from Russia and have had to permit certain actions which we did not like.' As an illustration of the autonomy of the police, it is interesting to learn that even with a signed order from the Director of Prisons and the Minister of Justice, McGovern and the others could not obtain admission to one of the 'secret prisons' maintained by the Communist Party in Barcelona.[1]

I think this should be enough to make the matter clear. The accusation of espionage against the POUM rested solely upon articles in the Communist press and the activities of the Communist-controlled secret police. The POUM leaders, and hundreds or thousands of their followers, are still in prison, and for six months past the Communist press has continued to clamour for the execution of the 'traitors'. But Negrín and the others have kept their heads and refused to stage a wholesale massacre of 'Trotskyists'. Considering the pressure that has been put upon them, it is greatly to their credit that they have done so. Meanwhile, in the face of what I have quoted above, it becomes very difficult to believe that the POUM was really a Fascist spying organisation, unless one also believes that Maxton, McGovern, Prieto, Irujo, Zugazagoitia, and the rest are all in Fascist pay together.

Finally, as to the charge that the POUM was 'Trotskyist'. This word is now flung about with greater and greater freedom, and it is used in a way that is extremely misleading and is often intended to mislead. It is worth stopping to define it. The word Trotskyist is used to mean three distinct things:

(i) One who, like Trotsky, advocates 'world revolution' as against 'Socialism in a single country.' More loosely, a revolutionary extremist.

(ii) A member of the actual organisation of which Trotsky is head.

(iii) A disguised Fascist posing as a revolutionary who acts especially by sabotage in the USSR, but, in general, by splitting and undermining the Left-wing forces.

In sense (i) the POUM could probably be described as Trotskyist. So

---

[1] For reports on the two delegations see *Le Populaire*, 7 September, *La Flèche*, 18 September, Report on the Maxton delegation published by *Independent News* (219 Rue Saint-Denis, Paris), and McGovern's pamphlet, *Terror in Spain*.

can the English ILP, the German SAP, the Left Socialists in France, and so on. But the POUM had no connection with Trotsky or the Trotskyist ('Bolshevik-Leninist') organisation. When the war broke out the foreign Trotskyists who came to Spain (fifteen or twenty in number) worked at first for the POUM, as the party nearest to their own viewpoint, but without becoming party-members; later Trotsky ordered his followers to attack the POUM policy, and the Trotskyists were purged from the party offices, though a few remained in the militia. Nin, the POUM leader after Maurín's capture by the Fascists, was at one time Trotsky's secretary, but had left him some years earlier and formed the POUM by the amalgam-ation of various Opposition Communists with an earlier party, the Workers' and Peasants' Bloc. Nin's one-time association with Trotsky had been used in the Communist press to show that the POUM was really Trotskyist. By the same line of argument it could be shown that the English Communist Party is really a Fascist organisation, because of Mr John Strachey's one-time association with Sir Oswald Mosley.

In sense (ii), the only exactly defined sense of the word, the POUM was certainly not Trotskyist. It is important to make this distinction, because it is taken for granted by the majority of Communists that a Trotskyist in sense (ii) is invariably a Trotskyist in sense (iii) – i.e. that the whole Trotskyist organisation is simply a Fascist spying-machine. 'Trotskyism' only came into public notice at the time of the Russian sabotage trials, and to call a man a Trotskyist is practically equivalent to calling him a murderer, *agent provocateur*, etc. But at the same time anyone who criticises Communist policy from a Left-wing standpoint is liable to be denounced as a Trotskyist. Is it then asserted that everyone professing revolutionary extremism is in Fascist pay?

In practice it is or is not, according to local convenience. When Maxton went to Spain with the delegation I have mentioned above, *Verdad, Frente Rojo*, and other Spanish Communist papers instantly denounced him as a 'Trotsky-Fascist', spy of the Gestapo and so forth. Yet the English Communists were careful not to repeat this accusation. In the English Communist press Maxton becomes merely a 'reactionary enemy of the working class', which is conveniently vague. The reason, of course, is simply that several sharp lessons have given the English Communist press a wholesome dread of the law of libel. The fact that the accusation was not repeated in a country where it might have to be proved is sufficient confession that it is a lie.

It may seem that I have discussed the accusations against the POUM at greater length than was necessary. Compared with the huge miseries of a civil war, this kind of internecine squabble between parties, with its inevitable injustices and false accusations, may appear trivial. It is not really so. I believe that libels and press-campaigns of this kind, and the habits of mind they indicate, are capable of doing the most deadly damage to the anti-Fascist cause.

Anyone who has given the subject a glance knows that the Communist tactic of dealing with political opponents by means of trumped-up accusations is nothing new. Today the key-word is 'Trotsky-Fascist'; yesterday it was 'Social-Fascist'. It is only six or seven years since the Russian State trials 'proved' that the leaders of the Second International, including, for instance, Léon Blum and prominent members of the British Labour Party, were hatching a huge plot for the military invasion of the USSR. Yet today the French Communists are glad enough to accept Blum as a leader, and the English Communists are raising heaven and earth to get inside the Labour Party. I doubt whether this kind of thing pays, even from a sectarian point of view. And meanwhile there is no possible doubt about the hatred and dissension that the 'Trotsky-Fascist' accusation is causing. Rank-and-file Communists everywhere are led away on a senseless witch-hunt after 'Trotskyists', and parties of the type of the POUM are driven back into the terribly sterile position of being mere anti-Communist parties. There is already the beginning of a dangerous split in the world working-class movement. A few more libels against life-long Socialists, a few more frame-ups like the charges against the POUM, and the split may become irreconcilable. The only hope is to keep political controversy on a plane where exhaustive discussion is possible. Between the Communists and those who stand or claim to stand to the Left of them there is a real difference. The Communists hold that Fascism can be beaten by alliance with sections of the capitalist class (the Popular Front); their opponents hold that this manoeuvre simply gives Fascism new breeding-grounds. The question has got to be settled; to make the wrong decision may be to land ourselves in for centuries of semi-slavery. But so long as no argument is produced except a scream of 'Trotsky-Fascist!' the discussion cannot even begin. It would be impossible for me, for instance, to debate the rights and wrongs of the Barcelona fighting with a Communist Party member, because no Communist – that is to say, no 'good' Communist – could admit that I have given a truthful account of the facts. If he followed his party 'line' dutifully he would have to declare that I am lying or, at best, that I am hopelessly misled and that anyone who glanced at the *Daily Worker* headlines a thousand miles from the scene of events knows more of what was happening in Barcelona than I do. In such circumstances there can be no argument; the necessary minimum of agreement cannot be reached. What purpose is served by saying that men like Maxton are in Fascist pay? Only the purpose of making serious discussion impossible. It is as though in the middle of a chess tournament one competitor should suddenly begin screaming that the other is guilty of arson or bigamy. The point that is really at issue remains untouched. Libel settles nothing.

---

[378]

'Spilling the Spanish Beans'
New English Weekly, *29 July and 2 September 1937*

I

The Spanish War has probably produced a richer crop of lies than any event since the Great War of 1914–18, but I honestly doubt, in spite of all those hecatombs of nuns who have been raped and crucified before the eyes of *Daily Mail* reporters, whether it is the pro-Fascist newspapers that have done the most harm. It is the left-wing papers, the *News Chronicle* and the *Daily Worker*,[1] with their far subtler methods of distortion, that have prevented the British public from grasping the real nature of the struggle.

The fact which these papers have so carefully obscured is that the Spanish Government (including the semi-autonomous Catalan Government) is far more afraid of the revolution than of the Fascists. It is now almost certain that the war will end with some kind of compromise, and there is even reason to doubt whether the Government, which let Bilbao fall without raising a finger, wishes to be too victorious; but there is no doubt whatever about the thoroughness with which it is crushing its own revolutionaries. For some time past a reign of terror – forcible suppression of political parties, a stifling censorship of the Press, ceaseless espionage and mass-imprisonment without trial – has been in progress. When I left Barcelona in late June the jails were bulging; indeed, the regular jails had long since overflowed and the prisoners were being huddled into empty shops and any other temporary dump that could be found for them. But the point to notice is that the people who are in prison now are not Fascists but revolutionaries; they are there not because their opinions are too much to the Right, but because they are too much to the Left. And the people responsible for putting them there are those dreadful revolutionaries at whose very name Garvin[2] quakes in his goloshes – the Communists.

Meanwhile the war against Franco continues, but, except for the poor devils in the front-line trenches, nobody in Government Spain thinks of it as the real war. The real struggle is between revolution and counter-revolution; between the workers who are vainly trying to hold on to a little of what they won in 1936, and the Liberal-Communist bloc who are so successfully taking it away from them. It is unfortunate that so few people in England have yet caught up with the fact that Communism is now a counter-revolutionary force; that Communists everywhere are in alliance with bourgeois reformism and using the whole of their powerful machinery to crush or discredit any party that shows signs of revolutionary tendencies. Hence the grotesque spectacle of Communists assailed as wicked 'Reds' by right-wing intellectuals who are in essential agreement with them. Mr. Wyndham Lewis,[3] for instance, ought to love the Communists, at least temporarily. In Spain the Communist-Liberal alliance has been almost completely victorious. Of all that the Spanish workers won for themselves in 1936 nothing solid remains, except for a few collective farms and a certain amount of land seized by the peasants last year; and presumably even the peasants will be sacrificed later, when there is no longer any need to placate them. To see how the present situation arose, one has got to look back to the origins of the civil war.

Franco's bid for power differed from those of Hitler and Mussolini in that it was a military insurrection, comparable to a foreign invasion, and therefore had not much mass backing, though Franco has since been trying to acquire one. Its chief supporters, apart from certain sections of Big Business, were the land-owning aristocracy and the huge, parasitic Church. Obviously a rising of this kind will array against it various forces which are not in agreement on any other point. The peasant and the worker hate feudalism and clericalism; but so does the 'liberal' bourgeois, who is not in the least opposed to a more modern version of Fascism, at least so long as it isn't called Fascism. The 'liberal' bourgeois is genuinely liberal up to the point where his own interests stop. He stands for the degree of progress implied in the phrase 'la carrière ouverte aux talents'. For clearly he has no chance to develop in a feudal society where the worker and the peasant are too poor to buy goods, where industry is burdened with huge taxes to pay for bishops' vestments, and where every lucrative job is given as a matter of course to the friend or the catamite of the duke's illegitimate son. Hence, in the face of such a blatant reactionary as Franco, you get for a while a situation in which the worker and the bourgeois, in reality deadly enemies, are fighting side by side. This uneasy alliance is known as the Popular Front (or, in the Communist press, to give it a spuriously democratic appeal, People's Front). It is a combination with about as much vitality, and about as much right to exist, as a pig with two heads or some other Barnum and Bailey[4] monstrosity.

In any serious emergency the contradiction implied in the Popular Front is bound to make itself felt. For even when the worker and the bourgeois are both fighting against Fascism, they are not fighting for the same things; the bourgeois is fighting for bourgeois democracy, *i.e.*, capitalism; the worker, in so far as he understands the issue, for Socialism. And in the early days of the revolution the Spanish workers understood the issue very well. In the areas where Fascism was defeated they did not content themselves with driving the rebellious troops out of the towns; they also took the opportunity of seizing land and factories and setting up the rough beginnings of a workers' government by means of local committees, workers' militias, police forces, and so forth. They made the mistake, however (possibly because most of the active revolutionaries were Anarchists with a mistrust of all parliaments), of leaving the Republican Government in nominal control. And, in spite of various changes in personnel, every subsequent Government had been of approximately the same bourgeois-reformist character. At the beginning this seemed not to matter, because the Government, especially in Catalonia, was almost powerless and the bourgeoisie had to lie low or even (this was still happening when I reached Spain in December) to disguise themselves as workers. Later, as power slipped from the hands of the Anarchists into the hands of the Communists and right-wing Socialists, the Government was able to reassert itself, the bourgeoisie came out of hiding and the old division of society into rich and poor reappeared, not much modified. Henceforward every move, except a few dictated by military emergency, was directed towards undoing the work of the first few months of revolution. Out of the many illustrations I could choose, I will cite only one, the breaking-up of the old workers' militias, which were organised on a genuinely democratic system, with officers and men receiving the same pay and mingling on terms of complete equality, and the substitution of the Popular Army (once again, in Communist jargon, 'People's Army'), modelled as far as possible on an ordinary bourgeois army, with a privileged officer-caste, immense differences of pay, etc., etc. Needless to say, this is given out as a military necessity, and almost certainly it does make for military efficiency, at least for a short period. But the undoubted purpose of the change was to strike a blow at equalitarianism. In every department the same policy has been followed, with the result that only a year after the outbreak of war and revolution you get what is in effect an ordinary bourgeois State, with, in addition, a reign of terror to preserve the status quo.

This process would probably have gone less far if the struggle could have taken place without foreign interference. But the military weakness of the Government made this impossible. In the face of Franco's foreign mercenaries they were obliged to turn to Russia for help, and though the quantity of arms supplied by Russia has been greatly exaggerated (in my first three months in Spain I saw only one Russian weapon, a solitary machine-gun), the mere fact of their arrival brought the Communists into power. To begin with, the Russian aeroplanes and guns, and the good military qualities of the International Brigades (not necessarily Communist but under Communist control), immensely raised the Communist prestige. But, more important, since Russia and Mexico were the only countries openly supplying arms, the Russians were able not only to get money for their weapons, but to extort terms as well. Put in their crudest form, the terms were: 'Crush the revolution or you get no more arms.' The reason usually given for the Russian attitude is that if Russia appeared to be abetting the revolution, the Franco-Soviet pact (and the hoped-for alliance with Great Britain) would be imperilled; it may be, also, that the spectacle of a genuine revolution in Spain would rouse unwanted echoes in Russia. The Communists, of course, deny that any direct pressure has been exerted by the Russian Government. But this, even if true, is hardly relevant, for the Communist Parties of all countries can be taken as carrying out Russian policy; and it is certain that the Spanish Communist Party, plus the right-wing Socialists whom they control, plus the Communist Press of the whole world, have used all their immense and ever-increasing influence upon the side of counter-revolution.

II

In the first half of this article I suggested that the real struggle in Spain, on the Government side, has been between revolution and counter-revolution; that the Government, though anxious enough to avoid being beaten by Franco, has been even more anxious to undo the revolutionary changes with which the outbreak of war was accompanied.

Any Communist would reject this suggestion as mistaken or wilfully dishonest. He would tell you that it is nonsense to talk of the Spanish Government crushing the revolution, because the revolution never happened; and that our job at present is to defeat Fascism and defend democracy. And in this connection it is most important to see just how the Communist anti-revolutionary propaganda works. It is a mistake to think that this has no relevance in England, where the Communist Party is small and comparatively weak. We shall see its relevance quickly enough if England enters into an alliance with the U.S.S.R.; or perhaps even earlier, for the influence of the Communist Party is bound to increase – visibly is increasing – as more and more of the capitalist class realise that latter-day Communism is playing their game.

Broadly speaking, Communist propaganda depends upon terrifying people with the (quite real) horrors of Fascism. It also involves pretending

– not in so many words, but by implication – that Fascism has nothing to do with capitalism. Fascism is just a kind of meaningless wickedness, an aberration, 'mass sadism', the sort of thing that would happen if you suddenly let loose an asylum full of homicidal maniacs. Present Fascism in this form, and you can mobilise public opinion against it, at any rate for a while, without provoking any revolutionary movement. You can oppose Fascism by bourgeois 'democracy', meaning capitalism. But meanwhile you have got to get rid of the troublesome person who points out that Fascism and bourgeois 'democracy' are Tweedledum and Tweedledee. You do it at the beginning by calling him an impracticable visionary. You tell him that he is confusing the issue, that he is splitting the anti-Fascist forces, that this is not the moment for revolutionary phrase-mongering, that for the moment we have got to fight against Fascism without enquiring too closely what we are fighting *for*. Later, if he still refuses to shut up, you change your tune and call him a traitor. More exactly, you call him a Trotskyist.[5]

And what is a Trotskyist? This terrible word – in Spain at this moment you can be thrown into jail and kept there indefinitely, without trial, on the mere rumour that you are a Trotskyist – is only beginning to be bandied to and fro in England. We shall be hearing more of it later. The word 'Trotskyist' (or 'Trotsky-Fascist') is generally used to mean a disguised Fascist who poses as an ultra-revolutionary in order to split the left-wing forces. But it derives its peculiar power from the fact that it means three separate things. It can mean one who, like Trotsky, wishes for world-revolution; or a member of the actual organization of which Trotsky is head (the only legitimate use of the word); or the disguised Fascist already mentioned. The three meanings can be telescoped one into the other at will. Meaning No. 1 may or may not carry with it meaning No. 2, and meaning No. 2 almost invariably carries with it meaning No. 3. Thus: 'XY has been heard to speak favourably of world-revolution; therefore he is a Trotskyist; therefore he is a Fascist.' In Spain, to some extent even in England, *anyone* professing revolutionary Socialism (*i.e.*, professing the things the Communist Party professed until a few years ago) is under suspicion of being a Trotskyist in the pay of Franco or Hitler.

The accusation is a very subtle one, because in any given case, unless one happened to know the contrary, it might be true. A Fascist spy probably *would* disguise himself as a revolutionary. In Spain, everyone whose opinions are to the Left of those of the Communist Party is sooner or later discovered to be a Trotskyist, or at least, a traitor. At the beginning of the war the P.O.U.M., an Opposition Communist party roughly corresponding to the English I.L.P., was an accepted party and supplied a minister to the Catalan Government; later it was expelled from the Government; then it was denounced as Trotskyist; then it was suppressed, every member that the police could lay their hands on being flung into jail.

Until a few months ago the Anarcho-Syndicalists were described as 'working loyally' beside the Communists. Then the Anarcho-Syndicalists were levered out of the Government; then it appeared that they were not working so loyally; now they are in the process of becoming traitors. After that will come the turn of the Left-wing Socialists. Caballero,[6] the Left-wing Socialist ex-premier, until May, 1937, the idol of the Communist Press, is already in outer darkness, a Trotskyist and 'enemy of the people'. And so the game continues. The logical end is a régime in which every opposition party and newspaper is suppressed and every dissentient of any importance is in jail. Of course, such a régime will be Fascism. It will not be the same as the Fascism Franco would impose, it will even be better than Franco's Fascism to the extent of being worth fighting for, but it will be Fascism. Only, being operated by Communists and Liberals, it will be called something different.

Meanwhile, can the war be won? The Communist influence has been against revolutionary chaos and has therefore, apart from the Russian aid, tended to produce greater military efficiency. If the Anarchists saved the Government from August to October, 1936, the Communists have saved it from October onwards. But in organizing the defence they have succeeded in killing enthusiasm (inside Spain, not outside). They made a militarized conscript army possible, but they also made it necessary. It is significant that as early as January of this year voluntary recruiting had practically ceased. A revolutionary army can sometimes win by enthusiasm, but a conscript army has got to win with weapons, and it is unlikely that the Government will ever have a large preponderance of arms unless France intervenes or unless Germany and Italy decide to make off with the Spanish colonies and leave Franco in the lurch. On the whole, a deadlock seems the likeliest thing.

And does the Government seriously intend to win? It does not intend to lose, that is certain. On the other hand, an outright victory, with Franco in flight and the Germans and Italians driven into the sea, would raise difficult problems, some of them too obvious to need mentioning. There is no real evidence and one can only judge by the event, but I suspect that what the Government is playing for is a compromise that would leave the war-situation essentially in being. All prophecies are wrong, therefore this one will be wrong, but I will take a chance and say that though the war may end quite soon or may drag on for years, it will end with Spain divided up, either by actual frontiers or into economic zones. Of course, such a compromise might be claimed as a victory by either side, or by both.

All that I have said in this article would seem entirely commonplace in Spain, or even in France. Yet in England, in spite of the intense interest the Spanish war has aroused, there are very few people who have even heard of the enormous struggle that is going on behind the Government lines. Of course, this is no accident. There has been a quite deliberate conspiracy (I could give detailed instances) to prevent the Spanish situation from being understood. People who ought to know better have lent themselves to the deception on the ground that if you tell the truth about Spain it will be used as Fascist propaganda.

It is easy to see where such cowardice leads. If the British public had been given a truthful account of the Spanish war they would have had an opportunity of learning what Fascism is and how it can be combated. As it is, the *News Chronicle* version of Fascism as a kind of homicidal mania peculiar to Colonel Blimps bombinating in the economic void has been established more firmly than ever. And thus we are one step nearer to the great war 'against Fascism' (cf. 1914, 'against militarism') which will allow Fascism, British variety, to be slipped over our necks during the first week.

1. The *News Chronicle* was politically aligned to the Liberal Party's viewpoint. In his column, 'As I Please', 30, *Tribune*, 23 June 1944 (*2492*), Orwell described its politics as 'a very pale pink – about the colour of shrimp paste'. It ceased publication on 17 October 1960 when it was merged with the right-wing *Daily Mail*. The latter, founded by Alfred Harmsworth

(later Lord Northcliffe) in 1896, introduced popular journalism to the United Kingdom; it is still in circulation. The *Daily Worker* represented Communist Party views and politics and ran from 1 January 1930 to 23 April 1966; it was then incorporated in the *Morning Star*. It was suppressed by government order from 22 January 1941 to 6 September 1942.

2. J. L. Garvin was the right-wing editor of the *Observer*, 1908–42.

3. Percy Wyndham Lewis (1882–1957) was a painter, author, satirist and critic. His review *Blast* (1914 and 1915) espoused Vorticism. He supported Franco and flirted with Nazism, recanting in 1939; see *Time and Tide*, 17 January and 14 February 1939, and *The Hitler Cult, and How it will End* (1939). In Orwell's words, 'Lewis attacked everyone in turn; indeed, his reputation as a writer rests largely on these attacks' (see 'Inside the Whale', 600).

4. P. T. Barnum (1810–91) was a great American showman one of whose major attractions was General Tom Thumb. His circus, 'The Greatest Show on Earth', 1871, amalgamated with that of J. A. Bailey as Barnum and Bailey's ten years later.

5. See the documents presented to the Tribunal for Espionage and High Treason reproduced above, in which, unbeknown to Orwell, he, Eileen and Charles Doran are described as 'confirmed Trotskyists' (*trotzkistas pronunciados*).

6. Francisco Largo Caballero (1869–1946), a left-wing Socialist and Prime Minister and Minister of War in the Popular Front government of Socialists, Communists, Anarchists and some liberal Republicans from 4 September 1936 to 17 May 1937. He is described by Thomas as 'a good trade-union organizer without vision' whose 'political errors of judgement . . . were at the heart of the problems of the republic in the months before the conflict' (933). The Germans imprisoned him in a concentration camp for four years; he died in Paris, not long after his release, in 1946.

[378A]

Eileen Blair to John McNair
29 July 1937   Carbon copy

Although the letters written by George Kopp to Laurence O'Shaughnessy, Lieutenant-Colonel Burillo and Eileen that follow this letter are dated 7 and 8 July, their contents were only known to Eileen (and Orwell) on 29 July, and they are therefore best placed here, to provide a context for letters written thereafter.

The Stores, Wallington, Near Baldock, Herts

Dear John,

Herewith two enclosures. Number 1 is a copy of an ultimatum sent by George Kopp to the Chief of Police in Barcelona, together with the letter which accompanied it to my brother. Number 2 is an extract from a letter written by George Kopp to me, which is to some extent repetition of Number 1 but which gives more details of the conditions of imprisonment and will interest you personally by its reference to individuals.

You will see that the important facts emerging from all the documents are that George intended to go on hunger strike on the 9th or 10th July unless he obtained some satisfaction from the Chief of Police and that he wishes his action to be given publicity. Partly because you know the conditions in Spain, I think you will be best able to decide the manner of this publicity – there is of course a strong possibility that George will be made to suffer for it however it is done, but he will have considered that himself; the main doubt appears to be whether his name should be given or not.

It seems almost certain that the hunger strike has occurred, but actually these letters, although written on the 7th and 8th of July, only reached me this morning. In any case, if there is no further news before the next issue of the *New Leader*, we may assume that he is on strike and unable to communicate. As for publicity outside the *New Leader*, you and Fenner will know better than we what hope there is. Judging from Eric's experiences in attempting to publish the most conservative truth, we shall not find the English-press the least enthusiastic.[1]

Jock Branthwaite[2] proposed to come over to Letchworth on Monday[3] on a bicycle to hear you speak and to see you. We only have one bicycle; so he will represent the whole party on that day, but you could perhaps tell him what you think. Apparently George Tioli[4] still being helpful, which is really a magnificent gesture.

I hope to see you myself some time during next week – indeed I hope to see you *here*. Apart from all the sentimental considerations, there are a few hundred things I want to know.

Yours ever,
[Unsigned]

I forgot to say that the two earlier letters to which George refers never arrived.

George Kopp to Dr Laurence O'Shaughnessy
7 July 1937   Handwritten

Dear Mr O'Shaughnessy,

Will you please transmit to your sister the enclosed copy of a letter I am sending to the Chief of Police and tell her that if I have not received a satisfactory reply to same within 48 hours I shall begin a hunger strike. The way myself and my friends are treated makes it a duty for me to volunteer in the only way of protest which is left to us. In the case I am reduced to this measure, I want my friends in England and the I.L.P. people to give this fact the publicity without which it would be useless. You will receive further news after the 48 hours have elapsed. In the case you have no news within a week, it means I am on strike but put in a place where unable to send messages from.

I have written two letters to Eileen which have been posted at[5] your address and I hope you have been able to forward at least the first; the second, perhaps, never reached you, Ethel Macdonald,[6] who took care of my mail, having been arrested without my knowing if this particular message has been posted before her detention.

I am sorry to have to trouble you with all this, but I agreed with your sister to communicate with her through you. Tell her I am intensely thinking of her and give her my love. Shake hands to Eric.

Sincerely yours
(Signed) George Kopp

Translation of letter written in Spanish by George Kopp to Lieutenant-Colonel Burillo,[7] Chief of Police, Barcelona
7 July 1937

I was arrested on the 20th June when I had just got back from Valencia on a military commission and was prepared to carry out the orders of my superior officers. The police-agents who detained me told me that it was a question of furnishing the police with certain information which they believed it was in my power to give them, in order to help them with the investigation of a case of espionage, which I am always ready and delighted to do.

In the course of the day on which I was arrested I addressed to you a letter which I entrusted to the Captain of Assault Guards who was charged with my detention. The reason for this letter was that, in spite of the urgency of the military mission that had been entrusted to me, I had not yet been interrogated at 6 in the evening. I asked you to have me interrogated immediately or, if that was not possible, to do me the favour of receiving me personally.

I presume that my letter has been duly delivered to you, but your answer has never reached me.

It is now eighteen days that I have been imprisoned and I [have] not yet been interrogated, nor have I been told the reason for my arrest – I should rather say the supposed reason, for there is no reason for it in my actions.

I am detained in conditions which are intolerable for any decent individual, and which, in the case of an officer of the Spanish Army who has served for eight months at the front, amount to an insult. I am mixed up with pickpockets, tramps, thieves, fascists and homosexuals. I am, like the rest of the principal prisoners, confined in a room where as many as 18 persons are put and where there is only room for 3 or 4; all species of exercise is denied us; the food, consisting of 2 plates of soup and 150 grammes of bread, is distributed at unsuitable hours (4 in the afternoon and 11 at night); the guards, although I personally have no serious ground for complaint and though some of them carry out their duties in a decent manner, treat us like cattle, beating the prisoners and insulting them even to the point of insulting their mothers.

It appears to me that a foreign volunteer, an officer of the Belgian Army, who, after aiding the legal Government of Spain by secretly manufacturing munitions in his own country, comes to enlist in the anti-fascist militia and fights at the front where he is successively commander of a company, a battalion and a regiment, does not merit this kind of treatment. Nor is such treatment merited by the prisoners whom I have seen here and who after weeks of imprisonment do not know why they have been arrested.

I do not know how far the patience of these other prisoners will stretch, nor do I know what opinion they entertain of your sense of justice, but for my own part I have come to the end of the time when I could regard my experiences with good humour, and I have no reason for doubting your integrity. I therefore address you for the second time, asking you to give me the chance of clearing myself of any accusations that can be made against me, and to do so without loss of time, since I am needed at the front.

Awaiting your reply, I remain your servant and that of the anti-fascist cause.

(Signed) Commandante Jorge Kopp

George Kopp to Eileen Blair

8 July 1937   Typed copy of handwritten original (which has not been traced)

Barcelona, in jail

I have written you two letters c/o Laurence O'Shaughnessy but am not sure the second one reached you because Ethel Macdonald has been arrested and part of the mail she was in charge of had to be destroyed; it is not known if my letter was in that case.

I still have not been interrogated which is very bad sign; all the others have and most of the questions aimed to establish *my* attitude during the May Days. Absolutely frightened people have made wild statements and some of the Moka's guards state that on each of the Poliorama's towers[8] I had a machine gun and that a heavy barrage of fire and bombs was unceasingly produced from this position during three days. I have written yesterday a sort of ultimatum to Lt. Colonel Burillo, chief of the police, and if I do not get a proper answer within 48 hours, I shall start a hunger strike as a protest not only for my case but principally for the way we all are treated here. The prisoners are beaten and insulted and I know that if actual offence should be done to me, I shall kill the guard with bare fists, which will not be a solution for the rest of us. I have sent to Laurence (for you) the copy of my ultimatum and a short note stating that I want this hunger strike business to be given a broad publicity in England and France and that further news will be sent to let you know if really I was compelled to this measure. Without publicity, my sacrifice will be useless. We are now 18 in the 10' by 15' room and not allowed even to take a short walk in the passage. Nobody visits me; David[9] has sent me a French poetry book with the mention 'from an almost subterranean swine'; no news from George[10] who is my only hope for sending out of Spain my correspondence. I sent out messages to the Hotel Victoria to be transmitted but do not know if they are duly forwarded. My money has got out last week but Harry Milton[11] lets me share some of his. We are all mixed up with thieves, confidence-tricksters, lousy tramps and homosexuals – and 18 to a small apartment! I am not at all downhearted but feel my patience has definitely gone; in one or another way I shall fight to freedom for my comrades and myself. Harry Milton wishes to be known; I promoted him from a gamma minus to an alpha plus status.

1. Eileen refers to Kingsley Martin's refusal to publish Orwell's review of Franz Borkenau's *The Spanish Cockpit* in the *New Statesman & Nation* because it 'controverts the political policy of the paper'.

2. Jock Branthwaite served with Orwell in Spain. His father was a miner and he recalled copies of *The Road to Wigan Pier* arriving at the front. The book 'didn't seem to offend his working-class sensibilities'. Branthwaite thought Orwell had no political leanings when he arrived in Spain, 'except he was more left than right . . . leaning slightly towards the communists'. He told Stephen Wadhams that Orwell was not a snob: 'I thought he was a wonderful man.' Branthwaite got out of Spain on the last refugee boat from Barcelona for Marseilles. See *Remembering Orwell*, 83–4, 93, 99.

3. For the ILP Conference, 1–13 August 1937; Monday was the 1 August.

4. George Tioli is described by Orwell in *Homage to Catalonia* as 'an Italian journalist, a great friend of ours' He was himself wounded while tending a wounded man in Barcelona in May 1937 (p. 115 [VI/116].

5. at = to.

6. Ethel Macdonald (1909–60), leading social activist in Scotland. During the Spanish Civil War she was the English-speaking announcer for CNT (Confederación Nacional del Trabajo – the Anarcho-Syndicalist Trade Union) in Barcelona. She was arrested during the purge of the POUM and CNT in 1937 but escaped and helped others to escape, earning the nickname of 'Spanish Pimpernel'. On her return to Scotland she made 'outspoken claims' about the death of Bob Smillie and was heavily critical of the ILP (especially David Murray: see note 9); see Tom Buchanan. 'The Death of Bob Smillie, the Spanish Civil War, and the Eclipse of the Independent Labour Party', *Historical Journal*, 40 (1997), 452–3, for an excellent account of the controversy over Smillie's death and this period.

7. Col. Ricardo Burillo Stolle (1891–1939), described by Thomas as 'a left-wing aristocrat, puritanical, anti-clerical, and romantic, soon became virtually a communist' (245, n. 1). After the Events of May in Barcelona, effective control of the police was handed over to Burillo, who became director-general of security in Catalonia (672). He later commanded the army of Estremadura (779). After Franco's victory, he was one of many who was executed (925).

8. See *Homage to Catalonia*, pp. 110–21 [VI/109–24].

9. Possibly David Murray, the ILP representative in Valencia at the time of Bob Smillie's death, allegedly from appendicitis. Murray was refused permission to see Smillie's body. See *Homage to Catalonia*, pp. 155–6 [VI/170–71]. And see Tom Buchanan. n. 6 above.

10. George: presumably George Tioli (see n. 4.)

11. Harry Milton was the only American serving with the British ILP group on the Aragon Front. It was to him ('The American sentry') that Orwell was talking when he was shot through the throat (*Homage to Catalonia*), p. 131 [VI/137–8]. He regarded Orwell as 'politically virginal' on arrival in Spain. Stafford Cottman recalls that only Milton was proud to boast of being a Trotskyist. Milton and Orwell spent hours discussing politics. He tried, very forcefully, to argue Orwell out of his determination to transfer to the International Brigade on the Madrid Front, convinced that the Communists would kill him: 'But he was cool as a cucumber, and he just walked away from me. He was a very disciplined individual.' See *Remembering Orwell*, 81, 85, 90.

---

[379]

Review of The Spanish Cockpit *by Franz Borkenau;* Volunteer in Spain *by John Sommerfield*
Time and Tide, *31 July 1937*

Dr. Borkenau[1] has performed a feat which is very difficult at this moment for anyone who knows what is going on in Spain; he has written a book about the Spanish war without losing his temper. Perhaps I am rash in saying that it is the best book yet written on the subject, but I believe that anyone who has recently come from Spain will agree with me. After that horrible atmosphere of espionage and political hatred it is a relief to come upon a book which sums the situation up as calmly and lucidly as this.

Dr. Borkenau is a sociologist and not connected with any political party. He went to Spain with the purpose of doing some 'field work' upon a country in revolution, and he made two trips, the first in August, the second in January. In the difference between those two periods, especially the difference in the social atmosphere, the essential history of the Spanish revolution is contained. In August the Government was almost powerless, local soviets were functioning everywhere and the Anarchists were the main revolutionary force; as a result everything was in terrible chaos, the churches were still smouldering and suspected Fascists were being shot in large numbers, but there was everywhere a belief in the revolution, a feeling that the bondage of centuries had been broken. By January power had passed, though not so completely as later, from the Anarchists to the Communists, and the Communists were using every possible method, fair and foul, to stamp out what was left of the revolution. The pre-revolutionary police-forces had been restored, political espionage was growing keener and keener, and it was not long before Dr. Borkenau found himself in jail. Like the majority of political prisoners in Spain, he was never even told what he was accused of; but he was luckier than most in being released after a few days, and even (very few people have managed this lately) saving his documents from the hands of the police. His book ends with a series of essays upon various aspects of the war and the revolution. Anyone who wants to understand the Spanish situation should read the really brilliant final chapter, entitled 'Conclusions'.

The most important fact that has emerged from the whole business is that the Communist Party is now (presumably for the sake of Russian foreign policy) an anti-revolutionary force. So far from pushing the Spanish Government further towards the left, the Communist influence has pulled it violently towards the Right. Dr. Borkenau, who is not a revolutionary himself, does not particularly regret this fact; what he does object to is that it is being deliberately concealed. The result is that public opinion throughout Europe still regards the Communists as wicked Reds or heroic revolutionaries as the case may be, while in Spain itself –

It is at present impossible . . . to discuss openly even the basic facts of the political situation. The fight between the revolutionary and non-revolutionary principle, as embodied in Anarchists and Communists respectively, is inevitable, because fire and water cannot mix . . . But as the Press is not even allowed to mention it, nobody is fully aware of the position, and the political antagonism breaks through, not in open fight to win over public opinion, but in backstairs intrigues, assassinations by Anarchist bravos, legal assassinations by Communist police, subdued allusions, rumours . . . The concealment of the main political facts from the public and the maintenance of this deception by means of censorship and terrorism carries with it far-reaching detrimental effects, which will be felt in the future even more than at present.

If that was true in February, how much truer it is now! When I left Spain in late June the atmosphere in Barcelona, what with the ceaseless arrests, the censored newspapers and the prowling hordes of armed police, was like a nightmare.

Mr. Sommerfield was a member of the International Brigade and fought heroically in the defence of Madrid. *Volunteer in Spain* is the record of his experiences. Seeing that the International Brigade is in some sense fighting for all of us – a thin line of suffering and often ill-armed human beings standing between barbarism and at least comparative decency – it may seem ungracious to say that this book is a piece of sentimental tripe; but so it is. We shall almost certainly get some good books from members of the International Brigade, but we shall have to wait for them until the war is over.

1. Following his review of *The Spanish Cockpit*, Orwell greatly admired Franz Borkenau's work. Borkenau (1900–1957) had been a member of the Communist Party for eight years and an official of the Comintern, but 'reverted to a belief in liberalism and democracy', as Orwell put it in his review of *The Communist International* in 1938 (*485*). Unfortunately, none of their letters have survived. Orwell recommended Borkenau as a writer to the Foreign Office's Information Research Department in April 1949 (see XX/320, 322). He refers to *The Spanish Cockpit* in *Homage to Catalonia*, p. 178 [VI/200].

[*381*]

To Rayner Heppenstall
31 July 1937

The Stores, Wallington, Near Baldock, Herts

Dear Rayner,[1]

Thanks so much for your letter. I was glad to hear from you. I hope Margaret[2] is better. It sounds dreadful, but from what you say I gather that she is at any rate up and about.

We had an interesting but thoroughly bloody time in Spain. Of course I would never have allowed Eileen to come nor probably gone myself if I had foreseen the political developments, especially the suppression of the P.O.U.M., the party in whose militia I was serving. It was a queer business. We started off by being heroic defenders of democracy and ended by slipping over the border with the police panting on our heels.[3] Eileen was wonderful, in fact actually seemed to enjoy it. But though we ourselves got out all right nearly all our friends and acquaintances are in jail and likely to be there indefinitely, not actually charged with anything but suspected of 'Trotskyism'. The most terrible things were happening even when I left, wholesale arrests, wounded men dragged out of hospitals and thrown into jail, people crammed together in filthy dens where they have hardly room to lie down, prisoners beaten and half starved etc., etc. Meanwhile it is impossible to get a word about this mentioned in the English press, barring the publications of the I.L.P., which is affiliated to the P.O.U.M. I had a most amusing time with the *New Statesman* about it. As soon as I got out of Spain I wired from France asking if they would like an article and of course they said yes, but when they saw my article was on the suppression of the P.O.U.M. they said they couldn't print it. To sugar the pill they sent me to review a very good book which appeared recently, *The Spanish Cockpit*, which blows the gaff pretty well on what has been happening. But once again when they saw my review they couldn't print it as it was 'against editorial policy', but they actually offered to pay for the review all the same – practically hush-money. I am also having to change my publisher, at least for this book.[4] Gollancz is of course part of the Communism-racket, and as soon as he heard I had been associated with the P.O.U.M. and Anarchists and had seen the inside of the May riots in Barcelona, he said he did not think he would be able to publish my book, though not a word of it was written yet. I think he must have very astutely foreseen that something of the kind would happen, as when I went to Spain he drew up a contract undertaking to publish my fiction but not other books. However I have two other publishers on my track and I think my agent is being clever and has got them bidding against one another. I have started my book but of course my fingers are all thumbs at present.

My wound was not much, but it was a miracle it did not kill me. The bullet went clean through my neck but missed everything except one vocal cord, or rather the nerve governing it, which is paralysed. At first I had no voice at all, but now the other vocal cord is compensating and the damaged one may or may not recover. My voice is practically normal but I can't shout to any extent. I also can't sing, but people tell me this doesn't matter. I am rather glad to have been hit by a bullet because I think it will happen to us all in the near future and I am glad to know that it doesn't hurt to speak of. What I saw in Spain did not make me cynical but it does make me think that the future is pretty grim. It is evident that people can be deceived by the anti-Fascist stuff exactly as they were deceived by the gallant little Belgium stuff, and when war comes they will walk straight into it. I don't, however, agree with the pacifist attitude, as I believe you do. I still think one must fight for Socialism and against Fascism, I mean fight physically with weapons, only it is as well to discover which is which. I want to meet Holdaway[5] and see what he thinks about the Spanish business. He is the only more or less orthodox Communist I have met whom I could respect. It will disgust me if I find he is spouting the same defence of democracy and Trotsky-Fascist stuff as the others.

I would much like to see you, but I honestly don't think I shall be in London for some time, unless absolutely obliged to go up on business. I am just getting going with my book, which I want to get done by Xmas, also very busy trying to get the garden etc. in trim after being so long away. Anyway keep in touch and let me know your address. I can't get in touch with Rees. He was on the Madrid front and there was practically no communication. I heard from Murry[6] who seemed in the weeps about something. Au revoir.

Yours

Eric

1. Rayner Heppenstall (1911–81), novelist, critic, crime historian and BBC feature-writer and producer (1945–67). He shared a flat with Orwell in 1935 and though they came to blows they remained lifelong friends. He produced Orwell's radio adaptation of *Animal Farm* in 1947 and later versions in 1952 and 1957. He also commissioned and produced Orwell's radio feature, 'The Voyage of the *Beagle*', in 1946. His *Four Absentees* (1960) has reminiscences of Orwell; see *Orwell Remembered*, 106–15. See also Shelden, 225.

2. Mrs Rayner Heppenstall.

3. In *Homage to Catalonia*, Orwell tells how his hotel room was searched by six plain-clothes policemen, who took away 'every scrap of paper we possessed', except, fortunately, Eileen's and his passports and their cheque-book. He learned later that the police had seized some of his belongings, including a bundle of dirty linen, from the Sanatorium Maurín; pp. 151, 162–3 [VI/164, 178–9].

4. *Homage to Catalonia*.

5. N. A. Holdaway, schoolmaster and Marxist theorist. He was a member of the Independent Socialist Party, a contributor to *The Adelphi* and Director of the Adelphi Centre.

6. John Middleton Murry (1889–1957) was nominally the editor of *The (New) Adelphi*, which

he had founded in June 1923, for fourteen years but he was associated with the journal throughout its life (1923–55). The journal published about fifty contributions by Orwell and did much to foster his career as a writer. Murry was successively a fervent disciple of D. H. Lawrence, an unorthodox Marxist, a pacifist and a back-to-the-land farmer. He also edited *Peace News* from July 1940 to April 1946. Despite his deeply entrenched pacifism, over which he and Orwell disagreed, they remained on good terms.

---

[382]

'Eye-Witness in Barcelona'

Controversy: The Socialist Forum,[1] *vol. I, no. 11, August 1937*

This article was published as 'J'ai été témoin à Barcelone . . .', translated by Yvonne Davet, in La Révolution Prolétarienne: Revue Bimensuelle Syndicaliste Révolutionnaire, *no. 255, 25 September 1937. It was this article that the* New Statesman *refused to publish; see Orwell's letter to Rayner Heppenstall, 31 July 1937, above. Yvonne Davet (born* c. *1895) was for many years secretary to André Gide. She and Orwell corresponded before and after World War II, and she translated several of his books into French in the hope that she could find a publisher for them in France. Her translation of* Homage to Catalonia, *completed before the outbreak of war and read by Orwell, was not published until 1955. At the time it had notes by Orwell not found in English editions until 1986. She also translated Jean Rhys, Graham Greene and Iris Murdoch. She and Orwell never met.*

Orwell's article was preceded in Controversy *by this note:*

George Orwell, author of *The Road to Wigan Pier*, has been fighting with the ILP Contingent on the Aragón front. Here he contributes a personal account of events in Barcelona during the May Days and of the suppression of the POUM in the following month.

I

Much has already been written about the May riots in Barcelona, and the major events have been carefully tabulated in Fenner Brockway's pamphlet, *The Truth About Barcelona*, which so far as my own knowledge goes is entirely accurate. I think, therefore, that the most useful thing I can do here, in my capacity as eye-witness, is to add a few footnotes upon several of the most-disputed points.

First of all, as to the purpose, if any, of the so-called rising. It has been asserted in the Communist press that the whole thing was a carefully-prepared effort to overthrow the Government and even to hand Catalonia over to the Fascists by provoking foreign intervention in Barcelona. The second part of this suggestion is almost too ridiculous to need refuting. If the P.O.U.M. and the left-wing Anarchists were really in league with the Fascists, why did not the militias at the front walk out and leave a hole in the line? And why did the C.N.T.[2] transport-workers, in spite of the strike, continue sending supplies to the front? I cannot, however, say with certainty that a definite revolutionary intention was not in the minds of a few extremists, especially the Bolshevik Leninists (usually called Trotskyists) whose pamphlets were handed round the barricades. What I can say is that the ordinary rank and file behind the barricades never for an instant thought of themselves as taking part in a revolution. We thought, all of us, that we were simply defending ourselves against an attempted *coup d'état* by the Civil Guards,[3] who had forcibly seized the Telephone Exchange and might seize some more of the workers' buildings if we did not show ourselves willing to fight. My reading of the situation, derived from what people were actually doing and saying at the time, is this:–

The workers came into the streets in a spontaneous defensive movement, and they only consciously wanted two things: the handing-back of the Telephone Exchange and the disarming of the hated Civil Guards. In addition there was the resentment caused by the growing poverty in Barcelona and the luxurious life lived by the bourgeoisie. But it is probable that the opportunity to overthrow the Catalan Government existed if there had been a leader to take advantage of it. It seems to be widely agreed that on the third day the workers were in a position to take control of the city; certainly the Civil Guards were greatly demoralised and were surrendering in large numbers. And though the Valencia Government could send fresh troops to crush the workers (they did send 6,000 Assault Guards when the fighting was over), they could not maintain those troops in Barcelona if the transport-workers chose not to supply them. But in fact no resolute revolutionary leadership existed. The Anarchist leaders disowned the whole thing and said 'Go back to work', and the P.O.U.M. leaders took an uncertain line. The orders sent to us at the P.O.U.M. barricades, direct from the P.O.U.M. leadership, were to stand by the C.N.T., but not to fire unless we were fired on ourselves or our buildings attacked. (I personally was fired at a number of times, but never fired back.) Consequently, as food ran short, the workers began to trickle back to work; and, of course, once they were safely dispersed, the reprisals began. Whether the revolutionary opportunity *ought* to have been taken advantage of is another question. Speaking solely for myself, I should answer 'No'. To begin with it is doubtful whether the workers could have maintained power for more than a few weeks; and, secondly, it might well have meant losing the war against Franco. On the other hand the essentially defensive action taken by the workers was perfectly correct; war or no war, they had a right to defend what they had won in July, 1936. It may be, of course, that the revolution was finally lost in those few days in May. But I still think it was a little better, though only a very little, to lose the revolution than to lose the war.

Secondly, as to the people involved. The Communist press took the line, almost from the start, of pretending that the 'rising' was wholly or almost wholly the work of the P.O.U.M. (aided by 'a few irresponsible hooligans', according to the New York *Daily Worker*). Anyone who was in Barcelona at the time knows that this is an absurdity. The enormous majority of the people behind the barricades were ordinary C.N.T. workers. And this point is of importance, for it was as a scapegoat for the May riots that the P.O.U.M. was recently suppressed; the four hundred or more P.O.U.M. supporters who are in the filthy, verminous Barcelona jails at this moment, are there ostensibly for their share in the May riots. It is worth pointing, therefore, to two good reasons why the P.O.U.M. were not and could not have been the prime movers. In the first place, the P.O.U.M. was a very small party. If one throws in Party members, militiamen on leave, and helpers and sympathisers of all kinds, the number of P.O.U.M. supporters on the streets could not have been anywhere near ten thousand – probably not five thousand; but the disturbances manifestly involved scores of thousands of people. Secondly, there was a general or nearly general strike for several days; but the P.O.U.M., as such, had no power to call a strike, and the strike could not have happened if the rank and file of the C.N.T. had not wanted it. As to those involved on the other side, the London *Daily Worker* had the impudence to suggest in one issue that the 'rising' was suppressed by the Popular Army. Everyone in Barcelona knew, and the *Daily Worker* must have known as well, that the Popular Army remained neutral and the troops stayed in their barracks throughout the disturbances. A few soldiers, however, did take part as individuals; I saw a couple at one of the P.O.U.M. barricades.

Thirdly, as to the stores of arms which the P.O.U.M. are supposed to have been hoarding in Barcelona. This story has been repeated so often that even a normally critical observer like H. N. Brailsford accepts it without any investigation and speaks of the 'tanks and guns' which the P.O.U.M. had 'stolen from Government arsenals' (*New Statesman*, May 22).[4] As a matter of fact the P.O.U.M. possessed pitifully few weapons, either at the front or in the rear. During the street-fighting I was at all three of the principal strongholds of the P.O.U.M., the Executive Building, the Comité Local and the Hotel Falcón. It is worth recording in detail what armaments these buildings contained. There were in all about 80 rifles, some of them defective, besides a few obsolete guns of various patterns, all useless because there were no cartridges for them. Of rifle ammunition there was about 50 rounds for each weapon. There were no machine-guns, no pistols and no pistol ammunition. There were a few cases of hand-grenades, but these were sent to us by the C.N.T. after the fighting started. A highly-placed militia officer afterwards gave me his opinion that in the whole of Barcelona the P.O.U.M. possessed about a hundred and fifty rifles and *one* machine-gun. This, it will be seen, was barely sufficient for the armed guards which at that time all parties, P.S.U.C., P.O.U.M., and C.N.T.-F.A.I. alike, placed on their principal buildings. Possibly it may be said that even in the May riots the P.O.U.M. were still hiding their weapons. But in that case what becomes of the claim that the May riots were a P.O.U.M. rising intended to overthrow the Government?

In reality, by far the worst offenders in this matter of keeping weapons from the front, were the Government themselves. The infantry on the Aragón front were far worse-armed than an English public school O.T.C.[5] but the rear-line troops, the Civil Guards, Assault Guards and Carabineros, who were not intended for the front, but were used to 'preserve order' (i.e., overawe the workers) in the rear, were armed to the teeth. The troops on the Aragón front had worn-out Mauser rifles, which usually jammed after five shots, approximately one machine-gun to fifty men, and one pistol or revolver to about thirty men. These weapons, so necessary in trench warfare, were not issued by the Government and could only be bought illegally and with the greatest difficulty. The Assault Guards were armed with brand-new Russian rifles; in addition, every man was issued with an automatic pistol, and there was one sub-machine-gun between ten or a dozen men. These facts speak for themselves. A Government which sends boys of fifteen to the front with rifles forty years old, and keeps its biggest men and newest weapons in the rear, is manifestly more afraid of the revolution than of the Fascists. Hence the feeble war-policy of the past six months, and hence the compromise with which the war will almost certainly end.

II

When the P.O.U.M., the Left Opposition (so-called Trotskyist) off-shoot of Spanish Communism, was suppressed on June 16–17, the fact in itself surprised nobody. Ever since May, or even since February, it had been obvious that the P.O.U.M. would be 'liquidated' if the Communists could bring it about. Nevertheless, the suddenness of the suppressive action, and the mixture of treachery and brutality with which it was carried out, took everyone, even the leaders, completely unaware.

Ostensibly the Party was suppressed on the charge, which has been repeated for months in the Communist press though not taken seriously by anyone inside Spain, that the P.O.U.M. leaders were in the pay of the Fascists. On June 16 Andrés Nin, the leader of the Party, was arrested in his office. The same night, before any proclamation had been made, the police raided the Hotel Falcón, a sort of boarding-house maintained by the P.O.U.M. and used chiefly by militiamen on leave, and arrested everybody in it on no particular charge. Next morning the P.O.U.M. was declared illegal and all P.O.U.M. buildings, not only offices, book-stalls, etc., but even libraries and sanatoriums for wounded men, were seized by the police. Within a few days all or almost all of the forty members of the Executive Committee were under arrest. One or two who succeeded in going into hiding were made to give themselves up by the device, borrowed from the Fascists, of seizing their wives as hostages. Nin was transferred to Valencia and thence to Madrid, and put on trial for selling military information to the enemy. Needless to say the usual 'confessions', mysterious letters written in invisible ink, and other 'evidence' were forthcoming in such profusion as to make it reasonably likely that they had been prepared beforehand. As early as June 19 the news reached Barcelona, via Valencia, that Nin had been shot. This report was, we hope, untrue, but it hardly needs pointing out that the Valencia Government will be obliged to shoot a number, perhaps a dozen, of the P.O.U.M. leaders if it expects its charges to be taken seriously.[6]

Meanwhile, the rank and file of the Party, not merely party members, but soldiers in the P.O.U.M. militia and sympathisers and helpers of all kinds, were being thrown into prison as fast as the police could lay hands on them. Probably it would be impossible to get hold of accurate figures, but there is reason to think that during the first week there were 400 arrests in Barcelona alone; certainly the jails were so full that large numbers of prisoners had to be confined in shops and other temporary dumps. So far as I could discover, no discrimination was made in the arrests between those who had been concerned in the May riots and those who had not. In effect, the outlawry of the P.O.U.M. was made retrospective; the P.O.U.M. was now illegal, and therefore one was breaking the law by having ever belonged to it. The police even went to the length of arresting the wounded men in the sanatoriums. Among the prisoners in one of the jails I saw, for instance, two men of my acquaintance with amputated legs; also a child of not more than twelve years of age.

One has got to remember, too, just what imprisonment means in Spain at this moment. Apart from the frightful overcrowding of the temporary jails, the insanitary conditions, the lack of light and air and the filthy food, there is the complete absence of anything that we should regard as legality. There is, for instance, no nonsense about Habeas Corpus. According to the present law, or at any rate the present practice, you can be imprisoned for an indefinite time not merely without being tried but even without being charged; and until you have been charged the authorities can, if they choose, keep you 'incommunicado' – that is, without the right to communicate with a lawyer or anyone else in the outside world. It is easy to see how much the 'confessions' obtained in such circumstances are worth. The situation is all the worse for the poorer prisoners because the P.O.U.M. Red Aid, which normally furnishes prisoners with legal advice, has been suppressed along with the other P.O.U.M. institutions.

But perhaps the most odious feature of the whole business was the fact that all news of what had happened was deliberately concealed, certainly for five days, and I believe for longer, from the troops on the Aragón front. As it happened, I was at the front from June 15 to 20. I had got to see a medical board and in doing so to visit various towns behind the front line, Siétamo, Barbastro, Monzón, etc. In all these places the P.O.U.M. militia headquarters, Red Aid centres and the like were functioning normally, and as far down the line as Lérida (only about 100 miles from Barcelona) and as late as June 20, not a soul had heard that the P.O.U.M. had been suppressed. All word of it had been kept out of the Barcelona papers, although, of course, the Valencia papers (which do not get to the Aragón front) were flaming with the story of Nin's 'treachery'. Together with a number of others I had the disagreeable experience of getting back to Barcelona to find that the P.O.U.M. had been suppressed in my absence. Luckily I was warned just in time and managed to make myself scarce, but other[s] were not so fortunate. Every P.O.U.M. militiaman who came down the line at this period had the choice of going straight into hiding or into jail – a really pleasant reception after three or four months in the front line. The motive for all this is obvious: the attack on Huesca was just beginning, and presumably the Government feared that if the P.O.U.M. militia knew what was happening they might refuse to march. I do not, as a matter of fact, believe that the loyalty of the militia would have been affected; still, they had a right to know the truth. There is something unspeakably ugly in sending men into battle (when I left Siétamo the fight was beginning and the first wounded were jolting in the ambulances down the abominable roads) and at the same time concealing from them that behind their back their party was being suppressed, their leaders denounced as traitors and their friends and relatives thrown into prison.

The P.O.U.M. was by far the smallest of the revolutionary parties, and its suppression affects comparatively few people. In all probability the sum total of punishments will be a score or so of people shot or sentenced to long terms of imprisonment, a few hundreds ruined and a few thousands temporarily persecuted. Nevertheless, its suppression is symptomatically important. To begin with it should make clear to the outside world, what was already obvious to many observers in Spain, that the present Government has more points of resemblance to Fascism than points of difference. (This does not mean that it is not worth fighting for as against the more naked Fascism of Franco and Hitler. I myself had grasped by May the Fascist tendency of the Government, but I was willing to go back to the front and in fact did so.) Secondly, the elimination of the P.O.U.M. gives warning of the impending attack upon the Anarchists. These are the real enemy whom the Communists fear as they never feared the numerically insignificant P.O.U.M. The Anarchist leaders have now had a demonstration of the methods likely to be used against them; the only hope for the revolution, and probably for victory in the war, is that they will profit by the lesson and get ready to defend themselves in time.

1. Raymond Challinor, in *Bulletin of the Society for the Study of Labour History*, 54 (Winter 1989), 40, states: 'Originally, *Controversy* was begun after the Independent Labour Party disaffiliated from the Labour Party in 1932. At first, it functioned as the Party's internal bulletin . . . In 1936, however, its character completely changed. From then onwards, *Controversy* sought to be – and largely was – a journal where the many diverse views held within the working-class movement could be openly discussed without rancour.' To acknowledge that its readership was much wider than that of the ILP, it changed its name in 1939 to *Left Forum* and then to *Left*. It ceased publication in May 1950. Challinor attributes much of its success to the character of its editor, Dr C. A. Smith, a London headmaster and later a University of London lecturer. Among those writing for the journal he lists Frank Borkenau, Max Eastman, Sidney Hook, Jomo Kenyatta, Victor Serge, August Thalheimer, Jay Lovestone, George Padmore, Marceau Pivert and Simone Weil.

2. For the significance of the groups represented by initials, see *Homage to Catalonia*, pp. 179–82 [VI/Appendix I, 201–5]. Relevant extracts and part of a letter from Hugh Thomas to the editors of *CJEL* are reprinted as a note to Orwell's 'Notes on the Spanish Militias', below.

3. Orwell later realized that it was not the Civil Guards, but a local section of Assault Guards, who seized the Barcelona Telephone Exchange. Shortly before he died, he gave instructions that the text of *Homage to Catalonia* be changed; see pp. 29–30 [VI/Textual Note].

4. For Orwell's later thoughts, see letters to H. N. Brailsford, 10 and 18 December 1937, below.

5. Officers' Training Corps, associated with the public-school system in England.

6. Andrés Nin (1892–1937) was leader of the POUM. He had at one time been Trotsky's secretary but broke with him when Trotsky spoke critically of the POUM (see Thomas, 523). He 'underwent the customary Soviet interrogation' suffered by those who were claimed to be 'traitors to the cause' and was then murdered, possibly in the royal park just north of

Madrid. In later months the remaining POUM leaders were interrogated and tortured, some in the convent of Saint Ursula in Barcelona, 'the Dachau of republican Spain', as one POUM survivor described it. Nin was the only POUM leader to be murdered. However, Bob Smillie was thrown into jail in Valencia without just cause (see *Homage to Catalonia*, pp. 155–6 [VI/170–1]), where he died, according to his captors, of appendicitis. Thomas gives this account of Nin's probable fate: 'He ... refused to sign documents admitting his guilt and that of his friends ... What should they do? ... the Italian Vidali (Carlos Contreras) suggested that a "nazi" attack to liberate Nin should be simulated. So, one dark night, probably 22 or 23 June, ten German members of the International Brigade assaulted the house in Alcalá where Nin was held ... Nin was taken away and murdered ... His refusal to admit his guilt probably saved the lives of his friends' (705).

Abstracts of Reports on the Spanish Civil War in the Daily Worker *and* News Chronicle, *1936–7*
[July and August 1937?]

In a footnote to Homage to Catalonia, *Orwell remarks, 'In connection with this book I have had to go through the files of a good many English papers' (p. 185 [VI/208]). Some of the notes he made in his search have survived. These are reprinted in* CW, X/290–306.

---

[384]

To Amy Charlesworth
1 August 1937

The Stores, Wallington, Near Baldock, Herts

Dear Miss Charlesworth,[1]

Once again a long delay in answering your letter, I am afraid. I can only excuse myself by saying I had a lot to do in the month after getting back from Spain, and that I have only recently got my health back. The damaged hand and Spain were only indirectly connected – ie. I had blood-poisoning at the front and this recurred. It is all right now. The wound I got in Spain was a bullet through the neck, but it is all healed up and well except that I have lost part of my voice.

You asked about the situation in Spain, and whether the rebels had not a case. I should not say that the rebels had *no* case, unless you believe that it is always wrong to rebel against a legally-established government, which in practice nobody does. Roughly speaking I should say that the rebels stand for two things that are more or less contradictory – for of course Franco's side, like the Government side, consists of various parties who frequently quarrel bitterly among themselves. They stand on the one hand for an earlier form of society, feudalism, the Roman Catholic Church and so forth, and on the other hand for Fascism, which means an immensely regimented and centralised form of government, with certain features in common with Socialism, in that it means suppression of a good deal of private property and private enterprise, but always ultimately in the interest of the bigger capitalists, and therefore completely unsocialistic. I am wholeheartedly against both of these ideas, but it is fair to say that a case can be made out for both of them. Some of the Catholic writers, such as Chesterton, Christopher Dawson etc., can make out a very appealing though not logically convincing case for a more primitive form of society. I would not say that there is any case for Fascism itself, but I do think there is a case for many individual Fascists. I had a lot to say about this in my last book. Roughly speaking I would say that Fascism has a great appeal for certain simple and decent people who genuinely want to see justice done to the working class and do not grasp that they are being used as tools by the big capitalists. It would be absurd to imagine that every man on Franco's side is a demon. But though the Fascist atrocities have probably been exaggerated, some of them undoubtedly happened and I think one can be certain that the Government has conducted the war much more humanely than the Fascists, even to the point of losing military opportunities, eg. by being unwilling to bomb towns where there were civilian populations.

Meanwhile on the Government side there is a very complicated situation and the most terrible things are happening, which have been kept out of the English papers and which I can't properly explain without expanding this letter into the size of a pamphlet. Perhaps I can summarise it like this: the Spanish war was not only a war but a revolution. When the Fascist rising broke out, the workers in various of the big towns, especially in Catalonia, not only defeated the local Fascists but took the opportunity of seizing land, factories etc. and setting up a rough form of workers' government. Ever since then, and especially since about December of last year, the real struggle of the Spanish Government has been to crush the revolution and put things back to where they were before. They have now more or less succeeded and there is now going on a most dreadful reign of terror directed against everyone who is suspected of genuinely revolutionary leanings. It is a little difficult for English people to understand, in so much that the Communist Party, which we are accustomed to regard as revolutionary, has been the principal mover in this, and is now more or less in charge of the Spanish Government, though not officially, and is conducting the reign of terror. This had begun when I left Spain on June 23rd. The party in whose militia I had been serving, the P.O.U.M., was suppressed and every person connected with it whom the police could lay their hands on, including even wounded men in the sanatoriums, was thrown into jail without any kind of trial. I was lucky enough to get out of Spain, but many of my friends and acquaintances are still in jail and I am afraid there is the greatest fear that some of them will be shot, not for any definite offence but for opposition to the Communist Party. If you want to keep in touch with Spanish affairs, the only paper you can more or less rely on to tell you the truth is the *New Leader*. Or if you come across it read an excellent book that appeared recently called *The Spanish Cockpit*, by Franz Borkenau. The chapters at the end of this sum up the situation much better than I could.

This seems to be quite a long letter after all. I must apologise for lecturing you about Spain, but what I saw there has upset me so badly that I talk and write about it to everybody. I am doing a book about it, of course. I suppose it will be out about next March.

Yours very sincerely,

Eric Blair ('George Orwell')

P.S. [handwritten] I might have told you before that George Orwell is only a pen-name. I would much like to meet you some time. You sound the kind of person I like to know, but goodness knows when I shall be in your part of the world. I am keeping your address. Let me know if you ever move down London-way.

1. Amy Charlesworth (1904–45), in a letter to Orwell of 6 October 1937, from Flixton, near Manchester, told him she had been married young, had had two children, had left her husband because he struck her so often, and was training to be a health visitor. She remarried,

and when she wrote to Orwell in June 1944, she signed herself Mrs Gerry Byrne. Her husband wrote to Orwell in June 1945 to tell him that his wife had died three months earlier. He may have been Gerald Byrne (1905), a crime reporter for the *Daily Herald* in the mid-1930s.

---

[386]

To Charles Doran
2 August 1937

The Stores, Wallington, Near Baldock, Herts

Dear Doran,[1]

I don't know your address, but I expect they will know it at the I.L.P. summer school, where I am going on Thursday. I was also there yesterday, to hear John McNair speak.

I was very relieved when I saw young Jock Branthwaite, who has been staying with us, and learned that all of you who wished to had got safely out of Spain. I came up to the front on June 15th to get my medical discharge, but couldn't come up to the line to see you because they kept sending me about from hospital to hospital. I got back to Barcelona to find that the P.O.U.M. had been suppressed in my absence, and they had kept it from the troops so successfully that on June 20th as far down the line as Lérida not a soul had heard about it, though the suppression had taken place on the 16th–17th. My first intimation was walking into the Hotel Continental and having Eileen and a Frenchman named Pivert,[2] who was a very good friend to everyone during the trouble, rush up to me, seize me each by one arm and tell me to get out. Kopp had just recently been arrested in the Continental owing to the staff ringing up the police and giving him away. McNair, Cottman and I had to spend several days on the run, sleeping in ruined churches etc., but Eileen stayed in the hotel and, beyond having her room searched and all my documents seized, was not molested, possibly because the police were using her as a decoy duck for McNair and me. We slipped away very suddenly on the morning of the 23rd, and crossed the frontier without much difficulty. Luckily there was a first class and a dining car on the train, and we did our best to look like ordinary English tourists, which was the safest thing to do. In Barcelona one was fairly safe during the daytime, and Eileen and I visited Kopp several times in the filthy den where he and scores of others, including Milton,[3] were imprisoned. The police had actually gone to the length of arresting the wounded P.O.U.M. men out of the Maurín, and I saw two men in the jail with amputated legs; also a boy of about ten. A few days ago we got some letters, dated July 7th, which Kopp had somehow managed to send out of Spain. They included a letter of protest to the Chief of Police. He said that not only had he and all the others been imprisoned for 18 days (much longer now, of course) without any trial or charge, but that they were being confined in places where they had hardly room to lie down, were half starved and in many cases beaten and insulted. We sent the letter on to McNair, and I believe after discussing the matter Maxton has arranged to see the Spanish ambassador and tell him that if something is not done, at any rate for the foreign prisoners, he will spill the beans in Parliament. McNair also tells me that there is a credible report in the French papers that the body of Nin, also I think other P.O.U.M. leaders, has been found shot in Madrid. I suppose it will be 'suicide', or perhaps appendicitis again.[4]

Meanwhile it seems almost impossible to get anything printed about all this. As soon as I crossed the French frontier I wired to the *New Statesman* asking if they would like an article, and they wired back Yes, but when they saw my article (on the suppression of the P.O.U.M.), they said they were sorry but they could not publish the article, as it would 'cause trouble'. To sugar the pill they sent me to review a very good book that was published recently, *The Spanish Cockpit*. But once again when they saw the review they were sorry they could not publish it as it 'controverted editorial policy', but they actually offered to pay for the article though unprinted – practically hush-money, you see. I am also having to change my publisher. As soon as Gollancz heard I had been with the P.O.U.M. he said he was afraid he would not be able to publish my book on Spain, though not a word of it was written yet. I haven't definitely fixed up, but shall probably take it to Secker. It ought to come out about March if all is well.

I went up to Bristol with some others to take part in a protest meeting about Stafford Cottman[5] being expelled from the Y.C.L.[6] with the words 'we brand him as an enemy of the working class' and similar expressions.

Since then I heard that the Cottmans' house had been shadowed by members of the Y.C.L. who attempt to question everyone who comes in and out. What a show! To think that we started off as heroic defenders of democracy and only six months later were Trotsky-Fascists sneaking over the border with the police on our heels. Meanwhile being a Trotsky-Fascist doesn't seem to help us with the pro-Fascists in this country. This afternoon Eileen and I had a visit from the vicar, who doesn't at all approve of our having been on the Government side. Of course we had to own up that it was true about the burning of the churches, but he cheered up a lot on hearing they were only Roman Catholic churches.

Let me know how you get on. Eileen wishes to be remembered.

Yours

Eric Blair

P.S. [handwritten] I forgot to say that when in Barcelona I wanted greatly to write to you all & warn you, but I dared not, because I thought any such letter would simply draw undesirable attention to the man it was addressed to.

1. This letter and that dated 26 November 1938 (*505*) were donated by Doran's widow, Mrs Bertha Doran, to Waverley Secondary School, Drumchapel, Glasgow, in December 1974. They are reproduced here with her kind permission. She and Dr James D. Young supplied details of Doran's life. Charles Doran (1894–1974) was born in Dublin and moved to Glasgow in 1915. After serving in World War I, he became active in Guy Aldred's Anti-Parliamentary Communist Federation. He joined the ILP in the early 1930s and served with Orwell in the POUM in Spain in 1937. They exchanged letters in 1938–9, but no others have been traced. Doran opposed World War II and joined a small anarchist group led by Willie MacDougall that engaged in anti-militarist and revolutionary socialist propaganda throughout the war. He also contributed to MacDougall's newspaper, the *Pioneer News*. In 1983 Mrs Doran told Dr Young that her late husband was impressed by Orwell's modesty and sincerity. 'I remember Charlie saying that Orwell was not an argumentative sort of person. He [Charlie] might voice an opinion about something, hoping to provoke Orwell into agreeing or disagreeing, but Orwell would just say: "You might be right, Doran!" Orwell at that time had not read Marx.' Alex Zwerdling, in *Orwell and the Left* (1974, 20), states that Orwell's work shows he had read Marx with care and understanding; he quotes from Richard Rees, *George Orwell: Fugitive from the Camp of Victory* (1961), who tells how Orwell astonished everyone at the Adelphi Summer School, 1936, by his knowledge of Marx (147). See Crick, 613, n. 49. By the mid-1940s, according to Mrs Doran, 'Charlie *classed* him [Orwell] as a rebel – not a revolutionary – who was dissatisfied with the Establishment, while remaining part of it' (*Bulletin of the Society for the Study of Labour History*, 51, part 1, April 1986, 15–17). See pp. 25–7, above, for charges against Doran.

2. Marceau Pivert contributed to *Controversy;* see 'Eye-Witness in Barcelona', n. 1, above.

3. Harry Milton, the only American in Orwell's section. See Eileen Blair's letter to John McNair, 29 July 1937, n. 11, above. He is sometimes referred to as Mike Milton.

4. The reference to appendicitis is to the supposed cause of death of Bob Smillie. Orwell gives an account of Smillie's death in *Homage to Catalonia*, pp.155–6 [VI/170–71]. He assumed that Smillie had been shot in prison, but it was later stated that he had died of appendicitis. The local ILP representative, David Murray, was refused permission to see Smillie's body, which 'may have been due to pure spite'. Orwell concludes: 'Smillie's death is not a thing I can easily forgive. Here was this brave and gifted boy, who had thrown up his career at Glasgow University in order to come and fight against Fascism, and who, as I saw for myself, had done his job at the front with faultless courage and willingness; and all they could find to do with him was to fling him into jail and let him die like a neglected animal.' For a full consideration of the controversy over Smillie's death, see Tom Buchanan, 'The Death of Bob Smillie, the Spanish Civil War, and the Eclipse of the Independent Labour Party', *Historical Journal*, 40 (1997), 435–61.

5. Stafford Cottman (1918–99) had been a clerk in local government before he joined the ILP contingent in Spain. He was Orwell's youngest colleague and escaped with him from Spain. Cottman's account of the journey is given in *Remembering Orwell*, 95–6; he was an adviser on Ken Loach's film *Land and Freedom*. He remained a loyal friend of Orwell's. See also *Orwell Remembered*, 148–55, for a transcript of an interview by him in a BBC *Arena* programme. A letter from Orwell to Cottman for 25 April 1946, when Cottman was serving in the RAF, survives (*2984*). He served as a rear gunner in Bomber Command and was fortunately invalided out of active duty the day before his bomber was shot down over Germany.

6. Young Communist League.

[386A]

Unpublished Response to Authors Take Sides on the Spanish War
[3–6 August 1937]   Typewritten copy

In June 1937, Left Review *solicited reactions of writers to the Spanish Civil War. A questionnaire, prefaced by an appeal to writers to take sides, 'For it is impossible any longer to take no side', was sent out by Nancy Cunard.¹ The appeal was issued over the names of twelve writers, who included Louis Aragon, W. H. Auden, Heinrich Mann, Ivor Montagu, Stephen Spender, Tristan Tzara and Nancy Cunard (who processed the replies). Lawrence & Wishart published the result as a pamphlet,* Authors Take Sides on the Spanish War, *in December 1937. Authors were asked, 'Are you for, or against, the legal Government and People of Republican Spain? Are you for,*

or against, Franco and Fascism?' Authors were asked to answer in half a
dozen lines. Although many wrote briefly (Samuel Beckett especially so,
turning three words into one: '¡UPTHEREPUBLIC!', and Rose Macaulay in
two words, 'AGAINST FRANCO'), many wrote more fully. Orwell's letter
to Nancy Cunard was believed to have been lost. On 18 March 1994, the
New Statesman *published an article by Andy Croft, 'The Awkward*
Squaddie', which included part of Orwell's reply to Nancy Cunard; it had
been written on the back of the appeal. She typed a copy (or had a copy
typed) of Orwell's reply and sent it to the editor of Left Review, *Randall*
Swingler, among whose papers it was found by Andy Croft, together with a
covering letter from Nancy Cunard to Swingler. The copy of Orwell's letter
is headed 'Letter received, addressed to me, at Paris address, Aug 6. 1937'; it
is not clear whether the 6 August is the date Orwell sent his letter or the date
of its receipt. In his article, Croft correctly sets the context of this letter
between the publication of the two parts of 'Spilling the Spanish Beans', 29
July and 2 September 1937 (see above). But there is a more specific, and more
significant, context, revealed by the letters published here. Orwell was
desperately anxious about the fate of his former colleagues rotting in jails in
Spain as a result of the 'reign of terror' to which he refers in his letter to
Nancy Cunard. For a much fuller note see XI/386A.

Will you please stop sending me this bloody rubbish. This is the second
or third time I have had it. I am not one of your fashionable pansies like
Auden and Spender, I was six months in Spain, most of the time fighting,
I have a bullet-hole in me at present and I am not going to write blah
about defending democracy or gallant little anybody. Moreover, I know
what is happening and has been happening on the Government side for
months past, i.e. that Fascism is being riveted on the Spanish workers
under the pretext of resisting Fascism; also that since May a reign of terror
has been proceeding and all the jails and any place that will serve as a jail
are crammed with prisoners who are not only imprisoned without trial
but are half-starved, beaten and insulted. I dare say you know it too,
though God knows anyone who could write the stuff overleaf would be
fool enough to believe anything, even the war-news in the *Daily Worker*.
But the chances are that you – whoever you are who keep sending me
this thing – have money and are well-informed; so no doubt you know

something about the inner history of the war and have deliberately joined in the defence of 'democracy' (i.e. capitalism) racket in order to aid in crushing the Spanish working class and thus indirectly defend your dirty little dividends.

This is more than 6 lines, but if I did compress what I know and think about the Spanish War into 6 lines you wouldn't print it. You wouldn't have the guts.

By the way, tell your pansy friend Spender[2] that I am preserving specimens of his war-heroics and that when the time comes when he squirms for shame at having written it, as the people who wrote the war-propaganda in the Great War are squirming now, I shall rub it in good and hard.

1.Nancy Cunard (1896–1965) was the daughter of the wealthy shipping magnate who gave his name to the Cunard line; hence the reference in Orwell's letter to her of defending 'your dirty little dividends'. She wrote poetry and literary reminiscences and devoted herself to socialist issues and the cause and arts of the blacks.

2.Stephen Spender (1909–95; Kt., 1993), poet, novelist, dramatist, critic and translator. He edited *Horizon* with Cyril Connolly, 1940–41, and was a co-editor of *Encounter*, 1953–65, remaining on the editorial board until 1967, when it was discovered that some of the money to launch *Encounter* had been provided by the US Central Intelligence Agency. Orwell counted Spender among parlour Bolsheviks and 'fashionable successful persons', whom he castigated from time to time, see Crick, 351. They later became friends and, on 15? April 1938, Orwell wrote Spender an explanation of how he changed his attitude after meeting him (*435*).

[397]
To Geoffrey Gorer
15 September 1937

The Stores, Wallington, Near Baldock, Herts

Dear Geoffrey,[1]

Thanks so much for your letter. I am glad you are enjoying yourself in Denmark, though, I must admit, it is one of the few countries I have never wanted to visit. I rang you up when I was in town, but of course you weren't there. I note you are coming back about the 24th. We shall be here till the 10th October, then we are going down to Suffolk to stay at my parents' place for some weeks. But if you can manage it any time between the 24th and the 10th, just drop us a line and then come down and stay. We can always put you up without difficulty.

What you say about not letting the Fascists in owing to dissensions between ourselves is very true so long as one is clear what one means by Fascism, also who or what it is that is making unity impossible. Of course all the Popular Front stuff that is now being pushed by the Communist press and party, Gollancz and his paid hacks etc., etc., only boils down to saying that they are in favour of British Fascism (prospective) as against German Fascism. What they are aiming to do is to get British capitalist-imperialism into an alliance with the U.S.S.R. and thence into a war with Germany. Of course they piously pretend that they don't want the war to come and that a French-British-Russian alliance can prevent it on the old balance of power system. But we know what the balance of power business led to last time, and in any case it is manifest that the nations are arming with the intention of fighting. The Popular Front boloney boils down to this: that when the war comes the Communists, labourites etc., instead of working to stop the war and overthrow the Government, will be on the side of the Government provided that the Government is on the 'right' side, ie. against Germany. But everyone with any imagination can foresee that Fascism, not of course called Fascism, will be imposed on us as soon as the war starts. So you will have Fascism with Communists participating in it, and, if we are in alliance with the U.S.S.R., taking a leading part in it. This is what has happened in Spain. After what I have seen in Spain I have come to the conclusion that it is futile to be 'anti-Fascist' while attempting to preserve capitalism. Fascism after all is only a development of capitalism, and the mildest democracy, so-called, is liable to turn into Fascism when the pinch comes. We like to think of England as a democratic country, but our rule in India, for instance, is just as bad as German Fascism, though outwardly it may be less irritating. I do not see how one can oppose Fascism except by working for the overthrow of capitalism, starting, of course, in one's own country. If one collaborates with a capitalist-imperialist government in a struggle 'against Fascism', ie. against a rival imperialism, one is simply letting Fascism in by the back door. The whole struggle in Spain, on the Government side, has turned upon this. The revolutionary parties, the Anarchists, P.O.U.M. etc., wanted to complete the revolution, the others wanted to fight the Fascists in the name of 'democracy', and, of course, when they felt sure enough of their position and had tricked the workers into giving up their arms, re-introduce capitalism. The grotesque feature, which very few people outside Spain have yet grasped, is that the Communists stood furthest of all to the right, and were more anxious even than the liberals to hunt down the revolutionaries and stamp out all revolutionary ideas. For instance, they have succeeded in breaking up the workers' militias, which were based on the trade unions and in which all ranks received the same pay and were on a basis of equality, and substituting an army on bourgeois lines where a colonel is paid eight times as much as a private etc. All these changes, of course, are put forward in the name of military necessity and backed up by the 'Trotskyist' racket, which consists of saying that anyone who professes revolutionary principles is a Trotskyist and in Fascist pay. The Spanish Communist press has for instance declared that Maxton[2] is in the pay of the Gestapo. The reason why so few people grasp what has happened in Spain is because of the Communist command of the press. Apart from their own press they have the whole of the capitalist anti-Fascist press (papers like the *News Chronicle*) on their side, because the latter have got onto the fact that official Communism is now anti-revolutionary. The result is that they have been able to put across an unprecedented amount of lies and it is almost impossible to get anyone to print anything in contradiction. The accounts of the Barcelona riots in May, which I had the misfortune to be involved in, beat everything I have ever seen for lying. Incidentally the *Daily Worker* has been following me personally with the most filthy libels, calling me pro-Fascist etc., but I asked Gollancz to silence them, which he did, not very willingly I imagine. Queerly enough I am still contracted to write a number of books for him, though he refused to publish the book I am doing on Spain before a word of it was written.

I should like to meet Edith Sitwell[3] very much, some time when I am in town. It surprised me very much to learn that she had heard of me and liked my books. I don't know that I ever cared much for her poems, but I liked very much her life of Pope.

Try and come down here some time. I hope your sprue[4] is gone.

Yours
Eric

1. Geoffrey Gorer (1905–85), social anthropologist and author of many books, including *Africa Dances* (1935), *The American People* (rev. edn 1964) and *Death, Grief and Mourning in Contemporary Britain* (1965). On 16 July 1935 he wrote to Orwell about *Burmese Days*: 'It is difficult to praise without being impertinent; it seems to me you have done a necessary and important piece of work as well as it could be done.' They met and remained lifelong friends.
2. James Maxton (1885–1946), Independent Labour MP, 1922–46; Chairman of the ILP, 1926–31, 1934–9. See his official biography by John McNair, *The Beloved Rebel* (1955).
3. Edith Sitwell (1887–1964; DBE, 1954), poet and literary personality. Her first book of poems was published at her own expense in 1915, and she continued to write throughout her life. She achieved lasting and widespread recognition for *Façade*, which was read in a concert version, with music by William Walton, in January 1922. She encouraged many young artists and was greatly interested in Orwell's work.
4. Here, a throat infection.

---

[401]

Review *of* Red Spanish Notebook *by Mary Low and Juan Brea;* Heroes of the Alcazar *by R. Timmermans;* Spanish Circus *by Martin Armstrong*
Time and Tide, *9 October 1937*

Red Spanish Notebook gives a vivid picture of Loyalist Spain, both at the front and in Barcelona and Madrid, in the earlier and more revolutionary period of the war. It is admittedly a partisan book, but probably it is none the worse for that. The joint authors were working for the P.O.U.M., the most extreme of the revolutionary parties, since suppressed by the Government. The P.O.U.M. has been so much vilified in the foreign, and especially the Communist press, that a statement of its case was badly needed.

Up till May of this year the situation in Spain was a very curious one. A mob of mutually hostile political parties were fighting for their lives against a common enemy, and at the same time quarrelling bitterly among themselves as to whether this was or was not a revolution as well as a war. Definitely revolutionary events had taken place – land had been seized by the peasants, industries collectivized, big capitalists killed or driven out, the Church practically abolished – but there had been no fundamental change in the structure of government. It was a situation capable of developing either towards Socialism or back to capitalism; and it is now clear that, given a victory over Franco, some kind of capitalist republic will emerge. But at the same time there was occurring a revolution of ideas that was perhaps more important than the short-lived economic changes. For several months large blocks of people believed that all men are equal and were able to act on their belief. The result was a feeling of liberation and hope that is difficult to conceive in our money-tainted atmosphere. It is here that *Red Spanish Notebook* is valuable. By a series of intimate day-to-day pictures (generally small things: a bootblack refusing a tip, a notice in the brothels saying, 'Please treat the women as comrades') it shows you what human beings are like when they are trying to behave as human beings and not as cogs in the capitalist machine. No one who was in Spain during the months when people still believed in the revolution will ever forget that strange and moving experience. It has left something behind that no dictatorship, not even Franco's, will be able to efface.

In every book written by a political partisan one has got to be on the look-out for one or another class of prejudice. The authors of this book are Trotskyists – I gather that they were sometimes an embarrassment to the P.O.U.M., which was not a Trotskyist body, though for a while it had Trotskyists working for it – and, therefore their prejudice is against the official Communist Party, to which they are not always strictly fair. But is the Communist Party always strictly fair to the Trotskyists? Mr. C.L.R. James,[1] author of that very able book *World Revolution*, contributes an introduction.

Heroes of the Alcazar re-tells the story of the siege last autumn, when a garrison mainly of cadets and Civil Guards held out for seventy-two days against terrible odds, until Toledo was relieved by Franco's troops. There is no need because one's sympathies are on the other side to pretend that this was not a heroic exploit. And some of the details of siege-life are very interesting; I particularly liked the account of the ingenious way in which a motor-bicycle engine was hitched onto a hand-mill to grind corn for the garrison. But the book is poorly written, in a glutinous style, full of piety and denunciations of the 'Reds'. There is an introduction by Major Yeats Brown, who generously concedes that not *all* the 'Red Militia' were 'cruel and treacherous'. The photographs of groups of defenders bring home one of the most pathetic aspects of the civil war. They are so like groups of Government militiamen that if they were changed round no one would know the difference.

Finally, Spain of a hundred years ago. *Spanish Circus* recounts the reign of Carlos IV, Godoy [2] (the 'Prince of Peace'), Napoleon, Trafalgar, palace intrigues, Goya's portraits – it is that period. At this particular moment I find it rather hard to read such a book. Spain is too much bound up in my mind with flooded trenches, the rattle of machine guns, food-shortage and lies in the newspapers. But if you want to escape from that aspect of Spain, this is probably the book you are looking for. It is written with distinction and, as far as I can judge, it is a piece of accurate historical research. The way in which Mr. Armstrong has *not* exploited the scandalous story of Godoy and Maria Luisa should be an example to all popular historians.

1. C.L.R. James (1901–89) was born in Trinidad but lived most of his life in England, where he died. A Marxist, but not a member of the Communist Party, he wrote on politics and cricket. He settled in Lancashire in the 1930s and wrote on cricket for the *Manchester Guardian* leading to the fine book *Beyond the Boundary* (1963). He worked for a British West Indian Federation (proposed 1947) and lectured in the USA, but fell victim to McCarthyism and was expelled.

2. Manuel de Godoy (1767–1851) was twice Prime Minister of Spain. When a member of the royal bodyguard, he became the lover of Maria Luisa of Parma, wife of future king, Charles IV. He sided with the French in the Napoleonic Wars, and in 1807 agreed to the partition of Portugal. The following year, Charles was forced to abdicate in favour of the heir apparent (later Ferdinand VII), and by a device, Godoy, with Charles and Ferdinand, became a prisoner of Napoleon. Martin Armstrong (1882–1974) was to be one of the contributors to Orwell's 'Story by Five Authors', 30 October 1942 *(1623)*.

[413A]

To H. N. Brailsford
10 December 1937

The Stores, Wallington, Near Baldock, Herts

Dear Mr Brailsford,[1]

I cannot exactly claim your acquaintance, though I believe I did meet you for a moment in Barcelona, and I know you met my wife there.

I have been trying to get the truth about certain aspects of the May fighting in Barcelona. I see that in the *New Statesman* of May 22nd you state that the P.O.U.M. partisans attacked the Government with tanks and guns 'stolen from Government arsenals'. I was, of course, in Barcelona throughout the fighting, and though I cannot answer for tanks I know as well as one can be certain about such a thing that no guns were firing anywhere. In various papers there occurs a version of what is evidently the same story, to the effect that the P.O.U.M. were using a battery of stolen 75 mm. guns on the Plaza de España. I know this story to be untrue for a number of reasons. To begin with, I have it from eye-witnesses who were on the spot that there were no guns there; secondly, I examined the buildings round the square afterwards and there were no signs of gunfire; thirdly, throughout the fighting I did not hear the sound of artillery, which is unmistakeable if one is used to it. It would seem therefore that there has been a mistake. I wonder if you could be kind enough to tell me what was the source of the story about the guns and tanks? I am sorry to trouble you, but I want to get this story cleared up if I can.

Perhaps I ought to tell you that I write under the name of George Orwell.

Yours truly
Eric Blair

---

1. Henry Noel Brailsford (1873–1958) was a socialist intellectual, author, political journalist and leader-writer for the *Manchester Guardian, Daily News* and the *Nation*; and editor of the *New Leader*, weekly organ of the ILP, 1922–6. His article in the *New Statesman & Nation* was published in two parts. In the first, 'Anarchists and Communists in Spain', 22 May 1937, he said that the POUM 'represented the older and now heretical Communist position. It opposed any alliance with the middle-class even for the salvation of the Republic: for the sake of political as distinct from social democracy it would make no sacrifices to unity. Against it, far more fiercely than against the Anarchists, the Communists waged a merciless feud, and charged it with all the treasons ascribed to Trotsky . . . the Anarchists with whom [the POUM] allied itself stand farther from its unbending Marxism than do the Socialists whom it assailed with its tanks and guns stolen from Government arsenals.'

[414]

Review of Storm Over Spain *by Mairin Mitchell;* Spanish
Rehearsal *by Arnold Lunn;* Catalonia Infelix *by E. Allison
Peers;* Wars of Ideas in Spain *by José Castillejo;*
Invertebrate Spain *by José Ortega y Gasset*
Time and Tide, *11 December 1937*

Storm Over Spain sounds like a war-book, but though it covers a period
that includes the civil war the author says very little about the war itself
– a subject which is obviously distasteful to her. As she very truly remarks,
the atrocity stories that are so eagerly circulated by both sides are an
indictment not of Right or Left, but simply of war.

Her book is valuable for a number of reasons, but especially because,
unlike almost all English writers on Spain,[1] she gives a fair deal to the
Spanish Anarchists. The Anarchists and Syndicalists have been persistently
misrepresented in England, and the average English person still retains
his eighteen-ninetyish notion that Anarchism is the same thing as anarchy.
Anyone who wants to know what Spanish Anarchism stands for, and the
remarkable things it achieved, especially in Catalonia, during the first few
months of the revolution, should read Chapter VII of Miss Mitchell's
book. The pity is that so much of what the Anarchists achieved has
already been undone, ostensibly because of military necessity, actually in
order to prepare the way for the return of capitalism when the war is over.

Mr. Arnold Lunn[2] writes as a supporter of General Franco and believes
life in 'Red' Spain (which he has not visited) to be one continuous
massacre. On the authority of Mr. Arthur Bryant,[3] who, 'as an historian,
is well accustomed to weigh evidence', he puts the number of non-
combatants massacred by the 'reds' since the beginning of the war as
350,000. It would appear, also, that 'the burning of a nun in petrol or the
sawing off of a Conservative tradesman's legs' are 'the commonplaces of
"democratic" Spain'.

Now, I was about six months in Spain, almost exclusively among
Socialists, Anarchists and Communists, and if I remember rightly I never
even once sawed off a Conservative tradesman's legs. I am almost certain
I should remember doing such a thing, however commonplace it may
seem to Mr. Lunn and Mr. Bryant. But will Mr. Lunn believe me? No, he

will not. And meanwhile stories every bit as silly as this are being manufactured on the other side, and people who were sane two years ago are swallowing them eagerly. That, apparently, is what war, even war in other countries, does to the human mind.

Professor Allison Peers[4] is the leading English authority on Catalonia. His book is a history of the province, and naturally, at the present moment, the most interesting chapters are those towards the end, describing the war and the revolution. Unlike Mr. Lunn, Professor Peers understands the internal situation on the Government side, and Chapter XIII of his book gives an excellent account of the strains and stresses between the various political parties. He believes that the war may last for years, that Franco is likely to win, and that there is no hope of democracy in Spain when the war is over. All of them depressing conclusions, but the first two are quite probably correct and the last is most assuredly so.

Finally, two books which really belong to an earlier period, but are relevant to the civil war in so much that they give certain glimpses of its origins. *Wars of Ideas in Spain* is primarily a treatise on Spanish education. I am not competent to judge it, but I can admire the intellectual detachment that has been able to produce it amid the horrors of civil war. Dr. Castillejo is a professor at the University of Madrid and for thirty years past has worked for educational reform in Spain. He is now watching his life-work going down into a sea of rival fanaticisms; for, as he rather sadly recognizes, whatever else survives the war, intellectual tolerance will not. *Invertebrate Spain* is a collection of essays, most of them first published about 1920, on various aspects of the Spanish character. Sr. Ortega y Gasset[5] is one of those writers of the type of Keyserling, who explain everything in terms of race, geography and tradition (in fact, of anything except economics), and who are constantly saying illuminating things without reaching any general conclusion. Open *Invertebrate Spain* and you realize immediately that you are in contact with a distinguished mind; go on reading it, and you find yourself wondering what the devil this is all about. Still, it *is* a distinguished mind, and if the book as a whole leaves behind an impression of vagueness, or even chaos, each separate paragraph is capable of starting an interesting train of thought.

1. Mairin Mitchell wrote to Orwell following the publication of this review (letter undated) thanking him for the generosity with which he had treated her book, especially because,

from her reading of *The Road to Wigan Pier*, she did not think they were in the same political camp. However, she did point out that she was 'unlike almost all English writers on Spain', in being Irish!

2. Arnold Lunn (1888–1974; Kt., 1952) incurred Orwell's wrath because he supported Franco. He was an authority on skiing and wrote books on travel and religion. With Monsignor Ronald Knox he published their correspondence about Roman Catholicism, *Difficulties* (1932).

3. Sir Arthur Bryant (1899–1985), conservatively inclined historian, whose books include *The Spirit of Conservatism* (1929), *Stanley Baldwin: A Tribute* (1937), *Unfinished Victory*, on Germany 1918–33 (1940), *The Years of Endurance, 1793–1802* (1942) and *The Years of Victory, 1802–12* (1944). Of *Unfinished Victory*, Kenneth Rose said, 'Goebbels himself could not have composed a more ingratiating apologia for the Nazis. Anti-semitism is a recurrent theme', yet he received 'a whole chestful of decorations' including a knighthood and the Companion of Honour (*Sunday Telegraph*, 1 August 1993).

4. E. Allison Peers (1891–1952), an Anglican scholar of English and French literature, was appointed in 1920 to the chair of Spanish at Liverpool University. His knowledge of Spain was extensive, and he wrote several distinguished studies on that country. He wrote on contemporary Spain from well before the outbreak of the civil war for the *Bulletin of Spanish Studies*. Under the pseudonym Bruce Truscot he wrote the influential *Redbrick University* (1943).

5. José Ortega y Gasset (1883–1955), Spanish essayist and philosopher. Of his many books and essays, *The Revolt of the Masses* (in Spanish, 1929–30; in English, 1932) is perhaps now best known. Orwell reviewed *Invertebrate Spain* at greater length in 'The Lure of Profundity', *New English Weekly*, 30 December 1937 (415).

---

[424]

H. N. Brailsford to Orwell
17 December 1937

Dear Mr. Blair,

The story about the theft of guns & tanks from an arsenal in the rear of the Aragón front came from the Russian Consul-General Ossienko°,[1] who has since been purged. He had his notes before him & gave me date, place & the details of the forged order by which it was worked. I also took notes but haven't got them now. The people who actually did this were Friends of Durruti[2] but I gathered they were acting then & later with Poum. I had this from him at the end of April, before the rising. I accepted it, because the Consul-General struck me as a fair-minded man, who had much good to say about Anarchists. About Poum he said very little, but was in general less prejudiced than most Communists. I had confirmation later of this story from the latter.

I'm puzzled when you now tell me that no guns were used in the rising. I hope I haven't been unwittingly unfair.

I hope your wife is well after her very trying time in Barcelona. You must both feel very sore.

Sincerely Yours

H. N. Brailsford

P.S. Is it conceivable that the guns *were* stolen, but were recovered before the rising?

1. Vladimir Antonov-Ovsëenko (1884–1937), Soviet Consul-General in Barcelona. He was recalled by Stalin to take up a high judicial post shortly after the May Events of 1937, but he disappeared soon after his return and was presumably murdered. He had led troops in the assault on the Winter Palace at St Petersburg in 1917. Orwell refers to him in *Homage to Catalonia*, p. 204 [VI/234].

2. The Friends of Durruti were an extreme anarchist group (see Thomas, 656, n. 1). Orwell refers to them in *Homage to Catalonia*, pp. 194–5 and 202–3 [VI/219–20 and 231–3].

[414B]

To H. N. Brailsford
18 December 1937

The Stores, Wallington, Near Baldock, Herts

Dear Mr Brailsford,

Thank you very much for your letter. I was very interested to know the source of the story about tanks and guns. I have no doubt the Russian ambassador told it you in good faith and from what little I know myself I should think it quite likely it was true in the form in which he gave it you. But because of the special circumstances, incidents of that kind are apt to be a little misleading. I hope it will not bore you if I add one or two more remarks about this question.

As I say, it is quite conceivable that at some time or other the guns *were* stolen, because to my own knowledge, though I never actually saw it done, there was a great deal of stealing of weapons from one militia to another. But people who were not actually in the militia do not seem to have understood the arms situation. As far as possible arms were prevented from getting to the P.O.U.M. and Anarchist militias, and they were left only with the bare minimum that would enable them to hold the line but not to make any offensive action. There were times when the men in the trenches actually had not enough rifles to go round, and at no time until the militias were broken up was artillery allowed to get to the Aragón front in any quantity. When the Anarchists made their attacks on the Jaca road in March–April they had to do so with very little artillery support and had frightful casualties. At this time (March–April) there were only about 12 of our aeroplanes operating over Huesca. When the Popular Army attacked in June a man who took part in the attack tells me that there were 160. In particular, the Russian arms were kept from the Aragón front at the time when they were being issued to the police forces in the rear. Until April I saw only one Russian weapon, a sub-machine gun, which quite possibly had been stolen. In April two batteries of Russian 75 mm. guns arrived – again possibly stolen and conceivably the guns referred to by the Russian ambassador. As to pistols and revolvers, which are very necessary in trench warfare, the Government would not issue permits to ordinary militiamen and militia officers to buy them, and one could only buy them illegally from the Anarchists. In these circumstances the outlook everyone had was that one had to get hold of weapons by hook or by crook, and all the militias were constantly pilfering them from one another. I remember an officer describing to me how he and some others had stolen a field gun from a gun-park belonging to the P.S.U.C.,[1] and I would have done the same myself without any hesitation in the circumstances. This kind of thing always goes on in war-time, but, coming together with the newspaper stories to the effect that the P.O.U.M. was a disguised Fascist organisation, it was easy to suggest that they stole weapons not to use against the Fascists but to use against the Government. Owing to the Communist control of the press the similar behaviour by other units was kept dark. For instance there is not much doubt that in March some partisans of the P.S.U.C. stole 12 tanks from a Government arsenal by means of a forged order. *La Batalla*, the P.O.U.M. paper, was fined 5000 pesetas and suppressed for 4 days for reporting this, but the Anarchist paper, *Solidaridad Obrera*, was able to report it with impunity. As to the guns, if stolen, being kept in Barcelona, it seems to me immensely unlikely. Some of the men at the front would certainly have heard of it and would have raised hell if they had known weapons were being kept back, and I should doubt if you could keep two batteries of guns concealed even in a town the size of Barcelona. In any case they would have come to light later, when the P.O.U.M. was suppressed. I do not, of course, know what was in all the P.O.U.M. strongholds, but I was in the three principal ones during the Barcelona fighting, and I know that they had only enough weapons for the usual armed guards that were kept on buildings. They had no machine guns, for instance. And I think it is certain that there was no artillery-fire during the fighting. I see that you refer to the Friends of Durruti being more or less under P.O.U.M. control, and John Langdon-Davies[2] says something to the same effect in his report in the *News Chronicle*. This story was only put about in order to brand the P.O.U.M. as 'Trotskyist'. Actually the Friends of Durruti, which was an extremist organisation, was bitterly hostile to the P.O.U.M. (from their point of view a more or less right-wing organisation) and so far as I know no one was a member of both. The only connection between the two is that at the time of the May fighting the P.O.U.M. are said to have published approval of an inflammatory poster which was put up by the Friends of Durruti. Again there is some doubt about this – it is certain that there was no *poster*, as described in the *News Chronicle* and elsewhere, but there may have been a handbill of some kind. It is impossible to discover, as all records have been destroyed and the Spanish authorities would not allow me to send out of Spain files even of the P.S.U.C. newspapers, let alone the others. The only sure thing is that the Communist reports on the May fighting, and still more on the alleged Fascist plot by the P.O.U.M., are completely untruthful. What worries me is not these lies being told, which is what one expects in war-time, but that the English left-wing press has refused to allow the other side a hearing. Eg. the papers made a tremendous splash about Nin and the others being in Fascist pay, but have failed to mention that the Spanish Government, other than the Communist members, have denied that there was any truth in the story. I suppose the underlying idea is that they are somehow aiding the Spanish Government by allowing the Communists a free hand. I am sorry to burden you with all this stuff, but have tried to do all I can, which is not much, to get the truth about what has happened in Spain more widely known. It does not matter to me personally when they say that I am in Fascist pay, but it is different for the thousands who are in prison in Spain and are liable to be murdered by the secret police as so many have been already. I doubt whether it would be possible to do much for the Spanish anti-Fascist prisoners, but some kind of organised protest would probably get many of the foreigners released.

My wife wishes to be remembered to you. Neither of us suffered any ill-effects from being in Spain, though, of course, the whole thing was terribly distressing and disillusioning. The effects of my wound passed off more quickly than was expected. If it would interest I will send you a copy of my book on Spain when it comes out.

Yours sincerely,
Eric Blair

1. Partido Socialista Unificado de Cataluña (The United Catalan Socialist Party, a communist party). For its 'line', *see Homage to Catalonia*, pp. 179–80 [VI/201–2].
2. John Langdon-Davies (1897–1971), journalist and author. He wrote for the *News Chronicle* in Spain and was joint secretary with the communist lawyer, Geoffrey Bing, of the Comintern-inspired Commission of Inquiry into Alleged Breaches of the Non-Intervention Agreement in Spain; see Thomas 397–8. Orwell's 'refusal to accept the politics of liquidation and elimination' led to sneering by 'harder Communists' – of which Langdon-Davies was one – at *Homage to Catalonia*: see Valentine Cunningham, *British Writers of the Thirties* (1988), 427.

[421]

Review of The Tree of Gernika *by G. L. Steer;* Spanish Testament *by Arthur Koestler*
Time and Tide, 5 February 1938

It goes without saying that everyone who writes of the Spanish War writes as a partisan. What is perhaps less obvious is that, because of the huge discords that have shaken and threatened to split the Government side, every pro-Government writer is really involved in several distinct controversies. He is writing *for* the Government, but he is also (though he generally pretends otherwise) writing *against* the Communists, or the Trotskyists, or the Anarchists, or what-not. Mr. Steer's book is no exception to the general rule, but he carries a different set of prejudices from the majority of pro-Government writers, because he happens to have seen the war not in eastern Spain but in the Basque country.

In a way the problems here were simpler. The Basques were Catholic and Conservative, the left-wing organizations were weak even in the large towns (as Mr. Steer says, 'there was no social revolution in Bilbao'), and what the Basques chiefly wanted was regional autonomy, which they were likelier to get from the Popular Front Government than from Franco. Mr. Steer writes entirely from the Basque standpoint, and he has, very strongly, the curious English characteristic of being unable to praise one race without damning another. Being pro-Basque, he finds it necessary to be anti-Spanish, i.e., to some extent anti-Government as well as anti-Franco. As a result his book is so full of gibes at the Asturians and other non-Basque loyalists as to make one doubtful of his reliability as a witness – a pity, for he has had opportunities that were shared by very few Englishmen.

His book is sub-titled 'A Field Study of Modern War', but as a matter of fact it is not at all clear how much he has seen with his own eyes and how much he is repeating from hearsay. Nearly every incident is described as though by an eye-witness, but it is obviously impossible that Mr. Steer can have been in all places at once. However, there is one very important and much-disputed event upon which he speaks with undoubted authority – the bombing of Guernica (or Gernika). He was in the immediate neighbourhood at the time of the aeroplane raids, and his account leaves no doubt that the little town was *not* 'burnt by Red militiamen' but systematically destroyed from the air, out of sheer, wanton brutality. Guernica was not even of much importance as a military objective. And the most horrible thought of all is that this blotting-out of an open town was simply the correct and logical use of a modern weapon. For it is precisely to slaughter and terrify the civilian population – not to destroy entrenchments, which are very difficult to hit from the air – that bombing aeroplanes exist. The photographs in this book are very good. All photographs in books on the Spanish war have a certain similarity, but these have much more character in them than most.

Mr. Arthur Koestler,[1] a *News Chronicle* correspondent, stayed in Málaga when the Republican troops had departed – a bold thing to do, for he had already published a book containing some very unfriendly remarks about General Queipo de Llano.[2] He was thrown into jail by the rebels, and suffered what must have been the fate of literally tens of thousands of political prisoners in Spain. That is to say, he was condemned to death without trial and then kept in prison for months, much of the time in solitary confinement, listening at his keyhole night after night for the roar of rifle-fire as his fellow prisoners were shot in batches of six or a dozen. As usual – for it really does seem to be quite usual – he knew that he was under sentence of death without knowing with any certainty what he was accused of.

The prison part of the book is written mainly in the form of a diary. It is of the greatest psychological interest – probably one of the most honest and unusual documents that have been produced by the Spanish war. The earlier part is more ordinary and in places even looks rather as though it had been 'edited' for the benefit of the Left Book Club. Even more than Mr. Steer's, this book lays bare the central evil of modern war – the fact that, as Nietzsche puts it, 'he who fights against dragons becomes a dragon himself'.[3]

Mr. Koestler says:

I can no longer pretend to be objective . . . Anyone who has lived through the hell of Madrid with his eyes, his nerves, his heart, his stomach – and then pretends to be objective, is a liar. If those who have at their command printing machines and printer's ink for the expression of their opinions, remain neutral and objective in the face of such bestiality, then Europe is lost.

I quite agree. You cannot be objective about an aerial torpedo. And the horror we feel of these things has led to this conclusion: if someone drops a bomb on your mother, go and drop two bombs on his mother. The only apparent alternatives are to smash dwelling houses to powder, blow out human entrails and burn holes in children with lumps of thermite, or to be enslaved by people who are more ready to do these things than you are yourself; as yet no one has suggested a practicable way out.

1. Arthur Koestler (1905–83), novelist and political and scientific writer, born in Hungary. He was a lifelong friend of Orwell's. See Orwell's essay on Koestler, September 1944 (*2548*), and the cumulative index in *CW*. XX.

2. General Gonzalo Queipo de Llano y Serra (1875–1951), Nationalist, who, on 18 July 1936 in Seville, when commander of carabineers, 'carried out an outstanding *coup de main*' and took Seville for Franco. From the radio station he made a 'notorious series of harangues. In a voice seasoned by many years' consumption of sherry, he declared that Spain was saved and that the rabble who resisted the rising would be shot like dogs' (Thomas, 221, 223). In

his most famous broadcast, he said, 'tonight I shall take a sherry and tomorrow I shall take Málaga' (520). In 1947, though now an avowed republican, he accepted a marquisate from Franco (948).

3. Nietzsche, *Jenseits von Gut und Böse* (Beyond Good and Evil, 1886), ch. 4, no. 146.

---

[422]

To the Editor, Time and Tide
5 February 1938

> 'Time-Tide *Diary' of 22 January 1938 included these paragraphs over the pen-name 'Sirocco' [unknown]:*

That nine thousand Left Book Club's members rallied to the Albert Hall on Sunday is gratifying or alarming, according to whichever way you look at it. Here is an organization both subtle and widespread, an embryo Catholic Church with Mr. Gollancz as Pope. I can imagine him seated at his desk with a map of England in front of him. Every time the telephone rings he sticks in a red flag – a new member for Blackpool, five for Manchester, a married couple for Stow-on-the-Wold. Presently there is no map left – only red flags.

It is hard to see why a club with such excellent principles should give one such a nightmare. The Left is kind. The Left has good intentions. Mr. Gollancz is only the spokesman of the Left. But is he also the censor? Why are there no orange volumes by anarchists? Who publishes the perorations of those nice young Trotskyites one meets at parties? What galvanizes all Left Book Club writers into total and unnatural agreement? Is the English intellectual already in training for the critical apathy of post-revolution?

> *Orwell responded two weeks later:*

'TROTSKYIST' PUBLICATIONS

SIR, – In 'Time-Tide Diary' of January 22nd, Sirocco remarks upon the 'unnatural agreement' of Left Book Club writers, and adds, 'Why are there no orange volumes[1] by anarchists? Who publishes the perorations of those nice young Trotskyites one meets at parties?'

As a matter of fact, a certain number of political books written from a

Left Wing but non-Communist standpoint do get published, in particular by Messrs. Secker & Warburg, who are coming to be known rather inaccurately as 'the Trotskyist publishers'. I have had the honour of reviewing several books of this type, dealing with the Spanish war, in your columns. One was *Red Spanish Notebook*, which was written actually by Trotskyists. I thought it, as I said at the time, a prejudiced book, but interesting in detail and giving a good picture of Catalonia in the early months of the war. Another was Mairin Mitchell's *Storm Over Spain*, written by a Catholic, but very sympathetic to the Spanish Anarchists. And above all there was Franz Borkenau's *The Spanish Cockpit* (published by Faber's), which was written from a strictly non-party standpoint, except insomuch that the author was pro-Government and anti-Franco. This in my opinion is by a long way the ablest book that has yet appeared on the Spanish war or is likely to appear until the dust of conflict has died down. But the sequel to my review of it is rather interesting, and gives one a glimpse of the kind of censorship under which we are now suffering and of which the Left Book Club is a symptom.

Shortly after my review of *The Spanish Cockpit* appeared in *Time and Tide*, the author wrote and thanked me, saying that though the book had been widely praised I was the only reviewer who had drawn attention to one of its central themes, i.e., to the real part played by the Communist Party in Spain. Simultaneously I had had the book to review for another well-known weekly paper, and had said much the same as I said in *Time and Tide*, but at greater length. My review was refused publication on the ground that it 'controverted editorial policy'.[2] Meanwhile I had already discovered that it was almost impossible to get any publicity in the English press for a truthful account of what had been happening in Catalonia in May–June, 1937. A number of people had said to me with varying degrees of frankness that one must not tell the truth about what was happening in Spain, and the part played by the Communist Party, because to do so would be to prejudice public opinion against the Spanish Government and so aid Franco. I do not agree with this view, because I hold the outmoded opinion that in the long run it does not pay to tell lies, but in so far as it was dictated by a desire to help the Spanish Government, I can respect it. But what I think is interesting is this. The pro-Government papers covered up the disreputable happenings in Spain, the mass impris-onments without trial, assassinations by the secret police, etc., but so did the pro-Franco papers. The huge 'Trotsky-Fascist' plot which the Communist press claimed to have discovered was given wide publicity; the fact that Prieto[3] and other members of the Government denied that there was any truth whatever in the 'plot' story, and said roundly that the police were practically an independent body under Communist control, was carefully unmentioned. It will be seen, therefore, that the pro-Communist censorship extends a great deal further than the Left Book Club. The newspapers of the Right, although professing to lump all 'Reds' together and to be equally hostile to all of them, are in fact perfectly well aware which parties and individuals are or are not dangerous to the structure of Capitalism. Ten years ago it was almost impossible to get anything printed in favour of Communism; today it is almost impossible to get anything printed in favour of Anarchism or 'Trotskyism'. Did not Miss Ellen Wilkinson remark in your number of January 22nd that in Paris 'one can meet a Pertinax and a former Chef du Cabinet, Poincaré, at a lunch with Communist leaders without any sense of strain'?[4] And does she really see no more in this than that Pertinax and Thorez[5] are both frightened of Hitler?

1. Left Book Club copies intended for members were bound in limp orange-coloured covers.

2. See Orwell's letter to Raymond Mortimer, 9 February 1938, following.

3. Indalecio Prieto y Tuero (1883–1962) was a Socialist. He was Minister of Defence in the Negrín Government, and a fountainhead of defeatism; see Thomas, 809. He founded the SIM, the counter-espionage police of ill-repute, and died in exile in Mexico.

4. Ellen Cicely Wilkinson (1891–1947) was a leading Labour Party MP, first elected in 1924. She had written: 'there is an influential section of French opinion which, though completely reactionary at home, is passionately patriotic as against the old enemy Germany. M. de Kérillis and Pertinax are the best-known voices of this current of opinion. In France today, however, one cannot be anti-German without also being anti-Fascist. Anti-Fascism immediately links up with the most uncompromising anti-Hitlerites who are the Communists. So one can meet a Pertinax . . .' Henri de Kérillis was a journalist and right-wing politician. He was the only non-communist member of the Chamber of Deputies to vote against ratification of the Munich Agreement with Hitler. Pertinax was the pen-name of journalist André Géraud (1882–1956). He was London correspondent of the right-wing *Echo de Paris*, 1905–14, and foreign-affairs editor, 1917–38. He went to the United States after the fall of France in 1940. After the war, he became diplomatic correspondent for *France-Soir*. Raymond Poincaré (1860–1934), a lawyer, was both Premier and Foreign Minister of France from

January 1912 to January 1913, and President from 1913 to 1920. Again Premier, 1926–9, he resigned because of ill health. His politics were conservative.

5. Maurice Thorez (1900–1964), a miner at the age of twelve, became Secretary-General of the Pas de Calais Communist Federation in 1923 and Secretary-General of the Communist Party of France in 1930. He went to the Soviet Union in 1939 and returned only in 1944. He had been elected a deputy in 1932, and from 1945 to 1946 was a minister of state. In 'As I Please', 48, 17 November 1944, Orwell devoted a section to Thorez and the falsification of history (see 2579).

---

[424]

To Raymond Mortimer
9 February 1938

On reading Orwell's letter of 5 February 1938 to the editor of Time and Tide, *Raymond Mortimer, critic and literary editor of the* New Statesman & Nation *and one of the best that paper had, wrote to Orwell, on 8 February 1938, in protest, saying: 'It is possible of course that the "well known weekly paper" to which you refer is not the* New Statesman, *but I take this as a reference to us, and so no doubt will the majority of those who read your letter.' The offices of the* New Statesman *were bombed during the war, so all the correspondence of that time has been lost. But among his papers Orwell kept the originals of letters from Kingsley Martin, editor of the* New Statesman, *and Raymond Mortimer and a carbon copy, reprinted here, of his reply to Mortimer.*

The Stores, Wallington, Near Baldock, Herts

Dear Mortimer,

With reference to your letter of February 8th. I am extremely sorry if I have hurt your or anybody else's feelings, but before speaking of the general issues involved, I must point out that what you say in it is not quite correct. You say, 'Your review of *The Spanish Cockpit* was refused, because it gave a most inadequate and misleading description of the book. You used the review merely to express your own opinions and to present facts which you thought should be known. Moreover, last time I saw you, you acknowledged this. Why then do you now suggest, quite mistakenly, that the review was refused because it "controverted editorial policy"? Are you confusing the review with the previous refusal of an article, which you submitted, and which the editor turned down because we had just printed three articles on the same subject.'

I attach a copy of Kingsley Martin's letter. You will see from this that the review *was* refused because it 'controverts the political policy of the paper' (I should have said 'political policy' not 'editorial policy'). Secondly, you say that my previous article had been turned down 'because we had just printed three articles on the same subject'. Now, the article I sent in was on the suppression of the P.O.U.M., the alleged 'Trotsky-Fascist' plot, the murder of Nin etc. So far as I know the *New Statesman* has never published any article on this subject. I certainly did and do admit that the review I wrote was tendentious and perhaps unfair, but it was not returned to me on those grounds, as you see from the letter attached.

Nothing is more hateful to me than to get mixed up in these controversies and to write, as it were, against people and newspapers that I have always respected, but one has got to realise what kind of issues are involved and the very great difficulty of getting the truth ventilated in the English press. So far as one can get at the figures, not less than 3000 political prisoners (ie. anti-Fascists) are in the Spanish jails at present, and the majority of them have been there six or seven months without any kind of trial or charge, in the most filthy physical conditions, as I have seen with my own eyes. A number of them have been bumped off, and there is not much doubt that there would have been a wholesale massacre if the Spanish Government had not had the sense to disregard the clamour in the Communist press. Various members of the Spanish Government have said over and over again to Maxton, McGovern, Félicien Challaye[1] and others that they wish to release these people but are unable to do so because of Communist pressure. What happens in Loyalist Spain is largely governed by outside opinion, and there is no doubt that if there had [been] a general protest from foreign Socialists the anti-Fascist prisoners would have been released. Even the protests of a small body like the

I.L.P. have had some effect. But a few months back when a petition was got up for the release of the anti-Fascist prisoners, nearly all the leading English Socialists refused to sign it. I do not doubt that this was because, though no doubt they disbelieved the tale about a 'Trotsky-Fascist' plot, they had gathered a general impression that the Anarchists and the P.O.U.M. were working against the Government, and, in particular, had believed the lies that were published in the English press about the fighting in Barcelona in May 1937. To mention an individual instance, Brailsford in one of his articles in the *New Statesman* was allowed to state that the P.O.U.M. had attacked the Government with stolen batteries of guns, tanks etc. I was in Barcelona during the fighting, and as far as one can ever prove a negative I can prove by eye-witnesses etc. that this tale was absolutely untrue. At the time of the correspondence over my review I wrote to Kingsley Martin to tell him it was untrue, and more recently I wrote to Brailsford to ask him what was the source of the story. He had to admit that he had had it on what amounted to no authority whatever. (Stephen Spender has his letter at present, but I could get it for you if you wanted to see it.) Yet neither the *New Statesman* nor Brailsford has published any retraction of this statement, which amounts to an accusation of theft and treachery against numbers of innocent people. I do not think you can blame me if I feel that the *New Statesman* has its share of blame for the one-sided view that has been presented.

Once again, let me say how sorry I am about this whole business, but I have got to do what little I can to get justice for people who have been imprisoned without trial and libelled in the press, and one way of doing so is to draw attention to the pro-Communist censorship that undoubtedly exists. I would keep silent about the whole affair if I thought it would help the Spanish Government (as a matter of fact, before we left Spain some of the imprisoned people asked us *not* to attempt any publicity abroad because it might tend to discredit the Government), but I doubt whether it helps in the long run to cover things up as has been done in England. If the charges of espionage etc. that were made against us in the Communist papers had been given a proper examination at the time in the foreign press, it would have been seen that they were nonsense and the whole business might have been forgotten. As it was, the rubbish about a Trotsky-Fascist plot was widely circulated and no denial of it was published except in very obscure papers and, very half-heartedly, in the *Herald* and *Manchester Guardian*. The result was that there was no protest from abroad and all these thousands of people have stayed in prison, and a number have been murdered, the effect being to spread hatred and dissension all through the Socialist movement.

I am sending back the books you gave me to review. I think it would be better if I did not write for you again. I am terribly sorry about this whole affair, but I have got to stand by my friends, which may involve attacking the *New Statesman* when I think they are covering up important issues.

Yours sincerely

Handwritten on a separate sheet is a note by Orwell which, because there is no salutation, was almost certainly sent to Raymond Mortimer with the typewritten letter above. Orwell enclosed the letter from H. N. Brailsford which he said Spender had. Brailsford's letter here follows this addendum.

I add this letter from H. N. Brailsford[2] because I think it is of interest as showing how stories get made up. In the *New Statesman* he spoke of P.O.U.M. adherents during the Barcelona fighting attacking the Government with stolen tanks & guns. I wrote & asked where he learned this, and it appears from his answer:

a. That he accepted Antonov-Ovseenko's statements about the Friends of Durruti, though obviously no Russian dare speak otherwise than unfavourably about a 'Trotskyist' organisation.

b. That on the same authority he assumed that the F. of D. was 'acting with' the P.O.U.M.

c. That he added this onto some statements in *Inprecor*[3] & elsewhere & so produced the story about guns in the streets of Barcelona.

Meanwhile it is always possible that guns *were* stolen, only for use at the front, not in Barcelona. Every unit was constantly stealing weapons from others, when it could, owing to the general shortage & in one case (the P.O.U.M.) because we were systematically starved of weapons & at times were not far from unarmed. About April 2 batteries of Russian guns did arrive, & conceivably they were stolen ones, as no Russian weapons had been allowed to get to us till then.

> *Raymond Mortimer quickly sent Orwell a handwritten note saying, 'Dear Orwell, Please accept my humble apologies. I did not know Kingsley Martin had written to you in those terms. My own reasons for refusing the review were those that I gave. I should be sorry for you not to write for us, and I should like to convince you from past reviews that there is no premium here on Stalinist orthodoxy.' On 10 February, Kingsley Martin wrote to Orwell: 'Raymond Mortimer has shown me your letter. We certainly owe you an apology in regard to the letter about* The Spanish Cockpit. *There is a good deal else in your letter which suggests some misunderstanding and which, I think, would be better discussed than written about. Could you make it convenient to come and see me some time next week? I shall be available on Monday afternoon, or almost any time on Tuesday.' It is not known whether Orwell accepted Martin's invitation, but he probably did; his letter to Moore of about 12 February (425) indicates that he expected to be in London on that Tuesday, 15 February. Orwell's review of Galsworthy's* Glimpses and Reflections *was published in the* New Statesman *on 12 March 1938 (see 430), and he contributed reviews to the journal from July 1940 to August 1943. However, as is recorded in conversation with friends, he never forgave Martin for his 'line' on the Spanish Civil War. See Crick, 340–42.*

1. John McGovern (1887–1963), ILP MP, 1930–47; Labour MP, 1947–59, led a hunger march from Glasgow to London in 1934. Félicien Challaye, French left-wing politician, member of the committee of La Ligue des Droits des Hommes, a liberal, anti-Fascist movement to protect civil liberty throughout the world. He resigned in November 1937, with seven others, in protest against what they interpreted as the movement's cowardly subservience to Stalinist tyranny.
2. The letter from Brailsford of 17 December, printed above.
3. For Orwell's references to *Inprecor* in *Homage to Catalonia*, see pp. 200 and 202–4 [V/228 and 231–3].

[434]

To Stephen Spender
2 April 1938   Handwritten

Jellicoe Ward, Preston Hall, Aylesford, Kent

Dear Spender,

I hope things go well with you. I really wrote to say I hoped you'd read my Spanish book (title *Homage to Catalonia*) when it comes out, which should be shortly. I have been afraid that having read those two chapters[1] you would carry away the impression that the whole book was Trotskyist propaganda, whereas actually about half of it or less is controversial. I hate writing that kind of stuff and I am much more interested in my own experiences, but unfortunately in this bloody period we are living in one's only experiences *are* being mixed up in controversies, intrigues etc. I sometimes feel as if I hadn't been properly alive since the beginning of 1937. I remember on sentry-go in the trenches near Alcubierre I used to say Hopkins's poem 'Felix Randal', I expect you know it, over and over to myself to pass the time away in that bloody cold, & that was about the last occasion when I had any feeling for poetry. Since then it's gone right out of my head. I don't know that I can give you a copy of my book because I've already had to order about 10 extra ones and it's so damned expensive, but you can always get it out of the library.

I have been in this place about 3 weeks. I am afraid from what they say it is TB. all right but evidently a very old lesion and not serious. They say I am to stay in bed and rest completely for about 3 months and then I shall probably be O.K. It means I can't work and is rather a bore, but perhaps is all for the best.

The way things are going in Spain simply desolates me. All those towns & villages I knew smashed about, & I suppose the wretched peasants who used to be so decent to us being chased to & fro & their landlords put back onto them. I wonder if we shall ever be able to go back to Spain if Franco wins. I suppose it would mean getting a new passport anyway. I notice that you and I are both on the board of sponsors or whatever it is called of the S.I.A.[2] So also is Nancy Cunard, all rather comic because it was she who previously sent me that bloody rot which was afterwards published in book form (called *Authors Take Sides*). I sent back a very angry reply in which I'm afraid I mentioned you uncomplimentarily, not knowing you personally at that time. However I'm all for this S.I.A. business if they are really doing anything to supply food etc., not like that damned rubbish of signing manifestos to say how wicked it all is.

Write some time if you get time. I'd like to meet again when I get out of here. Perhaps you will be able to come and stay with us some time.

Yours
Eric Blair

1. Probably what are now Appendixes I and II (pp. 169–215, above).
2. Solidaridad Internacional Antifascista, subtitled, on its letterhead, 'International Anti-Fascist Solidarity'. Other sponsors included W. H. Auden, Havelock Ellis, Sidonie Goossens, Laurence Housman, C. E. M. Joad, Miles Malleson, John Cowper, Llewelyn Powys, Herbert Read, Reginald Reynolds and Rebecca West. Ethel Mannin (see *575*) was the Honorary Treasurer; Emma Goldman, the Honorary Secretary. Goldman wrote to Eileen (as 'Miss Blair') on 14 April 1938 thanking her for her kind contribution and for help in distributing fifty of SIA's folders and bulletins. She also sent wishes for Orwell's recovery. The periodical *Spain and the World* for 8 April 1938 advertised, with Reg Groves's *But We Shall Live Again* (on Chartism) and Rudolf Rocker's *Anarcho-Syndicalism*, Ethel Mannin's *Women and the Revolution*, the last advertised as 'Biographies of great women rebels from Charlotte Corday to Emma Goldman, from Mary Wollstonecraft to Mme Sun Yat Sen and Maria Spridonova.' For Rudolf Rocker's *Anarcho-Syndicalism*, there was a commendation by Orwell: 'Of great value. It will do something towards filling a great gap in political consciousness.' See Nicolas Walter, 'Orwell and the Anarchists', *Freedom*, 42, no. 2, 30 January 1981; Crick, 351.

---

[436]

To Geoffrey Gorer
18 April 1938   Handwritten

Homage to Catalonia *was published on 25 April 1938 (see 438), but, as is customary, review copies had been sent out in advance. On a Saturday before Orwell's letter to Gorer, probably 16 April, Gorer sent him a short note to say how 'absolutely first-rate' he thought* Homage to Catalonia, *as well as a carbon copy of his review for* Time and Tide, *'in case they object to its inordinate length', and so that Orwell could let him know before the proof arrived if there were any errors. The review appeared on 30 April.*

Jellicoe Pavilion, Preston Hall, Aylesford, Kent

Dear Geoffrey,

I must write to thank you for your marvellous review. I kept pinching myself to make sure I was awake, but I shall also have to pinch myself if *T. & T.* print it – I'm afraid they'll think it's too long & laudatory. I don't think they'll bother about the subject-matter, as they've been very good about the Spanish war. But even if they cut it, thanks ever so for the intention. There were just one or two points. One is that you say the fighting in Barcelona was started by the Assault Guards. Actually it was Civil Guards.[1] There weren't any Assault Guards there then, & there is a difference, because the Civil Guards are the old Spanish Gendarmerie dating from the early 19th century & in reality a more or less pro-Fascist body, ie. they have always joined the Fascists where it was possible. The Assault Guards are a new formation dating from the Republic of 1931, pro-Republican & not hated by the working people to the same extent. The other is that if you are obliged to shorten or otherwise alter the review, it doesn't particularly matter to insist, as you do now, that I only took part in the Barcelona fighting to the extent of doing sentry. I did, as it happens, but if I had been ordered to actually fight I would have done so, because in the existing chaos there didn't seem anything one could do except obey one's own party & immediate military superiors. But I'm so glad you liked the book. Various people seem to have received review copies, but I haven't had any myself yet & am wondering uneasily what the dust-jacket is like. Warburg talked of decorating it with the Catalan colours, which are easily mistaken for *a.* the Spanish royalist colours or *b.* the M.C.C.[2]

Hope all goes well with you. I am much better, in fact I really doubt whether there is anything wrong with me.[3] Eileen is battling with the chickens etc. alone but comes down once a fortnight.

Yours
Eric Blair

1. Orwell was wrong about this. He was later to ask that if a second edition of *Homage to Catalonia* were ever published – there was one English edition in his lifetime; the US and French editions did not appear until after his death – this error should be rectified. The correction has been made in the *Complete Works* edition; see 'A Note on the Text', pp. 29–30 and 198, above.

2. Marylebone Cricket Club, the then ruling cricket authority. Its tie has broad red and yellow stripes.

3. According to Orwell's blood sedimentation test on 27 April (and on 17 May), his disease was 'moderately active'. It was not until 4 July that it became 'quiescent'. It is never shown as normal.

---

[439]

'Notes* on the Spanish Militias'

These notes may have been written when Orwell was working on Homage to Catalonia, *but more probably after its publication. The watermark of the paper on which they are typed is the same as that of letters to Lady Rees, 23 February 1939, and Herbert Read, 5 March 1939, and different from that of the letter to Read of 4 January 1939 and all earlier letters from Morocco. The ink in which Orwell wrote the footnotes and the few emendations (included here without notice) is similar to that of the letter to Lady Rees and one to Geoffrey Gorer, 20 January 1939, but is different from that of the letters to Read of 4 January and 5 March. It is possible, therefore, that they were typed early in 1939, but they could have been written earlier. Gorer, in a letter to Sonia Orwell,[1] 4 July 1967, guessed their date of composition as summer 1940, after Dunkirk, for someone at the War Office interested in the experience of militias as resistance fighters.[2] (These letters are not included in this selection.)*

I joined the POUM militia at the end of 1936. The circumstances of my joining this militia rather than any other were the following. I had intended going to Spain to gather materials for newspaper articles etc., and had also some vague idea of fighting if it seemed worth while, but was doubtful about this owing to my poor health and comparatively small military experience. Just before I started someone told me I should not be able to cross the frontier unless I had papers from some leftwing organisation (this was untrue at that time although party cards etc. undoubtedly

---

* N.B. that these notes refer only to the POUM militia, exceptional because of the internal political struggle, but in actual composition etc. probably not very dissimilar from the other militias in Catalonia in the first year of war [Orwell's handwritten footnote].

made it easier). I applied to John Strachey who took me to see Pollitt. P after questioning me evidently decided that I was politically unreliable and refused to help me, also tried to frighten me out of going by talking a lot about Anarchist terrorism. Finally he asked whether I would undertake to join the International Brigade. I said I could not undertake to join anything until I had seen what was happening. He then refused to help me but advised me to get a safe-conduct from the Spanish Embassy in Paris, which I did. Just before leaving England I also rang up the I.L.P., with which I had some slight connections, mainly personal, and asked them to give me some kind of recommendation. They sent me to Paris a letter addressed to John McNair at Barcelona. When I crossed the frontier the passport people and others, at that time Anarchists, did not pay much attention to my safe-conduct but seemed impressed by the letter with I.L.P. heading, which they evidently knew by sight. It was this that made me decide to produce my letter to McNair (whom I did not know) and through this that I joined the P.O.U.M. militia. After one glimpse of the troops in Spain I saw that I had relatively a lot of training as a soldier and decided to join the militia. At that time I was only rather dimly aware of the differences between the political parties, which had been covered up in the English leftwing press. Had I had a complete understanding of the situation I should probably have joined the CNT militia.

At this time the militias, though theoretically being recast on an ordinary army basis, were still organised in columna, centuria, seccion, the centuria of about 100 men more or less centring round some individual and often being called 'So-and-so's bandera'.[3] The commander of the centuria ranked more or less as captain, but below that there was no well-defined rank except corporal and private. People wore stripes etc. of rank in Barcelona but it was 'not done' to wear them at the front. Theoretically promotion was by election, but actually the officers and NCOs were appointed from above. As I shall point out later this does not in practice make much difference. One peculiar feature however was that a man could choose which section he should belong to and as a rule could also change to another bandera if he wanted to. At that time men were being sent into the line with only a few days' training and that of a parade-ground kind, and in many cases without ever having fired a rifle. I had brought with me ordinary British Army ideas and was appalled by the lack of discipline. It is [of] course always difficult to get recruits to obey orders and becomes much more so when they find themselves thrust into trenches and having to put up with cold etc. which they are not accustomed to. If they have not had a chance to familiarise themselves with firearms they are often much more afraid of bullets than they need be and this is an added source of indiscipline. (Incidentally a lot of harm was done by the lies published in the leftwing papers to the effect that the Fascists were using explosive bullets. So far as I know there is no such thing as an explosive bullet,[4] and certainly the Fascists weren't using them.) At the beginning one had to get orders obeyed (a) by appealing to party loyalty and (b) by force of personality, and for the first week or two I made myself thoroughly unpopular. After about a week a man flatly refused to go to a certain place which he declared was exposed to fire, and I made him do so by force – always a mistake, of course, and doubly so with a Spaniard. I was immediately surrounded by a ring of men calling me a Fascist. There was a tremendous argument, however most of the men took my side and I found that people rather competed to join my section. After this, for some weeks or months, both among the Spaniards and the few English who were on this front, this kind of thing recurred over and over again. Ie. indiscipline, arguments as to what was justifiable and what was 'revolutionary', but in general a consensus of opinion that one must have strict discipline combined with social equality. There was always a lot of argument as to whether it was justifiable to shoot men for desertion and disobedience, and in general people agreed that it was, though some would never do so. Much later, about March, near Huesca, some 200 CNT troops suddenly decided to walk out of the line. One could hardly blame them as they had been there about five months, but obviously such a thing could not be allowed and there was a call for some POUM troops to go and stop them. I volunteered though not feeling very happy about it. Fortunately they were persuaded to go back by their political delegates or somebody, so it never came to violence. There was a lot of argument about this, but again the majority agreed that it would be justifiable to use one's rifle against men doing this if necessary. Throughout this period, ie. January-April 1937 the gradual improvement in discipline was brought about almost entirely by 'diffusion of revolutionary consciousness', ie. endless arguments and explanations as to *why* such and such a thing was necessary. Everyone was fanatically keen on keeping social equality between officers and men, no military titles and no differences of food etc., and this was often carried to lengths that were rather ridiculous, though they seemed less ridiculous in the line where minute differences of comfort were very appreciable. When the militias were theoretically incorporated in the Popular Army[5] all officers were expected to pay their extra pay ie. anything over 10 pesetas a day, into the Party funds, and everyone agreed to do so, though whether this actually happened I don't know, because I am not certain whether anyone actually began drawing extra pay before the POUM militia was redistributed. Punishments for disobedience were, however, being used even at the time when I first reached the front. It is extremely difficult to punish men who are already in the front line, because short of killing them it is hard to make them more uncomfortable than they are already. The usual punishment was double hours of sentry-go – very unsatisfactory because everyone is already short of sleep. Occasionally men were shot. One man who attempted to cross to the Fascist lines and was clearly a spy was shot. Another caught stealing from other militiamen was sent back supposedly to be shot, though I don't think he actually was. Courts martial were supposed to consist of one officer, one NCO and one militiaman, though I never saw one in action.

Periodically political delegates used to be sent round by the Party to visit the men in the line and, when possible, deliver [some] sort of political discourses. In addition every centuria had one or more men in its own ranks who were called its political delegates. I never grasped what the function of these men had originally been – they had evidently at the beginning had some function for which there was afterwards no need. When with the ILP English I was appointed their political delegate, but by this time the political delegate was simply a go-between who was sent to headquarters to complain about rations etc., and therefore so far as the English were concerned it was simply a question of choosing among the few men who spoke Spanish. The English were stricter than the Spaniards about electing officers and in one or two cases changed an NCO by election. They also appointed a committee of 5 men who were supposed to regulate all the affairs of the section. Although I was voted onto the committee myself I opposed its formation on the ground that we were now part of an army being commanded from above in more or less the ordinary way, and therefore such a committee had no function. Actually it had no important function but was occasionally useful for regulating very small matters. Contrary to what is generally believed the political leaders of the POUM were very hostile to this committee idea and were anxious to prevent the idea spreading from the English to the Spaniards.

Before joining the English I was some weeks in a Spanish bandera, and of about 80 men in it some 60 were completely raw recruits. In these weeks the discipline improved a good deal, and from then on till the end of April there was a slow but fairly steady improvement in discipline throughout the militia. By April a militia unit when it had to march anywhere still *looked* like a retreat from Moscow, but this was partly because the men had been experienced solely in trench warfare. But by this time there was no difficulty in getting an order obeyed and no fear that it would be disobeyed as soon as your back was turned. Outwardly the special 'revolutionary' characteristics remained the same till the end of May, but in fact certain differences were showing themselves by this time. In May when I was commanding a seccion (which now meant a platoon) the younger Spaniards called me 'usted'. I pulled them up about it but the word was evidently coming back, and no doubt the universal use of tu in the early months of the war was an affectation and would seem most unnatural to a Latin people. One thing that seemed to stop abruptly about March was the shouting of revolutionary slogans to the Fascists. This was not practised at Huesca, though in many cases the trenches were very close together. On the Zaragoza front it had been practised regularly and probably had its share in bringing in the deserters who were very numerous there (at one time about 15 a week on a section of front held by about 1000 men). But the universal use of 'camarada' and the notion that we were all supposed to be equals persisted until the militia was redistributed.* It was noticeable that the first drafts of the Popular Army who came up to the line conformed with this. Between the POUM and PSUC militias, up to the time when I last saw the latter

---

* My medical discharge-ticket, signed by a doctor at Monzón (a long way behind the line) about 18th June, refers to me as 'Comrade Blair' [Orwell's handwritten footnote].

at the beginning of March, there was no perceptible difference in state of discipline and social atmosphere.

The general organisation was in some ways very good but in others quite unnecessarily incompetent. One striking feature about this war was the good food organisation. Up till May 1937 when certain things began to give out the food was always good, and it was always regular, a thing not easy to arrange even in a very stationary war. The cooks were very devoted, sometimes bringing food up under heavy fire. I was impressed by the food-organisation behind the lines and the way in which the peasants had been got to co-operate. The men's clothes were laundered from time to time, but it was not done very well or very regularly. The postal arrangements were good and letters which had started from Barcelona always got to the front promptly, though an extraordinary number of letters sent into Spain went astray somewhere on the way to Barcelona. Ideas of sanitation practically did not exist and no doubt only the dry climate prevented epidemics. There was no medical service worth mentioning till one got about 10 miles behind the lines. This did not matter so long as there was only a small trickle of casualties, but even so many lives were lost unnecessarily. Trenches were at the beginning extremely primitive but about March a labour battalion was organised. This was very efficient and able to construct long sections of trench very rapidly and without noise. Nevertheless up to about May there was not much idea of communication-trenches, even where the front line was near the enemy, and it was not possible, eg., to get wounded men away without carrying them under fire. No effort was made to keep the roads behind the line in repair, although, no doubt, the labour to do so was available. The POUM Red Aid, to which it was voluntary-compulsory to subscribe, were very good about looking after wounded men in hospital etc. In regard to stores, there was probably some peculation and favouritism, but I think extremely little. When cigarettes began to run short the little English section received rather more than their fair share, a tribute to the Spanish character. The grand and inexcusable mistake made in this war, at any rate on the Aragón front, was to keep the men in the line for unnecessarily long periods. By Xmas 1936 the war was almost entirely stationary and for long periods during the next six months there was little fighting. It should therefore have been perfectly possible to organise the four days in four days out, or even four days in two days out, system. On this arrangement men do not actually get more hours of rest but they do periodically get a few nights in bed or at any rate with the chance to take their clothes off. As it was men were sometimes kept as long as five months in the line continuously. It sometimes happened that trenches were a long way from the enemy, say 1000 yards, but this is more boring and therefore worse for morale than being at 50–100 yards. Meanwhile they were sleeping in trenches in intolerable discomfort, usually lousy and up till April almost always cold. Moreover even when one is 1000 yards from the enemy one is under rifle and occasional shell fire, causing a trickle of casualties and therefore fear which is cumulative. In these circumstances it is difficult to do more than keep on keeping on. During February-March, the period when there was little fighting round Huesca, attempts were made to train the men in various things, use of the machine gun, signalling, open-order work (advancing by rushes etc.) etc. These were mainly a failure because everyone was suffering from lack of sleep and too exhausted to learn. I myself at this time tried to master the mechanism of the Hotchkiss machine gun and found that lack of sleep had simply deprived me of the power to learn. In addition it would no doubt have been feasible to grant leave at shorter intervals, but the failure to do so probably had reasons other than incompetence. But it would have been quite easy to take the men in and out of trenches as I have indicated, and to provide some kind of amenities for the troops not in the line. Even as far back as Barbastro the life of the troops was much drearier than it need have been. With a little organisation it would have been possible to arrange immediately behind the lines for hot baths, delousing, entertainments of some kind, cafés (actually there were some very feeble attempts at these) and also women. The very few women who were in or near the line and were getatable were simply a source of jealousy. There was a certain amount of sodomy among the younger Spaniards. I doubt whether troops can simultaneously engage in trench warfare and be trained for mobile warfare, but more training would certainly have been possible if more care had been devoted to resting the men. As it was they were exhausted for nothing at a period when the war was stagnant. Looking back I see that they stood it extremely well, and even at the time it was the fact that they did *not* disintegrate or show mutinous tendencies under these intolerable conditions that converted me (to some extent) to the notion of 'revolutionary discipline'. Nevertheless the strain that was put upon them was partly unnecessary.

As to jealousies between the different militias, so far as the rank and file were concerned I myself did not see serious signs of these till May 1937. To what extent the Aragón front was sabotaged from political motives I suppose we shall learn sooner or later. I do not know how important the capture of Huesca would have been, but there is little doubt that it could have been taken in February or March with adequate artillery. As it was it was surrounded except for one gap about a km. wide, and this with so little artillery that preliminary bombardments were an impossibility, as they would only have served as a warning. This meant that attacks could only be surprise attacks delivered by a few hundred men at most. By the beginning of April Huesca appeared to be doomed, but the gap was never closed, the attacks petered out and a little later it became clear that the Fascist trenches were more strongly held and that they had improved their defences. At the end of June the big attack on Huesca was staged, clearly from political motives, to provide the Popular Army with a victory and discredit the CNT militia. The result was what could have been foreseen – heavy losses and an actual worsening of the position. But as far as rank and file were concerned party-feeling did not usually get beyond vague rumours that 'they', usually meaning the PSUC, had stolen guns etc. meant for ourselves. On the Zaragoza front where POUM and PSUC militia were distributed more or less alternately relations were good. When the POUM took over a sector from the PSUC at Huesca there were signs of jealousy, but this I think was purely military, the PSUC troops having failed to take Huesca and the POUM boasting that they were going to do so. The Guadalajara victory in February could be regarded as, and in fact was, a Communist victory, but everyone was unaffectedly glad and in fact enthusiastic. A little later than this one of our aeroplanes, presumably Russian, dropped a bomb in the wrong place and killed a number of POUM militiamen. Later, no doubt, it would have been said that this was 'done on purpose', but at the time this did not occur to anybody. About May, perhaps following on the Barcelona trouble, relations worsened. In Lérida, where large numbers of the new Popular Army formations were in training, when detachments of Popular

Army marched past, I saw militiamen of I do not know what militia giving them raspberries and bleating in imitation of sheep. As to victimisation of men known to have served with the POUM, I doubt whether it began until after the alleged espionage discoveries. Immediately after these there appear to have been one or two serious incidents. About the end of June it seems that a detachment of PSUC militia were sent or came of their own accord to attack one of the POUM positions outside Huesca, and the men at the latter had to defend themselves with their machine guns. I have not either the exact date or more than general facts of this, but the source from which I had it leaves me in no doubt that it happened. It was no doubt the result of irresponsible statements in the press about espionage, desertion, etc., which had caused or almost caused trouble on earlier occasions.

The fact that the militias were organised by and owed loyalty to different parties had bad effects after a certain date. At the beginning, when everyone was full of enthusiasm, inter-party rivalry was perhaps not a bad thing – this impression at least I derived from those who were in the earlier fighting when Siétamo etc. were taken. But when the militias were dwindling as against the Popular Army the effect was to make every party anxious to keep its strength up at no matter what cost. I believe that this was one reason for the fact, noted above, that leave was not granted as often as it might have been. Up till about June there was in reality no way of making a man who had gone on leave rejoin his unit, and conscription into the Popular Army, if[6] passed into law (I forget when exactly it was passed), was completely ineffective. Therefore a militiaman once on leave could simply go home, and he had the more motive to do so as he had just drawn a big wad of back-pay, or he could join another organisation, which was often done at that time. In practice most men returned from leave, but some did not, so that every spell of leave meant a dwindling of numbers. In addition, I am certain that anxiety to keep up numbers made local commanders over-anxious not to incur casualties when they could not gain eclat° by incurring them. On the Zaragoza front valuable minor opportunities – the kind of thing that would not have got into the papers but would have made a certain difference – were lost owing to this, while such casualties as did occur were completely pointless. Also the useless riff-raff, amounting to five or ten per cent, who are to be found in all bodies of troops and who should be got rid of ruthlessly, were seldom or never got rid of. In January when I complained about the state of discipline a higher-up officer gave me his opinion that all the militias competed in slackness of discipline in order to detach recruits from the others. I don't know whether this was true or said owing to momentary fed-upness.

As to the personnel of the POUM militia, I doubt whether it was much different from the others. In standard of physique, which is a rough test, they were about equal to the PSUC. The POUM did not ask party affiliation from their militiamen, doubtless because being a minority party they found it hard to attract recruits. When the men were in the line efforts were made to get them to join the party, but it is fair to say that there was no kind of pressure. There was the usual proportion of riff-raff, and in addition a certain number of very ignorant peasants and people of no particular political alignment who had probably joined the POUM militia more or less by accident. In addition there was a certain number of people who had simply joined for the sake of a job. The fact that in December 1936 there was already a serious bread shortage in Barcelona and militiamen got bread in plenty had a lot to do with this. Nevertheless some of these nondescripts afterwards turned into quite good soldiers. Apart from a rather large number of refugee Germans there was a sprinkling of foreigners of many races, even including a few Portuguese. Putting aside the Germans, the best soldiers were usually the machine-gunners, who were organised in crews of six and kept rather apart from the others. The fetishistic attitude which men in this position develop towards their gun, rather as towards a household god, is interesting and should be studied. A few of the machine-gunners were old soldiers who had done their service over and over again owing to the Spanish substitute system, but most of them were 'good party men', some of them men of extremely high character and intelligence. I came to the conclusion, somewhat against my will, that in the long run 'good party men' make the best soldiers. The detachment of in all about 30 English and Americans sent out by the ILP were divided rather sharply between old soldiers of no particular political affiliations and 'good party men' with no military experience. As I am nearer to the first type myself I am probably not prejudiced in saying that I believe the second to be superior. Old soldiers are of course more useful at the beginning of a campaign, and they are all right when there is any fighting, but they have more tendency to go to pieces under inaction and physical exhaustion. A man who has fully identified with some political party is reliable in *all* circumstances. One would get into trouble in left-wing circles for saying so, but the feeling of many Socialists towards their party is very similar to that of the thicker-headed type of public school man towards his old school. There are individuals who have no particular political feelings and are completely reliable, but they are usually of bourgeois origin. In the POUM militia there was a slight but perceptible tendency for people of bourgeois origin to be chosen as officers. Given the existing class-structure of society I regard this as inevitable. Middle-class and upper-class people have usually more self-confidence in unfamiliar circumstances, and in countries where conscription is not in force they usually have more military tradition than the working class. This is notably the case in England. As to age, 20 to 35 seems to be the proper age for front-line soldiers. Above 35 I would not trust anybody in the line as a common soldier or junior officer unless he is of known political reliability. As for the younger limit, boys as young as 14 are often very brave and reliable, but they simply cannot stand the lack of sleep. They will even fall asleep standing up.

As to treachery, fraternisation, etc., there were just enough rumours about this to suggest that such things happened occasionally, and in fact they are inevitable in civil war. There were vague rumours that at some time pre-arranged truces had been held in no man's land for exchange of newspapers. I do not know of an instance of this but once saw some Fascist papers which might have been procured in this manner. The stories circulated in the Communist press about non-aggression pacts and people coming and going freely between our lines and the Fascists were lies. There was undoubtedly treachery among the peasants. The reason why no attack on this front ever came off at the time scheduled was no doubt partly incompetence, but it was also said that if the time was fixed more than a few hours ahead it was invariably known to the Fascists. The Fascists always appeared to know what troops they had opposite them, whereas we only knew what we could infer from patrols etc. I do not know what method was used by spies for getting messages into Huesca, but the method of sending messages out was flash-lamp signalling. There were morse code signals at a certain hour every night. These were always recorded, but except for slogans such as Viva Franco they were always in cipher. I don't know whether they were successfully deciphered. The spies behind the lines were never caught, in spite of many attempts. Desertions were very rare, though up to May 1937 it would have been easy to walk out of the line, or with a little risk, across to the Fascists. I knew of a few desertions among our men and a few among the PSUC, but the whole number would have been tiny. It is noticeable that men in a force of this type retain political feeling against the enemy as they would not in an ordinary army. When I first reached the front it was taken for granted that officer-prisoners taken by us must be shot, and the Fascists were said to shoot all prisoners – a lie, no doubt, but the significant thing was that people believed it. As late as March 1937 I heard credibly of an officer-prisoner taken by us being shot – again the significant thing is that no one seemed to think this wrong.

As to the actual performance of the POUM militia, I know of this chiefly from others, as I was at the front during the most inactive period of the war. They took part in the taking of Siétamo and the advance on Huesca, and after this the division was split up, some at Huesca, some on the Zaragoza front and a few at Teruel. I believe there was also a handful on the Madrid front. In late February the whole division was concentrated on the eastern side of Huesca. Tactically this was the less important side, and during March–April the part played by the POUM was only raids and holding attacks, affairs involving at most two hundred men and a few score casualties. In some of these they did well, especially the refugee Germans. In the attack on Huesca at the end of June the division lost heavily, 4–600 killed. I was not in this show but heard from others who were that the POUM troops behaved well. By this time the campaigns in the press had begun to produce a certain amount of disaffection. By April even the politically uninterested had grasped that except in their own press and that of the Anarchists no good would be reported of them, whatever their actual performance might be. At the time this produced only a certain irritation, but I know that later, when the division was redistributed, some men who were able to dodge the conscription did so and got civilian jobs on the ground that they were tired of being libelled. A number of men who were in the Huesca attack assured me that General

Pozas[7] deliberately withheld the artillery to get as many POUM troops killed as possible – doubtless untrue, but showing the effect of campaigns like that conducted by the Communist press. I do not know what happened to the division after being redistributed, but believe they mostly went to the 26th division.[8] Considering the circumstances and their opportunities, I should say that the performance of the POUM militia was respectable though in no way brilliant.

1. Orwell's first wife, Eileen, died under anaesthetic in 1945. On 13 October 1949, he married Sonia Brownell in University College Hospital by special licence (because he was very ill, could not leave his bed and the hospital was not licensed for marriages). Sonia Brownell was born in Ranchi, India, some 250 miles from where Orwell was born (at Motihari). She died in 1980, by when she had created the Orwell Archive at University College London and done much to establish Orwell's reputation. See *CW*, XX/*3693* and *3736*.

2. The relevant section of *Homage to Catalonia* is pp.169–90 [VI/188–215], (Appendix I; formerly chapter V). Hugh Thomas commented in a letter to the editors of *The Collected Essays, Journalism and Letters of George Orwell* (1968), Sonia Orwell and Ian Angus: 'first, that the CNT and FAI were actually different organisations of which the latter was, broadly speaking, the leadership of the former, having been set up in the 'twenties to keep the CNT from revisionism. Secondly, where George Orwell said in *Homage to Catalonia* that the Communists' viewpoint and the right-wing Socialists' viewpoint could everywhere be regarded as identical, this was only the case for quite a short time, since Prieto, the leading right-wing Socialist, moved over into a very strong anti-Communist position quite soon. Thirdly, it is only very "roughly speaking" that the PSUC was the political organ of the UGT [the Socialist Trade Union]. Indeed, this is nearer a mistake than any of the other points, because the UGT was the nationwide labour organisation, admittedly led by Socialists, whereas the PSUC was simply confined to Catalonia.'

3. *bandera*: flag, colours or infantry unit.

4. Probably the soft-nosed or dum-dum bullet was meant, which expands on impact, with appalling effect.

5. 'Since February [1937] the entire armed forces had theoretically been incorporated in the Popular Army [by the Government], and the militias were, on paper, reconstructed along Popular Army lines' (*Homage to Catalonia*, p. 97 [VI/91].

6. Presumably 'when' is meant.

7. General Sebastián Pozas Perea (1876 – died in exile), a Republican, was Director-General of the Civil Guard, and Minister of the Interior for the Republicans in 1936.

8. Orwell probably meant the 29th Division.

[441]

To the Editor, The Times Literary Supplement
14 May 1938

Sir, – I know it is not usual to answer reviews, but as your review of my book *Homage to Catalonia* in *The Times Literary Supplement* of April 30 amounts to misrepresentation I should be greatly obliged if you would allow me space to answer it.

Your reviewer[1] begins:–

> [George Orwell] enlisted in the Militia, took part in the trench warfare round Huesca, was wounded, and after some disheartening experiences in the internal rising in Barcelona in May, 1937, was compelled to flee the country.

The implication here is, (*a*) that I had been wounded before the fighting in Barcelona, and (*b*) that I had to flee the country as a direct result of my 'disheartening experiences'. As was made perfectly clear in my book, I was wounded some little time *after* the fighting in Barcelona, and I had to leave the country as a result of events which I set out at considerable length and which, so far as I know, had no direct connexion with my 'disheartening experiences'.

The rest of his review is mainly an attempt to throw discredit upon the Spanish Militias who were holding the Aragón front with inadequate weapons and other equipment during the first year of war. He has distorted various things that I said in order to make it appear that I agree with him. For example:–

> Discipline did not exist in the Militia: 'if a man disliked an order he would step out of the ranks and argue fiercely with the officer'.

I never said that discipline 'did not exist in the Militia'. What your reviewer failed to mention is that in the passage quoted ('if a man disliked an order', &c.) I was describing the behaviour of raw recruits *their first day at the barracks*, when they behaved as raw recruits always behave, as anyone with military experience would expect.

Yours truly,
George Orwell

The reviewer replied:

Mr. Orwell is unduly sensitive. I stated that he was wounded in the trench warfare round Huesca and that he was compelled to flee the country after some disheartening experiences in the internal rising in Barcelona – all facts recorded at length in his book. If my necessarily brief sentence implied that he was wounded before the rising this was unintentional and does not seem to reflect on him or anyone else. I did not say he was compelled to flee *because* of his part in the May rising, or that there was any direct connexion between the two events. Actually, however, it seems clear that it was because Mr. Orwell was then, and subsequently, associated with the POUM organization, which was officially blamed for the rising, that he was obliged to leave the country.

Of the May rising and the subsequent period Mr. Orwell uses the words 'concentrated disgust', 'fury', 'miserable internecine scrap', 'cesspool', 'disillusionment' and 'a depressing outlook'. If that is not disheartenment, what is?

Finally, as to indiscipline, it is a question of point of view. Mr. Orwell speaks of 'a mob of ragged children in the front line', one of whom threw a hand grenade into a dugout fire 'for a joke'; of slapping generals on the back, of how when men refused to obey orders it was necessary to appeal to them in the name of comradeship, and of how '*You often had to argue for five minutes before you got an order obeyed.*' He says further:– '*Actually a newly raised draft of militia was an indisciplined mob . . .* In a workers' army discipline is theoretically voluntary,' &c. He adds that 'it is a tribute to the strength of revolutionary discipline that the Militias stayed in the field at all'.

On 28 May 1938, The Times Literary Supplement *published a second letter from Orwell:*

Sir, – I am very sorry to trouble you with this correspondence, but your reviewer has again resorted to misquotation. For example: 'Actually a newly raised draft of militia was an undisciplined mob.' In my book the sentence ran as follows: 'Actually, a newly raised draft of militia was an undisciplined mob not because the officers called the privates "Comrade" but because new troops are *always* an undisciplined mob.'

By suppressing the second half of the sentence he has given it a totally different meaning; and similarly with various other statements which he has picked out of their contexts. As for his rearrangement of the order of events in the book, he pleads that his account was 'necessarily brief', this does not seem any reason for altering the chronology.

Yours truly,

George Orwell

1. Reviews in *The Times Literary Supplement* were then customarily unsigned. Records show that the reviewer was Maurice Percy Ashley (1907–94; CBE, 1978), journalist, author and historian. He was Winston Churchill's research assistant in 1929, served in the Intelligence Corps, 1940–45, was Deputy Editor of *The Listener*, 1946–58 and Editor, 1958–67.

[445]

Sir Richard Rees to Orwell
25 *May* [1938]   Handwritten

c/o Thos Cook & Sons, Place de la Madeleine, Paris

Dear Eric

I have just reached Paris from Barcelona[1] and I learn by a letter from Eileen that you have been laid up since March 8 but are doing very well – which latter I am indeed glad to hear. I knew you had been ill, but didn't realise it was ever since March 8 (before I left for Barcelona). If I had known then I would have tried to get in touch with you before leaving.

I have sent you a book, which I hope you will enjoy – Georges Bernanos' *Les Grands Cimetières sous la Lune.*[2] You will, of course, like me, be infuriated by his sentimentality. He's a Royalist and his attitude to 'les pauvres' is imbecile. He says they must be 'honoured', as the middle ages honoured women, for their 'faiblesse'. All the same, he's a *very* good chap in many ways, as you'll find if you persevere with the book. His, and his son's experiences with the Phalangistes[3] are in a way analogous to your experience with the P.O.U.M. The fascist treatment of the Phalanges corresponds very much to the C.P. treatment of the P.O.U.M. and the idealistic anarchists.

And, by the way, if you want to read another really good book on

Spain – try Elliot Paul's *Life & Death of a Spanish Town*.[4] It is about the island of Ibiza before & up to the war and makes a good comparison to Bernanos, which is about the neighbouring island of Majorca and which, more or less, begins just where Elliot Paul's ends, with the first fighting in the Balearic Isles.[5] Both these books really *are* worth reading, and, with yours, they are the only books about Spain that can be said to be written by people with free (i.e. fundamentally honest, if often mistaken) minds. I read your book through at one sitting. It is painful reading, of course, but on the whole it convinced me that you were lucky, in spite of everything, to have got mixed up with the P.O.U.M. & not the C.P.

That short period when the untrained anarchist militia, almost unarmed, were holding the Aragón front, really was the only pure revolutionary experience of the whole sordid business.

However, even my own even more sordid though less exciting experiences were not without flashes of the same thing – and anyway I did not need convincing that 'equality' in the anarchist sense *can* work – though whether it ever will be allowed to in this world, God only knows. With all respect to God, I find it hard to believe that he will ever allow it to. I get more and more pessimistic.

Chamberlain[6] is going to sell Spain & Eastern Europe to Fascism in return for a (temporary) immunity for the British Empire & British Capitalism.

During my last visit to Spain I felt ashamed of being English. In my more catastrophically gloomy moods (which are frequent) I find myself hoping that hell will break loose soon. After all, it would be better than a few more decades of ignominious security which Chamberlain hopes to buy by his concessions to Fascism. All the same, your description of hand-to-hand fighting convinces me I could never be a good soldier. I had plenty of bombing & shelling & was sometimes under rifle fire, and I saw plenty of violent death – and I found it all more or less bearable.

But I never had to experience anything like that raid you describe, when the white armlets failed to arrive and somebody said 'couldn't we arrange for the fascists to wear white armlets?'! I should never have enough aggressive spirit (i.e. courage) to get through an experience like that, sitting tight while being bombed or machine gunned from the air is *quite* a different matter and infinitely easier.

I hope you are comfortable and have plenty to read. Eileen tells me you have written a Peace pamphlet.[7]

I can't imagine peace, I can only imagine negative war – i.e. the kind of peace you find in Paris & London when you return from Spain. And really I am not sure I don't prefer war to that kind of peace.

But I suppose it is nonsense to talk like that, really.

Well, au revoir, and I hope you'll find Bernanos interesting.

Yours Richard

1. Sir Richard Rees (1900–1970) had been an attaché at the British Embassy in Paris, 1922–3, and Honorary Treasurer and Lecturer, London District of the Workers' Educational Association, 1925–7. From October 1930 to 1937 he was editor of *The Adelphi* (1930–1932 with Max Plowman), and he introduced a more political and self-consciously literary tone to its pages. His generous nature is reflected in Ravelston of *Keep the Aspidistra Flying*. He gave much encouragement to Orwell in the thirties, was a partner to Orwell in his Jura farm, and he became, with Sonia Orwell, Orwell's joint literary executor. He was a painter; among the books he wrote is *George Orwell: Fugitive from the Camp of Victory* (1961). He served in the defence of Madrid, initially with the Communist Party, becoming unwittingly embroiled in 'the political business'.

2. Georges Bernanos (1888–1948) was a polemical novelist whose passionate stance was expressed with subtlety. *Les Grands Cimetières sous la Lune* (1938; English title, *Diary of My Times*, 1938) fiercely condemns the atrocities committed in Mallorca by the Fascists and sanctioned by his, the Roman Catholic, Church. He is best remembered for his novel *Journal d'un curé de campagne* (1936; English title, *Diary of a Country Priest*, 1937), made into a prize-winning film by Robert Bresson (1950).

3. Phalangistes: the Falange Española was founded by José Antonio Primo de Rivera (1903–36), son of Spain's dictator 1923–30, Primo de Rivera (1870–1930). He was tried and executed by the Republicans. The Falangists 'saw themselves as an heroic élite of young men, whose mission was to release Spain from the poison of Marxism, as from what they took to be the second-rate, dull, provincialism of orthodox liberal values' (Thomas, 115). On 18 April 1937 the Falange was united with all other Nationalist groups under Franco, whose brother-in-law, Ramón Serrano Súñer (b. 1901), was appointed Secretary-General.

4. Elliot Paul (1891–1958) was an American autobiographical novelist and journalist. He served with the American Expeditionary Force in World War I and then worked in Europe for the Associated Press and Paris editions of US newspapers. With Eugene Jolas, he founded the influential journal *transition* (1927–38). His *A Narrow Street* (1942; US title, *The Last Time I Saw Paris*) is chiefly set in the rue de la Huchette, where he lived for eighteen years.

5. 'In the Balearics, while Majorca had been secured by Goded for the [Nationalist] rebels, the NCOs and troops of the garrison at Minorca prevented the success of the rising there . . . In Ibiza, the rising triumphed, as in the other small Balearic islands' (Thomas, 242; July 1936). Bernanos states that 3,000 were killed by Nationalists (Thomas, 265, who also extracts from Bernanos horrifying details of summary executions, 259–62).

6. Neville Chamberlain (1869–1940) served several times as a Conservative minister and

was Chancellor of the Exchequer. He became Prime Minister in 1937 and was associated with the appeasement of Hitler, though he initiated the rearmament of Britain. Following the failure of the Norwegian campaign in April 1940, he was much criticized and resigned in May. He then served the new Prime Minister, Winston Churchill. Writing to Orwell's sister, Marjorie, from Marrakesh on 27 September 1938 (two days before the Munich Agreement was signed), Orwell's wife, Eileen, remarked, 'It's very odd to feel that Chamberlain is our only hope, but I do believe he doesn't want war either at the moment and certainly the man has courage' (*487*).

7. This was to be called 'Socialism and War'. See Orwell's letter to Leonard Moore, 28 June 1938 (*458*). The pamphlet was never published and no manuscript has been found.

---

[452]

To the Editor, The Listener
16 June 1938

Review of 'Homage to Catalonia'

Your reviewer's[1] treatment of facts is a little curious. In his review of my book *Homage to Catalonia* in *The Listener* of May 25 he uses about four-fifths of his space in resurrecting from the Communist Press the charge that the Spanish political party known as the P.O.U.M. is a 'fifth column' organisation in the pay of General Franco. He states first that this accusation was 'hyperbolical', but adds later that it was 'credible', and that the leaders of the P.O.U.M. were 'little better than traitors to the Government cause'. Now, I leave on one side the question of how it can be credible that Franco's 'fifth column' could be composed of the poorest of the working class, led by men most of whom had been imprisoned under the régime Franco was trying to restore, and at least one of whom was on Franco's special list of 'persons to be shot'. If your reviewer can believe in stories of that kind, he is entitled to do so. What he is not entitled to do is to repeat his accusation, which is incidentally an accusation against myself, without even indicating from whom it came or that I had had anything to say about it. He leaves it to be inferred all through that the absurd charges of treachery and espionage originated with the Spanish Government. But, as I pointed out in great detail (Chapter XI [pp. 190–215 above; *CW*, Appendix II] of my book), these charges never had any footing outside the Communist Press, nor was any evidence in support of them ever produced. The Spanish Government has again and again repudiated all belief in them, and has steadfastly refused to prosecute the men whom the Communist newspapers denounced. I gave chapter and verse from the Spanish Government's statements, which have since been repeated several times. Your reviewer simply ignores all this, no doubt hoping that he has so effectually put people off reading the book that his misrepresentations will pass unnoticed.

I do not expect or wish for 'good' reviews, and if your reviewer chooses to use most of his space in expressing his own political opinions, that is a matter between him and yourself. But I think I have a right to ask that when a book of mine is discussed at the length of a column there shall be at least some mention of what I have actually said.

Aylesford   George Orwell

We have sent the above letter to our reviewer, who replies:
Mr. Orwell's letter ignores the major fact that conditions in Barcelona at one time became so bad that the Spanish Government was forced to send in armed police to put down what amounted to an insurrection. The leaders of that insurrection were the extreme anarchist elements allied with the P.O.U.M. It is not a question of 'resurrecting' charges from the Communist Press, but of historic fact. I have spent a considerable part of the Spanish war in Spain, and have not relied upon newspaper reports for my information.

As I made clear in my review, it was not the intention of the rank and file of the P.O.U.M. to do other than fight against Franco. Being poor and ignorant men, the complexities of the revolutionary situation were beyond them; their leaders were to blame. As for being part of Franco's fifth column, there is no doubt that whoever declined to co-operate with the central government and to abide by the law was, in fact, weakening the authority of that government and thus aiding the enemy. I submit that in time of war ignorance is as reprehensible as malicious sabotage. It is effect that matters, not the reasons for action.

I am sorry if Mr. Orwell thinks that I wanted to put readers off a magnificently written book: I didn't: I want people to read it even if, in my opinion, his analysis is wrong. It is the essence of a democracy in peace time that all views should be available to everybody.

We are bound to say, in printing our reviewer's reply, that we consider it hardly

meets the points made by Mr. Orwell, to whom we express our regrets. – Editor, *The Listener.*²

1. Philip Furneaux Jordan (1902–51) was a journalist, novelist and reviewer. He had been for a time on the staff of the Paris *Daily Mail* and edited the Riviera edition of the *Chicago Tribune.* In 1936 he joined the staff of the *News Chronicle* and served as its correspondent in Spain, 1936–7. He later became the *News Chronicle*'s features editor and then its foreign correspondent. In 1946–7 he was First Secretary at the British Embassy in Washington, and thereafter Public Relations Adviser to Prime Minister Clement Attlee. He also reviewed for *The Times Literary Supplement* – anonymously, as for *The Listener.*

2. J. R. Ackerley (1896–1967) was literary editor, 1935–59. See *Ackerley* by Peter Parker (1989). The editor was R. S. Lambert.

---

[456]

Review of Spain's Ordeal¹ *by Robert Sencourt;* Franco's Rule *[anonymous]*
New English Weekly, *23 June 1938*

It is not easy for any thinking person to write in praise of dictatorships, because of the obvious fact that when any dictatorship gets into its stride the thinking person is the first to be liquidated. Possibly Mr. Wyndham Lewis still approves of Hitler, but does Hitler approve of Mr. Lewis? Which side would Hitler have been on in the recent set-to about Mr. Eliot's portrait?² It is true that over against the German dictatorship there is the Russian dictatorship, but to a western European that is less immediately menacing. We are still in the position of being able to admire it from beyond gunshot range.

Consequently, bad as the pro-Government books on the Spanish war have been, the pro-Franco ones have been worse. All or almost all that I have seen – I except those of Professor Allison Peers, who is only rather tepidly pro-Franco – have been written by Roman Catholics. Mr. Sencourt's book does not sink to the level of Arnold Lunn's *Spanish Rehearsal,* but its general thesis is the same. Franco is a Christian gentleman, the Valencia Government are a gang of robbers, the Badajoz massacre didn't happen, Guernica was not bombed but wantonly burnt by Red militiamen – and so on and so forth. The truth is that all the haggling about 'who started it' and who committed which atrocity that goes on in books of this kind is a waste of time, because it does not tell you anything about the real conflict of motives. It would be much simpler if everyone would say outright, 'My money is on Franco (or Negrín), atrocities or no atrocities.' For that is what everyone who takes sides really thinks.

Mr. Sencourt at any rate differs from Messrs. Lunn, Yeats-Brown, etc., in that he knows a great deal about Spain and loves the Spaniards, so that though he is hostile to the 'Reds' he is not vulgarly spiteful. But like almost everyone who has written of this war he suffers a great disadvantage from having only been able to study conditions on one side of the line. What he says of the pre-war situation is probably sound enough, but his account of internal conditions on the Government side during the war is very misleading. He enormously exaggerates the amount of civil disorder, and though he gives the main outline of the struggle between the various political parties he misunderstands the role and aim of most of them, because he feels himself obliged to equate 'Red' with 'bad'. Communism he speaks of as though it were a disruptive force and nothing else, and he uses 'Anarchism' indifferently with 'anarchy', which is a hardly more correct use of words than saying that a Conservative is one who makes jam. Still, this is not an ill-natured or dishonest book, and to say that of a book on a political subject is a great deal nowadays.

Franco's Rule is simply an enormous list of atrocities committed in all the territories that Franco has over-run. There are long lists of people who have been shot, and such statements as that 23,000 were massacred in the province of Granada, etc., etc. Now, I do not say that these stories are untrue; obviously I have no means of judging, and at a guess I would say that some are true and some are not. And yet there is something that makes one very uneasy about the appearance of books of this kind.

There is no doubt that atrocities happen, though when a war is over it is generally impossible to establish more than a few isolated cases. In the first few weeks of war, especially in a civil war, there are bound to be massacres of non-combatants, arson, looting and probably raping. If these things happen it is right that they should be recorded and denounced, but I am not so sure about the motives of people who are so enthralled by the subject that they will compile whole books of atrocity-stories. They usually tell you that they are trying to stir up hatred 'against Fascism' or 'against Communism'. But you notice that they seldom hate these things sufficiently to fight against them themselves; I believe no soldier has ever compiled a book of atrocity-stories. One is left with the suspicion that some of the atrocity-mongers rather like writing about rapes and summary executions.

And does anyone believe that in the long run this is the best way to combat either Fascism or what is bad in Communism? Mr. Arthur Koestler, whose nerves must have suffered horribly during his imprisonment by Franco, and who is to be forgiven much, tells us in his book, *Spanish Testament,* to abandon objectivity and cultivate hatred. The anonymous editor of *Franco's Rule* also speaks contemptuously of 'objectivity neurosis'. I wish these people would stop to reflect what they are doing. To fight, or even to ask others to fight, is one thing; to go round stirring up maniacal hatred is another. For:

He who fights too long against dragons becomes a dragon himself: and if thou gaze too long into the abyss, the abyss will gaze into thee.[3]

This book is subtitled 'Back to the Middle Ages', which is unfair to the Middle Ages. There were no machine-guns in those days, and the Inquisition was a very amateurish business. After all, even Torquemada only burnt two thousand people in ten years. In modern Russia or Germany they'd say he wasn't trying.

1. The title of the book was originally given as *Spanish Ordeal.*
2. Lewis's portrait of T. S. Eliot was rejected by the hanging committee of the 1938 Royal Academy Exhibition. In a letter to Lewis of 21 April 1938, Eliot wrote that he would be quite willing to be known to posterity through this portrait. See Walter Michel, *Wyndham Lewis, Paintings and Drawings* (1971), 132 and plate 132.
3. See review of Koestler's *Spanish Testament,* n. 3, above.

[462]

Review of The Civil War in Spain *by Frank Jellinek*[1]
New Leader, *8 July 1938*

Frank Jellinek's book on the Paris Commune[2] had its faults, but it revealed him as a man of unusual mind. He showed himself able to grasp the real facts of history, the social and economic changes that underlie spectacular events, without losing touch with the picturesque aspect which the bourgeois historian generally does so much better. On the whole his present book – *The Civil War in Spain* – bears out the promise of the other. It shows signs of haste, and it contains some misrepresentations which I will point out later, but it is probably the best book on the Spanish War from a Communist angle that we are likely to get for some time to come.

Much the most useful part of the book is the earlier part, describing the long chain of causes that led up to the war and the fundamental issues at stake. The parasitic aristocracy and the appalling condition of the peasants (before the war 65 per cent of the population of Spain held 6.3 per cent of the land, while 4 per cent held 60 per cent of it), the backwardness of Spanish capitalism and the dominance of foreign capitalists, the corruption of the Church, and the rise of the Socialist and Anarchist labour movements – all these are treated in a series of brilliant chapters. The short biography which Mr. Jellinek gives of Juan March,[3] the old tobacco-smuggler who is one of the men behind the Fascist rebellion (although, queerly enough, he is believed to be a Jew), is a wonderful story of corruption. It would be fascinating reading if March were merely a character in Edgar Wallace; unfortunately he happens to be a real man.

The chapter on the Church does not leave much doubt as to why practically all the churches in Catalonia and eastern Aragón were burnt at the outbreak of war. Incidentally, it is interesting to learn that, if Mr. Jellinek's figures are correct, the world organisation of the Jesuits only numbers about 22,000 people. For sheer efficiency they must surely have all the political parties in the world beaten hollow. But the Jesuits' 'man of affairs' in Spain is, or was, on the board of directors of forty-three companies!

At the end of the book there is a well-balanced chapter on the social changes that took place in the first few months of the war, and an appendix on the collectivisation decree in Catalonia. Unlike the majority of British observers, Mr. Jellinek does not under-rate the Spanish Anarchists. In his treatment of the P.O.U.M., however, there is no doubt that he is unfair, and – there is not much doubt of this either – intentionally unfair.

Naturally I turned first of all to the chapter describing the fighting in Barcelona in May, 1937, because both Mr. Jellinek and myself were in Barcelona at the time, and this gave me a measure of checking his accuracy. His account of the fighting is somewhat less propagandist than those that appeared in the Communist Press at the time, but it is certainly one-sided and would be very misleading to anyone who knew nothing of the facts. To begin with, he appears at times to accept the story that the P.O.U.M. was really a disguised Fascist organisation, and refers to 'documents' which 'conclusively proved' this and that, without telling us any more about these mysterious documents – which, in fact, have never been produced. He even refers to the celebrated 'N' document[4] (though admitting that 'N' probably did not stand for Nin), and ignores the fact that Irujo,[5] the Minister of Justice, declared this document to be 'worthless', i.e., a forgery. He states merely that Nin was 'arrested', and does not mention that Nin disappeared and was almost certainly murdered. Moreover, he leaves the chronology uncertain and – whether intentionally or not – gives the impression that the alleged discovery of a Fascist plot, the arrest of Nin, etc., took place *immediately after* the May fighting.

This point is important. The suppression of the P.O.U.M. did *not* occur immediately after the May fighting. There was a five weeks' interval. The fighting ended on May 7 and Nin was arrested on June 15. The suppression of the P.O.U.M. only occurred after, and almost certainly as a result of, the change in the Valencia Government. I have noticed several attempts in the Press to obscure these dates. The reason is obvious enough; however, there can be no doubt about the matter, for all the main events were recorded in the newspapers at the time.

Curiously enough, about June 20, the *Manchester Guardian* correspondent in Barcelona sent here a despatch[6] in which he contradicted the absurd accusations against the P.O.U.M. – in the circumstances a very courageous action. This correspondent must almost certainly have been Mr. Jellinek himself. What a pity that for propaganda purposes he should now find it necessary to repeat a story which after this lapse of time seems even more improbable.

His remarks on the P.O.U.M. occupy a considerable share of the book, and they have an air of prejudice which would be obvious even to anyone who knew nothing whatever about the Spanish political parties. He thinks it necessary to denigrate even useful work such as that done by Nin as Councillor of Justice, and is careful not to mention that the P.O.U.M. took any serious part either in the first struggles against the Fascist rising or at the front. And in all his remarks about the 'provocative attitude' of the P.O.U.M. newspapers it hardly seems to occur to him that there was any provocation on the other side. In the long run this kind of thing defeats its own object. Its effect on me, for instance, is to make me think: 'If I find that this book is unreliable where I happen to know the facts, how can I trust it where I don't know the facts?' And many others will think the same.

Actually I am quite ready to believe that in the main Mr. Jellinek is strictly fair besides being immensely well-informed. But in dealing with 'Trotskyism' he writes as a Communist, or Communist partisan, and it is no more possible for a Communist today to show common sense on this subject than on the subject of 'Social Fascism' a few years ago. Incidentally, the speed with which the angels in the Communist mythology turn into devils has its comic side. Mr. Jellinek quotes approvingly a denunciation of the P.O.U.M. by the Russian Consul in Barcelona, Antonov Ovseenko,[7] now on trial as a Trotskyist!

All in all, an excellent book, packed full of information and very readable. But one has got to treat it with a certain wariness, because the author is under the necessity of showing that though other people may sometimes be right, the Communist Party is always right. It does not greatly matter that nearly all books by Communists are propaganda. Most books are propaganda, direct or indirect. The trouble is that Communist writers are obliged to claim infallibility for their Party chiefs. As a result Communist literature tends more and more to become a mechanism for explaining away mistakes.

Unlike most of the people who have written of the Spanish war, Mr. Jellinek really knows Spain: its language, its people, its territories, and the political struggle of the past hundred years. Few men are better qualified to write an authoritative history of the Spanish war. Perhaps some day he will do so. But it will probably be a long time hence, when the 'Trotsky-Fascist' shadow-boxing has been dropped in favour of some other hobby.

> *Orwell was mistaken in thinking the* Manchester Guardian *correspondent was Jellinek. See his letter to Jellinek, 20 December 1938, below. On 13 January 1939, he wrote a letter of correction to the* New Leader, *which was printed under the heading 'A Mistake Corrected'.*

In my review of Mr. Frank Jellinek's *Civil War in Spain* I stated that Mr. Jellinek had expressed certain opinions which were in contradiction to one of his own despatches to the *Manchester Guardian*. I now find that this despatch was actually sent not by Mr. Jellinek, but by another correspondent. I am very sorry about this mistake and hope you will find space for this correction.

1. Frank Jellinek (1908–75) was an American correspondent in London for the *New York Herald Tribune* and in Spain for the *Manchester Guardian*. See Orwell's letter to Jellinek, below.

2. *The Paris Commune of 1871* (1937; reprinted 1973).

3. Primo de Rivera's government sold the Moroccan tobacco monopoly to Juan March Ordinas (1884–1962). See Thomas, 28.

4. The 'N' document was a forged letter to Franco, purported by the Communists to be from Andrés Nin (see pp. 210 and 241, n. 6, above), a prominent member of the POUM, on which they based their charges of conspiracy between the POUM and Franco to justify their suppression of the POUM.

5. Manuel de Irujo y Ollo was a Basque member of the Republican government, as Minister without Portfolio, from 25 September 1936, then Minister of Justice until he resigned in January 1938, remaining Minister without Portfolio. He had attempted to restore 'normal justice'; see Thomas, 701, 778.

6. 'Barcelona after the Rising', from 'Our Special Correspondent', *Manchester Guardian*, 26 June 1937.

7. Vladimir Antonov-Ovsëenko was one of those listed by Thomas as having 'either [been] executed or died in concentration camps' following service in Spain. He was for a time rehabilitated, and his death was 'regretted as a mistake, in passing, by Khrushchev in his speech denouncing Stalin in February 1956'; see letter from H.N. Brailsford to Orwell above, 17 December 1937, and n.1., and Thomas, 952.

[466]

Review of Searchlight on Spain *by the Duchess of Atholl*[1]
Time and Tide, 16 July 1938

Although no one who publishes books at seven and sixpence a time (with a profit of ninepence to the author) can regard such a venture without alarm, the Penguin Library have shown admirable judgment in their choice of 'specials'.[2] The Duchess of Atholl's *Searchlight on Spain* probably contains less original matter than *Germany Puts the Clock Back* or *Mussolini's Roman Empire*, but it is a worthy successor. As a short popular history of the Spanish war, simply written and well documented, it is not likely to be bettered until the war is over.

Its chief virtue is that it is well-balanced and keeps the main facts in the right perspective. Its chief fault is the fault of virtually all books on the Spanish war – political partisanship. As I have pointed out elsewhere, there is not even among Government supporters one simple and generally-accepted 'version' of the Spanish war. The Loyalists include Socialists, Communists, Anarchists and 'Trotskyists' – one might add Basques and Catalans – who have never been in quite perfect agreement as to what the war is about. Every English writer on the Government side adopts more or less unreservedly the 'line' of one or other political party, and unfortunately he usually does so while claiming to be strictly impartial. The Duchess of Atholl follows the Communist 'line' throughout, and this fact should be borne in mind in reading her book. So long as she is dealing with the origins of the rebellion, with the military side of the war and the scandal of non-intervention, all is well; but I would be a little cautious about accepting her account of the internal political situation, which is one-sided and very much over-simplified.

In her final chapter, 'What it means to us', she points out the probable consequence of a Fascist victory in Spain – that England may lose the command of the Mediterranean and France may be faced with another hostile frontier. This raises what is perhaps the most mysterious question of the whole Spanish war. Why has our Government behaved as it has done? Without any doubt the British Cabinet has behaved as though it wished Franco to win; and yet if Franco wins it may – to put it at its worst – mean the loss of India. The Duchess of Atholl states the facts but does not offer any explanation of Mr. Chamberlain's attitude. Other writers have been less cautious. The real meaning of British foreign policy in the last two years will not become clear until the war in Spain is over; but in trying to divine it I believe it is much safer to assume that the British Cabinet are not fools and that they have no intention of giving anything away.[3]

1. Katharine Stewart-Murray, Duchess of Atholl (1874–1960; DBE, 1918), was trained as a musician, but devoted her life to public service. She became the second woman, and first Conservative woman, to hold ministerial office: Parliamentary Secretary to the Board of Education, 1924–9. She campaigned ceaselessly against cruelty in many forms and conducted a campaign in 1929 against the practice of female circumcision in Africa. Opposed to her party's policy of appeasement of Hitler, she resigned her seat in Parliament in 1938 and campaigned, unsuccessfully, for re-election on a platform of resistance to Hitler.

2. In November 1937, Penguin Books began a series of Specials – 'books of urgent topical importance'. The first was an up-dated version of Edgar Mowrer's *Germany Puts the Clock Back*; the second, February 1938, was *Mussolini's Roman Empire* by G. T. Garratt; in the same month *Blackmail or War?* by Geneviève Tabouis, diplomatic editor of the Paris journal, *L'Oeuvre*. Tabouis (1892–1985) was a remarkably prescient international journalist. She correctly forecast on 9 July 1939 that the Soviet-French-British pact would not be signed, over a month before the British and French delegations arrived in Leningrad. A Soviet-German pact was signed on 24 August 1939 (see *CW*, XI/ 368, 389 and 398–9.) *Searchlight on Spain* (June 1938) was the fourth Special.

3. Orwell also briefly reviewed *The Civil War in Spain* by Frank Jellinek, and *Spain's Ordeal* by Robert Sencourt in this review; they are more fully reviewed above (and see *469* and *462*). He again reviewed *Searchlight on Spain* in the *New English Weekly*, 21 July 1938 (*469*).

---

[470]

To the Editor, Manchester Guardian
5 August 1938

The same letter was sent by Orwell to the Daily Herald *(a daily paper supporting the Labour Party) and the* New Statesman & Nation. *The latter acknowledged the letter but did not print it; the* Daily Herald *neither acknowledged nor printed it. For the vilification and suppression of the POUM and the torture of its leaders, see Thomas, Index, 1095.*

ESPIONAGE TRIAL IN SPAIN
'PRESSURE FROM OUTSIDE'

August 1.   New Hostel, Preston Hall, Aylesford, Kent

Sir, – News has recently reached England that a number of members of
the Executive Committee of the Spanish political party known as the
P.O.U.M. are shortly to be put on trial on the charge of espionage in the
Fascist cause. The circumstances of the case are peculiar, and should, I
think, be brought to public notice. The main facts are as follows: –

In June, 1937, following on the fall of the Caballero Government, the
P.O.U.M. was declared an illegal organisation and a large number of
people were thrown into prison. Simultaneously the Spanish Communist
party published accounts of what purported to be a 'Trotsky-Fascist spy
plot' which was given wide publicity in the Communist press, though
treated with reserve elsewhere. Later various delegations from France and
England, two of them headed by Messrs. James Maxton, M. P., and John
McGovern, M. P., visited Spain to inquire into the matter.

It appeared that most of the leading members of the Spanish Government disclaimed not only all belief in the alleged plot but also responsibility for the arrest of the P.O.U.M. leaders, which had been undertaken
on their own initiative by the Communist-controlled police. Irujo, the
then Minister of Justice, Prieto, Zugazagoitia[1] and others all took this
line, some stated that they considered the P.O.U.M. leaders responsible
for the fighting in Barcelona in May, 1937, but all declared the charge of
espionage to be nonsensical. As for the main piece of evidence produced
by the Communist press, a document known as the 'N document' and
supposed to give proof of treasonable activities, Irujo stated that he had
examined it and that it was 'worthless'.[2] More recently, in January, 1938,
the Spanish Government voted by five to two in favour of releasing the
P.O.U.M. prisoners, the two dissentients being the Communist Ministers.

I think these facts should make it clear that this prosecution is undertaken not at the will of the Spanish Government but in response to outside
pressure as a part of the world-wide campaign against 'Trotskyism'. As
Zugazagoitia put it in his interview with Mr. McGovern, 'We have

received aid from Russia, and so we have had to permit things we did not like.'[3]

And there are other unsatisfactory features about the case. To begin with, the accused men have been kept in close confinement for thirteen months without the formulation of any clear charge and, so far as is discoverable, without facilities for legal aid. The advocate who at the beginning was engaged for their defence was violently attacked in the Communist press and later forced to leave the country. Moreover, a number of the people arrested have since disappeared in circumstances that leave little doubt as to their fate. Among these was Andrés Nin,[4] who a short time previously had been Minister of Justice in the Catalan Generalidad.

In spite of all this it now appears that the accused men are to be tried for espionage after all and that the 'N document', previously declared 'worthless', is to be revived. I suggest therefore that it is the duty of all who call themselves Socialists to enter some kind of protest. I do not mean that we should protest against the Spanish Government's trying its own political prisoners; obviously it has every right to do that. I mean that we should ask for a clear assurance that thèse men will be tried in open court and not in secret by a special tribunal set up for the purpose. Given an open trial and the absence of faked evidence or extorted confessions, those of us who happen to know something about the facts will have little doubt that the accused men can clear themselves. But that is a small matter compared with the preservation of ordinary justice, without which all talk of the 'defence of democracy' becomes entirely meaningless – Yours, &c.,

George Orwell

1. Manuel de Irujo y Ollo, see p. 303, n. 5. Indalecio Prieto y Tuero (1883–1962) was a Socialist, Minister of National Defence in the Negrín government and a fountainhead of defeatism; see Thomas, 809. He founded the SIM, counter-espionage police of ill-repute, and died in exile in Mexico, Julián Zugazagoitia was editor of *El Socialista* and Minister of the Interior in Negrín's government. He was shot after being handed over to the Gestapo in occupied France in 1940.

2. For the 'N document,' see p. 303, n. 4.

3. During a cabinet meeting, 'Zugazagoitia demanded if his jurisdiction as minister of the interior were to be limited by Russian policemen', according to Thomas. 'Had they been able to purchase and transport good arms from US, British, and French manufacturers, the

socialist and republican members of the Spanish government might have tried to cut themselves loose from Stalin' (704).
4. For Andrés Nin, see 'Eye-Witness in Barcelona', n. 6, above.

---

[474]

To Yvonne Davet
18 August 1938

New Hostel, Preston Hall, Aylesford, Kent

Dear Comrade,

I am writing in English this time. Very many thanks for your letter, and for several pamphlets, copies of *La Flèche* etc. I greatly hope you and your father have not been at too much trouble in enquiring about a house for us. We had intended to go to the south of France, but they now say I ought to spend the winter in Africa, so as far as we have any definite plan we are arranging to go to Morocco. The only difficulty I fear is that just possibly the French authorities might make difficulties about allowing us to enter Morocco. Normally there is a lot of tourist traffic there, but I suppose that if the European situation gets any more threatening they may object to the entry of foreigners. However, when we have fixed the date of leaving we will enquire at the French consulate before booking passages. I am keeping your father's address in case we should have to consult him after all. We expect to leave England about the beginning of September.

I hope all your trouble in translating the book has not been for nothing. I know it is terribly difficult to get anyone to publish translations nowadays. In England I don't know how many books get translated from the French every year, but I doubt whether there are more than about three or four which have any success. I can also well understand that they don't want books about the Spanish war. There have been so many, and most of them so bad. The trouble is that as soon as anything like the Spanish civil war happens, hundreds of journalists immediately produce rubbishy books which they put together with scissors and paste, and later when the serious books come along people are sick of the subject. Freda Utley's[1] *Japan's Feet of Clay*, which you tried to get them to publish, had quite a success in England. As to my own book, I don't know yet how it has sold. I should be disappointed if it sold less than 3000 copies, but I don't suppose it would sell more than 4000. It had some good reviews, but the trouble is that books from small publishers never get the same amount of notice as the ones from the big publishers who buy up all the advertisement space. Possibly some paper would publish parts of it serially. I should hate to think of your having all that trouble for nothing. Certainly I would like it very much if Félicien Challaye[2] saw it. I admired him very much for making a stand on behalf of the P.O.U.M. prisoners. I gather that the protests made from France have taken effect, as our latest news is that the Spanish Government has again postponed the trial and that one member of the Government (I suppose either Prieto or Irujo) declared that he would give evidence in favour of the P.O.U.M. prisoners. I wrote recently to three left-wing papers asking people to demand that they should be given a free trial, but only one paper, the *Manchester Guardian*, printed my letter. In private everyone says to me, 'Yes, what you say is quite true, but it is not politic to mention it now.' I have nothing but contempt for this attitude.

There is not much news here. The general public is very little interested in the European situation, and I believe that if war were to break out in the near future the English people would refuse to fight, or at any rate would be very apathetic about it. The proposals for forming a Popular Front seem to have fallen through, though I think we may see some such combination on the eve of the next general election. In the form in which it was proposed in England it is a most pernicious idea, because the so-called Liberal party, with which it is proposed that the Labour Party should ally itself, represents some of the most powerful and reactionary sections of the capitalist class.

I hope all goes well with you and that you will manage to find some more congenial and remunerative work.[3] I will let you know later our date of departure and what our address will be abroad.

Yours fraternally
Eric Blair

1. Orwell refers several times to Freda Utley (1898–1978). She wrote on China and Japan in the 1930s, in particular on the relationship of Lancashire to the Far East. In another letter to Davet (19 June 1939, see below), he refers to *Japan's Gamble in China* (June 1938) and he

recommended her *The Dream We Lost: Soviet Russia Then and Now* (1940). In September 1940, four months before her death, he read her account of her experience in the Soviet Union, *Lost Illusions*. He usually spelt her name Uttley.

2. See p.273, n.1.

3. Yvonne Davet (see headnote to 'Eye-Witness in Barcelona', above) was in fairly desperate straits at this time; she was undertaking translations without certainty of payment or publication because of her belief in the value of what she was translating (private communication).

---

[497]

To Raymond Postgate
21 October 1938   Typewritten draft

Boîte Postale 48, Gueliz, Marrakesh, French Morocco[1]

Dear Mr Postgate,[2]

You may perhaps remember meeting me once at a party of Warburg's. You also wrote to me once about a book of mine, a letter that never got answered because I was in Spain at the time.

The trial of the Executive Committee of the P.O.U.M., which the Spanish Government has been postponing for about sixteen months, has just begun, and from such reports as I can obtain here I see that, as was to be expected, they are being accused of things which everyone with any knowledge of the facts knows to be untrue. I do not think that we can assume as yet that they will not get a fair trial, and obviously we have no right to obstruct or interfere with the Spanish Government even if we were able to do so. But at the same time in the French press (and I have no doubt it will be the same in the English) all kinds of untruthful statements are being made and it is extremely difficult to get an opportunity of answering them. I expect you have some inner knowledge of this affair and are aware that the accusations against the P.O.U.M. in Spain are only a by-product of the Russian Trotskyist trials and that from the start every kind of lie, including flagrant absurdities, has been circulated in the Communist press. It has been almost impossible to answer these because the Communist press, naturally, does not publish letters from opponents and the rest of the left-wing press has been held back by a desire not to embarrass the Spanish Government. At the same time it is difficult to see what good is done by malicious lies directed against innocent people. The accusation (which seems to be fully accepted by the French press of this country – pro-Franco, by the way) which especially troubles me is that the 29th division (the P.O.U.M. troops) deserted from the Aragón front. Everyone with any knowledge of the facts, including those who make the accusation, knows that this is a lie. I myself served with the 29th division from December 30 1936 to May 20 1937, and the I.L.P. could give you the addresses of from ten to twenty other Englishmen, some of whom remained at the front a good deal longer than I did – this in addition to the thousands of Spaniards who could contradict the story. This cowardly libel against brave men can only be circulated because of the perhaps well-meaning refusal of the left-wing press to have this affair properly ventilated.

If this accusation is also flung about in the English press, and any opportunity of contradicting it arises, could you not lend your weight to it? Any statement from such a person as yourself would come much better than from anyone like me, who am obviously a prejudiced witness. The I.L.P. can give you all the details of the affair. You would be perfectly safe in saying that you know on good authority that all the stories of desertion, collaboration with the enemy etc. are untrue.

I enclose a summary of an article from *La Flèche* giving the views of various members of the Spanish Government on the case. So far as I know it contains no inaccuracies. In any case Maxton and others can verify. Even if you cannot see your way to doing anything about this, please forgive me for writing.

Yours sincerely
[not signed]

Orwell made two copies of this summary of the article in La Flèche *of 14 October 1938, by L.-P. Foucaud.*

The act of accusation against the P.O.U.M. repeats the charge of espionage formulated by the Communist press. On this subject two international delegations have obtained statements from the principal members of the Spanish Government.

To the first delegation, composed of Fenner Brockway, general secretary of the I.L.P., Charles Wolff and R. Louzon, editor of *La Révolution Prolétarienne*:

M. Irujo, Minister of Justice, declared: 'That the accusations of espionage brought against the P.O.U.M. were not founded on any fact that could be taken seriously' (aucun fait serieux).

M. Miravitlles, general secretary of the Department of Propaganda of the Catalan Generalidad, declared: 'That the "Golfin" document* was for him and for President Companys a forgery so obvious that at the moment when it was presented to him, he burst into such a shout of laughter that no one dared make use of it any longer.'

M. Largo Caballero stated: 'That if at present the P.O.U.M. was being prosecuted for espionage, this was solely for political reasons and because the Communist Party wished the P.O.U.M. to be suppressed.'

To a second delegation, composed of Mr. Maxton, M.P., M. Weill-Curiel, M. Yves Levy and M. L.-P. Foucaud, various Spanish ministers made similar declarations.

M. Irujo, at 12 o'clock on the 20 August 1937 at the Ministry of Justice in Valencia, stated: 'That there was no proof of espionage against the P.O.U.M. and that the "Golfin" document was valueless.'

M. Ortega y Gasset expressed his disbelief in the P.O.U.M. leaders being Fascist spies. M. Prieto, then Minister of War, received the delegation on August 23 1937. Not having seen the dossier, he refused to speak of the accusation of espionage, but added that: 'The arrest of the P.O.U.M. leaders had not been decided by the Government, but by the police, which the Communists had infiltrated (noyautée) according to their usual custom.'

All these statements, in particular Prieto's, can be obtained in the report on the Maxton delegation published by *Independent News*. In addition there is the pamphlet *Terror in Spain* by Mr John McGovern M.P., dealing with a later delegation and confirming the above.

The fate of this draft is given in Orwell's own handwritten note at the head of the letter:

Draft of letter sent to Raymond Postgate at the time of POUM trial. Similar letters sent to J. F. Horrabin & C. E. M. Joad.[3] All, of course,

---

* Generally referred to in the English press as 'the N document' [Orwell's note].

Welcome to Streatham Library
Tel: 020 7926 6768
www.lambeth.gov.uk/libraries

Borrowed Items 28/08/2019 15:02
XXXXX3059

Item Title	Due Date
* Orwell in Spain :the full text of Homage to Cata	18/09/2019
* House of the rising sun	18/09/2019

* Indicates items borrowed today
Thankyou for using self service
Download ebooks
audiobooks:lambeth.oneclickdigital.eu
Download magazines:
www.rbdigital.com/lambeth

unable to do anything, but all answered sympathetically & appeared to accept my version. R. P. offered to give part of 'Fact'[4] to publicity about the 29th division if J. McNair supplied the facts.

On 14 November 1938, a letter by the General Secretary of the ILP, Fenner Brockway, was published in the Manchester Guardian. *This summarized a full report of the trial. He stated that the charge of espionage made against the prisoners 'completely collapsed during the trial' and was dropped by the prosecution. The charge that the POUM divisions 'had deserted the front' was also dropped'. Whatever the rights and wrongs of the final indictment (that members of the POUM 'had joined the uprising provoked by rebellious elements in Barcelona in May, 1937'), that was the only charge upon which anyone was found guilty. Four prisoners were sentenced to fifteen years' internment and one to eleven years'. Thus, he concluded, 'the accusations against the P.O.U.M. of Fascist espionage and desertion at the front, which have been spread throughout the world by the Communist International and some of its innocent allies, have been shown to have no basis in fact.' Full accounts of those accused, the trial, the dropping of the principal charges and the sentences for involvement in the May Events of Barcelona are given in various issues of the* New Leader; *see, for instance, 21 October, 4 and 11 November 1938. The accused sentenced to eleven years' imprisonment was Jordi Arquer, to whom Orwell had Leonard Moore send a copy of the Italian translation of* Homage to Catalonia *(published in Italy in December 1948); (see 3651).*

1. From 2 September 1938 to 26 March 1939, the Orwells were in French Morocco, mainly at Marrakesh. Orwell had been advised (incorrectly) that the climate would be good for his chest complaint. He was able to go because of an anonymous gift – which Orwell accepted as a loan and which he repaid from the proceeds of *Animal Farm* – from the novelist L. H. Myers. He never learned Myers was his benefactor. While in Marrakesh he wrote *Coming Up for Air*. See Crick, 369–74; Shelden, 328–34; and P. Davison, *George Orwell: A Literary Life*, 111–13.

2. Raymond Postgate (1896–1971) edited *Tribune*, 1940–42 (to which Orwell contributed). Among his best-known books was *The Common People, 1746–1938* (1938), written in collaboration with G. D. H. Cole. He also wrote on food and wine. Cole (1889–1959) was an economist and novelist, whose writing on economics was often effectively directed to the general reader – for example, *The Intelligent Man's Guide Through World Chaos* (1932) and *What Everybody Wants to Know About Money* (1933).

3. J. F. Horrabin was a journalist, illustrator, Labour MP, 1929–31, and a member of the editorial board of *Controversy*. (See p. 241, n. 1, above) C. E. M. Joad (1891–1953) was a philosopher and writer. He achieved particular fame as a member of the team of the BBC's radio programme *The Brains Trust*. From 1930 until his death, he was head of the Department of Psychology and Philosophy, Birkbeck College, University of London.

4. *Fact*, subtitled *A Monograph a Month*, was published, in twenty-seven issues, from April 1937 to June 1939.

---

[503]

Review of The Church in Spain, 1737–1937 *by E. Allison Peers;* Crusade in Spain *by Eoin O'Duffy*[1]

New English Weekly, *24 November 1938*

Professor Allison Peers, though a Franco partisan and of late rather an acrimonious one, is a writer who can be taken seriously. He is also, I gather, a Catholic, and he is quite naturally and rightly concerned about the fate of the Church in Spain. No one would blame him for being angry when churches are burned and priests murdered or driven into exile. But I think it is a pity that he has not looked a little more deeply into the reasons why these things happen.

In recounting the various persecutions of the Church in Spain, from the Middle Ages onward, he traces four main causes. The first three are the struggle between Church and King, the struggle between Church and State, and the liberal anticlericalism of the nineteenth century. The last is the 'development of what is broadly termed Communism, *i.e.*, a number of related but not identical proletarian movements, one common factor of which is disbelief in, and denial of, God'. All church-burning, priest-shooting and anticlerical violence generally are supposed to have their roots in Communism and its Spanish variant, Anarchism, which are inseparable from 'hatred of God'. It is not, Professor Peers thinks, a question of hostility to a corrupt church, but of 'a cold, calculated, determined attempt to destroy institutional religion throughout the country'.

Now, it is no use denying that churches have been destroyed all over Government Spain. Various Government partisans, in their efforts to make their cause respectable, have pretended that churches were only demolished when they had been used as fortresses in the street fighting at the beginning of the war. This is merely a lie. Churches were destroyed everywhere, in town and village, and except for a few Protestant churches none were allowed to open and hold services till about August, 1937. It is also useless to deny that both Anarchism and Marxian Socialism are hostile to all religion. But this does not really tell us why the Spanish churches were destroyed. Professor Peers's *Catalonia Infelix*[2] made it clear that he understands the internal political situation in Government Spain a great deal better than most writers on the Spanish War, and there are two facts bearing on this question which he is probably aware of. One is the fact that during the present war the Russian Government has used its influence in Spain *against* and not *for* anticlerical violence and revolutionary extremism generally. The other is that the sacking of churches happened during the early period when the proletariat were in control, and the churches began to re-open and the priests to come out of hiding, when the Caballero Government fell and the middle class was back in the saddle. In other words the anticlerical movement, in its violent form, is a popular movement and a native Spanish movement. It has its roots not in Marx or Bakunin,[3] but in the condition of the Spanish people themselves.

In Catalonia and Aragón, in the first year of war, there were two things that impressed me. One was the apparent absence of any religious feeling whatever among the mass of the people. Admittedly at the time it might have been dangerous to admit openly to religious belief – still, one cannot be altogether deceived about a thing like that. The second was the fact that most of the wrecked or damaged churches that I saw were new ones; their predecessors had been burnt down in earlier disturbances. And this raises the thought, when was the last church burnt down in England? Probably not since Cromwell. A mob of English farm hands sacking the parish church would be something next door to unthinkable. Why? Because at present the conditions of class warfare simply do not exist in England. In Spain, for a century past, millions of people had had to live in conditions that were beyond bearing. Over huge tracts of country peasants who were serfs in everything but name worked enormous hours for wages of sixpence a day. In these conditions you get something that we have not got in England, a real hatred of the status quo, a real willingness to kill and burn. But the Church was part of the status quo;

its influence was on the side of the wealthy. In many villages the huge garish church, with the cluster of miserable mud huts surrounding it, must have seemed the visible symbol of property. Naturally, Catholic writers have of late been denying this. The Church was not corrupt, it was anything but wealthy, the priests were often good Republicans, etc., etc. The answer is that the Spanish common people, whose opinion on this matter is worth something, did not think so. In the eyes of at any rate very many of them, the Church was simply a racket and the priest, the boss and the landlord were all of a piece. The national church had lost its hold on them because it had failed in its job. Catholics would probably do their Church a better service by facing this fact than by tracing everything to mere wickedness, or to Moscow, which persecutes its own religious believers but has its reasons for being slightly pro-clerical elsewhere.

General O'Duffy's adventures in Spain do seem in one way to have resembled a crusade, in that they were a frightful muddle and led to nothing in particular. Otherwise his book does not tell one much. For the most part it consists of the usual vapid tributes to General Franco ('the great leader and patriot, General Franco, at the head of the Nationalist Movement, composed of all that is great and noble in Spanish national life, fighting for Christian civilization', etc., etc.) and the usual ignorant misrepresentations of what is happening on the other side. General O'Duffy's information is so sketchy that he even gets the names of some of the Spanish trade unions and political parties wrong. Franco propaganda is often less irritating than the rather subtler type of lie that has been evolved by the other side, but I confess to getting tired of that story of the 'Russian troops' (it is not recorded whether they had snow on their boots[4]) who are supposed to have fought on the Madrid front.

After what I saw in Spain, and what I have read about it in England, I understand why Sir Walter Raleigh burned his History of the World.[5] If

> The truth is great and will prevail
> When none cares whether it prevail or not,[6]

then the sooner people stop feeling strongly about this Spanish struggle, the better it will be. At present the atmosphere of lies that surrounds every aspect of it is suffocating. Meanwhile O'Duffy's is a badly written and uninteresting book.

Orwell's review drew protests from both authors. On 4 December General O'Duffy wrote to the editor of New English Weekly, *asking that his letter not be published, but describing Orwell's review as scurrilous. The word 'review' is underlined and placed in single quotation marks, evidently to indicate an anomalous, to him, use of the word. His book had, he said, received twenty-four favourable reviews and only one other (in a 'Communist organ') that was critical. He enclosed copies of typical reviews and claimed that his book had 'a record circulation here & abroad', strange if, as Orwell claimed, the book was 'an ignorant representation and badly written'. The letter is marked 'Came while you were in Africa' and was evidently not sent to Orwell at the time, but it was answered. O'Duffy replied to the effect that the editor's letter merely added insult to injury, and he asked that his name be removed from* New English Weekly'*s circulation list.*

Professor Peers's letter was published on 8 December 1938. He made three points: he was not a Roman Catholic; he was not a 'Franco partisan', but had maintained that the Spanish conflict could be resolved permanently only by agreement; his conclusions as to 'why these things happen' were not the product of a visit of a few months but of twenty years' study of many aspects of Spanish life. Orwell's response, headed 'Spanish Clericalism', was published in the New English Weekly *on 22 December 1938:*

Sir, – I am very sorry to see that I have hurt Professor Peers' feelings. I did not mean to do so. But perhaps I had better answer the three points he raises:

1. I only said that I 'gathered' that Professor Peers was a Catholic. My reason was simply that he is much more friendly in his attitude to the Catholic Church than is usual in non-Catholics, even including Anglicans. But I freely admit that his not being a Catholic makes his testimony in favour of the Spanish Church stronger.

2. I described Professor Peers as 'a Franco partisan and of late rather an acrimonious one'. I do not think Professor Peers would deny that the tone of *The Church in Spain* is a good deal more bitter than that of *Catalonia Infelix*. As to the question of partisanship, Professor Peers claims to be

impartial on the ground that he has 'continually maintained . . . that the only solution to the Spanish conflict that can be permanent is a solution by agreement'. Well, I should regard that as being pro-Franco. After all, Franco is, at least technically, a rebel. What should we say of a person who suggested a 'solution by agreement' between the burglar and the policeman? We should say that he was at any rate to some extent pro-burglar. But I never for an instant meant to suggest that Professor Peers was unfair or dishonest. When I read *Catalonia Infelix*, I regarded it as a book written from the Franco standpoint but written with extreme fair-mindedness. I believe I said something to this effect in a short review that I did of it. Incidentally, it may amuse Professor Peers to learn that I have been in trouble in 'left' circles for not attacking him more severely.

3. I quite agree that Professor Peers knows infinitely more about the Church in Spain, and everything else in Spain, than I am ever likely to know. But I think that his explanation of modern anti-clericalism is altogether too simple to be true, and I do not see why my own observations, small as they are, should not be advanced as evidence.

1. Gen. Eoin O'Duffy (1892–1944) led an Irish Fascist movement, the Blue Shirts, founded by William Cosgrave (1880–1965), President of Eire until 1932. Most of O'Duffy's men in Spain were Blue Shirts. They fought for Franco. See Thomas, 592 and 602.

2. See pp. 257–8.

3. Mikhail Aleksandrovich Bakunin (1814–76), Russian anarchist and political writer who opposed Karl Marx.

4. Orwell refers to one of the famous, and more incongruous, myths of World War I. At a critical period on the Western Front, rumours abounded that Russian troops were being transferred there from the Eastern Front. The 'evidence' purported to be sightings of Russian troops travelling in darkened trains from the north of Britain 'with snow on their boots'.

5. This was written by Sir Walter Raleigh (1552?–1618) when he was imprisoned in the Tower of London; it was published in 1614. Orwell writes of Raleigh's imprisonment and his *History* in 'As I Please,' 10, 4 February 1944 (*2416*), not included in the extract below.

6. 'Magna est Veritas', lines 9–10, by Coventry Patmore (1823–96).

To Frank Jellinek
20 December 1938

Boîte Postale 48, Gueliz, Marrakesh, French Morocco

Dear Jellinek,[1]

Many thanks for your letter. I am extremely sorry that I attributed that note in the *Manchester Guardian* to you, but my reason for doing so was that the *M.G.* had not denied it. The facts were these. I was apparently semi-disabled by my wound (though actually it got all right soon afterwards) and had decided to go back to England, and on June 15 I went up to Siétamo to get my discharge-papers, which for some reason unknown to me one had to go up to the front to do. When I got there the P.O.U.M. troops besides the others in Siétamo were being got ready for an action which actually took place some days later, and it was only by a bit of luck that I did not get involved in the battle, though at the time I could hardly use my right arm. When I managed to get back to Barcelona on June 20, it was to find that the P.O.U.M. had been suppressed, everyone I knew was in jail or in hiding, I had to sleep two nights in the streets, and the police had been interfering with my wife in the most revolting manner. What really angered me about all this was that it had carefully been kept secret from the men at the front and even from people in Lérida (where I had been on June 20). On I forget which day I saw you in a café near the Hotel Oriente. I was going to cross the road and speak to you, but at this time, as was not unnatural in the circumstanc[es] I was ready to believe that every Communist was a spy, and I simply walked on. Then later in England, when I went through the files of the *M.G.*, I saw the note saying that the P.O.U.M. were not Fascists (or words to that effect), which I naturally attributed to you. I was greatly touched and wrote to the *M.G.* congratulating them and asking for your address. I suppose the man who replied didn't know who had sent that message, and he merely said that you were in Mexico and they didn't know your address. I am going to send a note to the *New Leader* saying I was wrong about who sent the message.[2] If they don't insert it, please believe it is only for lack of space.

They are quite honest, though often no doubt mistaken, but with only 8 pages per week one hasn't much space to spare.

I am writing at the same time as this asking my agent to send you a copy of my book on the Spanish war. Parts of it might interest you. I have no doubt I have made a lot of mistakes and misleading statements, but I have tried to indicate all through that the subject is very complicated and that I am extremely fallible as well as biassed. Without answering in detail all the points in your letter, I might indicate more clearly than I could do in the book my position on one or two questions that inevitably come up in a controversy of this kind. I entirely agree with you that the whole business about the P.O.U.M. has had far too much fuss made about it and that the net result of this kind of thing is to prejudice people against the Spanish Government. But my position has always been that this kind of controversy could die a natural death and cause comparatively little harm if people would refrain from telling lies in the beginning. The sequence of events is approximately this. The P.O.U.M. preach a 'line' which may or may not make it more difficult to secure military efficiency for the Spanish Government, and which is also rather too like what the C.P. were saying in 1930. The C.P. feel that they have got to silence this at all costs, and therefore begin stating in the press that the P.O.U.M. are Fascists in disguise. This kind of accusation is infinitely more resented than any ordinary polemic could be, with the result that the various people and parties who could be described as 'Trotskyist' tend to develop into mere anti-Communists. What complicates it and enormously increases the feeling of bitterness it causes is that the capitalist press will on the whole throw its weight on the Communist side of the controversy. I know that Communists don't as a rule believe this, because they have got into the habit of feeling that they are persecuted and have hardly noticed that since about 1936 (ie. since the change of 'line') the attitude towards them in the democratic countries is very different. Communist doctrine in its present form appeals to wealthy people, at least some wealthy people, and they have a very strong footing in the press in both England and France. In England, for instance, the *News Chronicle* and *New Statesman* are under direct Communist influence, there is a considerable press which is actually official C.P., and certain influential papers which are bitterly *anti-Socialist* nevertheless prefer 'Stalinism' to 'Trotskyism'. On the other side, of course, there is nothing, because what is now called 'Trotskyism' (using the word very widely) has no appeal to anyone with over £500 a year. The result is that the most appalling lies can be printed and except in a few papers like the *M.G.* which keep up the old traditions it is quite impossible to answer them. One's only resort is to start miserable little rags like the ones the Trotskyists run, which, necessarily, are nothing but anti-Communist papers. There is no question that appalling lies were published about the P.O.U.M., not only by the official C.P. press, but by papers like the *N.C.* and *N.S. & N.*, which after publishing refuse to print any answers in their correspondence columns. I don't know whether you have yet seen the accounts of the P.O.U.M. trial. The trial made it clear, as it was bound to do if fairly conducted, that there was no truth in the accusations of espionage, which were for the most part merely silly. One accusation, for instance, had been that several miles of the Aragón front had been entirely deserted for two months – this at a time when I was there myself. This witness broke down in the box. Similarly, after all the statements in papers of the type of the *Daily Worker* about 'two hundred signed confessions' etc., there was complete failure to produce any evidence whatever. Although the trial was conducted more or less in camera, *Solidaridad Obrera* was allowed afterwards to print a report, and it was made quite clear that the charges of espionage were dismissed and the four men who were sentenced were only convicted of taking part in the May fighting in Barcelona. In the face of all this the C.P. press printed reports that they had been condemned for espionage. In addition this was also done by some pro-C.P. papers, which significantly enough are also pro-Fascist papers. Eg. the *Observer* reported the verdict in such a way as to let it appear that the verdict was one of espionage, and the French press of this country, which of course is pro-Franco, reported the accusation, stated that it had been 'proved' and then failed to report the verdict. You must agree that this kind of thing is likely to cause resentment, and though in the heat of the moment it may seem 'realistic' to say 'These people are obstructing us – therefore they might as well be Fascists – therefore we'll say they *are* Fascists', in the end it may do more harm than good. I am not a Marxist and I don't hold with all this stuff that boils down to saying 'Anything is right which advances the cause of the Party'. On the title page of my book you will find two texts from Proverbs[3] which sum up the two prevailing theories of how to combat Fascism, and I personally agree with the first and not the second.

I think you'll find answers in my book to some of what you say. Actually I've given a more sympathetic account of the P.O.U.M. 'line' than I actually felt, because I always told them they were wrong and refused to join the party. But I had to put it as sympathetically as possible, because it has had no hearing in the capitalist press and nothing but libels in the left-wing press. Actually, considering the way things have gone in Spain, I think there was something in what they said, though no doubt their way of saying it was tiresome and provocative in the extreme.

I got over the wound with no ill-effects but now my lungs have been giving trouble and they sent me to spend the winter in this country. I think it's doing me good, and I expect to be back in England in April.

Yours

Eric Blair

('George Orwell')

P.S. I don't agree with you that there was no persecution of P.O.U.M. militiamen. There was a lot – even, later on, in hospitals, as I learned from a man who was wounded later than I. I have today heard from George Kopp, who was my commandant at the front, and who has just got out of Spain after 18 months in jail. Making all allowance for exaggerations, and I know people who have been in those circumstances always exaggerate, there is no question he has been shamefully treated, and there were probably some hundreds of others in the same case.

The chap who told you something about the I.L.P. militiamen signing some kind of statement was probably a man named Parker. If so it was probably a lie. Ditto if it was a man named Frankfort. If it was a man named Hiddlestone[4] it was probably not a lie but might have been some kind of mistake. I know nothing about it as I came to Spain quite independently of them.

1. Frank Jellinek wrote to Ian Angus, 10 June 1964, to explain that Orwell's letter was prompted by his (Jellinek's) protest that he had not falsified a despatch to the *Guardian* 'for propaganda purposes', as suggested by Orwell in his review of *The Civil War in Spain*. He had left Barcelona well before 20 June 1937 and he wrote nothing for the *Guardian* about the suppression of the POUM. He believes the article in question 'was more or less planted

on the *MG* by F. A. Voigt', who was a visiting correspondent in Barcelona. Voigt (1892–1957), an outstanding foreign correspondent, early drew attention to the dangers of Nazism; such was his analysis of the rise of National Socialism that he was unable to work for the *Manchester Guardian* in Germany again after Hitler's accession to power in 1933. After his book *Unto Caesar* (1938) was published, he was grouped by Orwell among 'The Pessimists' in 'The Intellectual Revolt', 1, 24 January 1946 (see *2875*). Orwell, in 'Notes on Nationalism', October 1945 (see *2668*), grouped him with other Anglophobes who suddenly became violently pro-British. Voigt edited *The Nineteenth Century and After* from 1938 to 1946.

2. See 'A Mistake Corrected', *New Leader*, 13 January 1939, p. 303 above.

3. 'Answer not a fool according to his folly, lest thou also be like unto him. / Answer a fool according to his folly, lest he be wise in his own conceit', Proverbs 26:4–5. Orwell gave the reference as xxvi, 5–6 in *Homage to Catalonia*. It was not corrected until the Penguin edition of 1989.

4. Buck Parker, Frank Frankfort and Reg Hiddlestone were members of the ILP contingent linked to the 3rd Regiment, Division Lenin, POUM, of which Orwell was also a member. For Frankfort (Frankford), see Orwell's reply to his accusations, 24 September 1937 (*399*).

---

[535]

'Release of George Kopp'

Among Orwell's papers were three issues of Independent News: *a special number of, probably, late November or early December 1938 devoted to 'The P.O.U.M. Trial in Barcelona'; No. 59, 16 December 1938, with an article titled 'After the P.O.U.M. Trial'; and No. 60, 23 December 1938, which included a report on George Kopp's imprisonment and release. Kopp was Orwell's commander in Spain, and Orwell and his wife visited him in prison (see pp. 156–62 [VI/171–8]). The account given must have been derived from Kopp, who was not the most reliable of witnesses, but Orwell would have taken it at face value. It shows that Orwell had a close friend who had suffered at the hands of the Cheka (the Soviet secret police), knew about false confessions and had read of 'torture by rats' in a confined space. In view of its significance this account is given in full (with two or three slight styling corrections). It should be noted that Kopp was questioned in Russian and that an interpreter was required, which seems natural. Kopp, however, was born in Russia and went to Belgium only when he was ten. He may have been able to speak Russian but not have revealed this to his captors.* Independent News, *'Service de Presse Hebdomadaire du Bureau d'Informations Franco-Britanniques', was issued from Paris; its editor was Lucien Weitz. It presented the POUM point of view.*

After an intensive campaign for the release of George Kopp our Belgian comrades have succeeded in saving one more revolutionary militant from the claws of the Spanish stalinists°.

George Kopp has been saved but for a long time he will carry on his body the marks of the sadistic cruelty of these twentieth century inquisitors. When George Kopp came to Spain he was a robust strapping young man, radiantly healthy and strong. Today he has emerged from his long calvary, thin, feeble and bent, walking slowly with the aid of a cane. His body is covered with scabs and bruises, the marks of the diseases he has contracted in the subterranean dungeons of the Stalinist 'checas', in the damp, airless holds of the prison ships, and in the Forced Labour Camps.

Kopp was arrested June 20, 1937 at the height of the P.O.U.M. repression. Arrested without a warrant, without the knowledge of any authority, he was released in the same manner, without an order from any Spanish Court, – but for the past year and a half he has been under the vigilance of the Communist Party watch dogs.

During this time Kopp has been in the following jails, hideouts, secret prisons etc. First, upon his arrest he was taken to Police Headquarters; from there to the Hotel Falcón; then to the 'checa' of Puerta del Angel; from there to Vallmajor (clandestine prison). He was later sent to Segorbe (near Valencia) to a Forced Labour Camp; then back again to Vallmajor; then to the prison ship *Uruguay*; then to Falset (Labour Camp No. 6); then to the Palacio de Misiones; back again to the *Uruguay*; then to the Barcelona Seminary; afterwards to the Preventorium of Colell; then to Tamarite in Bonanova (suburb of Barcelona); and back to the Seminary. He was finally released December 7, 1938.

In the 'checa' of Puerta del Angel he was interrogated 27 times during a total of ONE HUNDRED AND THIRTY FIVE hours. The questions were put in Russian and the Russian Communist agents in charge had to use an interpreter both for the questions and the answers.

When Kopp was taken to the Falcón Hotel (the POUM hotel stolen by the 'unofficial' police and turned into a prison), he was so exasperated with the entire situation and with his arbitrary arrest that he decided to go on a hunger strike as a protest. During 6 days he touched no food but was obliged to give it up as it only endangered his situation.

In the Vallmajor prison the Stalinists put on their best performance. They started by cajoling, then intimidation and finally coercion and open threats. They placed before him three documents to sign, – one, his promotion to Lieutenant Colonel; another, his affiliation to the Communist Party; and the third, a 'confession' saying that the P.O.U.M. was a nest of spies and traitors. When Kopp refused to sign he was put in a coal bin without light, air, or food where enormous rats ran in and out of his legs. For 12 days he remained in the black pit, seeing no one, hearing no one until one day a voice called out, 'Tonight we're going to shoot you!'

Kopp's long martyrdom was his reward for a clean revolutionary record in the Workers' Militia. He came to Spain from Belgium when the revolution broke out. He left immediately for the Aragón front with the Miguel Pedrola Column as 'Centuria' chief. He took part in the following military operations: Casetas (9–10–36); Huesca (21–10–36); Insane Asylum of Huesca (11–36); Vedado Zucra (5–12–36); Alcubierre (6–2–37); the Hermitage of Salas (13–4–37); Chimillas (13–6–37). He fought in this last battle only seven days before his arrest. At that time he was Major in the Popular Army and had occupied commanding posts in the 29th Division.

---

[534]

'Caesarean Section in Spain'
The Highway,[1] *March 1939*

When General Franco raised his rebellion in July, 1936, he threw a spanner into the works of a machine which was travelling in a fairly well-defined direction. How seriously he jammed it is still uncertain.

The revolution of 1931 had got rid of the Spanish monarchy but had failed to solve any of the country's fundamental economic problems. One of its effects, however, had been to create an atmosphere of liberalism and free speech in which ideas hitherto frowned upon could circulate widely. From then onwards it was clear to many observers that civil war in Spain was inevitable. The decisive moment came when a Government which could roughly be described as 'left' was returned by a rather narrow majority at the elections of February, 1936. This Government – the

Government of the Popular Front – was not by any means under the control of extremists. It did not precipitate a crisis by violence towards its political opponents; on the contrary, it actually weakened itself by its moderation. A more rigidly 'left' Government would have dealt earlier with the military plot which everyone knew was being prepared, and would probably have made some promise of independence to the Arabs in Spanish Morocco, thus preventing them from throwing in their lot with Franco. Nevertheless the Government's programme of reform menaced the big landowners and the Church, as any radical reform was bound to do. In the existing state of Spain it was not possible to move nearer to a real democracy without colliding with powerful vested interests. Consequently, the mere appearance of the Popular Front Government was enough to raise the most difficult problem of our time: the problem of making fundamental changes by democratic methods.

Parliamentary democracy, and especially the party system, developed in a period when no dispute between the different factions was really irreconcilable. Whigs and tories, or liberals and conservatives, are conducting what is in effect a family quarrel, and they will abide by one another's decisions; but when the issue is, for instance, between capitalism and socialism, the case is altered. Actually, in slightly varying guises, the same situation has arisen over and over again. A democratically elected government proceeds to make radical reforms; it is acting perfectly legally, but its opponents 'won't play'; they rise in rebellion, either by open violence, as in Spain, or, more usually, by financial sabotage. The peculiarity of this case was that the Spanish Government fought back.

The war has now lasted two-and-a-half years and caused perhaps a million deaths, besides unheard-of-misery. How much damage has it done to the cause of democracy? One has only to consider the possibilities of modern war, the kind of things that governments will have to do to hold their peoples together, to feel very doubtful whether there will be much democracy left anywhere after several years of 'all-in' warfare between great nations. Yet it is a fact that the Spanish war, in nearly every way so terrible, has been a hopeful portent in this respect. In Government Spain both the forms and the spirit of democracy have survived to an extent that no one would have foreseen; it would even be true to say that during the first year of the war they were developing.

I was in Catalonia and Aragón from Christmas, 1936, until about the middle of the following year. To be in Spain at that time was a strange and moving experience, because you had before you the spectacle of a people that knew what it wanted, a people facing destiny with its eyes open. The rebellion had plunged the country into chaos and the Government nominally in power at the outbreak of war had acted supinely; if the Spanish people were saved, it had got to be by their own effort. It is not an exaggeration to say that practically the whole resistance of the opening months was the direct and conscious action of the ordinary people in the street, via their trade unions and political organisations. Transport and major industries had devolved directly into the hands of the workers; the militias which had to bear the brunt of the fighting were voluntary organisations growing out of the trade unions. There was plenty of incompetence, of course, but also there were astonishing feats of improvisation. The fields were tilled, trains ran, life away from the fighting line was for the most part peaceful and orderly, and the troops, though poorly armed, were well fed and cared for. With all this there was a spirit of tolerance, a freedom of speech and the press, which no one would have thought possible in time of war. Naturally the social atmosphere changed, in some ways for the worse, as time went on. The country settled down to a long war; there were internal political struggles which resulted in power passing from the hands of socialists and anarchists into the hands of communists, and from the hands of communists into the hands of radical republicans; conscription was imposed and censorship tightened up – two inevitable evils of modern war. But the essentially voluntary spirit of the opening months has never disappeared, and it will have important after-effects.

It would be childish to suppose that a Government victory could have instantly brought a democratic regime into existence. Democracy, as we understand it in Western Europe, is not immediately workable in a country so divided and exhausted as Spain will be when the war is over. Certainly any Government which triumphs over Franco will be of liberal tendency, if only because it will have to sweep away the power of the great land-owners and most if not all of the power of the Church. But the task of governing the whole of Spain will be completely different from that of governing the present loyal fraction. There will be large dissident minorities and enormous problems of reconstruction; inevitably this implies a transition period during which the régime will be democratic chiefly in name. On the other hand, if Franco wins even the name will be abandoned. He has made perfectly clear his intention of setting up a corporative state on the Italian model – that is to say, a state in which the majority of people are openly and cynically excluded from having any voice in affairs.

And yet the situation may be less desperate than it looks. Obviously if Franco wins the immediate prospects are not hopeful; but the long-term effects of a Franco victory are hard to foresee, because a dictator in Franco's position would almost certainly have to depend on foreign support. And if the Government can win, there is reason to think that the evil results necessarily following on civil war may disappear quite rapidly. Wars are normally fought by soldiers who are either conscripts or professionals, but who in either case are essentially in the position of victims and who have only a very dim idea as to what they are fighting about. One could not possibly say the same of the armies of Government Spain. Instead of the usual process of conscripts being fed into a military machine, a civilian people has voluntarily organised itself into an army. It is the psychological after-effects of this that may make a return to democracy more easy.

It was impossible to travel in Spain in early 1937 without feeling that the civil war, amid all its frightful evil, was acting as an educational force. If men were suffering, they were also learning. Scores of thousands of ordinary people had been forced into positions of responsibility and command which a few months earlier they would never have dreamed of. Hundreds of thousands of people found themselves thinking, with an intensity which would hardly have been possible in normal times, about economic theories and political principles. Words like fascism, communism, democracy, socialism, Trotskyism, anarchism, which for the vast mass of human beings are nothing but words, were being eagerly discussed and thought out by men who only yesterday had been illiterate peasants or overworked machine-hands. There was a huge intellectual ferment, a sudden expansion of consciousness. It must be set down to the credit side of the war, a small offset against the death and suffering, and it is doubtful whether it can be completely stamped out, even under a dictatorship.

It is true that things have not fallen out as we expected them to do at that time. To begin with, up till the summer of 1937 everyone in Government Spain took it as a thing assured that the Government was going to win. I would be far from saying that the Government is beaten even now, but the fact is that a Government victory cannot any longer be regarded as certain. Secondly, great numbers of people took it for granted that the war would be followed by a definitely revolutionary movement in the direction of socialism. That possibility has receded. Given a Government victory, it seems much likelier that Spain will develop into a capitalist republic of the type of France than into a socialist state. What seems certain, however, is that no regression to a semi-feudal, priest-ridden régime of the kind that existed up to 1931 or, indeed, up to 1936, is now possible. Such régimes, by their nature, depend upon a general apathy and ignorance which no longer exist in Spain. The people have seen and learned too much. At the lowest estimate, there are several million people who have become impregnated with ideas which make them bad material for an authoritarian state. If Franco wins, he will hold Spain's development back, but probably only so long as it pays some foreign power to keep him in place. Shooting and imprisoning his political opponents will not help him; there will be too many of them. The desire for liberty, for knowledge, and for a decent standard of living has spread far too widely to be killed by obscurantism or persecution. If that is so, the slaughter and suffering which accompany a modern civil war may not have been altogether wasted.

1. *The Highway* was subtitled *A Review of Adult Education and the Journal of the Workers' Educational Association.* W. E. Williams, editor of a special number, called 'Democracy at Work', had written to Orwell, 22 November 1938, asking if he could contribute an article with this title. A note preceded the article: 'Two at least of Mr. Orwell's books are familiar to W.E.A. members: *The Road to Wigan Pier,* and *Down and Out in London and Paris.* This article was written before Catalonia collapsed.' Various dates for the collapse can be used. Thomas has a map showing the advances made by Nationalist forces in the campaign for Catalonia, December 1938–January 1939 (870); Barcelona was occupied on 26 January 1939; Nationalist troops reached the French border at all points by 10 February (873, 881). Sir William Emrys Williams (1896–1977) was Chief Editor and Director of Penguin Books, 1935–65. He was also, from 1934–40, Secretary of the British Institute of Adult Education; Director of the Army Bureau of Current Affairs, 1941–5, and the Bureau of Current Affairs, 1946–51. He was so closely associated with the Pelican series that he was known in-house as 'Pelican Bill'. He can be seen in Rodrigo Moynihan's painting of the Penguin Editors (reproduced in *The Penguin Story,* 1956) and on p. 26 of *Fifty Penguin Years* (1985).

[550]

To Yvonne Davet

19 June 1939   *Typewritten in French; translation given below*

The Stores, Wallington, Near Baldock, Herts, Angleterre

TRANSLATION

I am sending you chapters 7–10,[1] and I shall send the others in a few days when I have corrected them. In these four chapters I have made notes on pages 120, 126, 128, 141, 164, 165, 168, 174, 207. There is not very much to alter anywhere, and I think the translation expresses the feeling of the original very well. I do hope that all your work will not be in vain. If we cannot find a publisher, I do not see why we should not publish some chapters in a magazine. I like the introduction by Georges Kopp very much,[2] but here I shall be guided by the wishes of the publisher, if we can find one. If necessary I am quite prepared to write an introduction myself. I shall let Warburg know he must not ask too much. I am surprised he asked £40 for Freda Utley's book[3] – it is probably because the book was quite successful in England.

Until the other day I didn't know you did not have a copy of *Homage to Catalonia.* A year ago I asked Warburg to send you one and he promised he would, but he probably forgot. The other day I sent you a proof copy, but I shall send you a proper copy of the book as soon as I can get one. Anyway there is no textual difference between the book and the manuscript. The name of Monte Oscuro could be changed to Monte Trazo[4] – I was definitely mistaken.

My latest book[5] came out a week ago. I don't yet know how it will be received. You will have noticed that I am still with Gollancz, that Stalinist publisher!

---

1. Chapters from *Homage to Catalonia* as originally published; these are chapters 6 to 9 and Appendix I, as rearranged in line with Orwell's wishes in the *Complete Works* edition. Yvonne Davet's translation was not published until 1955, five years after Orwell's death. See Note on the Text, above [VI/251–3].
2. George Kopp evidently wrote an introduction, because Orwell told Moore, 15 April 1947 (see *3216*), that it had been sent to the publisher (Gallimard). By 1947 Orwell thought it

'was not a very suitable one and in any case would have no point now'. Kopp's introduction has not been traced.

3. Freda Utley's *Japan's Gamble in China* (June 1938).
4. This change was made in *CW* [VI/38], and see p. 58.
5. *Coming Up for Air*.

---

[578]

Review *of* Hotel in Flight *by Nancy Johnstone*
The Adelphi, *December 1939*

How many millions of people in Spain and elsewhere are now looking back on the Spanish war and asking themselves what the devil it was all about? The thing had begun to seem meaningless even before the European kaleidoscope had twisted itself into its new pattern, and practically every foreigner who was involved seems to have brought away the impression of having been mixed up in a nightmare. Some months ago I was talking to a British soldier who was coming home from Gibraltar on a Japanese liner. A year earlier he had deserted from the Gibraltar garrison and with great difficulty made his way round to Valencia to join the Spanish Government forces. He had no sooner got there than he was arrested as a spy, flung into prison and forgotten about for six months. Then the British consul managed to extricate him and ship him back to Gibraltar, where he received another six months for desertion. This might almost be an allegorical history of the Spanish war.

Mrs. Johnstone's book, sequel to an earlier one, deals with the last eighteen months of the war, the period during which the Spanish Government's cause was becoming more and more obviously hopeless. She and her husband kept a hotel at Tossa on the Catalan coast, which became a rendezvous for journalists and visiting literary men, besides insufferable 'politicals' of all colours. Starting off with the comic-opera conditions which still prevailed in 1937, the book becomes increasingly a story of food-shortage and tobacco-shortage, air-raids, spy-mania and refugee children, and ends with the terrible retreat into France and the stench and misery of the concentration camps round Perpignan. Much of the atmosphere will be horribly familiar to anyone who was in Spain at any period of the war. The sense of never having quite enough to eat, the muddle, the inefficiency, the inability to understand what is happening, the feeling that everything is fading away into a sort of mist of fear, suspicion, red tape and obscure political jealousies – it is all there, with plenty of crude physical adventure into the bargain. Mrs. Johnstone's picture of the concentration camps on the French-Spanish border is dreadful enough, but there is one observation that she makes and which ought to be underlined, and that is that the French Government is the only one that has actually done anything appreciable for the refugees from Fascist countries. Whereas the British Government made a grant of £12,000 for the Spanish refugees, their keep at the beginning was costing the French Government £17,000 *a day*, and presumably is not costing much less even now. It is worth remembering that at any time during the past ten years close on 10 per cent of the population of France has consisted of foreigners, quite largely political refugees. After all, there is something to be said for 'bourgeois' democracy.

This book gives a valuable picture of the retreat and will no doubt help to stop up some historical gaps, but it does not seem to me a very good book, *as* a book. Why is it that autobiographical journalism of this type always has to be so chirpily facetious? As soon as I glanced into the book and saw the style in which it was written I began looking for the dog. Books of this kind almost always have a comic dog which is a great filler-up of paragraph-ends; however, the part is filled by Mrs. Johnstone's husband. The probability is that if a really good book is ever written about the Spanish war it will be by a Spaniard, and probably not a 'politically conscious' one. Good war books are nearly always written from the angle of a *victim*, which is just what the average man is in relation to war. What vitiated the outlook of most of the foreigners in Spain, and especially the English and Americans, was the knowledge at the back of their minds that they would probably succeed in escaping from Spain in the end. Moreover, if they had gone there deliberately to take part, they knew what the war was about, or thought they did. But what did it mean to the great mass of the Spanish people? We simply do not know as yet. Looking back on casual contacts with peasants, shopkeepers, street-hawkers, even militiamen, I now suspect that great numbers of these people had no feelings about the war whatever, except a wish that it were over. Mrs. Johnstone's picture of the stolid inhabitants of the little seaport town of Tossa half-consciously confirms this. One question that is still not satisfactorily answered is why the war went on so long. After the beginning of 1938 it was obvious to anyone with any military knowledge that the Government could not win, and even by the summer of 1937 the odds were in Franco's favour. Did the mass of the Spanish people really feel that even the atrocious sufferings of the later part of the war were preferable to surrender – or did they continue to fight at least partly because the whole of left-wing opinion from Moscow to New York was driving them on? Perhaps we shall know the answer when we begin to hear what the war looked like to Spanish conscripts and non-combatants, and not merely to foreign volunteers.

---

[586]

Review of The Last Days of Madrid *by S. Casado, translated by Rupert Croft-Cooke;* Behind the Battle *by T. C. Worsley*
Time and Tide, *20 January 1940*

Although not many people outside Spain had heard of him before the beginning of 1939. Colonel Casado's name[1] will always be among those that are remembered in connection with the Spanish Civil War. He it was who overthrew the Negrín Government[2] and negotiated the surrender of Madrid – and, considering the actual military situation and the sufferings of the Spanish people, it is difficult not to feel that he was right. The truly disgraceful thing, as Mr. Croft-Cooke says forcibly in his introduction, was that the war was ever allowed to continue so long. Colonel Casado and those associated with him were denounced all over the world in the left-wing press as traitors, crypto-Fascists, etc., etc., but these accusations came very badly from people who had saved their own skins long before Franco entered Madrid. Besteiro,[3] who took part in the Casado administration and afterwards stayed behind to face the Fascists, was also denounced as 'pro-Franco'. Besteiro was given thirty years' imprisonment! The Fascists certainly have a strange way of treating their friends.

Perhaps the chief interest of Colonel Casado's book is the light it throws on the Russian intervention in Spain and the Spanish reaction to it. Although well-meaning people denied it at the time, there is little doubt that from the middle of 1937 until nearly the end of the war the Spanish Government was directly under the control of Moscow. The ultimate motives of the Russians are uncertain, but at any rate they aimed at setting up in Spain a Government obedient to their own orders, and in the Negrín Government they had one. But the bid that they had made for middle-class support produced unforeseen complications. In the earlier part of the war the main adversaries of the Communists in their fight for power had been the Anarchists and left-wing Socialists, and the emphasis of Communist propaganda was therefore on a 'moderate' policy. The effect of this was to put power into the hands of 'bourgeois Republican' officers and officials, of whom Colonel Casado became the leader. But these people were first and foremost Spaniards and resented the Russian interference almost as much as that of the Germans and Italians. Consequently the Communist-Anarchist struggle was followed by another struggle of Communists against Republicans, in which the Negrín Government was finally overthrown and many Communists lost their lives.

The very important question that this raises is whether a western country can in practice be controlled by Communists acting under Russian orders. It is a question that will probably come to the front again in the event of a revolution of the Left in Germany. The inference from Colonel Casado's book seems to be that a western or westernized people will not for any length of time allow itself to be governed from Moscow. Making all allowance for the prejudice he undoubtedly feels against the Russians and their local Communist agents, his account leaves very little doubt that the Russian domination was widely and deeply resented in Spain. He also suggests that it was the knowledge of the Russian intervention that decided Britain and France to leave the Spanish Government to its fate. This seems more doubtful. If the British and French Governments had really wanted to counter the Russian influence, by far the quickest way was to supply the Spanish Government with arms, for it had been obvious from the start that any country that supplied arms could control Spanish policy. One must conclude that the British and French Governments not only wanted Franco to win, but would in any case have preferred a Russian-controlled Government to a Socialist-Anarchist combination under some such leader as Caballero.[4]

Colonel Casado's book gives a detailed account of all the events leading up to the capitulation, and it is one of those documents that will always have to be studied by future historians of the Spanish War. As a book it is not and does not pretend to be anything very remarkable. Mr. Worsley's book⁵ is better written, by a more practised hand; but the subject-matter is more familiar – air-raids, Barcelona politics, etc., etc. The story begins with a singularly amateurish attempt at intelligence-work on behalf of the Spanish Government by the author and Mr. Stephen Spender. Later Mr. Worsley found more useful and congenial work with an ambulance and had some interesting experiences, which included being mixed up in the retreat from Málaga. But I think it is very nearly the close-season for this class of Spanish war-book.

1. Colonel Sigismundo Casado López (1893–1968), commander of the Republican Army of the Centre. He organized a campaign against Dr Juan Negrín, the Republican Prime Minister, and attempted, towards the end of the civil war, to gain better terms from Franco. He failed and took refuge in Britain; he later returned to Spain.
2. Dr Juan Negrín (1889–1956) was Socialist Prime Minister of Spain, September 1936–March 1938. He fled to France in 1939 and set up a Spanish Government in Exile; he resigned from its premiership in 1945 in the hope of uniting all exiled Spaniards. He died in exile. See Thomas, 949–50.
3. Julián Besteiro (1870–1940), President of the UGT (Socialist Trade Union) to 1931, Speaker of the Cortes (the Spanish Parliament) and temporarily President of Spain in 1931. He died in prison in 1940 while serving a thirty-year prison sentence imposed by Franco's government.
4. See p. 223, n. 6.
5. T. C. Worsley (1907–77) was an author and critic. He taught at Wellington (where Orwell spent a term in 1917). Orwell reviewed his *Philistines and Barbarians: Democracy and the Public Schools* in *Time and Tide*, 14 September 1940 (see *Orwell and the Dispossessed*), and he wrote the foreword to his *The End of the 'Old School Tie'*, May 1941 (XII/*793*). With W. H. Auden Worsley wrote *Education Today – and Tomorrow* (1939). He took part in a BBC broadcast to India on education with N. G. Fisher (1910–72), which was directed by Orwell, 1 September 1942 (see XIII/*1415*).

[726]

Review of The Spanish Dilemma by E. Allison Peers; A Key to Victory: Spain by Charles Duff
Time and Tide, 21 December 1940

Now that the British Government's pro-Fascist policy during the Spanish Civil War has had its inevitable result, some of the apologists of General Franco are noting with surprise and dismay that Franco is not a gentleman after all. It is curious that Professor Peers, who during the war itself was one of the most moderate and fair-minded of Franco's supporters, does not seem to share this feeling. He still appears to think that Franco's victory was all to the best, not only from the Spanish point of view but from our own. The strongest argument he can advance is that, had the Government won, Spain might have remained under the control of Russia, who is the friend of Germany.[1] So apparently it is better that Spain should remain in *direct* vassalage to Germany – and of the most slavish kind, as one can see by glancing at the Spanish press – than that she should retain any kind of connection with Germany's rather doubtful ally. He gives various quotations from the Spanish newspapers, and from the history textbooks which Franco has introduced into the schools, in which England and the U.S.A. are vilified as malignantly as Goebbels himself could wish, and yet on top of this alleges that Nationalist Spain is a possible friend of England. His book is, in fact, simply a re-hash of the 'anti-red' doctrines of three years ago, most manifestly false at the time and since exploded by events. If an attack on Gibraltar should begin, I should be interested to read Professor Peers's explanation of it. Meanwhile, after what happened in France, it is disquieting that people of such views should remain in any kind of position of influence.

Mr. Duff's book is at any rate a corrective to Professor Peers's, even if, like some others of the Victory Books, it is a little too easily optimistic. It is a vigorous plea for support of the Spanish Republicans, both as part of the general defence of democracy and because of the strategic importance of the Spanish peninsula. When one remembers how during the past three years we have been deluged with books on the Spanish war, mainly from a pro-Government angle, it might seem that the familiar Popular Front viewpoint is hardly worth re-stating. Unfortunately, this is not the case. The policy of Danegeld is still being followed towards Franco Spain, and there is no sign that the general public grasps even now what this suicidal policy must mean. Worse still, influence has been brought to bear on the press to prevent free criticism of the Spanish question. All through the winter of 1939–40 Italy was flattered and supplied with war materials, with the result, foreseen by every thinking person, that Italy came into the war against us in the spring. It is just possible that this might not have happened if the Italian danger had been freely publicized at the time. And so also with Spain. If the ordinary newspaper-reader can be brought to understand that Franco Spain is not neutral, is venomously hostile towards England and directly under the control of Germany, then it is at any rate conceivable that our policy may be changed by force of public opinion.

Mr. Duff is certainly right in saying that we should support the Spanish Republicans. Where it is impossible to follow him is in the way he proposes to set about it. He is actually advocating that we should invade Spain through Portugal, making use of the fact that Portugal is friendly to Britain! It does not seem to occur to him that the Portuguese Government might not remain friendly if such an invasion took place.

Meanwhile, Dr. Negrín is grudgingly allowed to remain in England on condition that he 'takes no part in politics'. Franco's seizure of Tangier is sleekly explained away by Mr. Butler,[2] and friendly talks are being exchanged with the Spanish Fascist Government at the same time as Súñer[3] is in Berlin and Republicans like Zugazagoitia are being shot in jail. How to reconcile all this with a 'war against Fascism' is a little difficult to see. The best hope lies in the rapid enlightenment of public opinion, and towards that Mr. Duff's book should help. I wish it, therefore, a larger sale than on purely literary grounds it deserves.

1. In August 1939, Russia and Germany signed a Non-Aggression Pact. The countries were therefore allies from the outbreak of war in September 1939 (when both invaded Poland) until Germany invaded the Soviet Union on 22 June 1941.
2. Presumably R. A. ('Rab') Butler (1902–84; Life Peer, 1963), who was Under-Secretary of State for Foreign Affairs, 1938–41. He was later Chancellor of the Exchequer and Foreign Secretary in the Conservative governments of 1951–64.
3. Ramón Serrano Súñer (b. 1901), brother-in-law of Franco and, as Minister of the Interior, second in importance to him until dismissed in 1942. He was a pro-German Falangist. On 18 October 1940, Hitler expressed to him his exasperation at Spain's failure to join the war on the side of the Axis. His experience as a prisoner of the Republicans embittered him for life. As Thomas puts it, they were such 'as to make him close his eyes to pity' (Thomas, 924, and see 633–4).

[749]

Extract from *War-time Diary*

22.1.41: A propos of what — says, it is at any rate a fact that the People's Convention[1] crew have raised a lot of money from somewhere. Their posters are everywhere, also a lot of new ones from the *Daily Worker*. The space has not been paid for, but even so the printing, etc., would cost a good deal. Yesterday I ripped down a number of these posters, the first time I have ever done such a thing. Cf. in the summer when I chalked up 'Sack Chamberlain', etc., and in Barcelona, after the suppression of the POUM, when I chalked up 'Visca POUM'.[2] At any normal time it is against my instincts to write on a wall or to interfere with what anyone else has written.

1. The People's Convention was organized in January 1941 by the Communists, ostensibly to fight for public rights, higher wages, better air-raid precautions and friendship with the USSR, but some historians have said its true purpose was to agitate against the war effort. In July 1941, after Russia's entry into the war, it immediately called for a second front. By 1942 its active work had ceased.

2. See *Homage to Catalonia*, p. 164 [VI/181].

---

[852]

Review of The Forge by *Arturo Barea,*[1] *translated and with an introduction by Sir Peter Chalmers Mitchell*[2]
Horizon, *September 1941*[3]

If some Russian writer were at this moment to produce a book of reminiscences of his childhood in 1900, it would be difficult to review it without mentioning the fact that Soviet Russia is now our ally against Germany, and in the same way it is impossible to read *The Forge* without thinking at almost every page of the Spanish Civil War. In fact there is no direct connection, for the book deals only with Señor Barea's early youth and ends in 1914. But the civil war made a deep and painful impression on the English intelligentsia, deeper, I should say, than has yet been made by the war now raging. The man in the street, misled by frivolous newspapers, ignored the whole business, the rich mechanically sided with the enemies of the working class, but to all thinking and decent people the war was a terrible tragedy that has made the word 'Spain' inseparable from the thought of burnt bodies and starving children. One seems to hear the thunder of future battles somewhere behind Señor Barea's pages, and it is as a sort of prologue to the civil war, a picture of the society that made it possible, that his book is most likely to be valued.

He was born into a very poor family, the son actually of a washerwoman, but with uncles and aunts who were slightly richer than his mother. In Catholic countries the clever boy of a peasant family finds his easiest escape from manual labour in the priesthood, but Señor Barea, who had anticlerical relatives and was an early unbeliever himself, after winning a scholarship at a Church school, went to work at thirteen in a draper's shop, and afterwards in a bank. All his good memories are of country places, especially of the forge belonging to his uncle in Mentrida, a magnificent independent peasant of the type now extinct in the industrialized countries. On the other hand his memories of Madrid are low and squalid, a tale of poverty and overwork far more extreme than anything to be found in England. And here, perhaps, in his descriptions of the Madrid slums, of hordes of naked children with their heads full of lice and lecherous priests playing cards for the contents of the poor-boxes, he gives half-consciously the clue to the Spanish Civil War: it is that Spain is a country too poor to have ever known the meaning of decent government. In England we could not have a civil war, not because tyranny and injustice do not exist, but because they are not obvious enough to stir the common people to action. Everything is toned down, padded, as it were, by ancient habits of compromise, by representative institutions, by liberal aristocrats and incorruptible officials, by a 'superstructure' that has existed so long that it is only partly a sham. There are no half-tones in the Spain that Señor Barea is describing. Everything is happening in the open, in the ferocious Spanish sunlight. It is the straightforward corruption of a primitive country, where the capitalist is openly a sweater, the official always a crook, the priest an ignorant bigot or a comic rascal, the brothel a necessary pillar of society. The nature of all problems is obvious, even to a boy of fifteen. Sex, for example:

My cousin is taking advantage of my being a boy. But she is right. She would be a whore if she were to go to bed with anyone . . . I'd like to go to bed with the girls, and they would like to come with me, but it is impossible. Men have whores for that; women have to wait until the priest marries them, or they become whores themselves. And, naturally, meantime they get excited. Those who get too excited have to become whores.

Or politics:

They were always fighting in Parliament, Maura, Pablo Iglesias, and Lerroux, and they painted on the walls slogans such as 'Down with Maura'. Sometimes they would write in red, 'Maura, up!' The workers were those who wrote 'Down with Maura!' Those who wrote 'up' were the gentry . . . At nightfall, when Alcalá Street is crowded, a group of young gentlemen will appear shouting 'Maura, up!' Then a group of workers and students is formed at once, and begins to shout 'Maura, down!' . . . The civil guards charge, but they never attack the gentry.

When I read that last phrase, 'the civil guards never attack the gentry', there came back to me a memory which is perhaps out of place in a review, but which illustrates the difference of social atmosphere in a country like England and a country like Spain. I am six years old, and I am walking along a street in our little town with my mother and a wealthy local brewer, who is also a magistrate. The tarred fence is covered with chalk drawings, some of which I have made myself. The magistrate stops, points disapprovingly with his stick and says, 'We are going to catch the boys who draw on these walls, and we are going to order them SIX STROKES OF THE BIRCH ROD.' (It was all in capitals in my mind.) My knees knock together, my tongue cleaves to the roof of my mouth, and at the earliest possible moment I sneak away to spread the dreadful intelligence. In a little while, all the way down the fence, there is a long line of terror-stricken children, all spitting on their handkerchiefs and trying to rub out the drawings. But the interesting thing is that not till many years later, perhaps twenty years, did it occur to me that my fears had been groundless. No magistrate would have condemned me to SIX STROKES OF THE BIRCH ROD, even if I had been caught drawing on the wall. Such punishments were reserved for the Lower Orders. The Civil Guards charge, but they never attack the gentry. In England it was and still is possible to be unaware of this, but not in the Spain that Señor Barea writes of. There, injustice was unmistakable, politics was a struggle between black and white, every extremist doctrine from Carlism to Anarchism could be held with lunatic clarity. 'Class war' was not merely a phrase, as it has come to be in the Western democracies. But which state of affairs is better is a different question.

This is not primarily a political book, however. It is a fragment of autobiography, and we may hope that others will follow it, for Señor Barea has had a varied and adventurous life. He has travelled widely, he has been both worker and capitalist, he took part in the civil war and he served in the Riff War[4] under General Franco. If the Fascist powers have done no other good, they have at least enriched the English-speaking world by exiling all their best writers. Sir Peter Chalmers Mitchell's translation is vivid and colloquial, but it was a pity to stick all the way through to the 'dramatic present', which seems all right in a Latin language but rapidly becomes tiresome in English.

1. Arturo Barea (1897–1957) had been Head of Foreign Press Censorship and Controller for Broadcasts, Madrid, in 1937. Orwell knew him personally. See Orwell's review of *The Clash*, below.
2. Sir Peter Chalmers Mitchell (1864–1945; Kt., 1929) was an eminent zoologist. He was responsible for rebuilding much of London Zoo and for the creation of the 'open' zoological garden at Whipsnade. He retired to Malaga but the civil war forced his return to England.
3. Orwell also reviewed this book in *Time and Tide*, 28 June 1941 (see *821*).
4. The Riff (or Rif) is an area of north-eastern Morocco occupied by Berber tribes. Under Abd-el-Krim they maintained their independence against the Spanish until 1926 when they were defeated by a combined French and Spanish army. Franco served with distinction in the Rif War. The tribesmen are noted warriors and have served in the French and Spanish armies.

---

[854]

Extract from letter to Partisan Review
23 September 1941

When I said that the belief in international working class solidarity doesn't exist any longer, I was not thinking of what may or may not be said at the 'parties' which Mr. [Nicholas] Moore supposes I frequent. I was thinking of the history of Europe during the past ten years and the utter failure of the European working class to stand together in the face of Fascist aggression. The Spanish civil war went on for two and a half years, and during that time there was not one country in which the workers staged even a single strike in aid of their Spanish comrades. So far as I can get at the figures the British working class subscribed to various 'aid Spain' funds about one per cent of what they spent during the same period in betting on football and horse-races. Anyone who actually talked to working men at the time knows that it was virtually impossible to get them to see that what happened in Spain concerned them in any way. Ditto with Austria, Manchuria, etc. During the past three months Germany has been at war with Russia and at the time of writing the Germans have overrun the greater part of the Russian industrial areas. If even the shadow of international working class solidarity existed, Stalin would only have to call on the German workers in the name of the Socialist Fatherland for the German war-effort to be sabotaged. Not only does nothing of the kind happen, but the Russians do not even issue any such appeal. They know it is useless. Until Hitler is defeated in the field he can count on the loyalty of his own working class and can even drag Hungarians, Rumanians and what-not after him. At present the world is atomised and no form of internationalism has any power or even much appeal. This may be painful to literary circles in Cambridge, but it is the fact.

[1173]

Extract from BBC Weekly News Review for India, 22 [Comparison with the Spanish Civil War] 16 May 1942

This is not the only heroic fight against Fascist aggression which has happened during the last ten years. The Spanish people fought for two-and-a-half years against their own Quislings and against the German and Italian invaders, actually fought against odds which – relatively speaking – were greater than those facing China. Their resistance was the resistance of almost unarmed peasants and working men against hordes of trained soldiers with the resources of the German war machine behind them. [At the beginning of the Spanish Civil War, the Republic had practically no army at all, for it was precisely the regular army, under Fascist officers, which had staged the revolt and this army was soon reinforced by great numbers of Italian mercenaries sent by Mussolini, and by German tanks and bombing planes. The ordinary working men of the factories, led by their Trade Union Officials, began to organize themselves into Companies and Battalions to make such weapons as they could manage with the rather backward industrial equipment of Spain, and to learn the art of war literally by practice. Men, who in private life were factory workers, or lawyers or orange-growers, found themselves within a few weeks officers, commanding large bodies of men and in many cases commanded them with great competence. Apart from the inequalities of equipment, the Spanish people had great hardships to face. The food situation was none too good even from the first, and the Nazi airmen, serving with General Franco, carried out, wherever they went, the most atrocious raids on open towns, deliberately aiming their bombs on residential working-class districts, with the idea of terrorising the people into surrender.][1] Yet [in the face of all these difficulties,] they[2] fought for two-and-a-half years, and, though at the end, Franco managed to win a kind of victory, his position is now so insecure that it is thought that about a million people – that is about four per cent of the population – are in concentration camps.

1. The passages between square brackets were not broadcast. For a full discussion of whether cuts were to assist in accurate timing or censorship, see *892*, XIII/82–92, especially 87.
2. Originally 'they' read 'the Spanish people' but the last two words were crossed out and a 'y' was added to 'the'.

[1421]

'Looking Back on the Spanish War'
[*1942?*]

It has not proved possible to date this essay, nor even to discover exactly when it was first published. When it appeared in New Road,[1] *probably in June 1943, sections IV, V and VI were omitted, much to Orwell's annoyance. On 23 July 1944, Orwell wrote to Dwight Macdonald[2] that 'the little beasts' at* New Road *'cut it about without informing me'*

*(2518, XVI/298). The complete essay was published in New York in
1953 in* Such, Such Were the Joys, *and in London in the same year in*
England Your England. *An editorial note in* New Road *dates the
essay 1942:*

> *As a representative of the* NEW WRITING *school in English literature during 1942,
> we print excerpts from an essay on the Spanish Civil War, by George Orwell. The
> sections omitted from this essay dealt with the danger that, by the falsification of
> history, political leaders might obtain control of the past as well as of the future, and
> with the political attitude of the Great Powers during the Civil War. Political writing
> as a literary form is becoming a neglected art. Mr. Orwell is probably its most talented
> contemporary exponent.*

I

First of all the physical memories, the sounds, the smells and the surfaces
of things.

It is curious that more vividly than anything that came afterwards in
the Spanish War I remember the week of so-called training that we
received before being sent to the front – the huge cavalry barracks in
Barcelona with its draughty stables and cobbled yards, the icy cold of the
pump where one washed, the filthy meals made tolerable by pannikins of
wine, the trousered militiawomen chopping firewood, and the roll-call in
the early mornings where my prosaic English name made a sort of comic
interlude among the resounding Spanish ones, Manuel González, Pedro
Aguilar, Ramón Fenellosa, Roque Ballaster, Jaime Domenech, Sebastián
Viltrón, Ramón Nuvo Bosch. I name those particular men because I
remember the faces of all of them. Except for two who were mere riff-raff
and have doubtless become good Falangists by this time, it is probable
that all of them are dead. Two of them I know to be dead. The eldest
would have been about twenty-five, the youngest sixteen.

One of the essential experiences of war is never to be able to escape
from disgusting smells of human origin. Latrines are an overworked
subject in war literature, and I would not mention them if it were not that
the latrine in our barracks did its necessary bit towards puncturing my
own illusions about the Spanish Civil War. The Latin type of latrine, at

which you have to squat, is bad enough at its best, but these were made of some kind of polished stone so slippery that it was all you could do to keep on your feet. In addition they were always blocked. Now I have plenty of other disgusting things in my memory, but I believe it was these latrines that first brought home to me the thought, so often to recur: 'Here we are, soldiers of a revolutionary army, defending Democracy against Fascism, fighting a war which is *about* something, and the detail of our lives is just as sordid and degrading as it could be in prison, let alone in a bourgeois army.' Many other things reinforced this impression later; for instance, the boredom and animal hunger of trench life, the squalid intrigues over scraps of food, the mean, nagging quarrels which people exhausted by lack of sleep indulge in.

The essential horror of army life (whoever has been a soldier will know what I mean by the essential horror of army life) is barely affected by the nature of the war you happen to be fighting in. Discipline, for instance, is ultimately the same in all armies. Orders have to be obeyed and enforced by punishment if necessary, the relationship of officer and man has to be the relationship of superior and inferior. The picture of war set forth in books like *All Quiet on the Western Front*[3] is substantially true. Bullets hurt, corpses stink, men under fire are often so frightened that they wet their trousers. It is true that the social background from which an army springs will colour its training, tactics and general efficiency, and also that the consciousness of being in the right can bolster up morale, though this affects the civilian population more than the troops. (People forget that a soldier anywhere near the front line is usually too hungry, or frightened, or cold, or, above all, too tired to bother about the political origins of the war.) But the laws of nature are not suspended for a 'red' army any more than for a 'white' one. A louse is a louse and a bomb is a bomb, even though the cause you are fighting for happens to be just.

Why is it worth while to point out anything so obvious? Because the bulk of the British and American intelligentsia were manifestly unaware of it then, and are now. Our memories are short nowadays, but look back a bit, dig out the files of *New Masses*[4] or the *Daily Worker*, and just have a look at the romantic warmongering muck that our left-wingers were spilling at that time. All the stale old phrases! And the unimaginative callousness of it! The sang-froid with which London faced the bombing of Madrid! Here I am not bothering about the counter-propagandists of the Right, the Lunns, Garvins *et hoc genus*; they go without saying. But here were the very people who for twenty years had hooted and jeered at the 'glory' of war, at atrocity stories, at patriotism, even at physical courage, coming out with stuff that with the alteration of a few names would have fitted into the *Daily Mail* of 1918. If there was one thing that the British intelligentsia were committed to, it was the debunking version of war, the theory that war is all corpses and latrines and never leads to any good result. Well, the same people who in 1933 sniggered pityingly if you said that in certain circumstances you would fight for your country, in 1937 were denouncing you as a Trotsky-Fascist if you suggested that the stories in *New Masses* about freshly wounded men clamouring to get back into the fighting might be exaggerated. And the Left intelligentsia made their swing-over from 'War is hell' to 'War is glorious' not only with no sense of incongruity but almost without any intervening stage. Later the bulk of them were to make other transitions equally violent. There must be a quite large number of people, a sort of central core of the intelligentsia, who approved the 'King and Country' declaration in 1935, shouted for a 'firm line' against Germany in 1937, supported the People's Convention in 1940, and are demanding a Second Front now.[5]

As far as the mass of the people go, the extraordinary swings of opinion which occur nowadays, the emotions which can be turned on and off like a tap, are the result of newspaper and radio hypnosis. In the intelligentsia I should say they result rather from money and mere physical safety. At a given moment they may be 'pro-war' or 'anti-war', but in either case they have no realistic picture of war in their minds. When they enthused over the Spanish War they knew, of course, that people were being killed and that to be killed is unpleasant, but they did feel that for a soldier in the Spanish Republican Army the experience of war was somehow not degrading. Somehow the latrines stank less, discipline was less irksome. You have only to glance at the *New Statesman* to see that they believed that; exactly similar blah is being written about the Red Army at this moment. We have become too civilised to grasp the obvious. For the truth is very simple. To survive you often have to fight, and to fight you have to dirty yourself. War is evil, and it is often the lesser evil. Those who take the sword perish by the sword,[6] and those who don't take the sword perish by smelly diseases. The fact that such a platitude is worth writing down shows what the years of *rentier* capitalism have done to us.

II

In connection with what I have just said, a footnote on atrocities.

I have little direct evidence about the atrocities in the Spanish Civil War. I know that some were committed by the Republicans, and far more (they are still continuing) by the Fascists. But what impressed me then, and has impressed me ever since, is that atrocities are believed in or disbelieved in solely on grounds of political predilection. Everyone believes in the atrocities of the enemy and disbelieves in those of his own side, without ever bothering to examine the evidence. Recently I drew up a table of atrocities during the period between 1918 and the present;[7] there was never a year when atrocities were not occurring somewhere or other, and there was hardly a single case when the Left and the Right believed in the same stories simultaneously. And stranger yet, at any moment the situation can suddenly reverse itself and yesterday's proved-to-the-hilt atrocity story can become a ridiculous lie, merely because the political landscape has changed.

In the present war we are in the curious situation that our 'atrocity campaign' was done largely before the war started, and done mostly by the Left, the people who normally pride themselves on their incredulity. In the same period the Right, the atrocity-mongers of 1914–18, were gazing at Nazi Germany and flatly refusing to see any evil in it. Then as soon as war broke out it was the pro-Nazis of yesterday who were repeating horror-stories, while the anti-Nazis suddenly found themselves doubting whether the Gestapo really existed. Nor was this solely the result of the Russo-German Pact. It was partly because before the war the Left had wrongly believed that Britain and Germany would never fight and were therefore able to be anti-German and anti-British simultaneously; partly also because official war-propaganda, with its disgusting hypocrisy and self-righteousness, always tends to make thinking people sympathise with the enemy. Part of the price we paid for the systematic lying of 1914–18 was the exaggerated pro-German reaction which followed. During the

years 1918–33 you were hooted at in left-wing circles if you suggested
that Germany bore even a fraction of responsibility for the war. In all the
denunciations of Versailles I listened to during those years I don't think I
ever once heard the question 'What would have happened if Germany
had won?' even mentioned, let alone discussed. So also with atrocities.
The truth, it is felt, becomes untruth when your enemy utters it. Recently
I noticed that the very people who swallowed any and every horror story
about the Japanese in Nanking in 1937 refused to believe exactly the same
stories about Hong Kong in 1942. There was even a tendency to feel that
the Nanking atrocities had become, as it were, retrospectively untrue
because the British Government now drew attention to them.

But unfortunately the truth about atrocities is far worse than that they
are lied about and made into propaganda. The truth is that they happen.
The fact often adduced as a reason for scepticism – that the same horror
stories come up in war after war – merely makes it rather more likely that
these stories are true. Evidently they are widespread fantasies, and war
provides an opportunity of putting them into practice. Also, although it
has ceased to be fashionable to say so, there is little question that what
one may roughly call the 'whites' commit far more and worse atrocities
than the 'reds'. There is not the slightest doubt, for instance, about the
behaviour of the Japanese in China. Nor is there much doubt about
the long tale of Fascist outrages during the last ten years in Europe. The
volume of testimony is enormous, and a respectable proportion of it comes
from the German press and radio. These things really happened, that is the
thing to keep one's eye on. They happened even though Lord Halifax said
they happened. The raping and butchering in Chinese cities, the tortures in
the cellars of the Gestapo, the elderly Jewish professors flung into cesspools,
the machine-gunning of refugees along the Spanish roads – they all happened, and they did not happen any the less because the *Daily Telegraph* has
suddenly found out about them when it is five years too late.

III

Two memories, the first not proving anything in particular, the second, I
think, giving one a certain insight into the atmosphere of a revolutionary
period.

Early one morning another man and I had gone out to snipe at the Fascists in the trenches outside Huesca. Their line and ours here lay three hundred yards apart, at which range our aged rifles would not shoot accurately, but by sneaking out to a spot about a hundred yards from the Fascist trench you might, if you were lucky, get a shot at someone through a gap in the parapet. Unfortunately the ground between was a flat beetfield with no cover except a few ditches, and it was necessary to go out while it was still dark and return soon after dawn, before the light became too good. This time no Fascists appeared, and we stayed too long and were caught by the dawn. We were in a ditch, but behind us were two hundred yards of flat ground with hardly enough cover for a rabbit. We were still trying to nerve ourselves to make a dash for it when there was an uproar and a blowing of whistles in the Fascist trench. Some of our aeroplanes were coming over. At this moment a man, presumably carrying a message to an officer, jumped out of the trench and ran along the top of the parapet in full view. He was half-dressed and was holding up his trousers with both hands as he ran. I refrained from shooting at him. It is true that I am a poor shot and unlikely to hit a running man at a hundred yards, and also that I was thinking chiefly about getting back to our trench while the Fascists had their attention fixed on the aeroplanes. Still, I did not shoot partly because of that detail about the trousers. I had come here to shoot at 'Fascists'; but a man who is holding up his trousers isn't a 'Fascist', he is visibly a fellow creature, similar to yourself, and you don't feel like shooting at him.

What does this incident demonstrate? Nothing very much, because it is the kind of thing that happens all the time in all wars. The other is different. I don't suppose that in telling it I can make it moving to you who read it, but I ask you to believe that it is moving to me, as an incident characteristic of the moral atmosphere of a particular moment in time.

One of the recruits who joined us while I was at the barracks was a wild-looking boy from the back streets of Barcelona. He was ragged and barefooted. He was also extremely dark (Arab blood, I dare say), and made gestures you do not usually see a European make; one in particular – the arm outstretched, the palm vertical – was a gesture characteristic of Indians. One day a bundle of cigars, which you could still buy dirt cheap at that time, was stolen out of my bunk. Rather foolishly I reported this to the officer, and one of the scallywags I have already mentioned promptly came forward and said quite untruly that twenty-five pesetas had been stolen from his bunk. For some reason the officer instantly decided that the brown-faced boy must be the thief. They were very hard on stealing in the militia, and in theory people could be shot for it. The wretched boy allowed himself to be led off to the guardroom to be searched. What most struck me was that he barely attempted to protest his innocence. In the fatalism of his attitude you could see the desperate poverty in which he had been bred. The officer ordered him to take his clothes off. With a humility which was horrible to me he stripped himself naked, and his clothes were searched. Of course neither the cigars nor the money were there; in fact he had not stolen them. What was most painful of all was that he seemed no less ashamed after his innocence had been established. That night I took him to the pictures and gave him brandy and chocolate. But that too was horrible – I mean the attempt to wipe out an injury with money. For a few minutes I had half believed him to be a thief, and that could not be wiped out.

Well, a few weeks later, at the front, I had trouble with one of the men in my section. By this time I was a '*cabo*', or corporal, in command of twelve men. It was static warfare, horribly cold, and the chief job was getting sentries to stay awake and at their posts. One day a man suddenly refused to go to a certain post, which he said, quite truly, was exposed to enemy fire. He was a feeble creature, and I seized hold of him and began to drag him towards his post. This roused the feelings of the others against me, for Spaniards, I think, resent being touched more than we do. Instantly I was surrounded by a ring of shouting men: 'Fascist! Fascist! Let that man go! This isn't a bourgeois army. Fascist!' etc., etc. As best I could in my bad Spanish I shouted back that orders had got to be obeyed, and the row developed into one of those enormous arguments by means of which discipline is gradually hammered out in revolutionary armies. Some said I was right, others said I was wrong. But the point is that the one who took my side the most warmly of all was the brown-faced boy. As soon as he saw what was happening he sprang into the ring and began passionately defending me. With his strange, wild, Indian gesture he kept exclaiming, 'He's the best corporal we've got!' (*¡No hay cabo como el!*) Later on he applied for leave to exchange into my section.

Why is this incident touching to me? Because in any normal circumstances it would have been impossible for good feelings ever to be
re-established between this boy and myself. The implied accusation of
theft would not have been made any better, probably somewhat worse,
by my efforts to make amends. One of the effects of safe and civilised life
is an immense over-sensitiveness which makes all the primary emotions
seem somewhat disgusting. Generosity is as painful as meanness, gratitude
as hateful as ingratitude. But in Spain in 1936 we were not living in a
normal time. It was a time when generous feelings and gestures were
easier than they ordinarily are. I could relate a dozen similar incidents,
not really communicable but bound up in my own mind with the special
atmosphere of the time, the shabby clothes and the gay-coloured revolutionary posters, the universal use of the word 'comrade', the anti-Fascist
ballads printed on flimsy paper and sold for a penny, the phrases like
'international proletarian solidarity', pathetically repeated by ignorant
men who believed them to mean something. Could you feel friendly
towards somebody, and stick up for him in a quarrel, after you had been
ignominiously searched in his presence for property you were supposed
to have stolen from him? No, you couldn't; but you might if you had both
been through some emotionally widening experience. That is one of the
by-products of revolution, though in this case it was only the beginnings
of a revolution, and obviously foredoomed to failure.

IV

The struggle for power between the Spanish Republican parties is an
unhappy, far-off thing which I have no wish to revive at this date. I only
mention it in order to say: believe nothing, or next to nothing, of what
you read about internal affairs on the Government side. It is all, from
whatever source, party propaganda – that is to say, lies. The broad truth
about the war is simple enough. The Spanish bourgeoisie saw their chance
of crushing the labour movement, and took it, aided by the Nazis and by
the forces of reaction all over the world. It is doubtful whether more than
that will ever be established.

I remember saying once to Arthur Koestler, 'History stopped in 1936',
at which he nodded in immediate understanding. We were both thinking

of totalitarianism in general, but more particularly of the Spanish Civil War. Early in life I had noticed that no event is ever correctly reported in a newspaper, but in Spain, for the first time, I saw newspaper reports which did not bear any relation to the facts, not even the relationship which is implied in an ordinary lie. I saw great battles reported where there had been no fighting, and complete silence where hundreds of men had been killed. I saw troops who had fought bravely denounced as cowards and traitors, and others who had never seen a shot fired hailed as the heroes of imaginary victories; and I saw newspapers in London retailing these lies and eager intellectuals building emotional superstructures over events that had never happened. I saw, in fact, history being written not in terms of what happened but of what ought to have happened according to various 'party lines'. Yet in a way, horrible as all this was, it was unimportant. It concerned secondary issues – namely, the struggle for power between the Comintern and the Spanish left-wing parties, and the efforts of the Russian Government to prevent revolution in Spain. But the broad picture of the war which the Spanish Government presented to the world was not untruthful. The main issues were what it said they were. But as for the Fascists and their backers, how could they come even as near to the truth as that? How could they possibly mention their real aims? Their version of the war was pure fantasy, and in the circumstances it could not have been otherwise.

The only propaganda line open to the Nazis and Fascists was to represent themselves as Christian patriots saving Spain from a Russian dictatorship. This involved pretending that life in Government Spain was just one long massacre (*vide* the *Catholic Herald* or the *Daily Mail* – but these were child's play compared with the continental Fascist press), and it involved immensely exaggerating the scale of Russian intervention. Out of the huge pyramid of lies which the Catholic and reactionary press all over the world built up, let me take just one point – the presence in Spain of a Russian army. Devout Franco partisans all believed in this; estimates of its strength went as high as half a million. Now, there was no Russian army in Spain. There may have been a handful of airmen and other technicians, a few hundred at the most, but an army there was not. Some thousands of foreigners who fought in Spain, not to mention millions of Spaniards, were witnesses of this. Well, their testimony made no impression at all upon the Franco propagandists, not one of whom had set foot in Government Spain. Simultaneously these people refused utterly to admit the fact of German or Italian intervention, at the same time as the German and Italian press were openly boasting about the exploits of their 'legionaries'. I have chosen to mention only one point, but in fact the whole of Fascist propaganda about the war was on this level.

This kind of thing is frightening to me, because it often gives me the feeling that the very concept of objective truth is fading out of the world. After all, the chances are that those lies, or at any rate similar lies, will pass into history. How will the history of the Spanish War be written? If Franco remains in power his nominees will write the history books, and (to stick to my chosen point) that Russian army which never existed will become historical fact, and schoolchildren will learn about it generations hence. But suppose Fascism is finally defeated and some kind of democratic government restored in Spain in the fairly near future; even then, how is the history of the war to be written? What kind of records will Franco have left behind him? Suppose even that the records kept on the Government side are recoverable – even so, how is a true history of the war to be written? For, as I have pointed out already, the Government also dealt extensively in lies. From the anti-Fascist angle one could write a broadly truthful history of the war, but it would be a partisan history, unreliable on every minor point. Yet, after all, *some* kind of history will be written, and after those who actually remember the war are dead, it will be universally accepted. So for all practical purposes the lie will have become truth.

I know it is the fashion to say that most of recorded history is lies anyway. I am willing to believe that history is for the most part inaccurate and biased, but what is peculiar to our own age is the abandonment of the idea that history *could* be truthfully written. In the past people deliberately lied, or they unconsciously coloured what they wrote, or they struggled after the truth, well knowing that they must make many mistakes; but in each case they believed that 'the facts' existed and were more or less discoverable. And in practice there was always a considerable body of fact which would have been agreed to by almost everyone. If you look up the history of the last war in, for instance, the *Encyclopaedia Britannica*, you will find that a respectable amount of the material is drawn from German sources. A British and a German historian would disagree deeply on many things, even on fundamentals, but there would still be that body of, as it were, neutral fact on which neither would seriously challenge the other. It is just this common basis of agreement, with its implication that human beings are all one species of animal, that totalitarianism destroys. Nazi theory indeed specifically denies that such a thing as 'the truth' exists. There is, for instance, no such thing as 'science'. There is only 'German science', 'Jewish science' etc. The implied objective of this line of thought is a nightmare world in which the Leader, or some ruling clique, controls not only the future but *the past*. If the Leader says of such and such an event, 'It never happened' – well, it never happened. If he says that two and two are five – well, two and two are five. This prospect frightens me much more than bombs – and after our experiences of the last few years that is not a frivolous statement.

But is it perhaps childish or morbid to terrify oneself with visions of a totalitarian future? Before writing off the totalitarian world as a nightmare that can't come true, just remember that in 1925 the world of today would have seemed a nightmare that couldn't come true. Against that shifting phantasmagoric world in which black may be white tomorrow and yesterday's weather can be changed by decree, there are in reality only two safeguards. One is that however much you deny the truth, the truth goes on existing, as it were, behind your back, and you consequently can't violate it in ways that impair military efficiency. The other is that so long as some parts of the earth remain unconquered, the liberal tradition can be kept alive. Let Fascism, or possibly even a combination of several Fascisms, conquer the whole world, and those two conditions no longer exist. We in England underrate the danger of this kind of thing, because our traditions and our past security have given us a sentimental belief that it all comes right in the end and the thing you most fear never really happens. Nourished for hundreds of years on a literature in which Right invariably triumphs in the last chapter, we believe half-instinctively that evil always defeats itself in the long run. Pacifism, for instance, is founded largely on this belief. Don't resist evil, and it will somehow destroy itself. But why should it? What evidence is there that it does? And what instance is there of a modern industrialised state collapsing unless conquered from the outside by military force?

Consider for instance the re-institution of slavery. Who could have imagined twenty years ago that slavery would return to Europe? Well, slavery has been restored under our noses. The forced-labour camps all over Europe and North Africa where Poles, Russians, Jews and political prisoners of every race toil at road-making or swamp-draining for their bare rations, are simple chattel slavery. The most one can say is that the buying and selling of slaves by individuals is not yet permitted. In other ways – the breaking-up of families, for instance – the conditions are probably worse than they were on the American cotton plantations. There is no reason for thinking that this state of affairs will change while any totalitarian domination endures. We don't grasp its full implications, because in our mystical way we feel that a régime founded on slavery *must* collapse. But it is worth comparing the duration of the slave empires of antiquity with that of any modern state. Civilisations founded on slavery have lasted for such periods as four thousand years.

When I think of antiquity, the detail that frightens me is that those hundreds of millions of slaves on whose backs civilisation rested generation after generation have left behind them no record whatever. We do not even know their names. In the whole of Greek and Roman history, how many slaves' names are known to you? I can think of two, or possibly three. One is Spartacus and the other is Epictetus. Also, in the Roman room at the British Museum there is a glass jar with the maker's name inscribed on the bottom, '*Felix fecit*'. I have a vivid mental picture of poor Felix (a Gaul with red hair and a metal collar round his neck), but in fact he may not have been a slave; so there are only two slaves whose names I definitely know, and probably few people can remember more. The rest have gone down into utter silence.

v

The backbone of the resistance against Franco was the Spanish working class, especially the urban trade union members. In the long run – it is important to remember that it is only in the long run – the working class remains the most reliable enemy of Fascism, simply because the working class stands to gain most by a decent reconstruction of society. Unlike other classes or categories, it can't be permanently bribed.

To say this is not to idealise the working class. In the long struggle that has followed the Russian Revolution it is the manual workers who have been defeated, and it is impossible not to feel that it was their own fault. Time after time, in country after country, the organised working-class movements have been crushed by open, illegal violence, and their comrades abroad, linked to them in theoretical solidarity, have simply looked on and done nothing; and underneath this, secret cause of many betrayals, has lain the fact that between white and coloured workers there is not even lip-service to solidarity. Who can believe in the class-conscious international proletariat after the events of the past ten years? To the British working class the massacre of their comrades in Vienna, Berlin, Madrid, or wherever it might be, seemed less interesting and less important than yesterday's football match. Yet this does not alter the fact that the working class will go on struggling against Fascism after the others have caved in. One feature of the Nazi conquest of France was the astonishing defections among the intelligentsia, including some of the left-wing political intelligentsia. The intelligentsia are the people who squeal loudest against Fascism, and yet a respectable proportion of them collapse into defeatism when the pinch comes. They are far-sighted enough to see the odds against them, and moreover they can be bribed – for it is evident that the Nazis think it worth while to bribe intellectuals. With the working class it is the other way about. Too ignorant to see through the trick that is being played on them, they easily swallow the promises of Fascism, yet sooner or later they always take up the struggle again. They must do so, because in their own bodies they always discover that the promises of Fascism cannot be fulfilled. To win over the working class permanently, the Fascists would have to raise the general standard of living, which they are unable and probably unwilling to do. The struggle of the working class is like the growth of a plant. The plant is blind and stupid, but it knows enough to keep pushing upwards towards the light, and it will do this in the face of endless discouragements. What are the workers struggling for? Simply for the decent life which they are more and more aware is now technically possible. Their consciousness of this aim ebbs and flows. In Spain, for a while, people were acting consciously, moving towards a goal which they wanted to reach and believed they could reach. It accounted for the curiously buoyant feeling that life in Government

Spain had during the early months of the war. The common people knew in their bones that the Republic was their friend and Franco was their enemy. They knew that they were in the right, because they were fighting for something which the world owed them and was able to give them.

One has to remember this to see the Spanish War in its true perspective. When one thinks of the cruelty, squalor and futility of war – and in this particular case of the intrigues, the persecutions, the lies and the misunderstandings – there is always the temptation to say: 'One side is as bad as the other. I am neutral.' In practice, however, one cannot be neutral, and there is hardly such a thing as a war in which it makes no difference who wins. Nearly always one side stands more or less for progress, the other side more or less for reaction. The hatred which the Spanish Republic excited in millionaires, dukes, cardinals, play-boys, Blimps and what not would in itself be enough to show one how the land lay. In essence it was a class war. If it had been won, the cause of the common people everywhere would have been strengthened. It was lost, and the dividend-drawers all over the world rubbed their hands. That was the real issue; all else was froth on its surface.

VI

The outcome of the Spanish War was settled in London, Paris, Rome, Berlin – at any rate not in Spain. After the summer of 1937 those with eyes in their heads realised that the Government could not win the war unless there was some profound change in the international set-up, and in deciding to fight on Negrín and the others may have been partly influenced by the expectation that the world war which actually broke out in 1939 was coming in 1938. The much-publicised disunity on the Government side was not a main cause of defeat. The Government militias were hurriedly raised, ill-armed and unimaginative in their military outlook, but they would have been the same if complete political agreement had existed from the start. At the outbreak of war the average Spanish factory-worker did not even know how to fire a rifle (there had never been universal conscription in Spain), and the traditional pacifism of the Left was a great handicap. The thousands of foreigners who served in Spain made good infantry, but there were very few experts of any kind among them. The Trotskyist thesis that the war could have been won if the revolution had not been sabotaged was probably false. To nationalise factories, demolish churches, and issue revolutionary manifestos would not have made the armies more efficient. The Fascists won because they were the stronger; they had modern arms and the others hadn't. No political strategy could offset that.

The most baffling thing in the Spanish War was the behaviour of the great powers. The war was actually won for Franco by the Germans and Italians, whose motives were obvious enough. The motives of France and Britain are less easy to understand. In 1936 it was clear to everyone that if Britain would only help the Spanish Government, even to the extent of a few million pounds' worth of arms, Franco would collapse and German strategy would be severely dislocated. By that time one did not need to be a clairvoyant to foresee that war between Britain and Germany was coming; one could even foretell within a year or two when it would come. Yet in the most mean, cowardly, hypocritical way the British ruling class did all they could to hand Spain over to Franco and the Nazis. Why? Because they were pro-Fascist, was the obvious answer. Undoubtedly they were, and yet when it came to the final showdown they chose to stand up to Germany. It is still very uncertain what plan they acted on in backing Franco, and they may have had no clear plan at all. Whether the British ruling class are wicked or merely stupid is one of the most difficult questions of our time, and at certain moments a very important question. As to the Russians, their motives in the Spanish War are completely inscrutable. Did they, as the pinks believed, intervene in Spain in order to defend democracy and thwart the Nazis? Then why did they intervene on such a niggardly scale and finally leave Spain in the lurch? Or did they, as the Catholics maintained, intervene in order to foster revolution in Spain? Then why did they do all in their power to crush the Spanish revolutionary movements, defend private property and hand power to the middle class as against the working class? Or did they, as the Troskyists suggested, intervene simply in order to *prevent* a Spanish revolution? Then why not have backed Franco? Indeed, their actions are most easily explained if one assumes that they were acting on several contradictory motives. I believe that in the future we shall come to feel that Stalin's foreign policy, instead of being so diabolically clever as it is claimed to be, has been merely opportunistic and stupid. But at any rate, the Spanish Civil War demonstrated that the Nazis knew what they were doing and their opponents did not. The war was fought at a low technical level and its major strategy was very simple. That side which had arms would win. The Nazis and the Italians gave arms to their Spanish Fascist friends, and the western democracies and the Russians didn't give arms to those who should have been their friends. So the Spanish Republic perished, having 'gained what no republic missed'.[8]

Whether it was right, as all left-wingers in other countries undoubtedly did, to encourage the Spaniards to go on fighting when they could not win is a question hard to answer. I myself think it was right, because I believe that it is better even from the point of view of survival to fight and be conquered than to surrender without fighting. The effects on the grand strategy of the struggle against Fascism cannot be assessed yet. The ragged, weaponless armies of the Republic held out for two and a half years, which was undoubtedly longer than their enemies expected. But whether that dislocated the Fascist time-table, or whether, on the other hand, it merely postponed the major war and gave the Nazis extra time to get their war machine into trim, is still uncertain.

VII

I never think of the Spanish War without two memories coming into my mind. One is of the hospital ward at Lérida and the rather sad voices of the wounded militiamen singing some song with a refrain that ended:

> *¡Una resolución,*
> *Luchar hasta'l fin!*[9]

Well, they fought to the end all right. For the last eighteen months of the war the Republican armies must have been fighting almost without cigarettes, and with precious little food. Even when I left Spain in the middle of 1937, meat and bread were scarce, tobacco a rarity, coffee and sugar almost unobtainable.

The other memory is of the Italian militiaman who shook my hand in the guardroom, the day I joined the militia. I wrote about this man at the beginning of my book on the Spanish War,[10] and do not want to repeat what I said there. When I remember – oh, how vividly! – his shabby uniform and fierce, pathetic, innocent face, the complex side-issues of the war seem to fade away and I see clearly that there was at any rate no doubt as to who was in the right. In spite of power politics and journalistic lying, the central issue of the war was the attempt of people like this to win the decent life which they knew to be their birthright. It is difficult to think of this particular man's probable end without several kinds of bitterness. Since I met him in the Lenin Barracks he was probably a Trotskyist or an Anarchist, and in the peculiar conditions of our time, when people of that sort are not killed by the Gestapo they are usually killed by the GPU. But that does not affect the long-term issues. This man's face, which I saw only for a minute or two, remains with me as a sort of visual reminder of what the war was really about. He symbolises for me the flower of the European working class, harried by the police of all countries, the people who fill the mass graves of the Spanish battlefields and are now, to the tune of several millions, rotting in forced-labour camps.

When one thinks of all the people who support or have supported Fascism, one stands amazed at their diversity. What a crew! Think of a programme which at any rate for a while could bring Hitler, Pétain, Montagu Norman, Pavelitch, William Randolph Hearst, Streicher, Buchman, Ezra Pound, Juan March, Cocteau, Thyssen, Father Coughlin, the Mufti of Jerusalem,[11] Arnold Lunn, Antonescu, Spengler, Beverley Nichols, Lady Houston and Marinetti all into the same boat! But the clue is really very simple. They are all people with something to lose, or people who long for a hierarchical society and dread the prospect of a world of free and equal human beings. Behind all the ballyhoo that is talked about 'godless' Russia and the 'materialism' of the working class lies the simple intention of those with money or privileges to cling to them. Ditto, though it contains a partial truth, with all the talk about the worthlessness of social reconstruction not accompanied by a 'change of heart'. The pious ones, from the Pope to the yogis of California,[12] are great on the 'change of heart',[13] much more reassuring from their point of view than a change in the economic system. Pétain attributes the fall of France to the common people's 'love of pleasure'. One sees this in its right perspective if one stops to wonder how much pleasure the ordinary French peasant's or workingman's life would contain compared with Pétain's own. The damned impertinence of these politicians, priests, literary men, and what-not who lecture the working-class Socialist for his 'materialism'! All that the workingman demands is what these others would consider the indispensable minimum without which human life cannot be lived at all. Enough to eat, freedom from the haunting terror of unemployment, the knowledge that your children will get a fair chance, a bath once a day, clean linen reasonably often, a roof that doesn't leak, and short enough working hours to leave you with a little energy when the day is done. Not one of those who preach against 'materialism' would consider life livable without these things. And how easily that minimum could be attained if we chose to set our minds to it for only twenty years! To raise the standard of living of the whole world to that of Britain would not be a greater undertaking than this war we are now fighting. I don't claim, and I don't know who does, that that would solve anything in itself. It is merely that privation and brute labour have to be abolished before the real problems of humanity can be tackled. The major problem of our time is the decay of the belief in personal immortality, and it cannot be dealt with while the average human being is either drudging like an ox or shivering in fear of the secret police. How right the working classes are in their 'materialism'! How right they are to realise that the real belly comes before the soul, not in the scale of values but in point of time! Understand that, and the long horror that we are enduring becomes at least intelligible. All the considerations that are likely to make one falter – the siren voices of a Pétain or of a Gandhi, the inescapable fact that in order to fight one has to degrade oneself, the equivocal moral position of Britain, with its democratic phrases and its coolie empire, the sinister development of Soviet Russia, the squalid farce of left-wing politics – all this fades away and one sees only the struggle of the gradually awakening common people against the lords of property and their hired liars and bumsuckers. The question is very simple. Shall people like that Italian soldier be allowed to live the decent, fully human life which is now technically achievable, or shan't they? Shall the common man be pushed back into the mud, or shall he not? I myself believe, perhaps on insufficient grounds, that the common man will win his fight sooner or later, but I want it to be sooner and not later – some time within the next hundred years, say, and not some time within the next ten thousand years. That was the real issue of the Spanish War, and of the present war, and perhaps of other wars yet to come.

I never saw the Italian militiaman again, nor did I ever learn his name. It can be taken as quite certain that he is dead. Nearly two years later, when the war was visibly lost, I wrote these verses in his memory:

The Italian soldier shook my hand
Beside the guard-room table;
The strong hand and the subtle hand
Whose palms are only able

To meet within the sound of guns,
But oh! what peace I knew then
In gazing on his battered face
Purer than any woman's!

For the fly-blown words that make me spew
Still in his ears were holy,
And he was born knowing what I had learned
Out of books and slowly.

The treacherous guns had told their tale
And we both had bought it,
But my gold brick was made of gold –
Oh! who ever would have thought it?

Good luck go with you, Italian soldier!
But luck is not for the brave;
What would the world give back to you?
Always less than you gave.

Between the shadow and the ghost,
Between the white and the red,
Between the bullet and the lie,
Where would you hide your head?

For where is Manuel González,
And where is Pedro Aguilar,

And where is Ramón Fenellosa?
The earthworms know where they are.

Your name and your deeds were forgotten
Before your bones were dry,
And the lie that slew you is buried
Under a deeper lie;

But the thing that I saw in your face
No power can disinherit:
No bomb that ever burst
Shatters the crystal spirit.

---

1. *New Road: New Directions in English Arts and Letters* was published 1943–49. Vols. I and II (1943–44) were edited by Alex Comfort (1920–2000, who later gained a certain fame as author of *The Joy of Sex*, 1972) and John Bayliss.

2. Dwight Macdonald (1906–82), libertarian critic, pamphleteer and scholar. He was for a time associate editor of *Partisan Review*, for which journal Orwell wrote his London Letters. He later founded *Politics*, which he edited 1944–49, and to which Orwell also contributed.

3. *All Quiet on the Western Front*, a novel based on the experiences of front-line German troops in the First World War trenches, was written by Erich Maria Remarque and published as *Im Westen nichts Neue* in 1929. It was immediately translated into English by A. W. Wheen and published in the same year. It is still in print, in a new translation. A film of the novel was made in 1930 (featuring Lew Ayres and Louis Wolheim). It was censored in Britain because regarded as too horrific (in particular a scene featuring a rat; if Orwell had seen it, he would have been particularly impressed, given his antipathy to rats).

4. US weekly journal devoted to proletarian literature. It ran from 1926 to 1948.

5. The Oxford Union's motion in 1935 supporting the refusal to fight 'for King and Country' initiated a series of alternating demands that Britain abstain from and engage in military action.

6. Jesus said: "for all they that take the sword shall perish with the sword", Matthew, 26: 52.

7. See War-time Diary, *1218, 11.6.42*.

8. The source of this quotation has not been traced.

9. 'A resolution, / To fight to the end!'

10. *Homage to Catalonia*.

11. Mohammed Amin al-Husseini (1893–1974), Mufti of Jerusalem from 1921. He was arrested in 1937 for instigating anti-Semitic riots. He escaped and later broadcast for the Nazis from Berlin and encouraged the deportation of Jews to concentration camps. He was charged with war crimes but found refuge first in Egypt and then in Palestine. Six thousand Bosnian Muslims who formed the S.S. Handzar Division in Yugoslavia in 1943 to fight for the Nazis saw him as their spiritual leader. A 'Mufti' is a Muslim canon lawyer.

12. Orwell possibly had in mind Gerald Heard (1889–1971), whom he mentions in his September 1943 review in *Horizon* of Lionel Fielden's *Beggar My Neighbour* (see *2257*, and see also headnote to 'Can Socialists be Happy?', *2397*); also Aldous Huxley (see *600*, section

3), and possibly Christopher Isherwood (see *2713*), all of whom settled in Los Angeles just before the war. In California, Isherwood developed an interest in yoga and vedanta (though whether Orwell knew this is uncertain), edited and introduced *Vedanta for the Western World* (Hollywood, 1945; London, 1948) and with Swami Prabhavananda translated *The Bhagavad-Gita* (1944) and other related works. It is possible that this reference was inspired by Orwell's preliminary arrangements for G. V. Desani to talk on the *Bhagavad-Gita* in his BBC series *Books that Changed the World* (see *1970*).

13. 'New style of architecture, a change of heart', from W. H. Auden, 'Sir, No Man's Enemy' (1930).

Proposed BBC Broadcast on the Spanish Civil War
3 December 1942

While a Talks Producer for the BBC's India Section, Orwell arranged many series of talks. One of these was on 'The History of Fascism'. The fifth in the series was to be on the Spanish Civil War and, on 7 October 1942, Orwell asked Mulk Raj Anand whether he would be willing to write and broadcast such a talk (1551). Anand (1905–　), novelist, short-story writer, essayist and critic, was born in India and had fought for the Republicans in the Spanish Civil War, though he and Orwell did not meet there. He taught literature and philosophy to London County Council adult-education classes and wrote scripts and broadcast for the BBC, 1939–45. After the war he lectured in a number of Indian universities and was appointed Professor of Fine Arts, University of Punjab, 1963. He was awarded an International Peace Prize from the World Council of Peace in 1952. At the time of writing (1999) he is living in Bombay. He and Orwell remained friends and their relationship is discussed in Abha Sharma Rodrigues, 'George Orwell, the BBC and India: A Critical Study' (Edinburgh University, Ph.D, 1994).

Anand was formally booked to give the talk on 3 December 1942 for a fee of £8 8s. (1595) but his talk was not passed by the censor. Orwell wrote to E. W. D. Boughen of the Talks Booking Department on 10 December (1729) to ask that Anand be paid a proportion of his fee because the 'subject is a particularly delicate one at the present time' and it was not practicable to modify its 'angle'. It was agreed that he be paid £5 5s. – but as he had already received his full fee his next fee would be reduced by £3 3s.

[2380]

Review of Spain in Eclipse, 1937–1943 *by E. Allison Peers;* Behind the Spanish Mask *by Lawrence Dundas*
Observer, *28 November 1943*

The titles of both of these books are symptomatic of the fact that we know very little of what has been happening in Spain since the end of the Civil War. There have been hunger and pestilence, great numbers of people are in gaol, and the régime has been markedly friendly to the Axis – that is about as far as common knowledge extends. Opinions on anything else are likely to be coloured by the political sympathies of the writer, and one must keep it in mind that Mr. Dundas is vigorously pro-Republic, while Professor Peers should rather be described as mildly and regretfully pro-Franco.

Professor Peers devotes part of his book to the Civil War, but his best chapters are those dealing with the last four years. He considers that the Franco regime for a while enjoyed majority support, that its political persecutions have probably been exaggerated, and that it has not in fact given much solid aid to the Nazis. He does not, however, believe that it will last much longer, and though he himself hopes for some kind of Liberal monarchist régime, he thinks that a swing to the extreme Left is not impossible.

It is noticeable that Professor Peers seems surprised as well as pained that the 'non-belligerent' Spanish Government has been so consistently unfriendly to ourselves. He lists the endless provocations, and the inspired campaigns of libel in the Spanish Press, as though these in some way contradicted Franco's earlier record. But, in fact, there was never very much doubt as to where the sympathies of Franco and his more influential followers lay, and the time when it might have been useful to point out that Franco was the friend of our enemies was in 1936. At that time Professor Peers did nothing of the kind. No one would accuse him of falsifying facts, but the tone of the books he was then writing did, there is little doubt, tend to make the Nationalist cause more respectable in British eyes. In so far as books influence events, Professor Peers must be held to have done something towards establishing Franco's régime, and he ought not now to be astonished because Franco has behaved in very much the manner that every supporter of the Republic foretold at the time.[1]

Mr. Dundas's book is written round the speculative but interesting thesis that a quite different kind of rebellion – a Conservative but not Fascist rebellion – had been planned in the beginning, and that events only took the course they did because of Sanjurjo's[2] death and because the Nationalists, having failed in their first coup, had to apply for help to the Germans and Italians, who imposed their own terms. The importance of this is that the régime which has actually been set up is, as Mr. Dundas says, 'not Spanish'. It is a régime modelled on foreign lines and intolerable from the point of view of an ordinary Spaniard, even an aristocrat; it might therefore turn out to be brittle in a moment of emergency. The book contains some interesting details about Civil War events in Majorca. But Mr. Dundas is surely wrong in suggesting that Franco will fight for the Axis if the Allies invade Europe. Fidelity is not the strong point of the minor dictators.

1. Also in 1943, under the name of Bruce Truscot, Professor Peers published *Redbrick University*. This included 'The Nature and Aims of a Modern University', which proved influential in post-war British university development. A more modest publication, under the name E. Allison Peers, was *A Skeleton Spanish Grammar* (1917). See also p. 259, n. 4.
2. General José Sanjurjo Sacanell (1872–1936), a Nationalist (as was Franco), led a coup against the government of the Second Spanish Republic in August 1932. This failed; he was captured, tried, sentenced, then, in 1934, reprieved. He was killed when a plane sent to bring him from Lisbon to Burgos crashed on take-off. Sabotage was suspected, but the cause was more mundane. The plane, a small Puss Moth, was overloaded because Sanjurjo 'insisted on taking with him a heavy suitcase, which contained a full-dress uniform for his use as head of the new Spanish State'. The plane, which had been diverted by the Portuguese authorities to a small outlying airfield, failed to clear the surrounding pine trees. The pilot was injured but thrown clear; Sanjurjo was burned to death, a 'victim of conformity rather than sabotage' (Thomas, 254).

[2416]

Extract from 'As I Please', 10 [How the lie becomes truth]
Tribune, 4 February 1944

During the Spanish Civil War I found myself feeling very strongly that a true history of this war never would or could be written. Accurate figures, objective accounts of what was happening, simply did not exist. And if I felt that even in 1937, when the Spanish Government was still in being, and the lies which the various Republican factions were telling about each other and about the enemy were relatively small ones, how does the case stand now? Even if Franco is overthrown, what kind of records will the future historian have to go upon? And if Franco or anyone at all resembling him remains in power, the history of the war will consist quite largely of 'facts' which millions of people now living know to be lies. One of these 'facts', for instance, is that there was a considerable Russian army in Spain. There exists the most abundant evidence that there was no such army. Yet if Franco remains in power, and if Fascism in general survives, that Russian army will go into the history books and future schoolchildren will believe in it. So for practical purpose the lie will have become truth.

This kind of thing is happening all the time . . .

[2510]

'The Eight Years of War: Spanish Memories'
Observer, 16 July 1944

The Spanish Civil War, curtain-raiser of the present struggle and one of the most tragic as well as one of the most sordid events that modern Europe has seen, began eight years ago next Friday.

The issue of the Spanish war was decided outside Spain, and by the time that it was a year old realistic observers were able to see that the elected government could not win unless there were some radical change in the European situation. In the first period of the war, which lasted just under a year, the struggle was essentially between Franco's professional soldiers and Moors on the one side and the hurriedly-raised militias of peasants and factory workers on the other.

In this period honours were about even, and no objective of first-rate importance changed hands.

Franco, however, was being reinforced on a massive scale by the Axis Powers, while the Spanish Government was receiving only sporadic doles of arms from Soviet Russia and the help of a few thousand foreign volunteers, mostly refugee Germans. In June, 1937, the resistance of the Basques collapsed and the balance of forces tipped heavily against the Government.

In the meantime, however, the Government had quelled the revolutionary disorder of early days, smoothed out the struggles between factions, and trained its raw forces. Early in 1938 it had a formidable army, able to fight on for the year or so that food supplies would last out.

Dr. Negrín and the other rulers of Government Spain probably realised that they could not win by their own efforts, but they were justified in fighting on, since the political outlook in Europe still might change. The obviously approaching world war might break out during 1938; the British Government might abandon its policy of non-intervention.

Neither event happened, and towards the end of 1938 the Russians withdrew their help. Government Spain had long been hungry, and was now definitely starving.

As the Fascist forces drove across Catalonia, hordes of refugees streamed into France, machine-gunned by Italian aeroplanes and interned behind barbed-wire as soon as they arrived.

Early in 1939 Franco entered Madrid, and used his victory with the utmost ruthlessness. All political parties of the Left were suppressed, and countless people executed or imprisoned. If recent reports are true, half a million people, or 2 per cent of the population of Spain, are still in concentration camps.

The story is a disgusting one, because of the sordid behaviour of the Great Powers and the indifference of the world at large. The Germans and Italians intervened in order to crush Spanish democracy, to seize a strategic keypoint for the coming war, and, incidentally, to try out their bombing planes on helpless populations.

The Russians doled out a small quantity of weapons and extorted the maximum of political control in return. The British and French simply looked the other way while their enemies triumphed and their friends were destroyed. The British attitude is the hardest to forgive, because it was foolish as well as dishonourable.

It had been obvious from the start that any foreign country which supplied arms to the Spanish Government could control or at least influence that Government's policy. Instead, the British preferred to make sure that Franco and Hitler should win, and at the same time that the affection and gratitude of the Spanish people should be earned by Russia and not by Britain.

For a year or more the Spanish Government was effectively under Russian control, mainly because Russia was the only country to come to the rescue. The growth of the Spanish Communist Party from a few thousands to a quarter of a million was directly the work of the British Tories.

There has been a strong tendency to push these facts out of sight and even to claim Franco's hostile 'non-belligerency' as a triumph for British diplomacy. Rather should the true history of the Spanish war be kept always in mind as an object-lesson in the folly and meanness of Power Politics. Nothing, indeed, redeems its story except the courage of the fighting-men on both sides, and the toughness of the civilian population of Loyalist Spain, who for years endured hunger and hardship unknown to us at the worst moments of war.

[2593]

Review of An Interlude in Spain *by Charles d'Ydewalle, translated by Eric Sutton*
Observer, *24 December 1944*

Unwilling witnesses are generally accounted the most reliable, and Mr. Charles d'Ydewalle is at least partly an unwilling witness against Franco's Spain. He is a Belgian journalist (evidently a devout Catholic), and during the Spanish Civil War he was a warm partisan of General Franco, in whose territory he appears to have spent some months. When his own country was subjugated by the Germans and he set out on the roundabout journey to England, he was quite confident that Nationalist Spain, whose 'crusade' he had supported as best he could, would offer no obstacle. It was therefore with some surprise that he found himself arrested and flung into jail almost as soon as he had set foot on Spanish soil.

This was towards the end of 1941. He was not released until eight months later, and at no time did he discover what offence, if any, he was charged with. Presumably he had been arrested because his flight to England indicated Allied sympathies. He was incarcerated first of all in the Model Prison in Barcelona, which had been built to hold 700 prisoners and at this time was holding 8,000. Later he was placed in a concentration camp among refugees of many different nationalities. Here the conditions were comparatively sympathetic; it was possible to buy small luxuries; one could choose one's hut mates, and there was international rivalry in the matter of digging tunnels under the barbed wire. It was the Model Prison that opened or partially opened Mr. d'Ydewalle's eyes to the nature of the régime.

At the end of 1941, nearly three years after the ending of the civil war, people were still being shot, in this prison alone, at the rate of five or six a week. In addition there was torture, presumably for the purpose of extracting confessions, and on occasion the torturer 'went too far'. Political prisoners and ordinary criminals were more or less mixed up together, but the majority of the prisoners were left-overs from the civil war, usually serving sentences of thirty years. In many cases, Mr. d'Ydewalle noted, this would take them to the ripe age of ninety-five or so. The shootings were carried out with the maximum of cruelty. No one knew, until the actual morning of execution, whether he was to be shot or not.

Early every morning there would be a trampling of boots and a clanking of bayonets along the corridor, and suddenly this door or that would be thrown open and a name called out. Later in the day the dead man's mattress would be seen lying outside the cell door. Sometimes a man was reprieved and then shot a day or two later for some different offence. But there were no shootings on Sundays or holidays. The display of religiosity with which the life of the prison was conducted stuck in Mr. d'Ydewalle's gizzard almost more than the cruelty.

Mr. d'Ydewalle spent only a day or two in Spain as a free man, but in the concentration camp he noted that the wretched Spanish soldiers who guarded them were glad to beg scraps of food from the better-off internees. He does not record things like this with any satisfaction, and is reluctant to draw their full moral. To the end, indeed, he seems to have remained convinced that in the civil war Franco was in the right, and that it was only afterwards that things went wrong. In prison he sometimes comforted himself with the thought that the wretched victims round about him had been doing the same thing to Nationalist sympathisers only a few years before. He reiterates his belief in 'red atrocities', and shows more than a trace of anti-Semitism.

The main impression that the book conveys is one of bewilderment. Why had he been locked up? How could the 'glorious crusade' have led to this kind of thing? He even expresses astonishment that a régime calling itself Catholic could lend its support to Hitler and Mussolini: which does seem to be carrying simplicity rather far, since General Franco can hardly be accused of having concealed his political affiliations.

Naturally it is not easy for someone who in good faith supported the Nationalist cause at the time of the civil war to admit that the horrors of the Model Prison were implicit in the Nationalist régime from the beginning. But Mr. d'Ydewalle also had the handicap of coming from a comparatively orderly and well-governed country and therefore not having any preliminary understanding of totalitarianism.

The essential fact about a totalitarian régime is that it has no laws. People are not punished for specific offences, but because they are considered to be politically or intellectually undesirable. What they have done or not done is irrelevant. It took Mr. d'Ydewalle some time to get used to this idea, and, as he observed, there were other Western European prisoners who had difficulty in grasping it as well. When he had been several months in jail some British soldiers, escaped from France, came to join him. He told them about the shootings. At the beginning they flatly disbelieved him, and only gradually, as mattress after mattress appeared outside this cell or that, came to realise that what he said was true: whereupon they commented, not inaptly, 'Well, give me England every time.'

This book is a useful footnote to history. The author's simplicity of outlook is an advantage to him as a narrator. But, if one may make a guess, the next variant of General Franco who appears will not have Mr. d'Ydewalle's support.

[2944]

Review of The Clash *by Arturo Barea*[1]

Observer, *24 March 1946*

The third and final volume of Arturo Barea's autobiography covers the period 1935–9, and is therefore largely a story of civil war. His private struggle and the failure of his first marriage cannot be separated from the general social tension of which the war was a result; and in his second marriage, which took place about the end of 1937, personal and political motives are even more closely intermingled. The book starts off in a Castilian village and ends up in Paris, but its essential subject is the siege of Madrid.

Mr. Barea was in Madrid from the very start of the war, and remained there almost continuously until vague but irresistible political pressures drove him out of the country in the summer of 1938. He saw the wild enthusiasm and chaos of the early period, the expropriations, the massacres, the bombing and shelling of the almost helpless city, the gradual restoration of order, the three-sided struggle for power between the common people, the bureaucracy, and the foreign Communists. For about two years he held an important post in the Foreign Press Censorship, and for a while he delivered the 'Voice of Madrid' broadcasts, which scored a considerable success in Latin America. Before the war he had been an engineer employed in the Patent Office, a would-be writer who had not actually written anything, a believing Catholic disgusted by the Spanish Church, and a temperamental Anarchist with no close political affiliations. But it is most of all his peasant origin that fits him to describe the war from a specifically Spanish point of view.

At the beginning fearful things happened. Mr. Barea describes the storming of the Madrid barracks, the flinging of live people out of upper windows, the revolutionary tribunals, the execution ground where the corpses lay about for days. Earlier, in describing the condition of the peasants and the behaviour of the landlords in the little village where he used to spend his week-ends, he has indicated part of the reason for these barbarities. His work in the Censorship Department, although he realised it to be useful and necessary, was a struggle first against red tape and then against backstairs intrigues. The censorship was never watertight, because most of the embassies were hostile to the Republic, and the journalists, irked by stupid restrictions – Mr. Barea's first orders were not to let through 'anything which did not indicate a Government victory' – sabotaged in every way they could. Later, when the Republic's prospects temporarily improved, there was further sabotage of the news at the editorial end, Italian prisoners being tactfully described as 'Nationalists' in order to keep up the fiction of non-intervention. Still later the Russians tightened their grip on the Republic, the bureaucrats who had fled when Madrid was in danger came back, and the position of Mr. Barea and his wife was gradually made impossible.

At this period of the war there was a general elbowing-out of those who had borne the brunt in the early months, but there was the added trouble that Mr. Barea's wife was a Trotskyist. That is to say, she was not a Trotskyist, but she was an Austrian Socialist who had quarrelled with the Communists, which, from the point of view of the political police, came to much the same thing. There were the usual episodes: sudden incursions by the police in the middle of the night, arrest, reinstatement, further arrest – all the peculiar, nightmare atmosphere of a country under divided control, where it is never quite certain who is responsible for what, and even the heads of the Government cannot protect their own subordinates against the secret police.

One thing that this book brings home is how little we have heard about the Spanish civil war from Spaniards. To the Spaniards the war was not a game, as it was to the 'Anti-Fascist Writers' who held their congress in Madrid and ate banquets against a background of starvation. Mr. Barea had to look on helplessly at the intrigues of the foreign Communists, the antics of the English visitors and the sufferings of the Madrid populace, and to do so with a gradually growing certainty that the war was bound to be lost. As he says, the abandonment of Spain by France and Britain meant in practice that Nationalist Spain was dominated by Germany and Republican Spain by the U.S.S.R.: and as the Russians could not then afford to provoke open war with Germany, the Spanish people had to be slowly bombed, shelled and starved into a surrender which could be foreseen as early as the middle of 1937.

Mr. Barea escaped into a France where foreigners got black looks and the man in the street heaved a sigh of relief at the Munich settlement;

finally he left France for Britain on the eve of the larger war. This is an exceptional book, and the middle section of it must be of considerable historical value.

1. See p. 341, n. 1, above.

Orwell's Pamphlet Collection

Orwell probably started collecting pamphlets about 1935–7 and carried on until at least March 1947. He thought he had between 1,200 and 2,000 and made more than one attempt to classify and catalogue them. He wished that after his death they should be donated to the British Museum and they are now held by the British Library, call number 1899 ss 1–21, 23–48, item 48 being a typed but incomplete catalogue. Orwell made a handwritten classified list of 364 pamphlets about 1946–7. He classified his nineteen Spanish Civil War pamphlets as Anarchist (An), Labour Party (LP), Left Socialist (LS) and Trotskyist (Tr). For a full account see Complete Works, *3733,* XX/*259–86. The pamphlets listed under the heading 'Spanish Civil War' have Orwell's classifications and the boxes in which they are to be found; notes within square brackets or smaller type are editorial. See also* Orwell and Politics.

SPANISH CIVIL WAR

1. Civil War in Spain (B[ertram] D. Wolfe) [*2932, n. 5*] [WAP,   (Tr) Box 3 (2)
   USA, 1937]
   Crick quotes from Wolfe's eulogy of Andrés Nin; this, he says,
   'has several obvious parallels to *Nineteen Eighty-Four*' (634)

2. Le Stalinisme en Espagne (K[atia] Landau [Edition   (Tr) Box 3 (7)
   Spartacus, 2 francs, 1937]
   The typed catalogue notes, 'very rare'; see headnote; for Kurt
   Landau, see *2648, n. 4.*[1]

3. Spotlight on Spain (J. Hatz) [ILP, 1938]   (Tr) Box 3 (17)

4. Democracy or Revolution in Spain? (J. Matteo) 2 [ILP,   (Tr) Box 3 (33)
   1937]

5. The Lesson of Spain ([L.] Trotsky) [WAP, 1937]   (Tr) Box 3 (34)

6. The Truth About Barcelona (F. Brockway) [ILP, 1937]   (Tr) Box 3 (35)

7. Terror in Spain (J. McGovern) [see p. 273, n. 1, above]   (Tr) Box 3 (44)
   [ILP, 1937]

8. Why Bishops Back Franco (J. McGovern) [ILP, 1936]   (Tr) Box 3 (45)

9. The Trotskyist Position on Spain [LL, 1943]   (Tr) Box 3 (67)

10. Buenaventura Durruti [CNT-FAI, Barcelona, 1937]   (Tr) Box 3 (70)
    CNT: 'Syndicalist unions controlled by the Anarchists'; FAI: 'an
    actual Anarchist organisation'; Orwell, *Homage to Catalonia*,
    pp. 174, 181 [VI/195, 203].

11. Spain – Anarchism [Anarcho-Syndicalist Union (CNT),   (An) Box 4 (37)
    1937]

12. Social Reconstruction in Spain [Gaston] (Leval) [*Spain and*   (Tr) Box 4 (38)
    the World, 1938]
    French anarchist who went to Moscow in 1921 with a Spanish
    delegation led by Andrés Nin, and wrote on the Spanish Civil
    War. See Thomas, 67, 117, 1025. Orwell wrote 'Level' in the
    manuscript but typescript has 'Gaston Leval'.

13. Catholics & the Civil War in Spain [National Council of   (LP) Box 5 (10)
    Labour, 1936]

14. A Catholic Looks at Spain [S. Gurrea; Labour Publications   (LP) Box 5(11)
    Dept., 1937]

15. Tempête sur l'Espagne [L'Homme Réel, 1936, 3 francs]   (LS) Box 6 (6)
    This is inscribed 'Henry Swanzy, Paris 1936'. Swanzy was one of
    Orwell's colleagues at the BBC; see *845, n. 2*.

16. Impressions of Franco's Spain (J. R. Vega) 2 [United   (LP) Box 6 (9)
    Editorial Ltd, 1943]

17. Franco's 'Neutrality' & British Policy [UDC, 1944]   (LS) Box 6 (13)

18. Spain: the moral touchstone of Europe (C. Duff) 2   (LS) Box 6 (23)
    [Gollancz, 1944]

19. Romancero de la Guerra Civil (Series 1) [verse; Madrid   (LS) Box 7 (6)
    Gov.t, 1936]

1. Kurt Landau, Austrian socialist, was to die 'in mysterious circumstances', as did a number
of other international sympathizers of the POUM; see Thomas, 706.

*A summary of letters from and to David Astor, 4 and 5
March 1949*

*On 4 March 1949, David Astor asked Orwell, then in the Cotswold
Sanatorium, Cranham, whether he would contribute an article for the
Observer on the tenth anniversary of the end of the Spanish Civil War.
Alternatively, Orwell could suggest who might be approached to write one
or perhaps two articles. Orwell replied the following day to say he would
rather not write an article because, owing to illness, he had not started any
work yet. Among those whom he suggested were Franz Borkenau and Arturo
Barea. On 15 March, Astor told Orwell that the Observer was trying to
contact Borkenau (then in Germany at Marburg University). See 3562,
XX/54–5.*

Further Reading

The longer items in *The Complete Works of George Orwell* on the Spanish Civil War are included here, except for his abstracts from reports on the war taken from the *Daily Worker* and the *News Chronicle* in 1936–7 (Appendix 2 to Volume XI, 290–306, with full annotations) and the article (not by Orwell), 'Night Attack on the Aragón Front', *New Leader*, 30 April 1937 (*366*, XI/18–20), which displeased him. However, the memory of his time in Spain was never far from his mind and *The Complete Works* contains a number of passing references that might interest readers, especially in Volume XII. Thus, in his Diary for 13 June 1940, he believes a poster recruiting for the Pioneer Corps cribbed its idea from 'a Government poster of the Spanish war' (*637*, XII/183); in a letter to John Lehmann, founder and editor of *New Writing*, 6 July 1940, he says that the War Office no longer holds it against a man that he fought in the Spanish Civil War (*653*, XII/208); he thinks Hugh Slater's *Home Guard for Victory!* relies 'too much on the experience of the Civil War' (*768*, XII/440), though some of his own lectures to the Home Guard are informed by that experience (*730–35*, XII/328–40); writing to American readers of *Partisan Review*, 15 April 1941, he tells them that 'in our own [British] papers there is certainly nothing to compare with the frightful lies that were told on both sides in 1914–18 or in the Spanish civil war' (*787*, XII/472), and there is a similar statement in 'English Writing in Total War', *New Republic*, 14 July 1941 (*831*, XII/527); a later letter to *Partisan Review*, 17 August 1941, remarks on a leavening of Home Guard recruits who are class-conscious factory-workers or the 'handful of men who had fought in the Spanish civil war' (*843*, XII/550). The Spanish Civil War was a point of reference for 'The Prevention of Literature' (e.g., *2792*, XVII/373 and 374; and especially his claim that English intellectuals could not write sincerely about that experience but had to resort to 'palpable lies', XVII/376). Also in volume XVII, in 'As I Please', 54, 12 January 1945, Orwell compares with experience in Spain, the way 'reputable British newspapers' connived at 'what amounted to forgery' in order to discredit Draja Mihailovich, whom they had been backing a few months earlier (XVII/19). Orwell's review of *Freedom was Flesh and Blood* by José Antonio de Aguirre, 19 July 1945 (*2704*, XVII/219–20) touches

377

on the civil war. The Cumulative Index in Volume XX of *CW* will reveal more examples.

The principal source for this volume is *The Complete Works of George Orwell*, edited by Peter Davison, assisted by Ian Angus and Sheila Davison, 20 vols. (1998; 2nd, paperback, edn, from 2000). Reference might also usefully be made to *The Collected Essays, Journalism and Letters of George Orwell*, edited by Sonia Orwell and Ian Angus, 4 vol. (1968; Penguin, 1970).

Volumes of *CW* in which items will be found are as follows:

X 1–355	XIV 1435–1915	XVIII 2832–3143
XI 355A–582	XV 1916–2377	XIX 3144–3515
XII 583–843	XVI 2378–2596	XX 3516–3715A
XIII 844–1434	XVII 2597–2831	

Vol. XX also includes in Appendix 15 the following supplementary items: 2278A, 2278B, 2420A, 2451A, 2563B, 2593A, 2625A, 3351A and 3715A. Each volume is indexed and vol. XX has a Cumulative Index, indexes of topics, and an index of serials in which Orwell's work appeared.

There is a wealth of literature devoted to the Spanish Civil War, not all of it in agreement. The following might be found helpful and, in the main, conveniently available.

Victor Alba, ed., *El Proceso del P.O.U.M.: Documentos Judiciales y Policiales* (Barcelona, 1989); this gives (in Spanish) many documents associated with the Tribunal Especial, June 1937 to October 1938

Victor Alba and Stephen Schwartz, *Spanish Marxism vs. Soviet Communism: A History of the POUM* (1988)

Bill Alexander, *British Volunteers for Liberty: Spain, 1936–1939* (1982)

Michael Alpert, *A New International History of the Spanish Civil War* (1994)

Frederick R. Benson, *Writers in Arms: The Literary Impact of the Spanish Civil War* (1967)

Burnett Bolloten, *The Spanish Civil War: Revolution and Counterrevolution* (1991)

Franz Borkenau, 'Spain: Whose Victory?', *Observer*, 27 March 1949, 4

Vincent Brome, *The International Brigade* (1965)

Tom Buchanan, 'The Death of Bob Smillie, the Spanish Civil War, and the Eclipse of the Independent Labour Party', *Historical Journal*, 40 (1997), 435–61

Audrey Coppard and Bernard Crick, eds., *Orwell Remembered* (1984)

David Corkhill and Stewart Rawnsley, eds., *The Road to Spain* (1981)

Bernard Crick, *George Orwell: A Life* (1980; 3rd edn 1992)

Valentine Cunningham, ed., *Spanish Civil War Verse* (1980); with a long introduction by Cunningham

Peter Davison, *George Orwell: A Literary Life* (1996)

Rayner Heppenstall, *Four Absentees* (1960)

Katherine B. Hoskins, *Today the Struggle: Literature and Politics in England during the Spanish Civil War* (1969)

James Joll, *The Anarchists* (2nd edn, 1980)

Jeffrey Meyers, ed., *George Orwell: The Critical Heritage* (1975)

—, *Orwell: Wintry Conscience of a Generation* (2000)

John Newsinger, *Orwell's Politics* (1999)

—, 'The Death of Bob Smillie', *Historical Journal*, 41 (1998), 575–8

Christopher Norris, ed., *Inside the Myth: Orwell: Views from the Left* (1984)

Paul Preston, *The Spanish Civil War, 1936–1939* (1986)

Sir Richard Rees, *For Love or Money* (1960)

—, *George Orwell: Fugitive from the Camp of Victory* (1961)

Patrick Reilly, *George Orwell: The Age's Adversary* (1986)

John Rodden, *The Politics of Literary Reputation: The Making and Claiming of 'St George Orwell'* (1989)

William Rust, *Britons in Spain: The History of the British Battalion of the XVth International Brigade* (1939)

Michael Seidmann, 'The Unorwellian Barcelona', *European History Quarterly*, 20 (1990), 163–80

Michael Shelden, *Orwell: The Authorised Biography* (1991)

Ian Slater, *Orwell: The Road to Airstrip One: The Development of George Orwell's Political and Social Thought from* Burmese Days *to* 1984 (1985)

Peter Stansky and William Abrahams, *Orwell: The Transformation* (1979)

Hugh Thomas, *The Spanish Civil War* (3rd edn, 1977; Penguin 1979)

Stephen Wadhams, ed., *Remembering Orwell* (1984)

George Woodcock, *The Crystal Spirit: A Study of George Orwell* (1967)

David Wykes, *A Preface to Orwell* (1987)

Alex Zwerdling, *Orwell and the Left* (1974)

Selective Index

This volume is concerned with Spain, its Civil War, Fascism and Catalonia; to index every reference to those, direct and indirect, would overwhelm the user. To some extent this is true of the POUM (the unit with which Orwell fought), Barcelona, Assault Guards, Anarchism, Trotskyism, Communism, and some other topics. The first group of topics is therefore not indexed, and most other topics are indexed selectively. Bracketed explanations are sometimes provided after line references (e.g., 'rev.' for Orwell's reviews, or, against 'POUM', after 180–81, 'POUM's line') to provide additional guidance. What the 'plague of initials' (p. 169) for the various formations stood for is often indicated by Orwell but, for convenience, they are spelt out in the Index in Spanish and English, drawn from Hugh Thomas, *The Spanish Civil War* (3rd edn, Penguin Books, 1982, p. xiii). Sources within footnotes are not usually indexed although a few exceptions have been made where it is thought these would help the user. Authors and titles in Orwell's Pamphlet Collection are not indexed. Page numbers for the text are given in roman type (e.g., 57, 168); notes are in italic (e.g., *33, 284*); bold italic is used for biographical and explanatory detail (e.g., ***44, 357***).